Da Capo

BEST

MUSIC

WRITING

2002

Da Capo
BEST
MUSIC
WRITING
2002

The Year's Finest Writing on
Rock, Pop, Jazz, Country & More

Jonathan Lethem
GUEST EDITOR

Paul Bresnick
SERIES EDITOR

DA CAPO PRESS
A Member of the Perseus Books Group

Thanks to M. Matos, W. Stace, and D. Ebdus for above-and-beyond assistance. And this book is for Paul Nelson.—JL

To the memory of Timothy White.—PB

❧

List of credits/permissions for all pieces can be found on page 351.

Copyright © 2002 by Da Capo Press

Designed by Jeffrey P. Williams
Set in 10-point Janson Text by the Perseus Books Group

Cataloging-in-Publication data for this book is available from the Library of Congress.

First Da Capo Press edition 2002
ISBN 0–306–81166–9

Published by Da Capo Press
A Member of the Perseus Books Group
http://www.dacapopress.com

Da Capo Press books are available at special discounts for bulk purchases in the U.S. by corporations, institutions, and other organizations. For more information, please contact the Special Markets Department at the Perseus Books Group, 11 Cambridge Center, Cambridge, MA 02142, or call (800) 255–1514 or (617) 252–5298, or e-mail j.mccrary@perseusbooks.com.

1 2 3 4 5 6 7 8 9—06 05 04 03 02

CONTENTS

Introduction   IX
by Jonathan Lethem

LENNY KAYE   I
A Ramone Leaves Home: Joey 1951–2001
Village Voice

NIK COHN   5
Soljas
Granta

KATE SULLIVAN   25
J. Lo vs. K. Sul
City Pages

DAVID CANTWELL   30
"Help Me Make It Through the Night":
    The Anatomy of a Record
The Journal of Country Music

FRANKLIN BRUNO   54
The DJ's New Lexicon
Feed

EDITORS OF *THE ONION*   62
Two from *The Onion*
    "God Finally Gives Shout-Out Back to All His Niggaz"

"Marilyn Manson Now Going Door-to-Door
Trying to Shock People"
The Onion

STEVE ERICKSON   68
L.A.'s Top 100
Los Angeles Magazine

MARK JACOBSON   89
Tangled Up In Bob
Rolling Stone

GARY GIDDINS   111
Boom!
Village Voice

KODWO ESHUN   119
N*E*R*D and the Rise of New Geek Chic
Hyperdub.com

CHARLES AARON   127
Don't Fight the Power
Spin

SASHA FRERE-JONES   138
Haiku for Eminem
Chicago Reader

JOHN LELAND   141
It's Only Rhyming Quatrains, But I Like It
The New York Times Magazine

RJ SMITH   151
The Many Faces of Korla Pandit
Los Angeles Magazine

JOEY SWEENEY 177
Days of the Nü
Salon.com

ERIK DAVIS 188
Only a Northern Song
Village Voice

SIMON REYNOLDS 193
Walking on Thin Ice
The Wire

VARIOUS 210
Strokes Thread
Ilovemusic.com

DAVID GATES 217
Constant Sorrow
New Yorker

LUC SANTE 232
England's Oldest Hitmakers
Village Voice

GEOFFREY O'BRIEN 237
Seven Years in the Life
NY Review of Books

MONICA KENDRICK 248
Gimme Shelter
Chicago Reader

GREIL MARCUS 253
Days Between Stations: Kelly Hogan
Interview

MICHAEL HALL 256
A Long, Strange Trip
Texas Monthly

KELEFA SANNEH 275
Gettin' Paid
New Yorker

MATTHEW C. DUERSTEN 292
The Moon Looks Down and Laughs
Flaunt

DAVID EASON 319
That Same Lonesome Blood
Oxford American

CARL WILSON 339
With Joey Gone, I Finally Get the Diana Fetish
Toronto Globe and Mail

Other Notable Essays of 2001 343
List of Contributors 345
Credits 351

Introduction

". . . Johnny made up his own job, varying the tasks to suit his eternally teenaged sense of what was and wasn't boring."
—Robert Christgau

Wait, before you flip to the contents page looking for a Christgau piece—the line quoted above isn't from this year's volume, wasn't even written in 2001. It's an attempt to characterize Johnny Thunders's guitar-playing, from Christgau's essay on the New York Dolls in *Stranded: Music For a Desert Island,* a volume edited by Greil Marcus in 1978. So, what's the quote doing there? Here's the thing: This book, the one you're holding in your hands, is haunted, for me, by the ghost of *Stranded.* That volume, a batch of commissioned pieces pegged on the beautifully dumb question "Which Single Rock-and-Roll Album Would I Take To A Desert Island?," not only sets a fine standard for any gathering of essays on music—though it certainly does that. *Stranded* is more: To my seventeen-year-old self in 1981, the book was itself a message in a bottle bumping ashore on my own little ahistorical teenage island. The message read something like this: *Hey, kid, listen. The music you've heard is just the tip of an iceberg.* The book was an overwhelming introduction to the idea of a Rock 'n' Roll Pantheon, one which might intelligibly sweep the Cream and Joni Mitchell albums I knew from my mother's collection into a continuum with the Talking Heads and Clash I was then so passionately making my own. The message on the other side of the bottle's slip of paper might have been: *What's more, my friend, there's a bunch of really hot-shit writers who've been arguing about this stuff for longer than you've been listening.* Those assembled in Marcus's book included many of the founding fathers (and a couple of mothers) of Rock Writing,

itself a pantheon: Christgau, Dave Marsh, M. Mark, John Rock-
well, Lester Bangs, Nick Tosches, Ellen Willis, Paul Nelson,
etcetera, etcetera. Even without the contextualizing hints in Marcus's introduction, it was easy to infer the sustained (and sustain-
ing) conversation these writers had been in with one another and
the music. It was also more than evident that the writers saw this
conversation as an opportunity for the conscious practice of an art
form, the essay. For a nascent music nerd and wannabe writer, this
was heady stuff. In one shot I'd learned that real writing could
alchemize with a passion for music, that some people had made
this precious fool's gold an avocation and even a sort of career, and
that there had been Kinks' records before *Low Budget*—several of
them, in fact.

So, in editing *Da Capo Best Music Writing*, it's been impossible for
me not to wonder how the results might fare as a message in a bottle—or, to change the metaphor slightly, as a time capsule of 2001—
or, to change the metaphor wildly, as a kind of hologram of popular
music culture, a microcosmic Sim City to represent in shrunken
proportion every facet of the larger World of Pop. Could a Martian
reconstruct our era solely from the evidence contained in this *Best
Music Writing* volume, as I had reconstructed the Founding Fathers'
worldview from the sole existence of *Stranded*? The answer's no,
absolutely. Popular music's history, like its present, is vastly more
complex in 2001 than in 1978. Not least because, as Nick Hornby
ably described in his introduction to last year's book, that history is
now intricately woven into its present, from samples to reissues.
Besides, even *Stranded* only intimated the world to my teenage-
Martian brain, it didn't actually contain it. I needed record stores
and hundreds of further books, as well as thousands of magazines
and liner notes and conversations, to enact the full reconstruction.
In truth, that project is still in progress, a life's work, though now it's
been muddled by the attempt to comprehend everything that's happened since 1978.

Oh, and I've tried to live in the present, too. Pop purists and Bud-
dhists concur, it's best to live in the present. I'm doing my best: *must
parse new record reviews, must get ass out of the reissue section in the*

record store: Be Here Now. I've so far skirted the whole looming question of *fuddy-duddyism*, destined to be wrestled with eternally in this field of study where the maximum impact between subject and object is ordinarily made somewhere in adolescence, say around age thirteen or fourteen. So, full disclosure: I'm thirty-eight. Though that's poor excuse for a paradigm shift, Da Capo ought to be congratulated on their progress: without actually consulting with a mathematician, I've calculated that the arc from Peter Guralnick (editor of the 2000 volume) through Hornby (last year) and now to me dictates that the editor of the 2004 *Da Capo Best Music Writing* will need to be thirteen years old, while the editor of the 2006 volume hasn't been born yet.

The point? I'm the first editor in this series who can fairly claim to be *faking it in both directions*. Sure, I've got a twelve-year-old niece who understands the radio better than I do—who doesn't? But I'll also admit that the first Rolling Stones song I heard on the radio *as a new single*, instead of an 'oldie,' was "Emotional Rescue" (I thought it was wonderful), a confession sure to chagrin anyone who's endured my discourses on the virtues of *Sticky Fingers* or *Exile On Main Street*, never mind *Aftermath*. My generation is the one jolted into solidarity in mourning Joey Ramone, and we were born into a world the giants, those both writing and written about in *Stranded*, had already made. What did our glorified punk-ineptitudes and leather-jacket poses mean if not this: To seize this music for ourselves, to seize a life for ourselves, was to embrace *faking it*, brazenly.

Not to say the giants have abandoned the field. A quarter-century later, four of *Stranded*'s contributors are collected in the first two volumes of this series (including the undead Lester Bangs). Also Richard Meltzer, who, thanks to his *Rock Aesthetics* in Paul Williams's early mimeographed issues of *Crawdaddy*, has a share of the claim to have invented the rock-crit form. What are the chances for the egg-sucking mammals of this planet when the dinosaurs are still so crafty, alert, and strong? It's as unfair as . . . well . . . as the tyranny of Bob Dylan's *Love and Theft* over the *Village Voice*'s Pazz and Jop Poll this past year. Muttering can be heard through the land: When will these guys take their jewels and binoculars and go home and take a nap?

No time soon, I hope. Let any revolution be incomplete while I'm in charge—that thirteen-year-old can clean house in 2004. Much of my favorite music writing last year was by the Usual Suspects, as was much of my favorite music. It happened, for instance, that 2001 was The Year Bluegrass Broke. Go figure. Besides, if picking a big fat pile of writing I loved was pure pleasure, the responsibility to create a snapshot of 2001 was mostly as distracting as it sounds. This is my chance to mention all the things this book could have been, and isn't: Rock Obituaries 2001, The Year's Best Dylan Writing, or Fifty Thousand Music Fans Array Themselves Like Iron Filings in Postures of Attraction and Repulsion Vis-à-vis The Strokes (though I did find a useful distillation of this element in an excerpt from the Ilovemusic online forum, where much of the impromptu chatter is as good as the best magazine writing). The book also isn't The Year's Best Capsule Reviews, Sidebars, Top Ten Lists, and Photo Captions. Though that stuff forms the regular work of a large number of talented writers, and is often smashingly clever, I'm helpless in my general preference for essays and profiles when it comes to re-reading, which is the point of binding this compendium with something more durable than staples. I've let Carl Wilson's poignant references to *which cool bands are coming to town this week* stand as a tribute to the yeoman work done by weekly columnists and listings writers everywhere, whose frontline efforts keep us all fresh and hopeful in our quest for a good show: Good show. Nor is this book What I Was Listening To and How Little It Mattered in September and October, though it easily could have been. 2001 was a year with a crater in it, and it seemed nearly every music writer, nearly every *writer* (myself included), contributed something to the vast collective howl of despair. But to include more than a few references was to feel the void open again under my feet, and then suddenly the subject wasn't music at all. The conclusion of many of the writers, anyway, was my conclusion in editing the book: 2001's music answered the needs of that moment better than music writing ever could. O Death, indeed.

So, welcome instead to Johnny's Graying Teenaged Sense of What Isn't Boring. I promise no objectivity: My tastes in music played a part here, as did my bullshit detector. I spent some money on new CDs to road-test claims for alluring new acts I hadn't heard. If the piece was a rave, I felt I ought to play official taster. Nice work, really, easier than trying to write about music from scratch or crashing vacuum cleaners for *Consumer Reports*. I also vetoed pieces, many of them appealingly written, even rhetorically strong, which were nevertheless pegged on listener's assertions I couldn't abide: Sorry, but if you want to claim that The Spinners' records don't hold up, do it on someone else's watch. Faking it and getting it wrong aren't the same thing. All we've got on this island—all anyone has in this archipelago of islands, here in this sea littered with urgent and impulsive communiqués, both musical and written—are two ears and the truth as we know it.

"When I found Steve Young, I had been heartsick a while," begins David Eason in his piece on the country singer, "and he was singing songs that told stories about a world I knew. It's a world where you go somewhere and aren't sure how you feel about it, where you feel the past pushing you away and pulling you back, where you cover sad feelings with crooked smiles and bitter words, where you make tough choices and always pay the price for them." In trying to explain the pull of Young's voice, Eason offers his own, and there's nothing more a writer can do. Music writing is an art of substitution, but perhaps so is any art. What we seek is the voice, and what's behind it. What we want is to be with ourselves, but not alone. This book, I hope, is a book of encounters, none of them predictable, whether the names are as familiar as The Beatles or Louis Armstrong or Jennifer Lopez, or as new to you as Kelly Hogan or Opeth were to me, or as unfamiliar and *unlikely* as Korla Pandit (I'll admit I searched the name on the Internet to be sure I wasn't being hoaxed by this account of a fake fakir). Take it as an invitation to an impossible, gabbling conversation, a party line, where every voice is unforgettable—vivid with a freight of confession, advocacy, sarcasm, dismay. The characters in these pieces are musicians and fans, sometimes also disc jockeys or producers or family members, but above all the characters in these stories are the writers themselves: chasing leads, pitching angles, making lists, constructing impossible gossamer theories, sprawled wrecked in depression on their couches, envying their heroes, arguing with their friends, changing stations, listening, listening, always listening. Faking it. We're all faking it, even Greil Marcus. Thank God, too. It's literally the best, and most human, thing we can do.

—JONATHAN LETHEM

A Ramone Leaves Home: Joey 1951–2001

The light has gone out of New York rock and roll.

Joey Ramone passed away on Easter Sunday, at 2:40 P.M., in the endgame of a long battle with lymphoma. Diagnosed in 1995 and given, at that time, three to six months to live, he managed to maintain his health and good spirits until a fall in the snow at the end of last year. He broke his hip, and after a painful replacement found that his body was unable to continue fighting on two fronts. The news during the past few months—passed around by his friends and followers the world over—was progressively less and less hopeful.

The end came at a time when the Ramones' flame has never burned brighter. With a quarter century of "punk"—the music they helped template and design, from black motorcycle jackets and chopped eighth-note chordings to the pop chants of "Hey ho let's go" and "Gabba gabba hey!"—now being celebrated atop the scrap heap of history, Joey was a Cover Boy. Even while his boundless energy was a-lyin' in a hospital bed ("Doctor, doctor!" you could hear the New York Dolls urge on), he graced England's *Mojo* and America's *Spin*. The music he played was beloved in garages in any part of the world where the guitar was revered as a magical totem.

Last fall, I turned on the Subway Series to hear "Hey ho" over the loudspeakers at Shea Stadium, galvanizing the crowd much as Joey did during dozens of nights at CBGB. It was too perfect, I thought, remembering the Ramones traveling past Shea on the Number 7 with their instruments in shopping bags. They'd come the long way around to get back home again.

It was the same with their music. They appeared on the scene at a time when your average rock and roll band was everything the Ramones were not. Hardly Promethean, they occupied the gawk end of geek, their sound minimalism to the max. They played what they hardly knew, and knew that was more than enough. Rock and roll can be as complex and arcane as you want, but stripped down, a chorus hooker reduced to a driving beat with nowhere to go but out of body, it can be slick and fast, like a quick fuck against a brick wall in an alley behind a Bowery club—the one you pose next to in your ripped jeans, emblazoned T-shirt, sneakers. A band.

Jeff Hyman was born in 1951, which would make him about 23 when he changed his name to Joey Ramone. They all transformed their names, Douglas to Dee Dee, John to Johnny, Tommy to Tommy. They became a cartoon family, piling 18 songs into the half-hour sitcom that was their early set. Only they had the last laugh. Every Ramones show kept you wanting more, which is the great drug of rock and roll. The sets stayed short even as their set lists grew lengthier. They just played faster. Louder. Like everyone else who followed them.

The Ramones were the great port of entry into the punk-rock kingdom. But unlike their brethren (and sistren; Joey, especially, had a feminine lilt to his voice), they were not merely about endurance and speed. Joey loved the romantic sing-alongs of the Brill Building; in another decade, he might have been Paul Simon, or even Shadow Morton. But he'd also heard the surfer birdsongs of the Beach Boys, the top-of-the-mops English Invasion, the trailer-park nihilism of the Stooges, the teen drive of the Bay City Rollers, the English glam of Gary Glitter and the Sweet. He styled his hair into the pageboy of the Hullabaloos' crowning glory. The Ramones wanted to write hit singles, and they did.

Oh, you couldn't hear them on Top 40, but that was their alternative cross to bear. Instead, the Ramones imagined their own stations of the cross, invoking a golden age of "Do You Remember Rock 'n'

Roll Radio" ("Let's go!"), situated in a "Rock 'n' Roll High School" with the Phil Spector production to prove it. The topics might have been a little bizarro, but gabba hey, truth is truth: "Sheena Is a Punk Rocker" and "Carbona Not Glue." That's all you need to know.

Listen to any of their songs three times and it would own you. Last December at the Continental, in what proved Joey's final appearance (though you wouldn't have guessed it at the time, so strong and confident did he seem), hosting one of his annual Christmas extravaganzas with the local bands he championed—the Independents, the Misfits, his sibling Mickey Leigh of the Rattlers—he poured forth Ramones tune after Ramones tune. To hear how immediate they were, how much a part of cultural occurrency they'd become—"I Wanna Be Sedated" in a Tokyo clothing store, "I Wanna Be Sedated" spit out by a band in Barcelona, "I Wanna Be Sedated" at three ayem in Anydisco, Anywhere, "I Wanna Be Sedated" in some random jam and having five musicians play along whether they know the song or not—had me doing the Blitzkrieg Bop, as I've been doing for lo these many years, punching my fist in the air at each O-word and singing along, because the words have the memorizing mesmerize of universal rhyme, and it's great to feel the wind from the amplifiers.

The Ramones kept their song on the road for more than 20 years, a remarkable achievement for any dysfunctional family, surviving world tours, new members—Joey was the last of the original Ramones, though each raw-boned recruit seemed cut in the image of the Ramonic ideal, blunt force wearing a sleeved heart—countless imitators and clichés. The Ramones stuck doggedly to their formula one, watching it become prototype. Joey was the frontman, and, ultimately, the band's biggest fan.

And a forever fan of New York rock and roll. One of the most supportive members of the local musicians' community, he loved to visit the nightclubs of his home turf, his lanky head bobbing over the crowd, out on the town with his friends. He would cheer the band on. Get up and do a tune. "Beat on the Brat"? *One-too-t'ree-faw!*

Everyone loved Joey. Especially Ronnie Spector. At a Christmas show at Life in 1999, she and Joey hosted a revue that included cretin-hopper Keith Richards. Joining in on "Bye Bye Baby," she became Cher to Joey's Sonny. He coproduced an EP for her, and for one who grew up in the echo chamber of the Brill Building, it must have been as fulfilling a circle as a spinning 45. He had also completed a solo album, working with producers Daniel Rey and Andy Shernoff, and though he had his "good days and his bad days," was an inspirational fount of future plans.

Yeah baby! We're watching ? and the Mysterians at Coney Island High that same year, another sun-glassed spectre with a gift for the simplistic epigram. Joey's birthday party had just been held there, a peer grouping that brought together several generations of New York scenesters. At Coney Island's "class reunion" last Friday night at Don Hill's, Joey's name hung in the Good Friday air. By Sunday the rock had rolled away.

I take a walk into Joey's Lower East Side on Sunday night, after the rain. Downstairs in a basement club on Avenue A, we put Ramones songs on the jukebox. We dance into the dawn, the end of the century now.

Soljas

On his twenty-ninth birthday, Baby Williams gave a party for two or three thousand in the New Orleans Superdome. Baby and his older brother Slim ran Cash Money, the hottest rap label in the city, and they liked to live large.

Every birthday Slim and Baby tried to outdo each other in the extravagance of their gifts. Baby, a man shaped like a 300-pound butt plug, had high expectations. "It better not be a helicopter. I don't need a motherfuckin' helicopter, I already got one," he told his entourage. But he needn't have worried. This year his gift was a Ferrari 360 Modena Berlinetta.

To show his appreciation, Baby jumped on the car and started to leap up and down. He was wearing combat boots and left a dent each time be landed. He reached into his jeans and pulled out two thick fistfuls of banknotes, tens and twenties and fifties, and started to fling them in the air. "I am the number-one stunna!" he cried. "Money ain't shit to me."

When the notes began to flutter overhead, Melvin was in the first row of the crowd, perfectly placed. A cluster was heading right at him, all he had to do was reach out, but he was stampeded. A wave of people slammed into his back and sent him sprawling. Melvin went down hard, face first. Someone kicked him in the skull, some- one else trod on his chest. He rolled up into a ball, arms curled over his head. He was calling on Bobby to help him, but Bobby wasn't there.

He could hear Baby Williams yelling, "Money ain't shit to me, money ain't shit," and the Hot 8 Brass Band blasting "Back that Azz Up." There was a floating feeling in his head, he may have lost consciousness. Then Bobby was shouting in his face. Bobby held his arms and dragged him along the floor till they were clear of the crowd. Melvin lay flat on his back, looking up at the lights in the roof, far off. His pants were wet.

Bobby had come away loaded: two fifties, a bunch of twenties and tens. And Melvin had nothing. Bobby kept thumbing the notes and calling him a bitch, and Melvin didn't have a word to say. A shorty, maybe ten years old, was standing next to his face in brand new Reeboks, his shoe a few inches from Melvin's eye. When he lifted his shoe, there was a crumpled twenty underneath. All Melvin had to do was reach out his hand.

Afterwards, he and Bobby hit a Popeye's on Canal Street, and Bobby ate three family dinners. Bobby was eighteen, five months older than Melvin, but he was close to Baby Williams's weight class and getting closer every day. He sat by the window with his big greasy hands and grease all over his face, and he wouldn't stop thumbing the banknotes. Two cops were outside and Bobby waved the notes at them. In Melvin's eyes that was purely stupid.

He was staying by his Uncle June's on Euterpe. June was the one who'd raised him, more or less. He wasn't really an uncle, but when Melvin was five, Melvin's mother had got herself sidetracked and couldn't keep him. He went to live with his grandma, but she got a cancer and died. After that he was fostered out. The first family couldn't handle him, they said he was too wild. The second family put him in a cage. They said it was the only way to stop his row, so they shut him up in a chicken coop with a tin roof over it. They took the chickens out first, but not the chickenshit. When Social Services found out, they put him in the House. He was eight years old, and he wouldn't speak. When he used to live with his moms he was never quiet. The way he chirped all hours of the day and night drove her crazy. Now he didn't say a word. The people at the House didn't know what to do. They sent him to a psychiatrist; it didn't help. They hit him; it didn't help.

The only person who could reach him was his mother's sister Maxine. She had a house on Orange Street, close to the St. Thomas projects, she shared with Uncle June. Sometimes she came to visit Melvin in the House and one day she took him home with her. She was a big fine woman with children of her own. They didn't want Melvin in the house, but Maxine wouldn't let them harm him. Once, when her kids were at school and Melvin was sick with the flu, she baked him peanut-butter cookies and they watched TV all day. Then Maxine lost the house and moved in with her boyfriend. The boyfriend didn't want Melvin, so Uncle June took him. June had two friends like himself, he-shes, who had a room to rent. It was just a closet, but it had a window and a bunk bed. Melvin slept on top, and Uncle June was the bottom.

Uncle June was almost young then, but shapeless and lumpy like a sack filled with mashed potatoes. He dressed like a man but he had a little girl's voice. One time when Melvin walked in on him naked, it looked like there was nothing down there, just shadows.

He was cool, though. There were men and women in his life that disrespected him, and this made him get evil at times, but he never got evil with Melvin. They moved in and out of projects, most often the St. Thomas. At some point, Melvin began to talk again. It turned out he had a stammer.

He couldn't say where the stammer came from. He didn't have it when he was in his mother's house. Maybe it was rust. But he never got rid of it.

When he was ten he topped five foot. Four years later he was the exact same height. The St. Thomas soljas gave him a hard time. They used to whale on him and imitate his stammer. The worst was 'Rilla. He was younger than Melvin, but he had a lot of gold chains and gold teeth, gold all over his person. He was tight with some heavy dealers, moving up the ladder, and one day he backed Melvin up in a breezeway and pissed on him. Melvin went back in the house and took Uncle June's Glock and walked over to 'Rilla's house and shot him. He didn't kill him, just winged him. He meant to kill him but he'd never used a Glock before.

Life was easier for a spell; he had some respect. Then Uncle June moved to the Calliope and Melvin was back in trouble. Calliope niggas made the St. Thomas look like church.

Bobby was living two houses down. He was big even then, and he had that winning attitude. His name was Bobby Mabry, but he went by Bobby Murda. Nobody messed with him. Bobby's younger brother Tyree had got killed the year before, and Bobby was still mad about it. The motherfucker that did the shooting got killed himself before Bobby could reach him. That was frustrating to Bobby.

Uncle June didn't take to Bobby. He never did care for soljas. According to June, that street life was only good to get you dead. He kept nagging on Melvin to do his homework and stay in school but Melvin wasn't hearing him. His dream was to be a rap star. Him and Bobby together. Lil Mel and Bobby Murda.

Many times he'd be out on the streets when some of Cash Money drove by. They'd be in their Bentleys or a fleet of bright yellow Hummers, bombing the bass, flossing mad gold and platinum too. When the girls on the street felt that bass, they threw themselves up against a wall and started shaking their booty. Then the Hummers moved on and those girls were left to dangle. Their asses would still be twitching when Cash Money was ten miles down the road.

Melvin planned to write a rap every day but he couldn't seem to have the knack. And Bobby was no big help. He was running the clubs every night and high every day, and sex, he was a pure hog for sex. How many songs had they finished so far? Not one.

Day and night, he thought about hitting big: the Hummers and Bentleys, the house at English Turn. English Turn was where Slim and Baby Williams had bought mansions and kept their families hid. Melvin drove out there with Bobby a few times when they'd stole a ride. There was a gate with a guardhouse and a golf course and landscaped gardens and a clubhouse with white pillars. In the evening you sat on a veranda and looked across a lagoon, and all your neighbours were white.

How you lovin' that? After Melvin walked in Uncle June's house with that twenty-dollar bill, he took it out and looked at it in the light for a long time. It was ugly-assed, one corner ripped, a sorry piece of paper. Used to be Baby's. Now it was his.

New Orleans rap is all about funk. It's lowdown and dirty, the greasier the better, and it has nothing to do with fashion. In the mid-Nineties, when the city first captured the national market, gangsta rap was said to be finished. The music press was full of stories claiming that the killings of Tupac Shakur and Biggie Smalls had reawakened hip-hop's social conscience. But New Orleans must not have heard the news. Instead of toning down, its raps became more brutal, its rhythms raunchier than ever.

The format was simple: unspeakable lyrics, irresistible beats. Slaughter met sex on the dance floor, and the Dirty South was born. Its first ruler was Master P from the Calliope. For two years his label, No Limit, was the bomb. Then Cash Money took over.

The Williams brothers rose from the Magnolia. To begin with, they were street hustlers, scuffling like everyone else. Later they came upon money, never mind how, and went into the music business. They started selling records out of the backs of vans, in the clubs and community centres, in mom-and-pop stores in the projects. They signed up Mannie Fresh, a veteran DJ with a genius for beats, and a stable of neighbourhood rappers, and, in 1997, they dropped their anthem, "Bling Bling": "I'm tattooed and barred up/Medallion iced up, Rolex bezelled up/And my pinky ring is platinum plus . . . "

"Bling Bling," a national hit, was the first of many, peaking with Juvenile's "Back that Azz Up," the hottest rap record of 1999. Depending on whose figures you believe, Cash Money grossed fifty million dollars, or eighty, or over a hundred million.

Master P, meanwhile, seemed to have lost his touch. Maybe the pressure had got to him. A full laundry list of New Orleans rappers—Pimp Daddy, DJ Irv, Yella Boy, Kilo G, MC T. T. Tucker, Warren Mays—had died by the gun. So P and his bodyguards moved away to Baton Rouge, and Cash Money owned the city.

Joyce lived in New Orleans East. She was a homecare nurse, and Edgar, her husband, was a shoe salesman. They had two daughters,

Gabrielle and Jalene; the whole family was strong in church. Their home was a ranch-style brick bungalow with its own driveway and a patch of St. Augustine grass out front. There was even a palm tree of sorts. More dead than alive, but Joyce gave praise for it. She didn't tell her age. She was in her prime, that's all she would say. She suffered with diabetes and had to watch her weight. This came hard to her, because she dearly loved chocolates and all sweet things, but how could she complain? Everyone had their cross.

When Joyce heard that Cash Money would be shooting a video at Garette Park, right down the block from her house, she was caught in two minds. She had no love for gangsta rap. Glorifying guns and killing, all that *language*, to her it was Satan at work. But Cash Money, well, she had to admit she liked those beats. Mannie Fresh, the man was blessed with a gift, no doubt. And Juvenile too. Don't nobody dare to tell her daughters this, but when "Back that *Thing* Up" was on the radio all the time, Joyce used to listen out for it.

The video featured Cash Money's rising star, Lil Wayne, known to his crew as Weezie. He was eighteen, and his first album had gone platinum. By Cash Money standards, its lyrics were tame, but that wasn't Weezie's fault. His mother didn't allow him to curse, he said.

The video wasn't due to start shooting for hours, but Joyce put on a pair of big old shorts and a Saints shirt, and carried a beach chair outdoors. She wanted to be sure not to miss anything, so she brought binoculars and a thermos. It was a lovely morning, crystal clear, and the sidewalk was crowded with neighbours. Kids were selling lemonade and sodas, it felt like carnival.

A Cash Money bus was already parked down the block. It had an outsize platinum '$' spray-painted on the back and every inch of the sides were covered with publicity for *Baller Blockin'*, the label's movie. According to Mannie Fresh, a baller blocker is "a nigga standin' in your way of ballin." In other words, a playa hata, and nothing was lower than that. "I think playa hating should be made a crime, I really do," said Fresh.

The painting on the bus showed the Cash Money Army, thugged up in bandanas and full bling bling, exploding out of the Magnolia in a flameburst. The bus had no windows that Joyce could tell. She thought this was strange, but maybe not. If you were Cash Money, you didn't need to look out.

When she turned her eyes to this street she lived on, though, she thought it was something worth seeing. All these tidy houses and tidy front gardens and driveways with cars in them; cars with wheels and hubcaps and working engines; new cars, some of them. It was a far cry from the inner city. Most of New Orleans these days was dead or dying. Tourists called this decadence; they thought it was romantic. Their New Orleans was the Big Easy, the City that Care Forgot. Crawfish and jazz brunches and Hurricanes at Pat O'Brien's, the French Quarter, the Garden District, mansions on St. Charles Avenue, the live oaks in Audubon Park. They rode the streetcar and shopped all day, and at night they got drunk and stupid on Bourbon Street. It was one big party to them.

Joyce could have taught them better. She was born and raised in the Sixth Ward, right by the St. Roch Cemetery, and she'd seen the city rot on the vine. Oh, there was still beauty all right. Sometimes it could fool you almost. She'd be a riding a bus, when she passed this or that place she knew as a child, it was like a hand clutched her throat. But she didn't get off the bus, no way.

Tourists and poverty, that's all there was. She read in the *Times-Picayune* where the population of Orleans Parish was close to sixty percent black, and over half lived below the poverty line. Hundreds of millions of dollars, billions, poured in every year, but none of it ever seeped down. Every cent was gobbled up by the politicians and the banks, old white money and new black money. That's right, black money. The mayor was black, the city council had a black majority, there were millionaire black businessmen. They were as bad as the whites. Worse, to her mind, because they betrayed their own people.

The lies; the bare-face lies. Politicians, black and white, kept announcing schemes to turn things around. Convention centres and casinos, museums, tourist malls. More jobs, they said; more money for education. But nothing ever changed.

Ask Joyce, it was deliberate. The schools were a crying shame, and why? Because they were planned that way. The whole idea was to keep people ignorant. Then they were fit for nothing but cleaning up the tourists' mess. That's what the politicians needed. Menial labour, dirt cheap.

Talking about it made Joyce so mad she forgot about her blood pressure and had to take a pill. She lay back in her beach chair, breathing deep and slow, and wished she could take one quick dip into a box of Russell Stover chocolates, just one.

Her husband was right; she took things too much to heart. She needed to count her own blessings, that she wasn't caught up in the projects, but safe in New Orleans East. This was next best to the promised land. Her own home, her own yard, her very own palm tree. Praise God, Joyce said. Praise Him.

Something was happening down the street. Word spread that Lil Wayne had arrived.

Today's video showcased a cut from his new album, *Lights Out*. To judge by its language, Wayne had managed to tear loose from his mother's apron strings. "You can look forward to me takin' over," he told *Da Rude*, a local rap magazine. "Some eye-opener shit, 'cause niggas be sleepin'' on Weezie, and Weezie "bout to wake niggas up, 'good mornin'.'"

When Joyce caught sight of him, he was behind the wheel of a mint purple Porsche. The Porsche wasn't moving, being perched on top of a flatbed, but Weezie kept twisting this way and that, as if cornering at ninety. The video crew took some test shots. "They started filming, they filming right now," Joyce said, and began to bounce up and down in her seat, but it proved a false alarm. The camera stopped whirring, the crew broke up. After a few seconds, Lil Wayne climbed down to the street.

He was tiny. In a full-length mink coat, with his wraparound shades and his baggy pants pulled low, he looked like a ten-year-old dressed up in his daddy's pimp clothes.

Watching him sashay down the block, Joyce let out her breath through her nose. "Would you look at that child?" she said. Wayne's new record was playing. People all around were dancing.

"What time is it?" she asked.

"Ricki Lake," she was told.

For a moment she felt stricken. Ricki Lake was her favorite TV talk show, the highlight of her day. When her sister Carla had a heart attack and was in the ICU, Joyce didn't leave the hospital for two days and nights, but she never missed Ricki Lake. And now? "Child," she said, and started to shake that thing.

Soljas lived and died by the G-Code. To be recognized as a G was the highest condition any hustla could aspire to. The G was a big-time gangsta, a godfatha, a don. He had all the cars and hoes and bling bling any man could dream of, yet he stayed true to his roots. He was a mighty warlord, but he had a project soul.

It was a matter of honour. "As far as what I mean by G-code," said Juvenile, "is the way we dress, the way we talk, the way we was raised. Traditions. When I say G-code, I'm talkin' about what you went through where you from."

Terrance "Gangsta" Williams, half-brother of Slim and Baby, was a G. Around the Magnolia he was a great hero, though he did not live there any more. He was serving life plus twenty years in a federal pen, for Continuing Criminal Enterprise, solicitation to commit murder, and conspiracy to sell six ounces of heroin.

From jail, he gave an interview to *F.E.D.S*, the magazine of "convicted hustlers/street thugs/fashion/sports/music/film/etc." Questioned by the mag's ace reporter, Cold Crushin' Kenny Rankin, Gangsta didn't deny the charges, though he tried to put them in context. When he was still on the streets, New Orleans had been known as Click Click, murder capital of the world, but he felt its status was deceptive. "That's only because New Orleans is a very small city," Gangsta argued. "Everybody's trying to build a reputation and get their hustle on—the city's not big enough for but so many gangsters. So, somebody had to go."

"How many people do they say you've killed?" Rankin asked.

". . . According to the streets they say I've murdered over forty people."

"How old were you when they started calling you a heartstopper?"

"I was about fifteen."

"What does 'heartstopper' mean?"

"When you penetrate someone with some iron."

All in all, he sounded upbeat. "I do thank God and I will admit that me having this life plus twenty was one of the best things that could've happened to me. It's all love in the federal system," he said. He was writing a book and planning a movie, warning the young not to follow his path. Meanwhile, he was grateful to be alive, and to have his brothers' support, and most of all to be who he was, "To Mister Terrance Gangsta Ooh-Wee Magnolia Williams," he concluded, "all I can say is, 'I'm jealous of myself.'"

The source of the G's strength was pride. Pride in his family, in his click, in his own legend. But if he came from a project, as most Gs did, pride in that project came first and last. It was what he represented.

Outsiders found this hard to understand. To them, the projects were dumping grounds. Driving through them, it seemed inconceivable that these tortured labyrinths of dung-colored buildings, with their scorched walls and boarded-up windows and stench of human rot, could be a source of pride to anyone. Yet they'd started out as model housing. When they were built, mostly in the 1940s, they were seen as a blessed escape. Ten of them ringed the inner city, each a small city to itself, each conceived in hope.

The G-Code was born of the 1980s, when crack first flooded the streets and raised up a new breed of drug lord, more murderous than any before. The projects turned into fiefdoms, ruled by guns and celebrated by rappers like Juvenile: "Welcome to the section where it's hotter than a bitch/Niggas breakin' up bricks, niggas tryin' to be rich/All day hustle, boocoo scuffle/Niggas huddle, AK–47s muffled/Blood in puddles, people scatter/Flying pieces of human matter . . . "

The G's gift was to harness the slaughter and ride it. But he needed soljas to protect his turf and run his games. Many of these were children; the younger they were, the less hang-ups they had about shooting people: "I ain't terrified from nuthin'/I'm young, wild, crazy and disgustin' . . . ."

Your project was who you were. It gave you a tribe, and a cause. Soljas called that love.

The enemy was everyone outside. New Orleans was an endless maze of rivalries and ancient feuds. Apart from the projects, there were also eighteen wards. Gerrymandered political districts, drawn up in the nineteenth century, their boundaries defied logic, but soljas held them sacred.

Some wards were allied, others at perpetual war. A story is told of a boy called Lawrence from the Sixth Ward, who went to a club in the Fourth Ward. The Fourth and Sixth Wards are friendly, the Fourth and Seventh are not. So when Lawrence got in the club, some niggas asked him his ward. Lawrence held both hands up, one with four fingers extended, the other with two. But he was dancing, and it was dark, and the niggas couldn't see that his thumb was down on the hand with the four fingers out. They thought he was saying seven. So they shot him once in the head, once in the chest and once in the stomach.

To soljas, the incident was regrettable, not tragic. Few of them conceived a long-term future; their life was minute by minute. They slung rocks (dealt crack), robbed gas stations and convenience stores, and served their time in the Orleans Parish Prison. Sooner or later, most likely, they were shot.

Even that was not all bad. When a solja died in battle, he was memorialized on a T-shirt. His image appeared in four-color glory, usually in combat gear, with the dates of his sunrise and sunset and a line of tribute from his click. In death, he achieved what life had denied him. He was someone; and he had the T-shirt to prove it.

June had trouble in his head. His brain was flooded with heavy water. He could feel it slopping behind his eyes every time he took a step. He needed to go see the doctor.

This new affair with Melvin didn't help none. The call had come in at three in the morning, Melvin phoning from jail. Him and Bobby Mabry had been in a bust-up on Orleans Avenue. Some dudes came out of the projects and tried to rob them. Melvin fought back. There was a maylay and somebody shot off a gun. The bullet hit a woman on the other side of the street. Passed straight through the flesh of her arm. She was lucky.

That was Melvin's story. But June could see the holes. What were those boys doing down on Orleans? And why did he fight back? He'd been robbed enough times before, he ought to know that tune. A man steps to you with a gun, you honor his request.

June saved his questions for later. He called Cheapie Bail Bonds, like he did all those times before, and carried Melvin home. The boy never thanked him, just hit him up for pizza. Heartaches was all it was. If June had a lick of sense, he'd put that boy in the street, but he knew he could never do it.

This morning they went to the courthouse, Tulane and Broad. Lord knows June despised that place. Big old ugly grey building like some kind of fortress, they might as well hang a sign, JAIL STARTS HERE. And the way these children walked the halls. In the time when June came up, he'd say he was black and proud. But these youths over here, that was some other something. Tatted up, slugged up, thugged up, even in the courthouse they strutted and talked that gangsta talk.

Not Melvin, though. He might signify on the street, but in here he walked real light.

Bobby Mabry was brought out from the cells, he had prison wear on. To June's way of thinking, he ought to keep wearing it all the time, save everyone a heap of trouble. The whole case was playtime to him, he never stopped yawning and flapping his mouth, but Melvin he was scared, he didn't want to be no man's wife.

The judge set the case back six weeks, and Bobby went back to jail, and Melvin was out on the street. Soon as he was out of the courthouse he went to laughing, doing that pimp-roll shit, with his pants pulled low to show off his drawers. Everyone he met, he called them nigga.

They had lunch at the Verdict Cafe. June had no appetite, but Melvin ate for them both. This was disturbing to June. Melvin never ate that way, most times he barely picked. It was like he was being Bobby, gluttoning and jabbering both at once, and with his stammer the food flew out as fast as he forked it in.

"What were you doing on Orleans Avenue?" June asked.

"Business," Melvin said.

June just raised up and left him there. Stood at the corner, waiting on the Broad Street bus, and he couldn't stop shaking. This was what loving got you. He needed to go see the doctor.

Before Master P or Cash Money there was bounce. It started in the late 1980s, a wild mix of rap and Mardi Gras Indian chants and second-line brass-band bass patterns and polyrhythmic drumming and gospel call-and-response. It was raw sex in dance, a music of summer block parties, of swelter.

On Sunday afternoons, when the temperature in the bricks was around 110 degrees and the humidity near a hundred per cent, the top DJs let blast for five hours straight, and the projects turned into giant mosh pits.

Big fine women and slim fine women hogged the spaces next to the speakers, action-ready in shorts and halter tops. Dancing to bounce was called twerking. To twerk meant shaking that thing till the sweat flew and the concrete underfoot was slick as an ice-rink.

The DJ shouted orders—walk it like a dog, walk it like a model, wobble in a circle—and the women jumped to obey. When the DJ told them to shake it on a stick, they bent over till their hands were flat on the ground, their buttocks high in the air, and twitched so fast they seemed plugged into a socket. All you saw was a blur of flying booty. "Now tiddy bop," the DJ ordered, and the women raised their T-shirts to shake their breasts. "Now show the globe," and the women bared their asses. "Now pop that pussy till the pussy goes pop . . . "

In the city's record stores, bounce outsold mainstream rap five-to-one. Since its first great hit, "Where Dey A" by DJ Irv and MC T. T. Tucker in '91, it had produced a succession of local heroes. Most of them had died untimely, but their legacy remained: both No Limit and Cash Money had made their fortunes by marrying bounce to hip-hop.

Mobo Joe was a rare survivor from the early days. In his prime he had produced classics like "Run Dat Shit" by Ruthless Juveniles and "Straight Up Villing" by Dog House Posse. When he passed by with Kenny, his 400-pound lieutenant, every G in town gave him space. But Joe fell on evil times. He got caught up in drugs, lost his money and his business, and ended up with a two-year stretch.

Now he was out again, and a billboard for his greatest hits, featuring his jail card—IVORY PAYNES, 79353–079—overlooked the interstate, near the Superdome.

In the flesh he looked shrunken, as if his frame no longer filled his skin, but he said he was not beaten. His girl had a job at Cachi Nails ("if your nails aren't becoming to you, you should be coming to me"), and he drove a Malibu, and when asked how much his billboard had cost, he smiled mysteriously. "I'm still Mobo Joe," he said. "I know how to work my jelly."

Maybe so. But younger bounce kings like Fifth Ward Weebie and Josephine Johnny, who was said to have shot up a bar and wounded two women in the legs to publicize his new album, *Out On Bail*, were stealing his spotlight. "Back in the day, I was the shit," Mobo Joe liked to say. Not any more.

Bounce was so all-powerful now that no event could flourish without it. On a Saturday afternoon King George, an uptown ruler, gave a children's party in the Magnolia. He provided free T-shirts and food but no DJ, so nobody came. Well, almost nobody. Some social workers showed up, and women dispensing condoms and AIDS pamphlets, plus a few hot girls with video cameras, but they barely made up a quorum.

King George, a mountainous man, held the party in a community playground. He owned a hip-hop clothing store and a record label, and some of his rappers sat around a picnic table, looking bored. Big Slack, the first among them, was short and stout and wore a T-shirt promoting *Ready For Combat*, his new CD. It showed a death's head in shades and a military beret, over crossed AK–47s, and the legend, MESS WITH THE BEST—DIE LIKE THE REST. This was his first album. "I been rappin' thirteen years but, due to incarceration, I fell behind my business," said Slack. Had he been in jail a lot? "Back and forth." He paused to reconsider. "Well, I'll be honest wit' ya," he said. "More back than forth."

King George started serving up turkey necks from a giant vat. Across the playground a small boy, no older than seven, came into view. He wore a football shirt down below his knees, he had a wall eye. As he approached, he could be heard rapping: "Motherfucka I'ma take you out/Bringin' the pain is what I'm about."

One of the hot girls, seeing but not hearing him, favored the child with a dazzling smile. "Trick bitch," said the child, "I'ma let you suck my dick."

DJ Jubilee would not have approved. His record label called him "King of Bounce," and he claimed to have created over a hundred dances, among them the Shake It Like a Dog, the Stick Your Booty Out and the Ee Wee Unk. He was also the anti-G.

Born Jerome Temple, he tutored handicapped children, coached basketball and football teams, and said he'd never touched drugs, not even marijuana. He had grown up in the St. Thomas and one of his brothers was doing life in Angola, but Jube was not a man who lied. His diligence and rigor were bywords. Even on stage, demonstrating the Shake It Like a Sissy or the Penis Pop, he carried himself like a traffic cop.

His record label, Take Fo', was equally righteous. The owner, Earl Mackie, was college-educated, a family man, church-going and low key. He'd graduated to bounce from *Positive Black Talk*, a local TV show, and was big on self-improvement. Sometimes his minister gave him grief about the lyrics Take Fo' put out, specially those by the transvestite Katy Red, who called herself the Millennium Sissy and liked to rap about cocksucking. Earl Mackie's defense was that it beat killing.

Most nights Mackie's artists gathered in a studio near the courthouse. The studio looked firebombed, with collapsing sofas and graffiti-splattered walls, but the atmosphere was restful. Henry the Man, Mackie's partner, manned the console in hospital scrubs, dandling his infant daughter; Junie B, the Magnolia Pepper Girl, who spat game like an uzi on record, talked about becoming a primary school teacher. Only Choppa acted the star.

He was the label's newest signing, a nineteen-year-old from suburban Marrero, good-looking and brash, dizzy with self-love, but he
was hardly a gangsta. His family was a unit, his father worked; at
home, he answered to Darwin.

"I'm bad," Choppa said. He'd got suspended in school, and he
was always in the clubs, and he had two gold teeth at $125 each.
Unlike Cash Money and No Limit, Take Fo' couldn't afford to hand
out precious metals and made do with faux-gold pendants. Choppa
wore his on all occasions. When a photographer appeared, he also
grabbed up his cellphone and posed with it, speed-talking, though
no one was on the other end.

He could never stand to stay home. If he heard that his click was
on some street, throwing bricks up against a wall, he had to be out
there with them. But a solja? He looked blank. He was a lover, not a
warrior. "Everyone lovin' Choppa," he said. "Everyone wantin' me,
wantin' me, it'll drive me crazy some day."

On Saturday night he played a dance at the gym of a community
fitness centre in LaPlace, an hour's drive outside the city. The night
was hot and steamy, and groups of teenage girls sat outdoors at picnic tables, catching any breeze they could. They seemed nice girls,
well-behaved. They talked about their nails, and boys, and Destiny's
Child, and boys. Then Choppa came on stage, and the girls flew
into the gym. "If you like your pussy ate, say Aaaahh," Choppa said.
And all the nice girls went, "Aaaahh."

Brandon Jones was a golden child. There was a light in him; just
seeing him made people smile. Everyone in Treme knew that he was
chosen.

Treme was a black neighborhood abutting the French Quarter.
Families had lived here for generations. The majority were poor, but
many owned their own houses, handed down from parents and grandparents. The houses were lovely to look at, old clapboard shotguns and
Creole cottages, but not so lovely to live in. Still, they were homes.

In the late Eighties, many of these homes were razed to make way
for Louis Armstrong Park, in hopes of luring the tourists who
thronged the Quarter. The people who were put out of their houses

to make room for the park were promised housing in New Orleans East but ended up in the projects. Treme never recovered.

The hoped-for tourists never came. A proposed Tivoli Gardens came to nothing; a casino opened and closed. Property speculators bought up homes on the cheap and resold them to white gentrifiers, but few of the incomers put down roots. Crack was taking over the streets. Soon everyone had a gun.

Due to a bureaucratic mix-up, Brandon's legal name was Benson. He was light-skinned, almost honey-colored. On the streets they called him Red.

His mother Regina was sixteen when she birthed him and already had a year-old daughter, Tiffany. Regina was a riotous woman, with a big laugh and a wild temper and an anarchic sense of humour. People said she should be a stand-up comic, but she was too busy working two jobs and wrestling demons. Brandon's father was up in Angola serving life for four murders. So Brandon was raised by a rotating committee: Regina, his mother's friend Booby, and his grandmother, Miss Rose.

From the time he could walk, he ran the streets. Treme streets were still safe then, you could use them to learn, and Brandon was wild for knowledge. He was also saddled with a sense of duty.

He was nine when he met Nan Parati. She was one of the white incomers, a graphic artist. One day she caught him smashing bottles in the street and told him to stop, because the glass ripped her bicycle tires. Brandon was furious. Not only had she ruined his pleasure, but now he felt responsible for the safety of her tires.

He went to work in Nan's studio, and she became part of his raising, too. She taught him history and philosophy, and Brandon taught her Treme. He'd never been outside Orleans Parish, so she took him travelling to Philadelphia and New York, to her family's home in North Carolina. Brandon told her there were mothers, moms, and maws. A mother said, "Brandon dear, get up"; a mom said, "Get up"; a maw said, "Boy, get yo ass outta bed." So Regina was his maw, and Nan was sometimes his mother, sometimes his mom.

They had many fights. The mood in the streets was changing, and Brandon started running with Peanut and Dookie and Fat Cory and UDog, who styled themselves the Sixth Ward Creepers. Cory had been shot and was stuck in a wheelchair for life. This was seen as an achievement.

At fifteen, Brandon had been shot at three times and could list twenty friends who'd died. He was arrested for shooting off a gun in the air, and again for breaking into a car. That time he was innocent, but the cops cuffed him so tight he lost circulation in his wrists. When Brandon complained, one of the cops said, "I hope they cut your motherfuckin' hands off." Then they beat a confession out of UDog, and Brandon was locked in a cell with a man who'd just killed his best friend for messing with his wife. He felt safer in there than he did with the cops.

On sunny days the Creepers used to sit out on some derelict porch and pose for pictures with their money and guns. That was Brandon's life. Then he would go to Nan and cry, and swear he was going to change. He sent her a letter saying, "I can't understand how stupid I acted for five years of your helping meracales that you gave me. I owe you so much first of all like a trillion dollars, my freedom." That was Brandon's life too.

School never agreed with him, but he could write. He started a hip-hop version of *Romeo and Juliet*, retitled "Homeyo and Ugliet." The opening scene began:

Corey: Chris, who do you think is the finest girl in school?

Chris: I like [Juliet]. That girl got the biggest tits in the world. I mean that butt! When she's walking up the street in the rain you can use her butt for an umbrella.

The arrests kept piling up, and he felt himself drowning. He checked himself into the Odyssey House, a drug rehab center that taught self-awareness and taking responsibility for one's own actions. He didn't have a drug problem, but he needed out of his home, out of Treme, so he stuck with the Odyssey programme, and when he emerged, he had acquired a direction. He still hung with Peanut and Fat Cory and the rest, but he got a job bagging groceries at an upscale healthfood store on Esplanade Avenue. This made him, in Treme, a high-flyer.

He learned therapeutic massage, read any book he could lay hands on, wrote poetry and journals. He also wrote raps, hundreds of them; his rap name was B-Red. With two other rappers, G-Sta and Casual T, he formed a group named Certified Hustlaz. Like every other click, they flashed bling bling for publicity pictures, but their music was politicized and self-aware, and Brandon's verses raged with an apocalyptic preacher's fire: "How many niggas you gonna kill before yo twenty-first birthday? . . . /Is it because you afraid to lose,/Or is yo 'hood full of niggas with something to prove?/Whatever it is, dog, you gotta stop/'Cos you're quick to kill yo boys, but you afraid of the cops . . . "

B-Red railed against the G-Code; to him, the 'G' stood for genocide. He preached the lessons he'd learned at Odyssey House: self-reliance, work, no excuses. Treme had become a prison to him. He was scared of getting shot, and slept in a different bed almost every night. Another family now shared Regina's home. They stole his money, destroyed his clothes, but he kept working, and at last he began to see some rewards. His live shows sold out, he was on the verge of a record deal. One last push and he'd be free, and he was driving home from work with his friend Dewitt, full of plans, when a cop car came speeding down the ramp from the freeway and rammed straight into them. Brandon Jones was twenty-three.

The T-shirts at Brandon's funeral, ignoring his true life, showed him in the camouflage gear of a Sixth Ward gangsta. B-RED, CERTIFIED HUSTLER, the inscription read. A COWARD DIES A THOUSAND DEATHS, A SOLDIER DIES BUT ONCE.

Bobby Murda also got a T-shirt that ignored his true life. When he went down on Orleans Avenue once too often, he had his head blown off. Melvin thought the T-shirt should say something about revenge, but Bobby's mother did not ask his opinion. Instead, she chose to use one of Bobby's baby pictures, captioned JESUS HAS A NEW FRIEND.

Melvin was at the burying. He even managed to drop a baggie of weed into the grave before they started shovelling. He wasn't invited to the food and drink after, but that was all right, he went anyway. He had some shrimps; nobody turned him away. But he started to have bad thoughts, he couldn't stay.

Truth? He was happy Bobby was gone. Not happy his head blew away, understand, but relieved he wasn't around. That first night they were on Orleans and those dudes tried to jack them, to Melvin that changed everything. When he felt that hand go in his pants and grab his money, he liked to snap. Baby's twenty was in there; he wasn't giving it up. They could kill his ass right there, he didn't give a fuck. But later, in lock-up, he saw the true facts. If he didn't cut loose from Bobby Murda, he'd be on a T-shirt himself or else in a wheelchair, either or.

Melvin was a person, he believed pretty much in signs. Uncle June had taught him that. June lived his whole life off of dream books and the stars. Well, you could take shit too far. But Baby's twenty, there was a meaning to it. Had to be.

When he left from the food and drink, it was coming on for evening. This hour of the day he liked to walk on Canal Street and watch the people come and go at the big hotels. Le Meridien was his first choice, it had the highest-class bitches.

He was standing outside the Burger King peeping when a sista with a gold dress and gold-streaked hair walked out, and Juvenile walked out right behind her. They got into Juvy's Bentley and drove away, and Melvin went in the Burger King. He ordered up a whopper, double fries and a large coke, then reached in his pocket and came up empty. Baby's twenty was all he owned.

He almost cancelled his order, but no, he had a better idea. He broke the twenty, let it go. Then he took a table by the window and sat down, Lil Mel, and started to write a rap.

J. Lo vs. K. Sul

Lots of people are fine with celebrity magazines. They read them to *unwind*—which sounds to me like eating live mice to unwind. They just don't take magazines seriously. They toss them out after they read them. They distinguish between the real world and the magazine world.

Me, not so much. I try, but it's no good: Magazines are real to me. I believe in them the way I believe in storybooks, which is a whole bunch. It hurts me to throw one away. So I've got to be careful, especially nowadays. Every issue of *Rolling Stone* in its most recent model (sleeker, faster, sexier) ends up in a cardboard box in the closet, because it makes me sad and lonely to have Britney, Christina, Kate Hudson, or that booby-rexic Brazilian model blinking at me from the coffee table like drugged teen hookers. I half believe that magazines and books have individual *vibes*, if you will, and that a magazine created without love transmits a jangly signal of desperation to those within its range. (The superstring theorists will prove me right, you'll see.) Let *Mojo* pile up next to the bed, no problem. But *Rolling Stone*'s got to go in the box.

Some people skim magazines to calm themselves while waiting for the shrink. For me, they're a big reason I'm at the shrink. How do these people do it? Maybe they just don't think to compare themselves to people in magazines. (They probably don't feel guilty for every bad thing that happens in the world, either. How do they do it? I carry around personal shame for Neil Diamond's work in

the early Eighties, just for starters, not to mention that version of
"Da Do Do Do, Da Da Da Da" with Sting singing in Spanish.) On
a bad day like yesterday, in the middle of my own, private Celebrate
Melancholy! Week, I was no match for the snorting beast of American psychosexual pathology in my mailbox: Jennifer Lopez on the
cover of *Rolling Stone*, in a metal Wonderbra.

I pull the thing out of the mailbox, and I know right away I'm
going to read it, despite laundry and deadlines and my best Girl
Power/Drew Barrymore/*Crouching Tiger* training. I mean, how
can I not? She's a one-woman freak show of metastasized success.
She might as well be wearing a sandwich board that reads: "I AM
RICHER, HOTTER, AND BETTER ORGANIZED THAN YOU COULD EVER
HOPE TO BE, YOU ROTTING CORPSE OF A NOBODY." An internal debate
ensues between two of my selves: the teen girl who loves to torture
herself with unfavorable comparisons to others, and the concerned
guru:

> TEEN: Whee! A celebrity-magazine article about a woman my
> age who's way more successful than me!
> GURU: Hmmm . . . what other mail is there? Look here, love,
> see the pretty pink stationery from—erm, the nice gas com-
> pany people . . .
> TEEN: She has a metal bikini!
> GURU: How about this keen *Get Organized!* catalog? Porn for
> obsessive-compulsives! C'mon, let's go grab some coffee—
> TEEN: She has golden skin!
> GURU: Do I have to give you the business—*again?* Okay. See,
> *Rolling Stone* pushes celebrity T&A in order to sell advertis-
> ing to the tobacco, liquor, and corporate-record industries,
> which consist of greedy bores and balding guys who wish
> they had been rock stars, who abuse and exploit *your people:*
> young people, and musicians! Furthermore, young lady,
> you're every bit as lovely as Jennifer Lopez and twice as
> smart. You're soulful and, and . . . and well, you're just a
> super person, and I don't want to hear another word about it.
> TEEN: She has a metal bikini.

And so on.

My mom always said, Don't compare yourself. But my mom's a Jedi master. I'm a 30-year-old late bloomer who couldn't even afford Ecstasy on New Year's, forgets her groceries in the back of the car, believes in magazines, obsesses over music trivia (and trivial musicians), and is convinced an alternate realm of perfection and beauty exists just on the other side of the air we breathe. I'm like one of those sleeping fetus-people in *The Matrix*, trying to find the rabbit hole to Reality. I don't have anything figured out, unlike Jennifer Lopez. She's got it sussed—even if what she's sussed is the manufacture of cold illusion and exploitation of human insecurity.

So I read the hideous thing. I regret it immediately but, unlike a bulimic food binge, you can't un-read a bad article once you've read it. It sits there, curdling your juju. For the rest of the day, comparisons with this chick haunt me.

Jennifer Lopez says, "I don't smoke because I don't have the three minutes it takes to smoke a cigarette!" I have plenty of time. I just don't have the three bucks for a pack.

Lopez has a kicky nickname: "J. Lo" (also the title of her new album). I wonder if I should try it. Call me K. Sul. Yo, I'm K. Sul.

J. Lo is a glamorous movie star. I have some glamorous moments too. Just the other night, my roommate said my dinner (fish sticks and spinach) was very *Erin Brockovich*.

J. Lo's famous ex-boyfriend is hoping he doesn't go to jail for fleeing the scene of a nightclub shooting, with guns ("it was an unfortunate situation," Lopez sighs), because it would mess with his recording career. The guy who used to kind of be my boyfriend (it was an unfortunate situation) is hoping he doesn't get dropped from his record label, because it would mess with his recording career. People call him "puffy" too, because of what his face looks like when he drinks too much Bud Light, which is most of the time.

J. Lo likes to stay in and nest. Hey, K. Sul does too. I'm at home writing on a Friday night when young Hollywood is out snorting coke and sucking face. You think I care?

J. Lo is ambitious. "I'm looking forward to the ninth album, the thirtieth movie," she says. I feel you, J. It's nice to collect stuff. I own, like, five movies right now, but I notice where they're selling used tapes now at Video Hut. You might want to check it out, too, sister. Just a tip.

J. Lo knows how to keep it real. Says one of her many producers: "[J. Lo] still comes to the Bronx and sleeps on her mother's couch." Up in my crib, we keep it so real, I even sleep on my own couch sometimes.

"When we're in the studio," says the producer, "she orders Chinese from, like, the place next door." Me too, totally! "One day she left the studio and got in a cab because she didn't want to wait for a car," he says. "She's got a little bit of thug in her." In that case, I'm a regular gang-banger—I walk, drive, *and* take cabs. I put the "hug" in "thug," yo.

J. Lo also likes to have fun: "Wherever she's at, she's got her crew that rolls with her," says the producer, "and they *party*." Apparently she spends more time with these dancers, managers, stylists, and publicists than with her family or boyfriend. Let's see. I must have a crew lying around here somewhere . . . I'm pretty sure I had a crew—

Good God! I forgot to let the crew out of the closet when I got home from Food 4 Less last week! They've had nothing to read but *Rolling Stone*!

Of course, J. Lo has a thoughtful side, too. She thinks about things, because she has lots of things to think about. Things like, you know, thoughts. For example: "Things I go through, things I see my friends go through. You get to a certain age and you start thinking about other things." Speak!

And still, I can't help but wonder what it would be like to be like J. Lo: "When she's not demanding everyone do as she does, everyone just seems to want to." That used to happen to me all the time—till I told everybody, *Look, Barbie—and Skipper, and you too, Cher: You're going to have to fend for yourselves some day*. It still happened after that, but at least I warned them.

Actually, I don't know J. Lo and I don't really mind if she pulls her Madonniest stunts to pop the superfame barrier. She's like an international diplomat for the shelf-asses of the world, and I'm personally grateful for that. She's an okay actress. She's not cloning babies or inventing sheep AIDS or giving money to the Scientologists (that we know of). So what the hell?

But still, she and her single, "Love Don't Cost a Thing"—in which her voice is reinvented by recording technology to resemble a set of robotic triplets, their programs set on "Destiny's Child-lite"— just leave me feeling cold and alone. When a person manages, after years of struggle, to capture the flaming baton of public attention, and they're really running with it, and they're actually starting to master it, I guess I kind of want them to do something with it. Say something. Give me something for my attention.

Not to be too predictable, but supposing you gave me a sign that you feel the things I feel: self-doubt, fear, loneliness, even wild obsession? (Sorry, but confessing you're "addicted to love!" doesn't cut the muffin.) Don't try to sell me that dorky lie that you're part of some immortal club of people who, having achieved humanity's lamest values—fame, wealth, and power—have shed all human qualities but greed and smugness. It only makes you look desperate.

If you can't do that, then sell me a dream, because I love dreams. But make it a goddamn beautiful one. Can you do that? Can you make a kick-ass dream that inspires ass kicking? Can you make it a multidimensional dream that contains hidden doors to larger dreams? Can you be a force for good in the world, and not just a force for you in the world?

You know what? I'd even be happy with a cool *bad* dream. Just don't give me this "I'm totally bland, have no imagination, and have been completely desalinated by the teams at corporate who have reprogrammed me for the pursuit of money and fame" bullshit.

When you get like that, J., you just remind me too much of reality.

DAVID CANTWELL

"Help Me Make It Through the Night": The Anatomy of a Record

In the spring of 1970, a veteran pop music sound engineer from Los Angeles, a rhythm section schooled in rock & soul, a classically trained Australian arranger, and an Oklahoma singer who loved pop and jazz all assembled in Nashville's Monument Studio to record— for a brand new label—a song written by a hippie Rhodes scholar. Through some combination of sweat, craft, ambition, and inspiration, this disparate group of individuals created a country classic called "Help Me Make It Through the Night."

By any standard, it was a great record. Thirty years later, it remains musically irresistible and emotionally compelling, and its grappling with complex human emotions continues to vibrate with country soul. Yet, even as it remains vital, it also speaks for its time. The late '60s through the early '70s was an exciting era for country music, a period when the genre had the eye and ear of the nation as never before. Country-identified performers such as Johnny Cash, Mac Davis, Glen Campbell, Buck Owens, and Roy Clark had landed highly visible TV gigs. On radio, it was possible for records that were unmistakably country to get Top Forty airplay. Quite a few country hits—including "Stand by Your Man," "Harper Valley

PTA," "Rose Garden," and "Kiss an Angel Good Morning"—crossed over to the pop charts.

Topping the country charts in the summer of 1971 and eventually climbing into the pop Top Ten, "Help Me Make It Through the Night" was one of these hits. Recorded the same week four Kent State University students were killed by national guardsmen during an anti-Vietnam War protest, it was a single born during one of the most tumultuous moments in American culture, and the contributions of its creators spotlight an important transitional moment in country music's history.

Kris Kristofferson's song—particularly the sexually frank detail of its lyrics—was emblematic of a new breed of rock-influenced country songwriting. The dynamic country soul of the recording—thanks to producer Jim Malloy, guitarist Chip Young, and arranger Bill Walker, among others—revealed the influences of a generation of Nashville music makers who had grown up listening not only to country music but to rock & roll, jazz, pop, r&b, and even classical music. Most indelible of all was the amazing performance of singer Sammi Smith. Her story illustrates the expanding opportunities for women in country music that developed during these years, while her intimate, vulnerable phrasing remains one of the most stirring interpretations in modern country music.

On the thirtieth anniversary of its recording, "Help Me Make It Through the Night" remains both a musical time capsule and a timeless expression of universal human needs. This is an anatomy of that record.

The Songwriter

The story of Kris Kristofferson has become one of Nashville's favorites. The son of a major general in the U.S. Air Force, he was born in Brownsville, Texas, on June 22, 1936, and grew up to be a football star at Pomona College and a Rhodes scholar at Oxford University. He was, it might be said, the very child of privilege that Creedence Clearwater Revival would one day rage against in "Fortunate Son." But for Kristofferson, it was writing—short stories and novels at first, but songs soon enough—that had won his heart. In June 1965, two weeks before he was to report to West Point as a professor of English literature, he said "No thanks" and set off for Nashville to make it as a songwriter. "I got a great future behind me," he liked to tell people.

He had an even greater future ahead of him, though it took a while to materialize. Over the next few years Kristofferson worked as a ditch digger, a bartender at Music Row's Tally Ho Tavern, and a janitor at Columbia Studios. But even though he made some promising connections—songwriter-publisher Marijohn Wilkin was an early supporter, as were Johnny Cash and June Carter Cash—he didn't seem to be getting anywhere. People weren't exactly racing to record his songs; his family had declared he embarrassed them; his wife had divorced him; and he was broke. Discouraged but still writing, he found himself in 1968 commuting back and forth between Nashville and the Gulf of Mexico, where he flew helicopters for the off-shore oil rigs. And then that job ended too.

"I was in this Evangeline Hotel, like something out of *Psycho*, a filthy place, just sitting there with this neon Jesus outside the door, in the swamps outside Lafayette, Louisiana," he recalled to *Esquire* magazine last year. "And I thought, 'Fuck. I'm on the bottom, can't go any lower.' I drove my car to the airport, left it there, and never went back to get it."

The thirty-two-year-old Kristofferson headed straight back to Nashville. The songs he began pitching now were ones he'd written on those lonely, worried drives from Nashville to Louisiana, or while shuttling oil workers over the Gulf. "The next moment, they cut three of my songs, and they were hits," he told *Esquire*. "I never had to go back to work again." First, Roger Miller recorded the song that is, thanks to a posthumously released version by Janis Joplin, Kristofferson's best-known composition, "Me and Bobby McGee." Then, in quick succession, Ray Price had a huge crossover single with "For the Good Times," Cash scored with "Sunday Morning Coming Down," and Waylon Jennings hit with "The Taker." The hits kept on coming. Five Kris Kristofferson–penned songs made the *Billboard* country Top Ten in 1970 alone; three of them reached #1 and also crossed over to the pop charts. "Sunday Morning Coming Down" was named Song of the Year by the Country Music Association. When he accepted his award, a long-haired Kristofferson, dressed in hipster-wear and looking disoriented, stumbled up on stage to mumble his thanks. Many in the Nashville establishment were reportedly shocked to see that country music's hottest young songwriter looked like a hippie.

It was Kristofferson's destiny to become the most visible symbol of the changing American culture's impact on country music. As the '60s came to a close, Merle Haggard's #1 country hit "Okie From Muskogee" seemingly struck back at the decade's rock-associated counterculture. But on campuses and even in the mainstream, America had begun to assimilate the counterculture in significant, if sometimes superficial, ways. Kristofferson arrived on the country scene at roughly the same moment as an emerging group of talented, individualistic songwriters (including Jimmy Webb, Tom T. Hall, John Hartford, Mickey Newbury, Curly Putman, Dolly Parton, and a reinvigorated Willie Nelson). More successfully than any of his contemporaries, though, Kristofferson was able to take the period's political and cultural impulses—of youth culture generally, and of rock music specifically—and boil them down to their emotional essence: our desires for community, freedom, and love, and the suffering that plagues us when they go unmet.

It is just such human alienation, and the acute loneliness that is its most crushing effect, that has been Kristofferson's great theme; his songs beat a path to the idea again and again. "There'll be time enough for sadness when you leave me." "There's something in a Sunday makes a body feel alone." "Freedom's just another word for nothing left to lose." These lines from his finest songs deliver their observations in the everyday language typical of great country songs. When unpacked by a great singer and arrangement, they reveal an existential weight. Estranged, frightened, filled with despair—Kristofferson's characteristic conflict is an ordinary person seeking freedom and confronting a dark night of the soul.

Even so, the greatest versions of his songs—Janis Joplin's "Me and Bobby McGee" and Sammi Smith's "Help Me Make It

Through the Night"—have been made by women, perhaps because
in our society women can understand even more concretely than
men that reaching for freedom exacts a heavy price.

"Help Me Make It Through the Night" tackles these issues with
remarkable directness. "It's sad to be alone," Kristofferson wrote,
and the line at first seems so simple, so circular in its logic, as to be
simpleminded. But then he follows it with the title phrase, "Help me
make it through the night," and the stakes are immediately ratcheted
higher—as high, for the song's narrator, as they could possibly be.

Kristofferson is often hailed as having brought a new depth to
country music. Perhaps what he most had to offer, though, was not
added dimension but fresh perspective. Like so many earlier country
classics, Kristofferson's best work simply gave contemporary names
to those timeless moments when human beings are so lonesome they
could die. "If there was one thing I could cure, it wouldn't be cancer
or war, it would be loneliness," Kristofferson told *Seventeen* magazine in 1971. "That kills more than the rest."

The Record Label President

Born in Manhattan in 1921, Brad McCuen was raised in a musical
environment. His father owned a bugle manufacturing company,
and bandleader Hal Kemp was a friend of the family and neighbor.
McCuen played guitar in a high school dance band, but when he
headed south to the University of North Carolina in 1939, it
seemed as if "every third student played guitar." There was a large
dance band scene, though, all up and down the southern Atlantic
coast—the Chapel Hill area alone was managing to support at least
five such outfits—and the young McCuen soon found a niche
behind the scenes, writing a music column for the school newspaper
and managing one of the orchestras.

After serving in Europe during World War II, McCuen landed a
job selling records throughout Long Island and Manhattan for the
Majestic label, an independent that specialized in popular dance
music such as bandleader Eddy Howard's "Rickety Rickshaw Man,"
a Top Ten hit in 1946. By 1948, though, he was back in the South.

"I was a southern field man for RCA," he remembers today, "because RCA used to send brilliant young Yankees down south and the southerners would chew 'em up and send 'em back up here every six months. But because I'd had four years of college down there, RCA hoped I knew something that the other Yankees didn't."

The strategy paid off. In 1954, McCuen, clued in by east Tennessee record merchants, was among the first people to notify RCA A&R director Steve Sholes about a phenomenon called Elvis Presley. McCuen would spend the next decade and a half in various positions at RCA—in the '60s he oversaw the label's Vintage reissue program—but in 1969 he struck out on his own to found Mega Records. "With the Elvis reputation behind me it was not hard to raise the money to start the label," he says.

According to its publicity materials, Mega Records was "Nashville's first total concept label." Its releases ranged from classical and jazz to rock & roll; its second release was by a now-forgotten rock band called Alan Rush & the Stonehouse. Mega's greatest success, though, would come with the label's first signing, country artist Sammi Smith, and the song "Help Me Make It Through the Night."

"Several other people had recorded the song," McCuen recalls, "and I had thought, 'My God, this is too great a song not to really be a major hit.' So we looked for a man to sing it, and we found Sammi Smith. She was a woman—boy, was she ever!—and the record turned out beautifully."

The Singer

Sammi Smith was born August 5, 1943, in Orange, California. Her mother and father's families were both from Oklahoma, and at age three Sammi moved with her parents back to their home state. The marriage soon ended in divorce, and Smith grew up on the move. "I guess you could call me a roamer," she says today. She followed her mother to New Mexico, Colorado, Arizona, and finally back to California. Encouraged by her mother's new husband, an eleven-year-old Smith began singing for a band at the local army base. But before long she was back in Oklahoma, and alone. "My mother moved on again," she remembers, "forgot to take me." She was thirteen.

"I worked in the nightclubs," she explains. "I sang and made enough money to have a room in Oklahoma City. I got by all right. That hotel was kinda in a bad part of town, but there were some gay guys that lived there. They helped me with my makeup and took care of me, pretty well watched out for me. And somehow I skated through.

"I had a steady job at the Some Place Else Club in Oklahoma City . . ." she continues. "At that time, I did big band stuff, you know, and just a little jazz and swing . . . We did Dorsey and all that kinda stuff and we did some country, some Hank Thompson swing. Six nights a week . . . I did Peggy Lee songs, 'Fever' and that kinda stuff. Some Brenda Lee songs I did. The band did waltzes like 'Fascination' and 'Westphalia Waltz,' just a typical, all-around dance band."

It was the mid-to-late '50s, so a few rock & roll numbers were soon added to the mix. "We did 'Blue Suede Shoes,' I remember, but of course we did Ray Price songs, too," she says. "It was really rockabilly that we did, which was just mainly at that time country music to me."

Over the next decade Smith remained on the move. She married the owner of Some Place Else and the two headed back to California; when the marriage bottomed out she returned to Oklahoma, alone again. Through it all she kept singing. In December of 1967 she took a tape of herself to promoter Hap Peebles, who was in town with the Johnny Cash show. Peebles played the tape for Cash's bass player, Marshall Grant, and Grant played it for Cash. "A week later I was in Nashville," she recalls, still amazed. After years of bouncing around, she found herself overnight in a Columbia Studios recording session backed by the Tennessee Three.

Debuting on the country charts during the last week of January 1968, Smith's first single, "So Long, Charlie Brown," had "Ring of Fire"-style mariachi horns and a thumping backbeat that was unmistakably Tennessee Three. Mostly, though, Smith's Columbia sides stayed within the narrow range of styles then available to country girl singers. Producer Frank Jones cut Smith in arrangements that had her sounding, alternately, like Patsy Cline, Loretta Lynn, and Connie Smith.

Although Sammi Smith respected the talent of those women, they weren't exactly the singers she would have identified as her musical influences. "I always loved Keely Smith, with Louie Prima," she says, citing the dusky-voiced pop singer who played straight-woman to jazz showman Prima on standards like "That Old Black Magic." "I got to meet her one time, thrilled me to death. I was at that time, though, mainly listening to Merle Haggard, all those guys. But I really don't have a female country influence. I liked Ella Fitzgerald and I liked Keely Smith and Della Reese, just a bunch of them. But the country women weren't a big influence on me, I don't think."

Smith's interest in jazz and pop, a remnant of her years singing for big bands in the Southwest, would become more apparent when she recorded "Help Me Make It Through the Night" in 1970. But on her earlier Columbia sides, her primary influences remained more or less buried. The three singles that resulted from these first sessions went largely unnoticed; the most successful of them, a version of John Hartford's "Why Do You Do Me Like You Do," crawled to #53 on the *Billboard* country chart. Although Smith's vocals were strong on these early recordings, the chief characteristics of her later success—her husky, smoky voice; her soulful ballad delivery; her startling vulnerability in song—had not yet fully emerged. Singing in other women's styles, Smith seemed unable to distinguish herself from any other "girl singer" of the period.

Not that there were a lot of slots on country radio for women in the late '60s, particularly not at the highest levels of visibility. During the eight years from 1963, when Patsy Cline died in a plane crash, to 1970, when "Help Me Make It Through the Night" debuted, female solo artists had managed to top *Billboard*'s Hot Country Singles chart just sixteen times (all but two of those by Loretta Lynn or Tammy Wynette), a track record that accounted for only 11 percent of all country chart-toppers in the period. But in the four years immediately following "Help Me Make It Through the Night," women's presence on country radio exploded. Between 1971 and 1974, solo women topped the country singles chart thirty-three times.

With the exception of Lynn, the women who led this charge to greater visibility were of a new generation: Tammy Wynette, most famously, as well as Smith, Bobbie Gentry, Donna Fargo, Jeannie C. Riley, Jeannie Seely, Lynn Anderson, Dolly Parton, and, later, Tanya Tucker. Born during World War II or in the years just after, these women came of age during a relatively more permissive postwar culture of economic expansion, a time when television and rock & roll—not to mention an increased awareness of women's rights—were changing America.

With this context in mind, the pop-influenced country music these women would soon make—not to mention the more assertive and even sexual themes they would explore—should have been no more surprising in the early '70s than the emergence of a rock-influenced country songwriter like Kris Kristofferson. This doesn't mean, however, that such developments weren't shocking to many country listeners, especially ones not accustomed to rock's expanded (though often no less oppressive) roles for women artists.

Smith had met Kristofferson when she was recording at Columbia Studios and he was still the janitor. "We were running buddies," she says. The pair remained in touch even after Columbia dropped Smith from its roster in 1968. Without a label and still unable to carve out a distinctive niche for herself, she went out on the road for a couple of years as Waylon Jennings's girl singer—"Girl Hero," he would call her—but eventually that job ended, too. She struck out alone, splitting her time between gigs at Nashville venues like the Black Poodle in Printer's Alley and in a variety of Arizona clubs. By 1970 the grind had Smith so discouraged that she seriously considered leaving the business. When Brad McCuen and Harry Pratt (Mega's primary investor) tracked her down in Arizona, and said they wanted her to come back to Nashville and be the first artist on their new label, Smith needed to have her arm twisted. "It was kinda off the wall, brand new label and all," she remembers. "I was burnt out. I was about ready to just toss it in." But she decided to give it a try.

"I'd heard her singing on the Columbia label," McCuen says of Smith. "My feeling was she wasn't being produced right to take benefit of her great talent. Number one, the selection of the songs weren't quite right for her." Smith agreed. She caught up with her old friend Kristofferson, who was just then enjoying the first blush of fame. "He and I went into the old Monument studio," she remembers. "He played guitar and I sang, and we put down six or seven of his songs, including 'For the Good Times' and 'Me and Bobby McGee' and 'Help Me Make It,' just about every song he had."

"I loved everything Kris wrote," she says today. "I just wanted to do one of his songs. I really didn't care which one. ['Help Me Make It'] is the one they let me do. They took it in to my producer Jim Malloy, and that's the one they said I could do."

The Producer

Jim Malloy was born in Dixon, Illinois, in 1931. Like Smith, he bounced around a good deal growing up, even enduring a period of homelessness when he was thirteen years old and living in Iowa. By his early twenties he had made his way to California to pursue a career in electronics.

"California had all the big electronics companies," Malloy remembers, "and in 1954, that just seemed like the coming thing, seemed like the future to me." He attended electronics school for two years, eventually landing a job at NBC in Burbank. From there Malloy moved to Radio Recorders as an electronics maintenance engineer, where he fell under the tutelage of Alan Emig, the head of Columbia's West Coast office and a former mixing engineer for Capitol Records. "Alan just started showing me about being a music mixer," Malloy says. "And so I started sitting at the board and doing preliminary mixes on all kinds of big-named acts."

Malloy was a quick study. "It's like putting," he says. "You just have to feel it. I knew guys who had done it for years before I started and who did it for years after me, and the stuff they did was just really blah, didn't have any spark or anything." By 1960 he had started to engineer sessions by himself, and in 1962 he became a full-time sound engineer at RCA studios in Los Angeles. For the next three years he engineered sessions for a Who's Who of early '60s pop and r&b stars, including Frank Sinatra, Sammy Davis Jr., Dean Martin, Paul Anka, Sam Cooke, and Doris Day. He was especially well known for his work with Henry Mancini; Malloy engineered "The Pink Panther Theme," and won the sound engineering Grammy in 1966 for his work on Mancini's *Charade* soundtrack. (He would be nominated five other times throughout the decade.)

It was, in part, the experience Malloy gained on these pop sessions—and on one session in particular—that would later translate into the distinctive sound of "Help Me Make It Through the Night." "Julie London had that real kind of intimate voice that Sammi does," he says, recalling the smoky pop singer. "I recorded an album one time with her back in the '50s. And I always thought that was a real great sound for somebody in the country field after I moved to Nashville." That came in 1965. Chet Atkins, in L.A. working with the Anita Kerr singers, asked Duane Eddy to recommend an engineer. Eddy suggested Malloy, and Atkins soon lured him to Music City where he began engineering sessions for such RCA acts as Eddy Arnold, Waylon Jennings, Charley Pride, Connie Smith, and Elvis Presley. By the end of the decade Malloy had gained enough of a reputation to strike out on his own as a freelance producer.

It was a good time for Malloy to make the move. As the '60s gave way to the '70s, many of Nashville's frontline producers were spending less time in the studio: Atkins, who became an RCA vice-president in 1968, had begun sharing much of his work load with Bob Ferguson. Other producers were being replaced altogether: At Columbia, Don Law was forced into retirement in 1967, in favor first of Bob Johnston—who had produced Bob Dylan's *Blonde on Blonde* the year before—and later Billy Sherrill. Many of these new faces—including Jerry Kennedy, Jack Clement, Glenn Sutton, and, on the West Coast, Al Delory—had extensive experience outside country music, experiences that would soon be reflected on country radio and, increasingly, pop radio, as well.

Malloy—who had already served as de facto producer on countless sessions in the Nashville system, and who was every bit as comfortable with rock & roll and old-school pop as he was with country music—could not have been better suited to this new environment. "Brad [McCuen] called me," Malloy remembers, "and said we signed a little girl who's a country music singer and we think she's really, really good. We'd like to play a demo tape for you of her and see if you would produce her for us. So I listened to it, and I thought she had just a fabulous voice. And so the first session I produced was for 'Help Me Make It Through the Night' with Sammi Smith."

The Band

Malloy set about putting together a band for the Smith sessions, and the first player he turned to was Chip Young, a guitarist he had worked with regularly through the years. Young (born Jerry Stembridge in 1938) had grown up in Atlanta, and like so many teenagers of the period, he was a fan of the new rock & roll. "I listened to Chuck Berry and of course Elvis and Carl Perkins and a lot of r&b records," he recalls. "I was a little more of a rocker then than a country guy." Young pursued his love for rock & roll by learning guitar and, by the late '50s, was working as a picker, song-writer, and producer for the various acts that had gravitated to Atlanta's Bill Lowery and his publishing firm Lowery Music Group: Jerry Reed, Billy Joe Royal, Ray Stevens, and, in particular, Joe South, with whom Young had toured.

After a two-year hitch in the army, Young was coaxed up to Nashville by Jerry Reed to pursue a performing career. "January 1st, 1963, I hit the road with Reed as a duo out of Nashville," Young remembers. He ultimately found more success catching session work and recording demos. His real break came when he recorded the demo for a song called "What Color (Is a Man)?" "It had a little rolling lick, a little finger lick that was real intricate," he recalls. Later, Grady Martin, attempting to duplicate Young's demo part on a session with pop singer Bobby Vinton, couldn't figure it out and so Young was summoned. "You little son of a bitch," Young remembers Martin saying. "Come here and play that for me!" Young did just that, and from then on, he and Martin were fast friends. Now properly initiated, Young also began to get more gigs. After a 1966 introduction by Scotty Moore, for whom Young had recorded jingles in Memphis, Young became a fixture at Elvis Presley's '60s recording sessions, along with engineer Jim Malloy.

To round out the group for the Smith sessions, Malloy chose guitarist Jerry Shook, pedal steel player Weldon Myrick (best known for his work with Connie Smith), and bassist and A-team staple Roy "Junior" Huskey. To complete his rhythm section Malloy went after players who, like Young, were every bit as versed in rocking soul as they were in country music. Pianist David Briggs and drummer Jerry Carrigan had both been part of the original Muscle Shoals rhythm section, backing singers such as Arthur Alexander, Tommy Roe, and Jimmy Hughes in the early '60s.

"I came [to Nashville] just a few years before they did," Young explains, "before they came up from Muscle Shoals, but I had known them in Muscle Shoals going over from Atlanta playing on things. And going from here in Nashville down to Muscle Shoals and playing on things after I moved up here. So I knew all those guys real well and when they moved up here, we kinda became a unit. We were a little more hungry, we wanted to be known, if that makes sense. All these other people, the 'A' players, were already pretty well known and so we wanted to do something that'd impress somebody.

"The young blood is what they called us," Young says. "The new guys."

The Arranger

Bill Walker, who Malloy chose to do the string arrangements for Smith's first Mega sessions, brought an even more unlikely background to Nashville. Born and raised in Australia, Walker graduated from the Sydney Conservatorium of Music and quickly took a job working for RCA in Johannesburg, South Africa. "When I worked there, between 1959 and 1964, all of the record companies at that time had big operations there," he says. "The job of each label was to cover the other label's stuff that was making hits in the states, as well as recording a lot of the local artists."

It was working on just such a project that would eventually lead him to America. Walker did the arrangement for Jim Reeves's cover of "From a Jack to a King" ("We beat Ned Miller's record in Africa and Europe," Walker remembers), and Reeves liked Walker's work so much he enlisted the young arranger for his *Kimberly Jim* film project. When Reeves needed an arranger for a television series he was scheduled to begin back in the states, he offered Walker the job. But the show never happened.

"Jim got killed the week I got [to Nashville]," Walker recalls. "He flew that little plane into the mountain, out here at Brentwood. And so that was a little bit of a rough time for me. RCA offered me my job back in Johannesburg, but I thought, 'Well, I'm here now, I've got a green card, and I'm in the musician's union, I'm going to give it a shot.' Because as far as I was concerned this was the place to be."

It was also the time to be there. In the mid-'60s, Nashville was beginning to employ strings on its sessions like never before. Walker would be among a small group of men—primarily Cam Mullins, Bergen White, and Bill McElhiney—who would arrange virtually every session in Nashville that called for more than a basic country rhythm section. Walker says the real turning point came for him in 1965 when he provided the string arrangements for Eddy Arnold's *My World* album, which included the pop crossover hits "What's He Doing in My World" and "Make the World Go Away." By the time of the "Help Me Make It Through the Night" sessions in 1970, Walker was perhaps the busiest arranger in town. "When Jim Malloy was the head engineer at RCA I was doing 60 or 70 percent of RCA's work at that time," Walker says. "I wrote all the arrangements, conducted the orchestra, played piano, did a bunch of stuff."

The most lasting thing he did was contribute to the countrypolitan sound created by Nashville's new breed of producers. "I didn't write to make it sound like country," Walker stresses. "My idea at that time [was], 'Look, we've got a country audience for these artists. Let's try to get some of the city folks as well and increase our sales.' And we did. I wrote always in mind to keep the country rhythm section sound and feel, and the vocal group sound and feel, but with the orchestra sometimes I'd use a flute or an oboe just to give it a different something that urban [listeners] could identify and wouldn't say, 'Well, that's hillbilly' and not listen to it and not buy it. I worked at that all the time. It was something that made me a little bit different and gave me a tool with which to work."

The Session

It's hardly surprising that most of the principals have only the most general sorts of memories regarding the recording of "Help Me Make It Through the Night." These were men and women, after all, who went to the studio every day the way most people go to the office, field, or factory: Malloy says he engineered or produced more than 1,000 albums in his time; Young says he averaged 200 to 250 sessions a year, for thirty years. The significance of most sessions would only become plain after the fact—when the song was, or wasn't, getting played on the radio.

Still, thirty years later, Smith, Malloy, and Young agree on the basics. When they entered the studio Wednesday evening, May 6, 1970, Malloy—who was assisted on the session by engineer Tommy Strong—was already hearing an intimate blend of pop, r&b, and country. He was particularly interested in applying his experience with pop singers such as Julie London and Frank Sinatra to help Smith take full advantage of the studio setting. "With the soul Sammi had," Malloy remembers, "I always wanted her to sing in close to the microphone and soft so we could get that real intimate sound on her."

This was a new approach for Smith. "The way I was singing then was for an audience," she remembers. "It wasn't quite as intimate as you can get just getting right up close to a microphone and forgetting about volume, forgetting about anything but emotion and just doing it the way you feel it. And as a result, it changed my whole way of singing, even for an audience. Malloy was very good at not letting me over-sing. Actually, on a lot of them, I had hardly any volume, I was just barely singing."

Smith found a depth of expression missing from her earlier Columbia sides. "Sammi was one of those people, she made you believe everything she sang," Malloy says. "You just knew that whatever it was she was singing about, that's what had happened. The thing that set her apart for me as being a truly great country singer is like being a truly great rhythm and blues singer: You just can't be mechanically correct and in tune, you've gotta have a lot of soul in yourself."

Singing softly and in tempos so slow she almost seems to be speaking at times, Smith was able to unleash that soul as never before. Malloy, Walker, Young, and the rest fashioned settings that emphasized the vulnerability of the singer and her stories. They turned first that evening to "With Pen in Hand," a Bobby Goldsboro composition about the end of a marriage, which had been a hit on both pop and country radio in the previous two years. From its opening notes, a hushed tone was established for the evening. David Briggs's piano intro could have been lifted whole from one of Malloy's L.A. jazz or pop sessions; he makes his notes bounce up and down, like a seesaw, and then Walker's strings quickly join in to hold a note that just quivers there, teetering. And so the stage was set for Smith to beg her husband, one final time, not to sign that paper. The spare, melancholy "Saunders Ferry Lane" was recorded next, followed by Kristofferson's "Sunday Morning Coming Down."

In all these tracks, the arrangements manage to suggest the inner turmoil of their narrators without once distracting from Smith's solitary voice. "The only thing I did for Sammi, it was really very simple," Malloy explains. "What I didn't want to have happen [was] to cover her up and get anything busy going on around her. Like most country records, you hear the phrase, then you hear some instrument play the phrase, maybe just a few notes behind them. But I tried to stay away from doing that kind of stuff because she was just a stylist, I mean a true, true stylist. I wanted just rhythm around her a lot of the time, and the things that were happening I kept pretty subdued. And I didn't use a lot of harmony with her. I tried to make Sammi's records very intimate."

In part, this intimacy came across through rhythm arrangements graced with a little bit of the soul that Malloy had recorded in L.A., and that came like breathing to Carrigan, Briggs, and Young. "They all knew r&b," Malloy says, "and so I purposely put Sammi with a rhythm section like that so I could get her country interpretations of things but I could get the r&b feeling at the same time.

"I would say, 'Guys, I want this to have a little rhythm & blues feel to it, don't make it like twelve-bar bucket blues but give me a little rhythm & blues feel to a country song.' And they all knew exactly what I was talking about, of course. We did everything with that r&b type of feel and laid the country song on top of it. And we cut 'Help Me Make It Through the Night' straight to two track."

They almost didn't cut it at all that first night. By the time Malloy had gotten takes of "With Pen in Hand," "Sunday Morning Coming Down," and "Saunders Ferry Lane," there were only about five minutes left on the three-hour session. Malloy played the band Smith and Kristofferson's demo while the string players looked over their charts. The group's first and only time completely through the song, Malloy believes, was the performance that became the record.

"They may have given me a few extra minutes on the end of [the session]," Malloy says. "No, it was the last song, we didn't have much time. No time at all. Yeah, five minutes. And those guys, of course, were fast as hell. Bill [Walker] had written the chart anyway, and they were all good readers."

"Walker had that thing kinda laid out with his string arrangement," Chip Young recalls, "but I put that little da dee doo, dee doo doo, that little suspended lick on there, which was a kind of popular thing in that day. To me, it ached for that gut-string."

"The song to me makes the whole record," Young says. "The playing just enhances the song, you try to not get in the way of the lyrics. And the soul sound of that record just happened, it's one of those things where the song kinda led us there. And you know that's the way she was singing it. She felt really bluesy on it, like a young Peggy Lee or something. A white soul singer. She poured her heart and soul into it. It's the meetings of all of these things: It's the arrangement, it's the playing, it's the performance, it's the sound in the studio.

"It was a good record," he says. "There's no doubt about that."

The Record

"Help Me Make It Through the Night" had been recorded several times before Smith's version hit. The first was an unissued version for Smash cut by Bill Nash in 1969, and Ray Price recorded an inexplicably jaunty version for his 1970 LP *For the Good Times*. All of these versions had been made by men—from his opening line, "Take the ribbon from your hair," Kristofferson had clearly written the song from his male viewpoint. But by the time Sammi recorded the song, she'd already altered the lyric, simply because she liked singing her friend's songs. Her edit—"Take the ribbon from my hair"—was simple yet significant. It not only switched the gender of the speaker, it transformed the relationship of the narrator to her intended lover. Instead of a man attempting to seduce a woman by asking her to do something he likes to watch, it is the woman who is doing the seducing. One reason the single would eventually be so shocking to some was that, at a moment when the women's movement was only just beginning to make its way into mainstream consciousness, Sammi Smith seemed to be so clearly advocating for a woman's right to initiate sex without apology.

What's most remarkable, though, is the way that—due to Smith's revision and performance, and the music surrounding it—the single becomes only superficially about sex. Kristofferson's sensual images—a woman's hair tumbling onto the bare skin of the lover who lies at her side—sets the listener up for a seduction, but then delivers on desires more profound: the fear that one cannot make it, will not even be able to go on, alone.

Kristofferson has said that he found the title for his song in a Frank Sinatra interview he'd read, where the singer talked about using liquor or a lover to get through the night. Smith is using the latter, but not in any tawdry sense. Rather, this is what Ralph Ellison meant when he wrote of "the mysteriousness of the blues," "their capacity to make the details of sex convey meanings which touch upon the metaphysical." Listening to "Help Me Make It Through the Night," we do not know what, exactly, has led the singer to her dark night of the soul; we only know that it is dark.

The record begins like the releasing of a breath—Junior Huskey's bass, Jerry Carrigan's cymbal, Chip Young's guitar, all playing one warm note that will return like a pulse. As Young picks out a delicate, urgent acoustic riff and Huskey's bass sounds the bottom, a string section enters playing Bill Walker's arrangement: The cellos play a low, earthy riff that will serve as a kind of motif or hook throughout the song, while the violins merely offer one long, high note suspended above.

"Take the ribbon from my hair," Smith sings in a husky drawl as the music pauses around her. Then Young and Huskey return, as Carrigan, now on wood block, keeps time. Smith calls to her lover, and the strings respond with increasingly more elaborate variations on their opening motif. Smith, her longing increasing with every line, rides the groove, asking her lover first merely to lay down by her side, then to stay with her 'til sunrise, and finally pleading for him to help her make it through the night. It is too personal a thing to have to say out loud, but when she does, her voice vibrates with a common need: To know that we are not alone because others note our pain, and are moved by it.

At the bridge, Smith begins to cry out in despair. She says she doesn't care about right or wrong or figuring out what it all means or what consequences tomorrow may bring. But the anxiety in her voice says she cares very much, or is at least painfully aware of the myriad disastrous consequences that can follow sex, especially for a woman. Yet she wants to do this anyway. She needs more than someone to sit up with her all night and hold her hand. She wants to be held in the most complete sense. And her voice conveys all of this.

The strings raise their voices here too, but now, driving through a fierce counter-melody, they are off on their own and no longer a comfort. The tension between the singer and the strings builds—a chasm underscored by Carrigan, who has now exchanged wood block for drum head—and there is no resolution, just the conflict ongoing. There's no narrative climax, just an emotional one: "Tonight I need a friend." Then Carrigan offers his version of the motif, and it drums the song to a halt.

The singer is terrified that she may not be able to make it through this crisis, but what seems to pull her onward is the absolute conviction that making it through the night will be worth it. She starts again. Smith has found her composure once more, but if anything she seems more trapped in this awful moment than ever—yesterday and tomorrow don't even exist to her now. Then she gives up on words altogether and begins to hum. David Briggs, on piano, enters for the first time, breathing out as she breathes in, finishing her lines. "It's sad to be alone," she sings. "I don't want to be alone." Behind her, the strings play their old parts but their notes tremble now and, here and there, Carrigan's bass drum punches up the rhythm like he's trying to keep the whole fragile thing from collapsing around them. There is something uncomfortably naked about it all. With her body and her wordless voice, she is begging for help, risking rejection, risking everything. Yet, as the record concludes, we know Smith has discovered, in the wisdom of rhythm and the generosity of melody, a way to emphasize the essential human dignity of her plea.

The Single

"We knew that Kris's songs were ahead of their time," Malloy remembers. "Sammi loved the songs, of course. She was a huge Kristofferson fan, the same as I was. You just didn't write those kind of songs for country music because it was all the Bible Belt, you know. But anyway we went ahead and when we got done with it and I played the album for the people who ran the label, they liked 'Help Me Make It Through the Night,' they liked the record, but realistically they felt they couldn't get it played because of the lyrics and also because of the fact that I didn't use any background singers." As Malloy related in the liner notes of the Varese Sarabande release *The Best of Sammi Smith*, "The people at Mega didn't think it sounded 'country' enough."

Though Malloy cannot recall for certain, he speculates, and Brad McCuen concurs, that such concerns may explain why the next two evenings of recording captured different sounds than the first. The versions of the songs the group recorded on Thursday, May 7

("Lonely Street," "This Room for Rent," "There He Goes," "If
Michael Calls"), and on Friday, May 8 ("Don't Blow No Smoke on
Me," "He's Everywhere," "But You Know I Love You," and a never-
released version of "Son of a Preacher Man"), still included elements of pop in Walker's strings, and of r&b in the bluesy fills of
Young, Briggs, and Carrigan. But these new songs sounded more
typically country. Predominantly uptempo with more traditional
country melodies, these versions found Smith singing louder as
well. Weldon Myrick's pedal steel guitar now played a prominent
role throughout.

This tension between the intimate pop-inflected approach perfected on the first night and the more characteristically country
sound they emphasized later was played out explicitly on Friday
night, when the group appears to have recorded two versions of
"He's Everywhere." One of these was in the style of the first night's
recordings, with strings; the other featured Myrick's pedal steel and
no strings at all. The pedal steel and no-strings version of "He's
Everywhere" was chosen to be Mega's first single. "We published
'He's Everywhere,' and so it was to our advantage to see it be a hit,"
McCuen says today. According to Malloy, "Mega released 'He's
Everywhere' because it had a steel guitar on it and sounded like a
country record." A review of the new release appeared in the August
8, 1970, issue of *Billboard:* "Debut of the Nashville based label is a
potent performance that should hit hard and fast. Much pop appeal
as well." Within the month, "He's Everywhere" had debuted on the
country singles chart ("Our first release is a happening," read a
Mega ad) where it peaked at #25 during the first week of November.
By that time, the *He's Everywhere* album had been issued as well. An
excited review in *Billboard* ("This girl has everything—looks, persuasive voice and, best of all, a hit record.") mentioned four especially strong tracks from the LP, but "Help Me Make It Through
the Night" was not among them.

Quickly, however, it became the only song anyone was talking
about. "I just got home one night," Malloy recalls. "It was around
10 or 10:30 and the phone rang and I picked it up. This voice said,
'Are you Jim Malloy?' I said, 'Yeah,' and he said, 'My name's Chris

Lane and I want you to know that on that *He's Everywhere* with
Sammi Smith you have a monster, monster record.' I said, 'What is
it?' He said, '"Help Me Make It Through the Night." I played it the
other night and it lit my phones up. Every phone line lit up. It's gotten so bad I have to announce that I'm going to play it every hour if
you will please stop calling in tying up all my phone lines.' [Lane] is
really the guy that broke that whole record."

Acting on such enthusiastic response. Mega released the recording as Smith's follow-up single, just ahead of Bobby Bare's upcoming version. "I was doing a show in Philadelphia," Bare told writer
Tom Roland. "Smith was on and she said, 'It's my next record.' She
beat me out with it, but of course, I had recorded it different. Mine
might not have been a hit."

The reaction to the Smith version was immediate. Two weeks
before the single would even chart, the December 5, 1970, issue of
Billboard predicted a hit for Smith. "She burst forth on the chart
with impact via her initial 'He's Everywhere,'" the magazine
enthused. "This strong Kris Kristofferson ballad material with a
powerful performance will put her right in the Top Twenty."

The Hit

"The first time I heard it on the radio," Smith recalls, "I was driving
on the way to a date and I was flipping the radio station around and
it came on and then I was really excited. Then about five minutes
later I was flipping it around and it came on again. Everywhere I
turned, that song was on. It just amazed me. I was in shock that it
had done anything at all. I guess you always are the first time."

According to a legend that has developed around the song, Smith
wasn't the only one who was shocked to hear "Take the ribbon from
my hair" come moaning out of the radio speakers; some listeners
were offended by the song's comparatively frank depiction of female
desire. Some country stations reportedly refused to play the sensual
ballad. The song's impact even reached the ivory tower. Writing in
1971, theologian Albert Outler cited Smith's hit as an example of
"defiant hedonism" and "self-conscious amoralism."

"It was banned in a couple of places," Smith says, "and that I could never understand because I don't see anything wrong with that song. I think it's a touching, honest song. I know Dottie West remarked [about it] one time on television. It was when we won the CMA award. [Somebody asked her] what she thought about it, and she said she thought it was great [but] she never would've recorded that song. Which kinda hurt my feelings. I just couldn't see a thing wrong with that song, and people said it was vulgar. I guess they think differently than I do.

"[Because] it's not about sex," Smith continues. "It's about someone who's lonely, who needs somebody to make it through another night. I don't think it's about sex at all. See, what people—here I'm on a soapbox now, but I'm gonna tell you this—people seem to think that everything in life revolves around sex. And if there is the merest hint of tenderness, or even if you talk about being held by somebody, immediately they think, 'Ah, sex!' That's not the case."

Brad McCuen also remembers some of the negative reaction. "There were people who said [the record was] dirty," he says. "I think that was one of the things why some disc jockeys didn't play it, or wouldn't play it, until they had to play it. But they fell in line real quickly."

Whatever backlash occurred, it wasn't extensive or long lasting enough to slow down the explosive trajectory of the record. On December 19, 1970, "Help Me Make It Through the Night" debuted at #64 on *Billboard*'s Hot Country Singles chart. Just a month later it had not only climbed to #9 on the country charts but had broken into the Hot 100 pop chart. By January 30—with the single now at #5 country and #64 pop—Mega had taken advantage of this success, reissuing Smith's *He's Everywhere* album under the new title *Help Me Make It Through the Night*. According to *Billboard*, by the following week the single was selling 18,000 copies a day. Then, on February 13, "Help Me Make It Through the Night" bumped Dolly Parton's "Joshua" from the #1 spot on the country charts and stayed there for three weeks. The single spent three months in the country Top Ten. Over on the pop charts, the recording climbed to #8 the first week of April, making it among the most successful recordings in a country-music era defined, in part, by its crossover successes.

In the wake of Smith's hit a number of other artists recorded versions of the song, including Joe Simon, O. C. Smith, Joan Baez, Jim Nabors, Bryan Ferry, Willie Nelson, and Elvis Presley. As soul singer Gladys Knight put it in a spoken introduction to her 1972 version, "Recently I heard a most beautiful song with a dynamic lyric that really expresses this feeling of loneliness." None of these later versions, however, matched Sammi Smith's hit on Mega Records—not in sales, not in intimacy, not in their feeling of loneliness.

Smith deserves much of the credit. "Sammi Smith, in my opinion, has got to be one of the all-time greatest women country singers that ever was, or ever will be," says Malloy. "I don't care who they want to talk about. Sammi was just fabulous." Although she continued to score hits (mostly minor ones) into the '80s, Smith never again approached the success of her signature hit.

The Country Music Association's Single of the Year in 1971, "Help Me Make It Through the Night" was more than just a great song put over by a great singer; it was a great record. In its grooves, song and singer—as well as arranger and musicians and producer—all came together, at a particular moment in Nashville history, to create something even more powerful than the sum of its parts would have predicted. The record addressed a universal condition; it captured a real human need.

"I don't think there's a one of them who were booing and hissing," Smith says, "who could've said they hadn't felt that way in their life at one point or another."

The DJ's New Lexicon

The hip-hop rank-and-file's introduction to the notion of skratch notation—a written system to represent turntable-based music—came last July at Skratchcon 2000, a one-day conclave held in San Francisco as a last act of community-building by the respected DJ team Invisible Skratch Picklz, just before their official breakup. (*Skratch* is the accepted spelling within the subculture; I'll adopt it here, at the risk of sounding like Mr. Kotter trying to "relate.") In the middle of a long afternoon of polite Q&A and virtuosic demos, two DJs took their turns behind a long row of direct-drive Technics 1200s and accompanying DMT mixers to hold forth on their respective—and perhaps competing—systems. First, Montreal's A-Trak talked through a series of hand-drawn overhead transparencies that resembled the output of a particularly busy seismograph, occasionally (and nimbly) translating an inscription into sound on the instruments in front of him. Next, Phoenix, Arizona's Radar delivered a sober lecture favoring the use of established Western notation, plus a few extra symbols, illustrated by sections of a thoroughly professional-looking score.

Both presentations, archived at www.skratch.com, were received with obvious interest, as well as some skepticism. (Radar, in particular, didn't score any points with such pronouncements as "This is music, and this is how it's done.") But the fact that they took place not in the context of musicological study, but among actual practitioners, marks this as an important moment in the development of skratch music or, more pretentiously, turntablism. It's not that the genre needs notation for individual practitioners to reach some arbitrary standard of maturity or complexity; a cursory listen to the technical mastery of X-Ecutioners' Rob Swift or the Picklz' own Q-Bert and Flare should convince even the classically-prejudiced that there's something going on here, whether or not it's amenable to being written down. It's far too early to predict how the development of skratch notation will affect the music, but the fact that DJs are willing to take the concept seriously marks a shift in how the community sees itself, and how it wants to be seen.

Despite a few avant-classical precursors (Pierre Schaeffer and John Cage both experimented with variable turntable speeds in compositions from the thirties and forties), the current use of the instrument *as* an instrument dates from the mid-seventies, when South Bronx club spinners began to develop more elaborate ways of keeping a party going by segueing between the most danceable portions of successive twelve-inches. (One origin story is even humbler, claiming that the first skratch occurred when Grand Wizard Theodore's mother told him to shut off his record player.) Paralleling the rise of the MC, the DJ's role quickly grew from a functional one to that of primary accompanist, with such eighties pioneers as DMT (of "Rockit" fame) and Barry B becoming as notorious as anyone they backed.

Contemporary turntablism is still tied to its roots by tradition and fashion-sense, though the sounds you'll hear behind most current commercial rap are more likely to be produced by a combination of samples, loops, and "real" instrumentation. As if in response, skratch music has become a world unto itself; its leading figures stand as recording and performing artists in their own right, while up-and-comers fight for supremacy in "battles" somewhere between a bebop cutting contest and a gymnastic heat. There's an irony here: The phonograph, which brought the reproduction of musical sound within reach of the musically maladroit, has entered the new century as the chosen tool of a new crop of virtuosos, as prone to the pitfalls of empty technique as any piano prodigy or fusion wonk.

It's this emphasis on speed and skill that has made the move to notation almost inevitable. As the skratch repertoire has expanded, so has the nomenclature that practitioners use to communicate with one another. There are "chirps," the high, birdlike skratches pioneered by Will Smith's pre-Hollywood partner DJ Jazzy Jeff; "flares" (named for their inventor) and "orbits," sub-categorized by number of quick cross-fader cuts or "clicks" per push or drag of the record; "crabs," Q-Bert's secret weapon, involving a many-fingered fader movement—to say nothing of "tears," "transforms," "combos" of all of the above, and two-handed techniques ("phasers," "lasers," "hydroplane"), successively more difficult both to execute and to describe in prose or conversation. Which is where we came in.

"I'm not creating anything new, I'm merely adapting the turntables to the scoring of instruments known within the 'Western standard' of music," insists DJ Radar (aka Jason Grossfeld) in the course of an email interview. A twenty-six-year-old rooted in the unlikely but vital Phoenix skratch scene, he traces his project to his training as a classical percussionist, which preceded his career behind the wheels of steel. "When I was learning to skratch, I found it easier to catch on because of my musical training. If I heard a complex skratch I couldn't do, I would write it out rhythmically just as I had when I played snare drum in junior symphony. That was one of the ways we learned."

The most visible fruit of his labors is "Anti-Matter," a 12-inch released in 1998 along with a fourteen-page score-plus-explanation that documents every note heard in the song's three minutes and twenty-six seconds. As with most studio-generated skratch music, its constituent sounds are all generated from pre-existing vinyl, transformed by mixing, overdubbing, and the DJ's hands. Entirely written out before recording began, the disc's raison d'être is to show the feasibility of fully-notated turntable composition. In this, "Anti-Matter" is heir to the techno-polemical tradition of Bach's *[The] Well-Tempered Clavier*, composed to prove that the system of just-intonation could render keyboard instruments playable in every key signature. Radar's heated accompanying manifesto makes his intent clear: "It is now possible with this score to show other musicians exactly how a turntable is actually an analog percussion instrument."

The score lives up to its author's billing of conventionality, complete with bar lines and standard note- and rest-values. Groups of staves represent, respectively, a kick and snare pattern that could appear in a *Modern Drummer* transcription, a hi-hat overdubbed from a second disc, and various bass and vocal ornaments (such as the phrase "Life support systems functional" recited in a calm female voice) with all unpitched percussion sounds resting in the middle of the staff, an octave above middle C. The real action is on a staff marked "wha skratch," which notates the song's turntable "solo." After pages of measure-long rests, the score (and record) erupts with a barrage of thirty-second note triplets. Translated back into DJ-speak, this is the rhythmic profile of a long series of crabs. All the major skratches and combos can be represented in some similar manner; a two-click flare turns out to look and sound like the snare drum rudiment known as a flamm tap.

Additionally, an extra line of symbols above the staff represents articulations, the movements of the hand, which actually produce the skratch. These could also be thought of as changes in the unimpeded motion of the record. "Anti-Matter" uses four main markings: "+" for a forward cue (pushing the record slightly faster than normal); "-" for a drag cue (slowing the record down slightly), "=" for a back-cue (dragging the record backwards), and "o" for passages where the DJ's hand should be off the record. With an "r" indicating a repeating pattern, these cover the basic moves from which skratches are built, though Radar freely admits that numerous symbols could be added to cover advanced and two-handed techniques, just as the conventions covering more established instruments have resources to notate accents, glissandos, and trills.

In contrast to Radar's notation, which builds on several centuries of Western tradition, A-Trak developed his—forgive me—from scratch. At 18, the former Alain Macklovitch has spun with both the Picklz and Canadian-American crew The Allies, as well as winning two prestigious International Turntable Federation

(ITF) solo championships. The impetus behind his first forays into notation was purely practical. Preparing for a studio session with Montreal rap group Obscure Disorder, he says, "I wanted to remember some patterns, and for lack of any system, I just kind of drew those skratches the first time. I wasn't aware of any other notation. Later on, talking to the Picklz, they were impressed at hearing that I had a system—that's when I realized I should put some work into it. I'd been using it a lot to do sessions, and keeping an inventory of all my patterns, but I never put the whole theory down on paper."

The central idea behind A-Trak's system is remarkably elegant. Imagine a graph with its horizontal (x) axis representing the regular forward motion of a record over time, and its vertical (y) axis representing the particular stretch of vinyl to be skratched. On this "staff," each record movement appears as an angled line, with a positive or negative slope representing, respectively, a push forwards or a drag backwards. Thus, a baby skratch (forward, back, forward, back at regular intervals) looks like a large capital "M." The speed and distance covered by each skratch is conveyed by the marks' height and steepness. As A-Track explains, "In general, everything is relative to what's around it. If you see that most of the skratches reach a certain height and then you have one that goes further vertically, you know that's a skratch that covers more of the record."

These variations in height do double duty by giving an admittedly imprecise picture of the pitches created. "There's a direct link between the portion of the record that you're covering and the sound of the skratch. If you're barely moving the record back and forth on a very small portion, you'll get a low-pitched skratch, but if you do the same motions in the same rhythm but covering a larger portion of the record, you'll get a higher-pitched skratch." Hence, the taller the line, the higher the sound, though A-Trak adds, "It would be irrelevant to get into more details with pitch. When you get on the table, the first skratch you do won't be exactly the pitch you want, and you have to play around until you get it." (Both DJs agree that there is little point in notating specific pitches unless you already know the pitch of the sound source. Since a given pattern can be executed on any record, both systems treat the turntable as, in Radar's words, "a percussion instrument with some control over pitch," not unlike a tympani.)

Fader "clicks," which add rhythmic nuance, appear as cross-hatches on the lines representing record-movement, while a double-slash, like Radar's "o," indicates that the record is to be released. Within this basic vocabulary certain techniques are represented much differently than their rhythmic profile would suggest. One example: The difference between a one-click orbit and a crab lies not in the motion of the record, but in how the fader is manipu-lated, which leads to a clever notational solution. Instead of Radar's daunting 32nd-note triplets, A-Trak writes out the simpler pattern, accompanied by a tiny drawing of—what else?—a crab.

As it stands, this system is intriguing but loose—but then so are many features of Western notation. For its most obvious uses as a short-term mnemonic, or for jotting down patterns when there's no turntable handy, A-Trak rarely bothers drawing in the guiding axes. "Right now I'm pretty ghetto with it. I've been using it for my own purposes, I haven't really been worrying about presentation." Hence the absence of visual examples in this article; during our interview, A-Trak discussed plans to pursue a patent and to post a version of the system on The Allies' website. (A third, somewhat similar, pro-ject can be found at www.battlesounds.net. A-Trak says that he and designer John Carluccio traded ideas about three years ago but arrived at the basic principles independently.)

One difference between Radar and A-Trak's systems bears emphasis: Unlike Western conventions for scoring rhythm, what a particular group of marks represents in a graphically-based system depends on how much space it occupies. Four quarter notes are four quarter notes wherever they're placed in a measure. But scrunched together or spread out, A-Trak's slashes will notate different rhythms. Taking a distinction from philosopher Nelson Goodman's *Languages of Art* (a lively examination of the various ways that repre-sentational codes operate), Radar's traditionally-based notation can be thought of as "digital," dividing time into discrete units, while A-

Trak's is "analog," as ultra-discriminating (and potentially vague) as the sweep second-hand of a wristwatch.

Still, both systems make possible transcription and reproduction of complicated, formerly nameless patterns, and both are an improvement over a mere lexicon of techniques. The most telling differences lie in what and whom they're for. Though Radar states that his main aim is "to communicate with other musicians," legitimacy is a concern as well. "The bottom line is that people, including musicians, don't think of the turntable as a legitimate instrument. Personally, I'm tired of people asking me, 'How do you make that wicki-wicki sound—doesn't it hurt the record?' So I've decided to use a system of theirs for them to better understand what we do." An artist's desire to be recognized beyond his or her immediate community is understandable, but wider acceptance might have institutional advantages as well. For their part, DJs "haven't thought about the benefits, which this Western classical system has to offer. Do people in the skratch community understand that you can get scholarships and grants for playing a harmonica? Why not a turntable?"

Radar may be getting somewhere: Soon after our interview, an emailed press release announced an Arizona State University performance of the first movement of a concerto for turntable and orchestra written in collaboration with composer Raul Yanez. But most collisions between hip-hop and concert hall lie firmly in the avant-garde tradition of Cage and Schaeffer. A recent Lincoln Center program paired Cage's early tape piece "Imaginary Landscapes No. 1," rearranged for turntables, with a new "commissioned work" by The X-Ecutioners—essentially, a DJ crew show under a classier name. In this context, a new-*looking* notation such as A-Trak's may get greater play than Radar's more assimilationist project. After all, the expansion and abandonment of traditional notation is a key chapter in twentieth-century serious music, from Stockhausen's maddening attempts to micromanage every aspect of sound to the aleatory scores of Cage, Feldman, and Browne.

For his part, A-Trak voices complaints similar to Radar's about how skratch musicians are perceived, though he uses "digga-digga" in place of "wicki-wicki," but expresses far more suspicion about the instrument's growing institutional prospects. "The way I am, I probably wouldn't have shown [the system] to people. It puts me in an awkward position because I'm not fully for DJ schools. It's subtle, because I think it's good for one DJ to be able to explain a skratch to another, but there's a difference between that and having DJs who learn all their skratches that way." There's something of the magician's unwillingness to reveal secrets to a lay public to this, as well as the fear of respectability common to every subculture, but there's a legitimate concern here as well. Turntablism may not be in its infancy, but it's still an awkward adolescent, despite its recent growth spurts. The premature adoption of a given notation could stifle further creativity, especially if the patterns it's best suited to representing become standard while those it doesn't are marginalized; think of the difficulty "serious" musicians and educators have had in validating the skills common to jazz players (from the use of bent pitches to improvisation itself). A-Trak shows little interest in creating an industry standard, grants and orchestras be damned: "I'm not trying to impose this on anybody. If people don't believe in using notation, then they won't use it. But if someone's actually willing to find a use for it in their DJing, the same way that I have uses for it in my world, then it's there."

Two from *The Onion*

God Finally Gives Shout-Out
Back to All His Niggaz

SOUTH BRONX, NY—The Lord Almighty finally responded to nearly two decades of praise in hip-hop album liner notes Monday, when He gave a shout-out back to all His loyal niggaz.

"Right about now, I want to send a shout-out to each and every nigga who's shown Me love through the years," said the Lord, His booming voice descending from Heaven. "I got mad love for each and every one of you niggaz. Y'all real niggaz out there, you know who you are. Y'all was there for me, and it's about time I'm-a give some love back to God's true crew."

"All y'all niggaz, y'all be My niggaz," the Lord added.

As of press time, God has thanked nearly 7,000 of His niggaz, including those in New York's Bad Boy and Ruff Ryders posses, the No Limit soldiers and Cash Money Millionaires holdin' it down in New Orleans, Nelly and the whole St. Lunatics crew, Busta and the rest of the Flipmode Squad, His peeps from back in the day, and all the real ruffneck niggaz in lockdown. He also sent shout-outs to everybody in the Old School, as well as to Lil' Bow Wow and all the other new niggaz just coming up.

"Mad props to P. Diddy, Jay-Z, DMX, Lil' Kim, Mystikal, Eve, Ja Rule, Jadakiss, Trick Daddy, and Xzibit. And one love to Meth, RZA, GZA, Ghostface, and the rest of My real niggaz in the Wu-

Tang Clan," the deity said. "These My beloved niggaz, with whom I be well-pleased."

Now nearing the 48-hour mark, the Lord's first-ever reciprocal shout-out shows little sign of slowing down. Based on estimates of the number of rappers who have thanked Him in liner notes over the past 20 years, hip-hop experts say the historic shout-out is likely to continue through early next week.

In addition to rap's current stars, God offered shout-outs to the original hip-hop heads, including such pioneers of the art form as Grandmaster Flash, Busy Bee, Melle Mel, Jazzy Jay, Kool Moe Dee, Afrika Bambaataa, DJ Red Alert, the Cold Crush Brothers, Fab 5 Freddy, Kurtis Blow, Kool Herc, and the Funky 4+1.

God also offered shout-outs to the many DJs, record labels, magazines, TV shows, and radio stations that have tirelessly supported hip-hop over the years. Among them are Def Jam, Tommy Boy, Jive, Roc-A-Fella, *Rap Pages*, *The Source*, *Right On!*, The Box, Funkmaster Flex, Ed Lover and Dr. Dre, WBLS 107.5, KISS-FM, and Hot 97.

"For supporting the many artists who have supported Me so faithfully, I say thank you," God said. "All praise to Devante Harrell, Wanda Simmons, LaShell Thomas, and everybody else at Uptown/MCA for making this possible."

As a further sign of His love for the hip-hop community, God assured the nation's rappers that He is taking good care of all their peers currently with Him in heaven.

"Tupac, Notorious B.I.G., Eazy-E, Scott LaRock—some of y'all niggaz are already up in this bitch," the Lord said. "For those of you who were left behind, know that the Lord has got your dead homies' backs. Faith [Evans], I promise I'm taking real good care of your Biggie. He resting in crazy peace, no doubt."

Thus far, God has not played favorites, thanking such fallen-off acts as Hammer and Vanilla Ice in the same breath as vital artists whose careers are still going strong. The Lord has also seen fit to thank the little-known likes of Baby Tragic, DJ Phreek Malik, and Da Ill Collector—MCs so obscure that virtually no one within the hip-hop community has heard of them. All rappers, God explained, are equal in His sight, and none are too small to escape His notice.

"God sees even the smallest sparrow fall," said Dr. Cornel West, Harvard University professor of African-American studies and philosophy of religion. "The same is true of MCs: Whether a major superstar or a complete unknown, all rappers are His children, and He loves them all."

The sheer volume of names notwithstanding, the nation's rappers are deeply touched by God's gesture of tribute and appreciation, with many stating that they "feelin' Him."

"God is the Original," Brooklyn-based rapper Mos Def said. "The world is ruled by the wealthy and the wicked, but all respect due to the Creator who made this world and who will one day bring justice to the wicked and righteous alike."

Despite the overwhelmingly positive response among rappers, the Lord is drawing fire in certain circles for His use of the word "nigga." On Monday's *Larry King Live*, conservative activist Rev. Calvin Butts, a longtime ally of the Lord, blasted Him for His "shocking, unexpected use of the racially loaded N-word." Some concerned parties, including decency crusader C. Delores Tucker, Sen. Orrin Hatch (R-UT), and members of the San Francisco–based What About The Children? Foundation, are calling for a boycott of church services until God issues an apology.

Reacting to the controversy, many in the hip-hop community are rushing to the Lord's defense.

"The word 'nigga' means different things depending on how it's used and who's saying it," rap legend and Public Enemy frontman Chuck D said. "Judging from context, God obviously wasn't being derogatory. He was using 'nigga' as a blanket term of affection for all His true supporters on the rap scene. At one point, He said, 'I wanna give a shout-out to Ad-Rock, MC Serch, and my man Dan The Automator—all y'all is real niggaz in My all-benevolent sight.' Considering the fact that Ad-Rock and Serch are Jewish, and the Automator is Asian-American, it's clear God isn't talking about race here. He's just paying respect to all those who have paid respect to Him."

"God's the ultimate playa, so naturally He's going to have some haters," rapper Ice Cube said. "But these haters need to realize that if you mess with the man upstairs, you *will* get your ass smote. True dat."

Marilyn Manson Now Going
Door-to-Door Trying to Shock People

OVERLAND PARK, KS—Stung by flagging album sales and Eminem's supplanting him as Middle America's worst nightmare, shock rocker Marilyn Manson has embarked on a door-to-door tour of suburbia in a desperate, last-ditch effort to shock and offend average Americans.

Accompanied by bandmates Twiggy Ramirez, Madonna Wayne Gacy, and Zim Zum, Manson kicked off his 50-city "Boo" tour Jan. 26 in Overland Park, a conservative, middle-class suburb of Kansas City.

"When we first laid eyes on Overland Park, with its neat little frame houses, immaculately landscaped lawns, and SUVs in the driveways, we couldn't wait to swoop down on it like the Black Death," said Manson, born Brian Warner in Canton, OH. "We were like, 'Welcome to our nightmare, you bloated, pustulent pigs.'"

Last Friday at 4 P.M., Mark Wesley, 46, a resident of Overland Park's exclusive Maple Bluff subdivision, heard the sound of "animal-like shrieking" coming from the vicinity of his front lawn. Upon opening his front door, he was greeted by the sight of a pale and shirtless Manson carving a pentagram into his chest with a razor blade.

"Look at me, suburban dung," Manson told Wesley. "Does this shock you?"

When Wesley replied no, he said Manson became "petulant." Recalled Wesley: "He started stamping his feet and shaking his fists, saying, 'What do you mean no? Aren't your uptight, puritanical sensibilities offended? Don't you want to censor me so you don't have to confront the ugly truth I represent?' So I say, 'Well, not particularly.' Then, after a long pause, he says, 'Well, screw you, jerk!' and walks off sulking."

That evening, Linda Schmidt was preparing to drive her daughter Alyssa to a Girl Scouts meeting when she found Manson standing on her porch draped in sheep entrails.

"I knew who he was, but I was kind of busy and didn't really have time to chat," Schmidt said. "He just kept standing there staring at me, expecting me to react in some way."

Added Schmidt: "I tried to be nice and humor him a little. I said, 'Yesiree, that sure is some shocking satanic imagery, no doubt about it. And that one eye with no color in the pupil, very disturbing. I'd sure like to suppress that.' I mean, what do you say to Marilyn Manson?"

A deflated Manson remained on Schmidt's porch as she and Alyssa drove off.

Subsequent attempts to provoke outrage were met with equal indifference.

"[Manson] was standing at my front door wearing those fake breasts he wore on the cover of *Mechanical Animals*," retiree Judith Hahn said. "He said, 'My name is Marilyn Manson, and I'm here to tear your little world apart.' I thought he was collecting for the Kiwanis food drive, so I gave him some cans of pumpkin-pie filling."

Undaunted, Manson and his entourage stepped up their assault on mainstream American sensibilities. On Tuesday, they arrived in the tiny Detroit suburb of Grosse Pointe Farms, where stockbroker Glenn Binford answered his doorbell to find Manson hanging upside-down on a wooden cross as Ramirez performed fellatio on him.

"I just stood there thinking, now there's a boy who tries way too hard," Binford said. "I mean, come on: Homoerotic sacrilege went out in the late '90s."

Other provocative acts by Manson—including dismembering a chicken, bathing in pig's blood, and wearing a three-piece suit of human noses—failed to arouse anyone's ire, instead prompting comments such as "sophomoric," "trite," and "so Alice Cooper."

Manson's lone brush with controversy occurred in Edina, MN, a suburb of Minneapolis. An unidentified neighborhood-watch volunteer phoned police after seeing a nude, feces-smeared Manson being led around on a leash by a dwarf dominatrix. Officers arrived on the scene, but let Manson go with a warning for parading without a city permit.

"I could have given him a citation, but I figured, how much harm is he really causing?" Edina Police Officer Dan Herberger said. "I mean, he's just Marilyn Manson, for the love of Mike."

The "Boo" tour was dealt a further blow when Manson learned that Eminem's *The Marshall Mathers LP* had been banned from all Kmart stores. Manson's current album, *Holy Wood (In The Shadow Of The Valley Of Death)*, is still available.

"Why are all you people outraged by Eminem? He's not scary!" Manson said. "He doesn't sport ghoulishly pale skin or wear gender-bending make-up. He's just some regular guy. I'm the one who people should be terrified by, not him! Me!"

"If you ban me," Manson continued, "I promise to rail against censorship and hypocrisy. Please? Pretty, pretty please?"

By Monday, the tour appeared to have lost all momentum. Sources close to Manson described him as "exhausted and discouraged," despite not having even completed the first leg of the three-month tour. By the time he arrived in Hoffman Estates, IL, Manson had resorted to leaving flaming bags of dog feces on doorsteps and shining a flashlight under his chin to make himself look "spooky." He was ultimately chased from a Hoffman Estates subdivision by a group of bicycle-riding teenagers who advised him to "get [his] chalk-white goblin ass" out of their neighborhood.

On Friday, Manson is slated to appear in Bethesda, MD, where many believe he will bring his tour to a premature end.

"Have you people forgotten already?" Manson told *The Washington Post*. "You all thought I was responsible for Columbine two years ago. Well, I was! I was! I know I vehemently denied it at the time, but, really, I personally told those two kids to shoot up the school. I'm serious. I sent them an e-mail. And I told them to worship Satan, too. You hear that, kids? Marilyn Manson says you should shoot your friends in the head with a gun! And everyone should eat babies! And rape their dead grandparents! And poop on a church! There, now will someone please be offended?"

L.A.'s Top 100

Every city has a soundtrack, but sometimes Los Angeles seems like a soundtrack that has a city. The songs that have come out of L.A. have an identity that often eludes the geography of L.A. These songs—100 soundtracks, actually, for a city that has always liked to think of itself as utopia or 100 utopias—were all recorded here, but beyond that they are not just from L.A., they're *of* L.A. They're not necessarily about L.A., or by longtime residents, let alone natives; in what must have been a paranormal occurrence I was actually born here, but I realize most of you are just squatters with pretensions. Rather these are records with the current of the city running through them. In other words, if they had been recorded anywhere else, in some fundamental way they would have been different.

And if that sounds a little subjective, of course that's just the half of it. Because while a number of writers—David Cantwell (*Heartaches by the Number*), Ben Edmonds (*Marvin Gaye: What's Going On & the Last Days of the Motown Sound*), Mikal Gilmore (*Night Beat*), Peter Guralnick (*Careless Love*), Greil Marcus (*The Old, Weird America*), Dave Marsh (*The Heart of Rock & Soul*), Steve Propes (*L.A. R&B Vocal Groups*), Michael Ventura (*Shadow Dancing in the U.S.A.*), Craig Hansen Werner (*Holler If Ya Hear Me*), Jonny Whiteside (*Ramblin' Rose*), Daniel Wolff (*You Send Me*)—were lifesavers when it came to hard history, hot tips, and invaluable leads, in the end all selections were made by a committee of, well, one. Which is to say that all laughable inclusions, contemptible omissions, and forehead-slapping lapses in taste are mine and mine alone. With these caveats out of the way, then, in the tradition of radio-station countdowns and cheesy VH1 specials, we begin with number . . .

100 "LOSER," Beck (1994) Before he became the most over-rated artist of the '90s, there was an even-money chance he might record a song that told you something about how he felt rather than how smart he was. That assumes the central sentiment of this record—"I'm a loser, baby/So why don't you kill me?"—wasn't completely a joke. For Beck it may have been, but not necessarily for the generation that embraced it as an anthem, including Kurt Cobain nursing that shotgun in the wilds of Seattle.

99 "WHITE CHRISTMAS," Bing Crosby (1941) Inevitable. From the land of yellow Christmases, written by Irving Berlin for the movie *Holiday Inn*, it was the biggest record of the 20th century. The first time Crosby heard the composer play it on the piano, he just nodded and said, "Well, I don't think you have to worry about this one, Irving."

98 "SIXTEEN TONS," Tennessee Ernie Ford (1955) On the cusp of becoming America's favorite male gospel artist, Ford cut this Merle Travis song to fulfill a contract and, snapping the beat to set the tempo, was upstaged by his own fingers.

97 "HARLEM NOCTURNE," the Johnny Otis Orchestra (1945) On the cusp of becoming a rhythm-and-blues star with songs like "Willie and the Hand Jive," a Greek American passing as African American slowed down a honky-tonk tune until it had nothing to do with Harlem anymore, and instead it became the definitive soundtrack for every mean street down which every L.A. private eye ever walked.

96 "THE HEART OF SATURDAY NIGHT," Tom Waits (1974) The soundtrack of Barney's Beanery—"Is it the crack of the pool balls, the neon buzzin?/Telephone ringin' it's your second cousin"—assuming the narrator ever got that far west of Cahuenga.

95 "JAMES BROWN IS DEAD," L.A. Style (1992) In keeping with the rave culture's aesthetic of anonymity, we'll probably never know whether there was anything truly L.A. about this—

made by six producers and one Scottish-born Nigerian female vocalist—other than that it was played from the clubs of Hollywood to the canyons of San Gabriel. James Brown survived in any event.

94 "ODE TO BILLIE JOE," Bobbie Gentry (1967) This was released during the psychedelic summer of '67 and couldn't have been more at odds with either its time or its genre—country blues with a cello. But soon all of America was trying to figure out what that guy threw off that damn bridge. Legend has it somewhere in Capitol's vaults is a seven-minute version that reveals all, but at this point would we really rather know?

93 "FADE INTO YOU," Mazzy Star (1993) A fin de siècle Kitten with a Whip, singer Hope Sandoval sounded like she looked: every man's doom.

92 "FEVER," Peggy Lee (1958) All sass and style, and having traveled a long road to stardom, she knew what she was about, and wrote her own words to this Little Willie John blues. If "Sixteen Tons" has the all-time best finger snapping by a male vocalist, this is champion of the female division, unless someone out there happens to know those aren't Peggy's sassy, stylish fingers—in which case keep it to yourself.

91 "THE LETTER," the Medallions (1954) It sounds suspiciously like a paean to matrimonial love, but no one has ever really been sure what lead singer Vernon Green is saying. Dadaist doo-wop.

90 "DOCTOR WU," Steely Dan (1975) Let's not delude ourselves. This was L.A. music for people who hate L.A., which is one reason critics loved it so much. Other reasons: wit, originality, general all-around weirdness, and cynicism laced with more compassion than these guys would usually cop to.

89 "'ROUTE 66' THEME," Nelson Riddle (1962) For an America still straining at the seams of self-repression, this was the soundtrack of freedom and the Road—not Kerouac's, but as close to it as either television or the early '60s was going to get.

88 "MOONLIGHT IN VERMONT," Willie Nelson (1978) Where else was a Texas boy going to sing a song about Vermont but Los Angeles? Actually, the L.A. recording execs thought the idea was folly, but Willie's favorite singer had always been Frank Sinatra, and the *Stardust* album, arranged by Booker T. Jones, made him a superstar. This was the gem of those sessions, and if it was better than Sinatra's version, Frank probably didn't mind. It was better than anyone else's, too.

87 "PEEL THEIR CAPS BACK," Ice-T (1989) Cinematic and horrific, a cold-blooded narrative of a drive-by that backed up all the rapper's "original gangster" boasts, while implicitly acknowledging how little they mattered.

86 "MACARTHUR PARK," Richard Harris (1968) Of course I'm not kidding, but more to the point neither was Harris, who sang this as if he thought he was still King Arthur in *Camelot*, or songwriter Jimmy Webb, for whom a run-down park was the obvious landscape for love melting away like a cake in the rain. If it's an axiom of both the city and pop music in general that authenticity is the enemy of audacity, then this was audacity taking no prisoners, and in a season otherwise dominated by Hendrix, Cream and "Jumpin' Jack Flash," it was the record everyone talked about.

85 "I CAN'T MAKE YOU LOVE ME," Bonnie Raitt (1991) Raitt hadn't sounded this emotionally naked since "Love Has No Pride" 20 years before, except that now 20 years of weary wisdom were thrown into the bargain.

84 "WELCOME TO THE JUNGLE," Guns N' Roses (1987) The '60s Sunset Strip riots two decades later, with the victors searching the rubble wondering what they won.

83 "THIS TOWN," the Go-Go's (1981) If you saw them at the now-departed Starwood Club down on Crescent Heights in the late '70s, when Belinda Carlisle was a chubby little girl from Thousand Oaks and twice as sexy for it, it was obvious they would be huge if anyone could get just half their energy on record. Only later did their *significance* sink in: an autonomous American girl group not only playing their instruments but writing their own material, particularly this deadly Valentine to their city—a Pop Tart with a razor blade in the middle.

82 "THE DARK TREE," Horace Tapscott (1989) Two years after the death of this postbop pianist and founder of Watts's Pan

Afrikan Peoples Arkestra, the public is only beginning to catch up with his legend. But anyone who was listening one late autumn night at Catalina's in Hollywood where this was recorded, already knew.

81 "LONG AGO (AND FAR AWAY)," Jo Stafford (1944) From the biggest-selling female vocalist of her time, a Jerome Kern—Ira Gershwin song, released near the end of the war, that struck a chord with an America yearning for its lost innocence. The melancholy in Stafford's voice knows not only isn't coming back, but that it was never there.

80 "SUE EGYPT," Captain Beefheart (1980) In the late '60s Don Van Vliet collapsed into a double album called *Trout Mask Replica* the entire musical history of America, or the America of his mind, anyway. By the end of the '70s, on the verge of calling it quits and returning to a successful career as a painter—and your music has to be pretty weird if you can make a better living in this country as a painter—he was collapsing into this three-minute five-part suite the entire musical history of oh, Mars maybe. Which might not have been that different from the America of his mind.

79 "SHE'S GOT IT," Little Richard (1956) The B-side to "The Girl Can't Help It" from the movie of the same name, this was written for the movie, too. The girl who couldn't help it and she who had it were both Jayne Mansfield, for whom three simply weren't enough dimensions—but that's only if you think for two seconds. Richard wasn't singing about himself.

78 "FARMER JOHN," the Premier (1964) Barrio-punk, from east of the L.A. River. By his own account, 4,000 miles away in Canada a still-obscure Neil Young heard it, played it onstage, and found the Meaning of Life.

77 "FOR A DANCER," Jackson Browne (1974) In the Hollywood Hills, where the Meaning of Life was more elusive, L.A.'s '70s romantic was trying to explain it to someone—"a reason you were alive/but you'll never know"—before she slipped away. He was too late, and the grief was palpable before anyone realized this was a eulogy.

76 "CHELSEA BRIDGE," Gerry Mulligan and Ben Webster (1959) Webster, one of the great old-school tenor sax players of his time, met Mulligan, king of the West Coast cool-school baritone sax, on this Billy Strayhorn rhapsody, as lovely and wistful as a morning fog off the Palisades.

75 "HEARTS OF STONE," the Jewels (1954) "They'll say no no no no no no no no no no no no no . . . hearts of stone / will never break," but amid the hottest rock-and-roll sax west of Little Richard, the singer didn't sound so sure. Sometimes in pop, artifact transcends history; like a nova vanishing into darkness, L.A.'s Great Lost Doo-Wop Classic came and went.

74 "FUCK THA POLICE," N.W.A (1988) This rap landmark may have had more rage than reason, but just off the top of your head: How many cops was it again who beat the crap out of Rodney King three years later?

73 "THEME FROM 'CHINATOWN,'" Jerry Goldsmith (1974) Released near the climax of the Watergate scandal, when all America's authority figures had gone bad, this was a shimmery requiem to a city that still belonged to the angels, before the angels went bad, too.

72 "TWELVE-THIRTY," the Mamas and the Papas (1967) The times they epitomized only a year earlier having passed them by, they made their best record. "Young girls are coming to the canyon," John Phillips wrote: thinking of his wife Mama Michelle, who had already walked out the door for other Papa Denny Doherty, Phillips probably didn't notice that the young girls coming to the canyon were named Kasabian and Krenwinkel and—escorted on the arms of Charles Manson—had death in their eyes.

71 "RISE ABOVE," Black Flag (1981) They were playing a Washington, D.C., gig when a crazed fan jumped onstage: weeks later, as writer and singer, the crazed fan, Henry Rollins, led the hardcore band to their defiant manifesto. Uplifting, actually, if you didn't mind that it made your ears bleed.

70 "MY FUNNY VALENTINE," Chet Baker (1954) On this Rodgers and Hart love song with a vicious streak, the genius of trumpeter Baker's vocal is its androgyny, hovering in the air between cruel humiliation and tender longing as surely as it seems to hover between genders.

69 "LOVER MAN," Charlie Parker (1946) To most jazz historians—this session was a catastrophe. A few hours later the sax man many consider the single most important figure in jazz after Louis Armstrong and Duke Ellington would, in a dementia born of heroin, set his bed on fire, wander his hotel naked, be beaten and arrested by police and shut away in the Camarillo mental institution. But if one word for "Lover Man" is *shambles* the other is *heroic:* Parker locked in a ferocious losing battle with his demons, and displaying in his defeat how great art is often not about chops or mastery or execution, but courage and character.

68 "RIOT IN CELL BLOCK #9," the Robins (1954) Arriving from the East Coast, two Jewish teenage songwriters named Jerry Leiber and Mike Stoller had a funny idea they were black. None of the groups who benefited from this whimsy, including the prototype of the Coasters who made this highly flammable piece of novelty sociology, saw any percentage in setting them straight.

67 "WHEN I FALL IN LOVE," Jeri Southern (1952) This unjustly forgotten singer had a voice described as "smoky," but it was really more like a vapor the distillation of reverie. Her singing was utterly guileless, generous, promiscuous: she slept with all her songs. If this doesn't reduce you to a puddle, you may be the Antichrist.

66 "WILD IS THE WIND," David Bowie (1976) As he was living the worst year of his life in L.A. "doing bad things with bad people," who knows when it seemed like a good idea to record this overwrought Dimitri Tiomkin theme to a crummy old Anthony Quinn film? While coked to the gills in the back of his limbo rolling down La Cienega? Staring out from the edge of some Hollywood cliffside wondering if he should plummet to earth like the alien he was always playing? But backed by the Phil Spector–cum–Kraftwerk production, he did the most sincere, desperate singing of his career thus far; a few months later he got out of town for good, snarling a heartfelt wish that "the fucking place should be wiped off the face of the earth."

65 "IT'S A LONESOME OLD TOWN," Frank Sinatra (1958) The flip side of Bowie's "Wild Is the Wind," separated by only a couple of decades and fewer degrees of sensibility than you might think, this was the obscure, desolate heart of Sinatra's greatest period. If anyone today recorded anything this bleak and uncompromising, his career would be over before it began.

64 "WHITTIER BLVD.," Thee Midnitors (1964) The greatest of the Latino garage bands, living legends before this explosive instrumental was half out of the radio, they influenced more musicians in East L.A. than Elvis and the Beatles combined.

63 "PUSHIN' TOO HARD," the Seeds (1966) Los Angeles may have considered itself the American Utopia of the mid '60s, but this didn't sound too utopian. Unhinged lead singer Sky Saxon thought he was singing to his girlfriend who was taking an unseemly amount of time in the supermarket, but a country increasingly engaged in an inexplicable war in Southeast Asia—that had other uses for young men than the making of savage records—might well have assumed Saxon was singing to it.

62 "STAN," Eminem (2000) We shouldn't make too many excuses for him. To do so in the name of irony or postmodernism or the hope that he's just kidding (yeah, maybe) is to trivialize the power of art to have consequences. But as not only written but performed by the musical godchild of Sky Saxon, this fable of a young hip-hop fan in search of a human connection while on his way to oblivion—and taking others with him—is a tour de force; riveting, scary, moving.

61 "EARTH ANGEL," the Penguins (1954) From the city of earth angels, when every 16-year-old girl was one.

60 "ROLL WITH ME, HENRY," Etta James (1955) Not nearly euphemistic enough for the times, this was retitled "Dance with Me, Henry," and when that wasn't coy enough either, it was called "The Wallflower," which James certainly wasn't. Born and raised in L.A., still practically jailbait, she recorded it with co-vocalist Richard Berry and arranger Johnny Otis. Immortality would come to James six years later in Chicago with "At Last," but the gods gave her a taste of it here.

59 "POWERHOUSE," Carl Stalling (1951) Industrial ambient by way of Stravinsky and Bugs Bunny, this was the soundscape

of chugging cartoon factories as written by 1930s American surreal-
ist Raymond Scott, considered by many the godfather of electronica. Scored by Stalling, who also made such other Looney Tune
classix as "Putty Tat Trouble," "Dinner Music for a Pack of Hungry
Cannibals," and, of course, the eternal "To Itch His Own."

**58 "PLEASE SEND ME SOMEONE TO LOVE," Percy
Mayfield (1950)** An extortion letter to God, with Mayfield holding
his own soul hostage in exchange for tranquillity in our time:
"Unless man puts an end to these damnable sins / Hate will put the
world in a flame / What a shame." For his temerity, a car accident
two years later left him scarred for life.

57 "BILLIE JEAN," Michael Jackson (1982) He's a joke now
of course, but there's no denying this electric moment in pop history, brilliantly produced by Quincy Jones, written and sung by a
man wearing all his paranoia on his rolled-up sleeve.

56 "$1000 WEDDING," Gram Parsons (1973) Inventing
country-rock while nobody noticed, Parsons was a man out of time
and place. With the Flying Burrito Brothers he wrote this devastat-
ing song about a wedding to the mother of his child that in fact
never happened, and singing it was more than he could stand; the
voice didn't catch up with the heart for another five years, when
musical soul mate Emmylou Harris was there to provide backup.
Two months after that from an overdose of tequila and morphine in
Joshua Tree he was dead.

**55 "AIN'T NOBODY'S BUSINESS," Jimmy Witherspoon
(1947)** Like Central Avenue compatriot Johnny Otis, Witherspoon
reincarnated himself any number of times. But he brought his great
blues spirit to whatever he was singing, from gospel to jazz, and this
R&B smash was its essence.

54 "THE MAN I LOVE," the Nat King Cole Trio (1944) A
slyly insurrectionist instrumental arrangement of the Gershwin
standard, with the flip side, "Body and Soul," only marginally less
impressive. Rumor has it the pianist later did some singing.

53 "LA BAMBA," Ritchie Valens (1959) As the Premiers'
"Farmer John" was a revelation for Neil Young, so this was for
Jimmy Page. Old Veracruz by way of electric bass, a Mexican tradi-

tional relegated to the B-side because it was sung in Spanish, it was bumping the Top 20 when Valens's tour plane went down in Iowa. While the rest of the country mourned fellow passenger Buddy Holly, L.A. mourned Valens, especially the Latino community that needed a survivor a lot more than another martyr.

52 "BIRDS," Neil Young (1970) Beginning with his days in Buffalo Springfield, the dangerbird of American rock was always expecting to fly, but no take-off was as sad or radiant as this. The soundtrack of Topanga Canyon, after the gold rush and before the flood that, sooner than anyone else, Young seemed to sense was coming.

51 "I DON'T NEED NO DOCTOR," Ray Charles (1966) After Charles went Hollywood, apparently leaving his gritty rhythm-and-blues period behind him, a lot of artists were under the impression they were picking up where he left off. Turned out he hadn't quite left yet. His last great record.

50 "A MATTER OF TIME," Los Lobos (1984) Dazed and confused, young Valens lifted his head from the Midwest snow to ponder the small plane's smoking rubble. Painfully he struggled to his feet and began to walk, where or for how long he didn't know: later, after his delirium had passed, he couldn't say exactly how it was he had come to find himself back in the land of his ancestors. For the next 25 years, as all the other promises he made to himself faded with youth, he held on to the one made to his Mexican family of a better life in the land of his birth. Many nights he risked everything on a futile attempt to cross an unforgiving border, from the other side of which, once having finally made it to safety, he would then send for his wife and children. "It's only a matter of time," he assured them. The evening of his final try, now well into middle age and slowing down. Valens held his wife close and whispered in her ear, as he always did, that everything would be all right. But this time he had a funny feeling, and she did, too.

49 "BLUE," Joni Mitchell (1971) "Acid, booze, and ass / Needles, guns, and grass / Lots of laughs. . . ." An epitaph for the '60s, to whomever didn't already know they were dead.

48 "CLOSER," Nine Inch Nails (1994) A love song. First a little atmosphere (the house where Sharon Tate was murdered), then the romantic part: "I want to fuck you like an animal / I want to feel you from the inside." Terrifying, depraved, and, God help you, sexier than you'll ever admit.

47 "CRY ME A RIVER," Julie London (1955) A love song. Intensely shy about her bombshell looks, apprehensive about her torrid singing, musically naked but for a bare bass and stark guitar. London invented a new genre: revenge-torch. Robert Johnson by way of Marilyn Monroe.

46 "I CAN'T GET STARTED," Lester Young (1942) In his time Young was the great tenor sax alternative to Coleman Hawkins. There's a lot of controversy about the impact on his sanity—and his art—of a horrific stint in an army none too happy about his marriage to a white woman. But there's no dispute that he was in full command of his powers here: With Nat Cole on piano, Young answered the brash Bunny Berigan rendition of the song with something more mournful. Seventeen years later, when Sinatra recorded his version, you know Young's was the one he was listening to.

45 "BOULDER TO BIRMINGHAM," Emmylou Harris (1975) Her mentor gone, the student assumed his inspiration and spirit in order to write this hymn to his passing and—for a moment, anyway—to surpass him. Though nobody else would agree, including Harris, Gram Parsons would have thought it was worth the price.

44 "FOR WHAT IT'S WORTH," Buffalo Springfield (1966) "There's something happening here / What it is ain't exactly clear"—but the first stinging guitar chords told the story before songwriter Stephen Stills opened his mouth. Mistaken by some at the time as the soundtrack of revolution, in fact it was the soundtrack of utopia's new unspoken doubts.

43 "NIGHT AND DAY," Fred Astaire and the RKO Orchestra (1934) The Cole Porter classic as recorded for *The Gay Divorcee*, Astaire and Ginger Rogers's second movie together. His singing was almost as elegant as his dancing. But where you knew the dancing couldn't be *that* easy, the singing sounded like it was, which made him the favorite of great songwriters who liked the idea of a singer smart enough to get out of the way of a great song.

42 "ALONE AGAIN OR," Love (1967) All the multiple personalities of this strange band never came together more effectively than here, with the lyric of hippie optimism offset by the ominous melody. Arthur Lee's black-punk harmony vocal overshadowing Bryan MacLean's folk-soul lead vocal, flamenco guitar threading psychedelic strings, and Spanish horns that the producer later felt compelled to apologize for when in fact they're the most inspired touch of all. If this was the soundtrack of the Sunset Strip—and it was—it was also a warning of paradise lost.

41 "OHIO," Crosby, Stills, Nash & Young (1970) Provoked by the shooting of four students by National Guardsmen at Kent State University, written, recorded, pressed, and in the stores in less than two weeks, it was delivered with the force of a bulletin, which is the way it was heard. Except for David Crosby's anguished cries of "How long?" at the end, this was all Neil Young, from the stormy guitar to the words he seemed to bite off as he sang them: "What if you knew her and / Found her dead on the ground?" Iconoclastic as opposed to ideological in the fashion of his three partners, he took his politics personally.

40 "LOS ANGELES," X (1980) Playing the Chinatown punk clubs of the late '70s the band could barely contain their sense of Armageddon, and soon every performance was just another advance in a scorching, triumphal march to the sea. When they recorded this John Doe–Exene Cervenka pièce de résistance about a brutal, merciless L.A. everyone knew existed but pretended not to, they weren't just the best band in the city or, for that matter, the country but—all due allowances made for the Clash, of course—the best on the planet.

39 "SAIL AWAY," Randy Newman (1972) From L.A.'s most original songwriter since Leiber and Stoller, sung from Eden's far shore, a slave trader's sales pitch for the promised land, as sweepingly lovely as it is appalling.

38 "I HAD TOO MUCH TO DREAM (LAST NIGHT),"
the Electric Prunes (1966) One night at the dinner table when I was 16, my father casually announced that at the aerospace company where he worked, there was a guy whose son was a member of some

group called—name uttered in disbelief—the Electric Prunes, who were then riding high on the national charts with this song, I was stunned: My dad knew an Electric Prune's dad? Was this conceivable? The quintessential psychedelic record, cut in that hotbed of acid, Studio City.

37 "MISIRLOU," Dick Dale and the Del-Tones (1962) World music before there was such a thing, surf guitar echoing out of the alleys of Istanbul.

36 "LET'S GET IT ON," Marvin Gaye (1973) Having freed himself from the dictates of the Motown music machine and moved to L.A., Gaye was in his hedonistic element. Yes, this is the soundtrack of sex—but also liberation.

35 "LOOSE," the Stooges (1970) Here's a good one: Their record company decided it would bring this Ann Arbor band out to L.A. to keep them under control, which was like bringing the Black Death to 14th-century Europe to contain the world's rodent population. After Jim Morrison's demise the Doors tried to recruit the Stooges' lead singer, one James Jewel Osterberg, aka Iggy Pop, but Iggy decided to have himself committed instead; when he got out of the loony bin, still very bent but certainly having left the bin a little loonier, he wrote songs about his adopted town with titles like "Kill City." Nothing, however, was as harrowing as this, a predatory rampage down Hollywood Boulevard.

34 "HOUND DOG," Big Mama Thornton (1953) It may be elitist to claim this original version is superior to that by a certain Tennessee truck driver a few years later. But given the trucks of money the Tennessee kid drove off with, it may also be justice.

33 "JAILHOUSE ROCK," Elvis Presley (1957) Leiber and Stoller thought they were kidding when they wrote this, after all, weren't they always kidding? Fortunately the Tennessee truck driver didn't get the joke and, for once, in his best moment in his best movie, branded onto celluloid all his incendiary magnetism.

32 "LET'S HAVE A PARTY," Wanda Jackson (1958) Eventually she would give her heart to Jesus, but for three very secular minutes it was up for grabs. Covering a song from the Elvis movie *Loving You*, this hot 20-year-old rockabilly princess kicked the

King's butt to the far corners of the realm and left Little Richard and Jerry Lee breathing hard, too.

31 "THE HONEYDRIPPER," Joe Liggins and His Orchestra (1945) The soundtrack of the Little Tokyo clubs where this number was a sensation, stripped down to something between a chain-gang chant and penthouse seduction, it had no beat per se but more than enough rhythm to suggest a little rock and roll on the horizon.

30 "LAURA," David Raksin (1944) Noir Tchaikovsky, the most transporting of all movie themes. As part of the great Otto Preminger film of the same name, it lifted Gene Tierney and Dana Andrews to the level of their most glamorous dreams; drifting through the bars and nightclubs of postwar L.A., it had a similar effect on the city at large, until it became a movie unto itself.

29 "CRUISIN'," Smokey Robinson (1979) Cruising Sunset Boulevard with Detroit well out of his rearview mirror, one of the great singer-songwriters had this epiphany. Legend has it that Bruce Springsteen made a tape loop of it so that while driving down his mythic highway, he could listen to Smokey sing the glorious chorus on and on and on into infinity.

28 "DON'T WORRY BABY," the Beach Boys (1964) Did God write this melody? If pop is finally nothing more than the mathematical possibilities of four chords, Brian Wilson has done things with four chords other songwriters are still trying to figure out, the most sublime example being the algebra of awe and heartbreak in this B-side to "I Get Around."

27 "MULE SKINNER BLUES," Jimmie Rodgers (1930) On a train somewhere from his 14th to his 33rd year when he recorded this most famous of his "blue yodels," he invented country music. Part of a Hollywood Follies revue that never made it west of Kansas, Rodgers kept going, already racked by the tuberculosis that would kill him; three years later, at the very end, he had a cot set up in the recording studio so that between spasms of blood he could wring out of his life every song he had left.

26 "I'M A LONESOME FUGITIVE," Merle Haggard (1966) Barely out of Bakersfield and already an icon, with a stay in

San Quentin—for a drunken, botched robbery attempt—only six years behind him, Haggard cut his first number-one record and irrevocably defined his persona; after that, everyone just got out of the way.

25 "EIGHT MILES HIGH," the Byrds (1966) It was an idea mind-boggling in its obviousness—Dylan crossed with the Beatles—and the 12-string guitar that announced "Mr. Tambourine Man" a year earlier fairly chimed, as though the millennium was at hand. But when the band then crossed their Beatled Dylan with John Coltrane, this supersonic record became the event horizon of L.A. music. Never before had there seemed so many possibilities. Afterward they all began imploding one by one.

24 "SUMMERTIME BLUES," Eddie Cochran (1958) If they have the summertime blues *in Los Angeles*—kids around the world must have wondered when they heard this frightening teenage howl—is there any hope for the rest of us? Between the nihilistic guitar lines that thrilled Pete Townshend was the answer: No.

23 "OVER THE RAINBOW," Judy Garland (1939) You hate it. You're sick of it. You never want to hear it again. Until you hear it again. While driving along Sunset Boulevard, in need of one more song for *The Wizard of Oz*, Harold Arlen pulled over to the curb and wrote down the melody, playing it for lyricist Yip Harburg a few days later. Harburg hated it. He was sick of it. He never wanted to hear it again. Louis B. Mayer hated it, preview audiences hated it. On more than one occasion as the film made its tortured way to the theaters, the song was floating like a feather down to the cutting room floor only to be lifted by some random breeze of destiny. But regular audiences heard in it the supreme example of the right song married to the right tremulous voice—that of an insecure 16-year-old girl who stepped in for beloved national treasure Shirley Temple at the last minute, and for whom the song was a window on the rest of her life, through which she saw nothing but sorrow and longing. Months later, when it won the Academy Award and a terrified Garland was sent up to accept the trophy, the Oscar audience wouldn't let her leave the stage without her singing it on the spot.

22 "BURNING LOVE," Elvis Presley (1972) Only weeks before, Priscilla had left him for another man. The soundtrack of spontaneous human combustion.

21 "CAROLINE, NO," Brian Wilson (1966) The *Great Gatsby* of pop, with a fading train in the night replacing the receding green light of East Egg's pier. Like Gatsby, at the age of 24 Wilson was already wandering dazed in a dream of the past where utopia was adolescence and, like Daisy, Caroline was the golden goddess who betrayed him by growing up. As he sat barefoot at a piano that he installed in a sandbox installed in the middle of his house, one can imagine the mortified glances shared by the other Beach Boys, each more blessedly uncomplicated by genius than the next. And though this was the coda to a classic album they finally deigned to associate themselves with, they insisted that if it must be a single, it be released under Brian's name alone.

20 "THE CRYSTAL SHIP," the Doors (1967) Tapping into the nocturnal side of the city in a way no one had before, they were dismissed by the rest of the L.A. rock community, pointedly *un*invited to the Monterey Pop Festival. After the Beach Boys and the Byrds, however, the Doors made more sense than anyone knew, and although the summer of Peace and Love wasn't half over before the band of Sex and Death had the biggest record of the year, it was the darkly gorgeous B-side of "Light My Fire" that best caught their vision of sensual anarchy, its promise lethal, its threat exquisite.

19 "LOUIE LOUIE," Richard Berry (1956) Covered by more than 1,000 artists who never have been completely clear what it's about, Berry's song was unanimously assumed to be pornographic if only because no one could absolutely prove it wasn't. Fittingly, the original seems to have disappeared from the face of the earth—or at least into the catacombs of degenerate collectors, who play it in secret corners at secret hours.

18 "THE CHASE," Dexter Gordon and Wardell Gray (1947) Tumultuous, ecstatic, the soundtrack of postwar Central Avenue, the Battle of the Great L.A. Tenor Saxes, and the first bebop rave.

17 "I'VE GOT YOU UNDER MY SKIN," Frank Sinatra (1956) Midway through, with the band starting to bubble over, you can almost hear arranger Nelson Riddle snort to himself, "I'll show this little punk a thing or two"—at which point the volcanic track erupts as though to blow the singer out of the studio. Of course America's Swinger held his own, but when it was all over the two men must have stared across the lava field between them in some amazement, accomplices in a cataclysm.

16 "BE MY BABY," the Ronettes (1963) Boom. Boom boom *boom*. Boom. Boom boom *boom*. *Bam!* and out cascades the most exciting opening in pop. Ten years later Martin Scorsese used it over the credits of *Mean Streets* to signal an urgent new aesthetic primitivism: one can picture all four Ramones sitting in the darkened movie theater looking at each other, the single collective lightbulb they had among them sputtering over their heads with inspiration. A decade after that, rad Brit band the Jesus and Mary Chain started so many songs the same way they practically made a concept out of it.

15 "FAMILY AFFAIR," Sly and the Family Stone (1971) The recording of this track is so notorious—Sly Stone ensconced in the Hollywood Hills in the old house of Jeanette MacDonald, now part pharmacy and part arsenal, part whorehouse and part bunker—that it's hard to know whether its dreadful power as the darkest record in the funk canon is a complete shock or completely predictable. The family he was singing about might have been his own or might have been America, but in any case, within a few miles and a few months of the Manson Family's reign of terror, *dysfunctional* was hardly the word for it.

14 "TOO MARVELOUS FOR WORDS," Art Tatum (1953) Given the sustained level of genius that informed Tatum's tone and virtuosity, that married technical invention to joyous expression, anyone born in the last 50 years might be forgiven for calling him the Hendrix of jazz piano; if anything of course, Hendrix was the Tatum of electric guitar. Blind and mostly self-taught, during his 47-year life he blazed his way from Ohio to New York to Los Angeles, from Fats Waller worship to a singular place in history: "God,"

Waller famously announced to his audience one night, on seeing his former protégé there, "is in the house."

13 "STORMY MONDAY," T-Bone Walker (1947) "They call it stormy Monday, but Tuesday's just as bad. . . ." Let's count the number of people who have recorded this—actually, let's not. Written by Walker, whose guitar taught B.B. King half of what he knows, this was a shot across the bow of blue history.

12 "SING ME BACK HOME," Merle Haggard (1967) After "Lonesome Fugitive" he established for himself a position in country music roughly analogous to Charlie Parker's in jazz. This was his stellar accomplishment, both a reach back to his bad old prison days and a leap of dark imagination, the thoughts of a condemned man walking to his death, as heard and sung by someone who had taken that walk in 1,000 nights of the soul.

11 "THAT LUCKY OLD SUN," Ray Charles (1963) The purists have it that after his period with Atlantic Records in the '50s, it was all musical Tomism: white songs with white strings and white arrangements. In fact, rendering the blackness of his voice all the more inescapable, these were some of the most subversive records ever made—the Trojan Herd smuggling into the gates of the White City the blind Negro who sneaked out at midnight singing in the voice of a slave. This overwhelming performance of a '40s standard is obscure relative to Charles's more popular hits of the time, such as "Born to Lose" and "I Can't Stop Loving You" (both recorded here), maybe because his vocal is too filled with a pain the White City couldn't stand to hear. But with all due respect to the purists and the indisputably brilliant Atlantic tracks, it's as great as anything the man ever did.

10 "PETER GUNN," Henry Mancini (1958) Absolutely, irresistibly, hands down, no contest, the coolest TV theme of all time. From its let's-rumble beginning to the Ride of the Motorcycle Valkyrie horns, it's all danger and sex, and it must have shocked the era's rockers. In last season's debut episode producer David Chase flattered himself that it might be the soundtrack of *The Sopranos*, before it became obvious *The Sopranos* couldn't hold Mancini's leather jacket. Chase switched to a Sting song.

9 "BLUE YODEL NO. 9," Jimmie Rodgers and Louis Armstrong (1930) Five weeks after eighth blue yodel, "Mule Skinner Blues," the father of country and the father of jazz recorded this, unfazed by the momentousness of it. Over the seven decades that followed, having started at the top, the fusion of the two most American forms of music had nowhere to go but down.

8 "A NIGHT IN TUNISIA," Charlie Parker (1946) Parker stayed behind in L.A. when his partner Dizzy Gillespie returned to New York: Was it as an homage, or retribution by a friend who felt abandoned, that Parker then recorded Gillespie's most famous song and took it away from him? His new hostile hometown a portal to more hospitable cities of the mind, this was a pulsing fantasia by which, as Bird took flight, he left not only the rest of the band down on terra firma but part of himself too; whether it was out of fear or relief, he later expressed the conviction that he would never again match it. Replacing Gillespie's horn in the septet was that of a 19-year-old who had come to L.A. just to play with Parker, Miles Davis.

7 "WHEN YOU WISH UPON A STAR," Cliff Edwards (1940) The most beautiful song in movies, as sung by a cricket. Though by now my four-year-old son has heard it, I hope to be around when he actually *hears* it. If he takes after his father, that will be when he's 40.

6 "ANGEL EYES," Frank Sinatra (1958) He was called the Voice, but that was a misnomer. It was never about his voice, which was at its best when as a singer, he was at his least impressive; in fact it was when he lost his voice for a year, his vocal cords hemorrhaging, that he reached inside for something no one had ever heard from him. In the years before the shtick, before the ring-a-ding-ding and dooby-dooby-doo, Sinatra would forge a relationship with his songs not unlike that between Brando and his greatest film roles: at once utterly dominant and utterly submissive, with the song as both slave and dominatrix. "Scuse me while I disappear," he sings at the end, his whisper of "Ava?" inaudible in the following darkness, not even knowing anymore whether he hopes she answers.

5 "EVERY GRAIN OF SAND," Bob Dylan (1981) With the vast bulk of his legacy scattered from New York to Nashville to

Minneapolis, nonetheless it was Los Angeles where the best American songwriter since Ellington wrote and recorded his best song. Not his most famous, to be sure, its power lying largely in the fact that it came at the lowest point of his career, from out of a spiritual confusion—"in the time of my confession / in the hour of my deepest need"—that exhausted all self-righteousness, at least for the moment. A hymn not to any religious ideology, then, but to the Mystery of it all, and to what may have been more his intuitive hope than certain conviction that there is indeed a Master's Hand, and that it hasn't passed him over.

4 "STARDUST," Nat King Cole (1956) Acknowledging Louis Armstrong's great 1931 rendition and Artie Shaw's famous 1940 celebration, Frank Sinatra's audacious 1962 deconstruction and Willie Nelson's canny 1978 reinvention, this is the definitive version of the most perfect of all pop songs. Written by Hoagy Carmichael in 1927, recorded more times than "Louie Louie" and "Stormy Monday" put together, it became such a grail for singers and musicians that Cole, a first-rate jazz pianist who never set out to be a singer and therefore underrated himself, probably didn't have the sense to be intimidated. As a result, his interpretation has no agenda. Intimate, serene, a little haunted, joined to a glistening Gordon Jenkins arrangement, it drifts somewhere above the twilight—and if none of that is convincing, well, Hoagy Carmichael thought it was the best version, too.

3 "LONELY WOMAN," Ornette Coleman (1959) A revolution, Coleman so defied conventional notions of harmony and pitch and chord change that Miles Davis called him "psychotic," though, coming from Miles, maybe it was a compliment. This is "Harlem Nocturne" with its senses deranged, drunk notes dripping in the air like rain running down a window, Coleman's sax careening between lyricism and pathos on the one hand and exhilaration and cacophony on the other. It converted not only trumpet man Don Cherry and bassist Charlie Haden (both of whom played on it) but—over the years that followed, thousands of miles away—a young Iggy Pop, still a model high school student, and Lou Reed, still a literature major in college, who heard it and felt the furniture in their heads turn upside down.

2 "YOU'VE LOST THAT LOVIN' FEELIN'," the Righteous Brothers (1964) The Righteous Brothers wanted to give this song to the Everly Brothers, and when Barry Mann, who wrote it with Cynthia Weil, heard the final result he thought it had been recorded at the wrong speed, because Bill Medley's voice was so low. But producer Phil Spector, who for the better part of a year had watched his pop empire fall to Anglo-Saxon hordes, knew what he had the moment he heard Mann and Weil play it for him at the Chateau Marmont; and for a Spector record the opening seconds are unprecedented in their humility: The first thing you hear isn't one of the producer's explosive orchestral crescendos but a single voice, Medley's rising out of the silence. The record builds, fades, builds again, fades again each resurrection ratcheting up the passion another unquantifiable notch, and it all goes on a good minute longer than anything radio was playing in those days. So when the record label was printed with the time on it, faced with the prospect of his master piece going unheard, Spector did the only morally responsible thing. He lied.

1 "A CHANGE IS GONNA COME," Sam Cooke (1964) In 1964, the most utopian year in American history—not in spite of John Kennedy's assassination but because of it, transforming the country by a martyrdom grander than he was—between the apotheosis of Martin Luther King's speech at the Lincoln Memorial in the summer of '63 and the rude awakening of L.A.'s Watts riots in the summer of '65, gospel/soul heartthrob Cooke made this record. By the time it was released as a B-side, in a truncated version that wasn't restored for another 20 years, Cooke himself was a martyr of sorts, murdered in an L.A. motel under tawdry circumstances. But when he soars from the bridge of the song into the final verse, the hair stands up on the back of your neck and he redeems not only anything he ever did, but everything you ever did, too. Ageless the very first time anyone heard it, shattering on every level, as a testament of personal struggle, racial justice, and spiritual transcendence, this became the national anthem of the Dream Deferred and the America that still hasn't come to pass, sung as though from the grave by a ghost who doesn't yet know he's dead.

MARK JACOBSON

Tangled Up In Bob

Someday, no doubt, when the keepers of the tower officially allow that Bob was one of the two or three greatest American artists of the second half of the twentieth century, Dylanology will be boiled down to a standard three credits, a dry bonepile of jewels and binoculars to squeeze in between the Yeatsology and Whitmanology. You might even be able to major in Dylanology, hand in papers on the interplay between Deuteronomy and Dock Boggs in Bob's middle period. But for now, even as the Dylan economy grows each day (a mint copy of the rare stereo version of *Freewheelin'*, which contains four extra songs, goes for $20,000), Dylanology, the semi–sub rosa info jungle of writers, fanzine publishers, collectors, Web page keepers, DAT tapers, song analyzers, old-girlfriend gossips and more, retains a bracing hit of democratic autodidacticism, a deep-fried aroma of overheated neocortices.

"We are fanatical because we are fanatics," says the indefatigable Paul Williams, author of more than twenty-five books, whose *Bob Dylan: Performing Artist 1960–1973*, *Bob Dylan: Performing Artist 1974–1986* and the ongoing *Bob Dylan: Performing Artist 1987–2000* will likely approach an aggregate 1,000 pages before he's done. Speaking of his Bob "compulsion," Williams, who is also the former literary executor of Philip K. Dick's estate, says, "If Shakespeare was in your midst, putting on shows at the Globe Theatre, wouldn't you feel the need to be there, to write down what happened in them?"

Williams, who put Dylan on the cover of *Crawdaddy* magazine, which Williams founded in 1966, is a believer in what he calls "the process." For him, the more than forty conventional, non-bootleg recordings put out by the artist since 1962 are just the blueprint, the starting point, since Dylan, famous for a restless ambivalence toward his own creations, is constantly changing these songs in performance. This means Williams, who solicits donations from Dylan fans so he might continue his work, spends a lot of time comparing and contrasting tapes made at the thousands of shows Bob has given since 1961, which adds up to a lot of alt.versions of "All Along the Watchtower" (1,125 live performances as of January 1st, 2001, according to Glen Dundas' *Tangled Up in Tapes*, as compared to 1,008 for "Like a Rolling Stone," 175 for "The Lonesome Death of Hattie Carroll," 53 for "Visions of Johanna," 22 for "Ring Them Bells," and one each for "Oxford Town" and "Bo Diddley").

"Writing a book about Bob Dylan is a twenty-four-hour-a-day, seven-day-a-week, 365-day-a-year project," Williams says.

This comprehensive approach is standard in D Studies. Bob is a big topic, getting bigger all the time, as he continues to flummox presumptions of reclusiveness by barnstorming 100 dates a year, churning up ever more Dylanology in his wake. Clinton Heylin's recent update of *Bob Dylan: Behind the Shades Revisited* now tips in at 780 pages, a strain on the bookshelf that also includes Heylin's *Bob Dylan: A Life in Stolen Moments*—a day-by-day account of Dylan's doings from the years 1941 to 1995. Even more colossal is Michael Gray's ever expanding revise of *Song and Dance Man III—The Art of Bob Dylan*, which now stretches to 918 pages, including a 111-page chapter titled "Even Post-Structuralists Oughta Have the Pre-War Blues." But even this seems curt compared with Oliver Trager's forthcoming (release is timed to Dylan's sixtieth birthday, on May 24th) *Bach Pages: The Definitive Encyclopedia of Bob Dylan*. Talk about bringing it all back home (the UPS man who delivered the 1,179-page manuscript to my house was puffing hard): This deeply annotated sprawl of song analysis and cool gossip is enough to keep D fans occupied through a short nuclear winter.

It does not stop, as witnessed by the more-than–5,000-item sales list put out by Rolling Tomes Inc., the Bob megalopolis run by the charming Mick and Laurie McCuistion out in Grand Junction, Colorado. In addition to their quarterly *On the Tracks*, the McCuistions, who have four full-time employees engaged in what Laurie calls "Bob work," recently added a monthly newsletter titled "Series of Dreams," because, as Laurie says, "there's just so much stuff happening all the time."

As everyone agrees, the current redhot center of Dylanology is Bill Pagel's Boblinks Web site, based in Madison, Wisconsin, which, in addition to posting a set list (and several highly personalized reviews) within a half-hour of Bob leaving the stage in any part of the world, also offers access to more than 300 other Dylan pages. Here, along with linkage to Sony's own "official" Bobdylan.com and its mighty lyric finder, one encounters the various personal Dylan shrines, cyber tours of Hibbing, Minnesota (where signs welcome the traveler to the "home of Kevin McHale"), hundreds of interviews with the Bobhead and numerous pages such as "A Lily Among Thorns: Exploring Bob Dylan's Christianity." "Lily" offers a compendium of Dylan's *Slow Train/Saved*–period brimstone preaching: On one particular tempestuous evening in Tempe, Arizona, the Rev. Bob, in a sin-killing lather over persistent cries of *"Rock & roll!!!"* screams, "If you want rock & roll, you can go down with rock & roll! You can see Kiss! You can rock & roll all the way down to the Pit!"

Displaying ecumenicalism befitting its seeker hero, Boblinks also features "Bob Dylan: Tangled Up in Jews." The site offers "highlights of Dylan's Judaic journeys," such as "changing his name from Zimmerman," "studying with Lubavitch Hasidim," and a description of the First Annual Bob Dylan Ceremonial New Year's Bread Toss, "in which Bob's rabbi shares where it's at and The Man himself blows the Jewish horn."

On Boblinks, one notes that a lot of the good Bob Web pages have already been claimed. Breadcrumbsins is taken. Foggyruinsoftime is taken. So is cowboyangelsings, powergreedandcorruptableseed, fantasticcollectionofstamps, and expectingrain.com. The latter is main-

tained by the genial Karl Erik Andersen, who works in the national
library in a small Norwegian town astride the Arctic Circle and is
happy to tell you how he rigged up a wireless system so he can listen
to Bob while he shovels snow, which is most of the time. Still, with
more than 500 Bob song titles to choose from, many site names
remain. As of this writing, such desirable addresses as huntedlike
acrocodile.com, bleachersoutinthesun.com, Istayedupallnightinthe
ChelseaHotelwritingSad-EyedLadyoftheLowlandsforyou.com, Iput
myfingerstotheglassbowedmyheadandcried.com and hitthatdrummer
withapiethatsmells.com are all available.

So many quotations, so many conclusions written on the wall, I
needed not remind myself as I went out walking through Green-
wich Village a few days ago. Dylan can spend the rest of his life
inside whatever gated Eden in Malibu, but the Village will always be
the mystic Mississippi Delta of Dylanology—Bob Ground Zero.
Over there, downstairs at 116 MacDougal, where a bar called The
Wreck Room is now, that was the Gaslight. Dylan sang "Talkin'
John Birch Paranoid Blues" there, before Dave Van Ronk did
"Cocaine Blues." Upstairs was the Kettle of Fish, the bar where
Dylan hung with the despondent Phil Ochs and once brought the
Supremes, blowing blowsy folkie minds. Around the corner was the
sainted Gerde's Folk City. Across Washington Square Park, now
outfitted with surveillance cameras by Rudy Giuliani, was the Hotel
Earle, currently renovated for tourists but then scruffy and bleak,
$19 a week, home to Bob back in 1962.

That was a whole other Dylanological epoch, I thought, strolling,
most positively, to the West 4th Street subway station to take the
ever-adventurous D train uptown to 59th Street. I was on the way to
talk to my old acquaintance A.J. Weberman, who is both the inventor of the term Dylanology and the discipline's most reviled figure.

As students of primeval D-ology know, A.J., who quit college in
1968 to create the first computer-generated Dylan Word Concor-
dance, is most famous for going through Bob's garbage. This "garbol-
ogy" action was part of a full-scale assault launched by the Dylan
Liberation Front, a bunch of Yippie pot smokers who thought Dylan,

the most angel-headed head of the generation, had fallen prey to a *Manchurian Candidate*-style government plot to hook him to sensibility-deadening hard dope. These findings were based on A.J.'s highly idiosyncratic interpretations of "Dylan's secret language," a code that, once cracked, revealed words like "rain" and "chicken" (as in "the sun is not yellow—it's chicken!") to actually mean "heroin." It was Dylan's addiction that led the poet to make sappy records like *Nashville Skyline* and *New Morning* when his great gift could have been better used speaking out against Vietnam, A.J. contended.

"Dylan's brain belongs to the People, not the Pigs!" was among the fervent cries back in 1970, as A.J. led the forty or so smelly hippies in his Dylanology class to Bob's home at 94 MacDougal Street, where they screamed for Dylan to "crawl out yer window" and answer charges that he had been co-opted. After an unsolicited DLF-inspired block party for Dylan's thirtieth birthday, which resulted in the NYPD shutting down Bleecker Street, and a long series of hectoring phone calls (the tapes were compiled on a Folkways Records release entitled *Bob Dylan vs. A.J. Weberman*, now a major Bob collectible), Dylan struck back.

Three decades later, A.J., now fifty-five, his once-wild mane receded to silver fringe (but still talking very fast), recalls the incident, one of the more colorful in the often drearily hagiographic Dylanological chronicles: "I'd agreed not to hassle Dylan anymore, but I was a publicity-hungry motherfucker. . . . I went to MacDougal Street, and Dylan's wife comes out and starts screaming about me going through the garbage. Dylan said if I ever fucked with his wife, he'd beat the shit out of me. A couple of days later, I'm on Elizabeth Street and someone jumps me, starts punching me.

"I turn around and it's like—Dylan. I'm thinking, 'Can you believe this? I'm getting the crap beat out of me by Bob Dylan!' I said, 'Hey, man, how you doin'?' But he keeps knocking my head against the sidewalk. He's little, but he's strong. He works out. I wouldn't fight back, you know, because I knew I was wrong. He gets up, rips off my 'Free Bob Dylan' button and walks away. Never says a word.

"The Bowery bums were coming over, asking, 'How much he get?' Like I got rolled. . . . I guess you got to hand it to Dylan, coming over himself, not sending some fucking lawyer. That was the last time I ever saw him, except once with one of his kids, maybe Jakob, and he said, 'A.J. is so ashamed of his Jewishness, he got a nose job,' which was true—at least in the fact that I got a nose job. . . ."

It was all too bad, A.J. said now, remembering how Dylan reportedly offered him a series of jobs if he would stop his "Free Bob" campaign. "He said I could be his chauffeur, but I told him I don't know how to drive. Then he said I could be his prompter. But I said, 'Forget it! It's not going to work! I'm the one person you can't buy out.' In retrospect, that was a sad mistake. I could have had a career as a rock critic or something, and not as a pot dealer, and not, you know, ended up where I'm going to end up."

This was the news. Just the week before, A.J. had been in the Union County Correctional Facility, finally busted by the Feds for allegedly running a marijuana-delivery service. He was out on $100,000 bail, looking at a possible ten years in the joint. When I called to ask if he was going to be home, he shouted, "Of course I'm going to be home, moron! I'm under fucking house arrest!" And there he was, the supposed Anton LaVey of Dylanology, with a plastic monitoring device snapped to his ankle, on the terrace of his apartment overlooking Central Park that had once been home to Antoine de Saint-Exupery, author of *The Little Prince*. It was a far cry from the old days at the Bleecker Street bunker, where A.J.'s famous Dylan Archives were zealously guarded by Dobermans.

"As fate would have it," A.J. noted with bitter amusement, "the Feds watched my office and saw me throw away these big huge wrappers from the pot in the garbage, and they used that to get a search warrant. So the garbologist got caught with his own garbage."

This irony was not missed by the current generation of Dylanologists, the postings of whom can be found on the popular Usenet site rec.music.dylan. Under the thread "Weberman in jail!! I bet Bob is laughing," D fans rejoiced with comments like "not so instant karma but I'll take it" and the inevitable "don't need a Weberman to know which way the wind blows."

Dismissing this, A.J. stood by his recent highly controversial claims, notably that Dylan is suffering from AIDS, supposedly contracted from a dirty needle. As always, the proof was in the song interpretation, A.J. contended, especially in "Disease of Conceit," "Dignity" and the overall doomsday pall of the 1997 *Time Out of Mind* album. To show me what he meant, A.J. rang up his own Bob page, Dylanology.com. But there was a problem. The site, written by A.J. himself almost exclusively in JavaScript, uses so much memory it often crashes computers. A.J. never noticed this until the Feds seized his high-powered system in their raid on his office. Now, forced to make do with a less zippy older machine, he found that Dylanology.com kept getting blown off the screen.

"Fuck this!" A.J. screamed, smacking the computer; the whole thing was a disaster, especially since, along with everything else, the government had confiscated the Web site's backup discs.

"Yeah, Dylan's going to be glad I'm going to jail all right," A.J. began to spritz, getting that look in his eye. "This is going to revitalize his career! He's going to be so inspired by my downfall he'll write five great songs by next week! Dylan'll owe me for this!"

But then Weberman's wife and kid came into the room. The idea that he might not see them for a long time stopped the old Dylanologist in his tracks.

After a moment, he said, "You know, I come from a people that, they looked at every word in the Bible, and they commented on it, then they commented on the comments. In the Torah, the Gemara, the Mishna. They know it so well, they look at a word on a page and tell you what word is behind it on the opposite page. They studied genes and interiors of things like maps of the heart. So it doesn't matter what people think about me and Bob Dylan. Because he's from the same place I'm from. And that's the real Dylanology ... and that never stops no matter what's gonna happen to me."

Rock is full of cults, but nothing—not collecting the Beatles, not documenting Elvis—rivals Dylanology. Back in his dark-sunglasses days, Dylan might have been the coolest, but Dylanology is not about cool. Neither is it a hobby, a fleeting affectation or indolent lord-it-over-you taste-making to get girls, like in *High Fidelity*. Dylanology is a risk, a gamble, a spiritual declaration, a life choice, and if you don't believe it, ask those real Weathermen, erstwhile college students who took the drama of "Subterranean Homesick Blues" to heart, maybe too much. A year after Rubin Carter addressed the United Nations, several of those forgotten revolutionaries continue to rot in jail, so ask them which way that wind blows. But this is how it is with Dylanology. To be a Bobcat is to acknowledge the presence of the extraordinary in your midst, to open yourself to its workings, to act upon it. In a world of postmod ephemera, this is a solemn bond.

In turns, a real folkie, a real rocker, a real lover, a real father, a real doper, a real shit, a real Christian, a real Jew, a real American from a real small town come to a real big town with real dreams and little false modesty, Dylan, big-tent preacher of millennial concerns both sacred and profane, has never offered less than authenticity to his variegated flock, no matter what peculiar ax they might grind. With Bob, you may feel betrayed, bitterly disappointed, but you never think it's a hustle. Because he has always been so willing to lay his heart on the line, so are we.

Nowadays it seems that without the Bible, McDonald's jingles and Bob Dylan, there'd be gaping holes in half the world's conversations. Couple of months ago I went with my mother to Romania. We were supposed to find our roots, but all we found were the vanished graves of murdered relatives, and dart-eyed Gypsy boys looking for someone's pocket to pick in front of the hideous palaces built by the dead Commie leader Nicolae Ceausescu. "When you got nothing, you got nothing to lose," a Gypsy boy said, standing beside a pile of red peppers in the market.

I see that Michael Douglas and Catherine Zeta-Jones named their baby Dylan, which is very nice, but half the kids in my son's class are named Dylan. There are even girl Dylans. Buy whatever apocryhpha you like about Bob taking the moniker from either Dylan Thomas or his gambling uncle Mr. Dillon—now it's just one more name on the birth-announcement card, like Ashley or Justin.

Dylanology marches on; it's a continuity thing. Last week, I was eating breakfast at a formerly run-down East Village diner with Josh Nelson, who is twenty-four and aspiring to be a psychology professor. In 1990, when Josh was thirteen, his father took him to see Bob for the first time at the Beacon Theater in New York. This was no surprise. As many fathers make a fetish out of taking their kid to their first ballgame, it is Dylanological ritual responsibility to bring *der kinder* to Bob shows. Only a few weeks before, I'd accompanied my own seventeen-year-old daughter, Rae, to her first Dylan show, at Jones Beach, the same funky stretch of sand where, thirty-five years ago, I used to come with my friends, our bodies stark and white, stupid Bob hats on our heads.

But still, it was tense. Dads and teens, it's always tense, all the more because we were seeing Bob, and nothing about Bob is simply casual. It could have been didactic, another lesson, one more bit of proof of how my hallowed pop youth exceeded hers. But Dylan speaks to all, equally. The show worked out fine. Just for that ole-time Bob atmosphere, it rained apocalyptically, the speakers nearly blew up, and Dylan sang Rae's favorite apocalyptic comedy, "Ballad of Frankie Lee and Judas Priest."

"The rest is up to her, you've done your part," commented Josh Nelson, who, since his dad took him to the Beacon, has seen Bob Dylan perform upward of 203 times, in St. John's, Newfoundland; Regina, Saskatchewan; Cottbus, Germany; and Starkville, Mississippi. "In my mind, Dylan was just another of the those older Jewish guys whom I had heard of only in name. It's scary, but, for some reason, I grouped him with Neil Diamond and Barry Manilow. Yes, in a word, I knew nothing. . . ." Josh once wrote in a college essay discussing his immersion in Bobdom. Soon enough, however, he decided that "'Boots of Spanish Leather' is no longer about sailing and 'Mama You Been on My Mind' is a song about the hopelessly unforgettable . . . no longer all foreign and ungraspable but rather now somehow understood and real."

"That's the difference," Josh said. "For me, Bob Dylan isn't the man who played Folk City and Forest Hills. The Bob Dylan I know is the man on the stage at the Beacon Theater, older, sadder maybe, but still him." It was one thing to regret the long-missed past, and another to make the most of the present and future, said Josh, who, like most younger Dylanologists, leans heavily to the study of Bob's stage performances. "We're there, keeping the flame," Josh says, proud that he'd heard that Dylan made *Time out of Mind* partially so his young fans would have some songs to hear for the first time, to call their own. Then, nervously pushing his kasha and eggs across his plate, Josh said that even if people called him "the walking Krogsgaard" (in reference to his encyclopedic recall of Michael Krogsgaard's authoritative listing of Dylan set lists), he didn't want to give the impression that "this" was his entire life. He'd graduated Phi Beta Kappa from Middlebury, after all. He didn't want to seem like some nut. It was a theme, skirting the edges of lunacy in service to the Bob Muse; this much was apparent upon visiting Mitch Blank, an old-time Village guy.

"Looking at this place, you'd think a normal person lives here," said Mitch, standing in the doorway of his remarkably neat (considering) walk-up apartment. Mitch's self-diagnosed mania is his Dylan collection, which includes: a magical set of sliding wall cabinets capable of handling more than 20,000 tapes of Bob Dylan concerts, a collection of every Bob interview dating back to the 1960s, the cover of each magazine on which Bob Dylan has ever appeared, nearly every Bob Dylan poster or show announcement (the November 11, 1961 playbill from Carnegie Chapter Hall says "All Seats— $2.00"), a xerox of the cover of Bob Dylan's copy of Woody Guthrie's *Bound for Glory*, a full collection of Bob Dylan postage stamps from Gambia and Tanzania (some of which Mitch arranged to have canceled by the Hibbing, Minnesota, post office on Dylan's 52nd birthday, May 24th, 1993), a Highway 61 sign from Minnesota DOT, a piece of the Big Pink piano, a Bob Dylan-signed baseball, a copy of a lease for an apartment Dylan moved into at 21336 Pacific Coast Highway that allows for "5" children and "t" dog. Also present is Mitch's typically complete database, which, among much else, catalogs covers of Dylan songs ("I Shall Be Released" was done by Marjoe Gortner, Coven, Telly Savalas and Big Mama Thornton; "Blowin' in the Wind" by Sebastian Cabot, Marlene Dietrich, Brian Hyland and the U.S. Navy Steel Band).

"It's just the tip of the iceberg," announced Mitch, who works as a photo researcher by day and is on the advisory board of the Museum of Folk Music in Greenwich Village, as he graciously copied a documentary on collectors of 8-track tapes so I'd see what "the really sick are like." Yet there is a line even Mitch will not cross, such as when a good friend called up saying he had several Marlboro butts freshly smoked by Dylan.

"'What do I want Bob's cigarette butts for?' I asked this degenerate," Mitch recalled. "And he said, 'Don't you see? Dylan's DNA is on those butts. Sometime in the future we'll be able to clone a whole new Bob Dylan. The ultimate collectible.' I told him he was disgusting. You know, even for me, there's a limit."

The limit. I was looking for the limit. I mean, it was fine thumbing through the hundreds of interviews Bob has given over the years, learning that on June 13th, 1984, Dylan told Robert Hilburn of the *Los Angeles Times* that he didn't think he'd be "perceived properly till 100 years after I'm gone." It was amusing to hear stories told by old Villagers about going shopping with Suze Rotolo, Bob's most mythic pre-Sara girlfriend (who was remembered as "quiet, pigeon-toed and very fond of the color green"), the day she bought those famous Boots of Spanish Leather. It was interesting also to read through many of the D novels written over the years, from Diane Di Prima's Olympia Press porno scenes about fucking along with "Highway 61" to Don DeLillo's *Great Jones Street*, onward to *The Dylanist*, a recent, well-received novel of (lefty) upper-middle-class manners, which, outrageously, does not even mention Bob until page 83, and then, on page 139, manages to have the main character quote Dylan's line: "He's an artist, he don't look back." *He?*

There was even a satisfying touch of terror, walking by the Morgan Library on East 36th Street in Manhattan, knowing the Red Notebook was almost certainly behind those stone walls. The Red Notebook: the fifty-nine-cent spiral pad in which Bob wrote, in his crabbed handwriting, the lyrics for the *Blood on the Tracks* songs. The Red Notebook: a document of the poet's most consummate pain, legendarily stolen from Bob's house, passed along on the black market, every collector's forbidden grail, then, by dint of the Dylan Office's demand, donated to the Morgan. The Red Notebook: the Maltese Falcon of Dylanology, the stuff dreams and nightmares were made of. To hold even a xerox in your hands was to risk any kind of karma.

I knew I was in too deep when I got a call from a friend in L.A. who said he knew the chauffeur who drove Michael Bolton to Dylan's Malibu house the day the two pop stars co-authored "Steel Bars." I had a head full of Dylanology that was driving me insane, and I hadn't even called on the academics yet, people like Christopher Ricks, the Boston University poetry professor, to grok his axial analysis of Dylan's pentameters. I hadn't listened to the complete works of the Wilburys, avoiding the whole Tom Petty period like the plague. Nor had I re-memorized the "11 Outlined Epitaphs," Bob's liner notes ("for I do not care to be made an oddball bouncin' past reporters' pens") on the back of my old vinyl of *The Times They Are A-Changin'*, which I retain, my high school girlfriend's phone number still visible in the upper-left-hand corner. I hadn't seen Mel Prussack's homemade "Dyl-clocks," each one marked with a Bob quote denoting the passage of "Dyl-time." I hadn't even established if "Quinn the Eskimo" was really written as Dylan watched Nicholas Ray's 1959 picture *The Savage Innocents*, in which Anthony Quinn played an Eskimo.

Amid the glut, a million legitimate Dylanological mysteries remained. Issues. Questions. Legends to either puncture or leave alone. For instance, even after all these years, no one seems to have conclusively ascertained exactly how hurt Dylan was after the 1966 motorcycle accident; whether, as some suggest, he exaggerated his injuries to derail the hectic schedule Albert Grossman had painted him into. Nor was it completely clear if Dylan is still a Christian. Clinton Heylin says yes—"Listen to the songs." Paul Williams says Dylan's current Christianity or Jewishness is secondary to his "overriding fundamentalism. . . . He is someone who believes in the literalness of the Word. He will be a fundamentalist in whatever he believes."

Whatever his current theology, I, for one, would like to know whatever happened to the Jewish jokes in Bob Dylan. Bob Dylan used to be as funny as Franz Kafka. "Motorpsycho Nightmare" (never performed live in concert) is one of the funniest songs ever written, a touchstone of surreal "dirt beneath my fingernails" *shtetl* humor. Maybe being born again beat the stand-up out of him, or maybe it was just the sheer weight of being Bob for so many years. But by the time Dylan got around to writing his "Lenny Bruce" song, as turgid a tune as he'd ever done, Bob had forgotten that Bruce, the old Jew junkie/First Amendment crusader, used to make people laugh for a living.

Still, when you came down to it, the biggest conundrum in Dylanology was Dylan himself. The Living Bob. How to deal with the fact that the most inspiring artist of the times still walks among us, after all these years. Written Dylanology breaks into three camps. Michael Gray's monumental, endlessly illuminating *Song and Dance Man III* most successfully places Dylan in his cultural context. (With resourceful scholarship, Gray finds the line "When you live outside the law you have to eliminate dishonesty" in the little-known 1958 Don Siegel noir film *The Lineup*, noting the obvious connection to the much better "to live outside the law you must be honest.") Gray ignores the Living Bob altogether. Referring almost exclusively to the fixed text of the "official" Columbia releases, he attempts no bridge to Bob the human, dealing only with the work, as if it were written by a poet in the thirteenth century.

Paul Williams, Clinton Heylin and others take the middle path, acknowledging the Living Bob's presence while warily wishing not to unduly trespass on the artist's personal space. This half-measure is a difficult tack, as Williams notes, describing the publishing of his well-known *Dylan—What Happened?*, a book seeking to come to terms with Dylan's mind-blowing born-again shows at San Francisco's Warfield Theater in 1979. Dylan liked Williams' book, reportedly buying 114 copies (114 happening to be the exact number of sayings of Christ to appear in the Gnostic Gospel of St. Thomas found at Nag Hammadi). Dylan invited Williams backstage and even performed the famously unperformed "Caribbean Wind" at the writer's request. However, Dylan was not much pleased with Williams' follow-up article, reportedly saying, "It happens every time—when I meet someone who's written something about me that I like, meeting me spoils them and the next thing they write doesn't work."

Williams, for his part, agrees with his subject. "After meeting him, I became very much aware that Bob Dylan would certainly read whatever I wrote. Maybe it took me away from what I usually do, which is only for fans. I think the idea that Bob Dylan might be looking over your shoulder damages a lot of writers."

Then, of course, there is the other approach to the Living Bob, which is to go forward, to stand naked before him, demanding his attention. Such was the methodology employed by Larry (Ratso) Sloman in his now out-of-print account of the Rolling Thunder Tour, *On the Road With Bob Dylan—Rolling With the Thunder.* Easily the most entertaining and strangely moving of Bob tomes, Sloman's book contains many good quotes. There is Dylan's mother, Beattie, saying, "He was born to us, but then he went away and did this on his own. . . . Bob Dylan is the writer, Dylan, not Zimmerman." And Bob himself, adding, "Well, I don't understand music, you know. I understand Lightning Hopkins. I understand Leadbelly, John Lee Hooker, Woody Guthrie, Kinky Friedman. I never claimed to understand music. . . . If you ever heard me play the guitar, you'd know that." To which Ratso, the fan, replies, "But I like the way you play the guitar."

But a key moment in all of Dylanology occurs when Sloman, in the midst of a book-wide freak-out about his inability to "get" the story, confronts Dylan in a hotel lobby.

"C'mere, schmuck," Ratso reports himself as saying, demanding that Dylan listen to his plea.

Dylan addresses the distraught reporter: "Well, what is it that you want? Be specific. What do you need?"

Ratso searches for the word. His eyes suddenly light up. "I need access," he screams at the superstar. "I need access. . . ."

Dylan then reportedly "rolls his eyes in amazement" and says, "Ex-Lax? . . . Why do you need Ex-Lax? What you been eating?"

This was it: access.

Access. What A.J. Weberman, in his dementia, called "the Brain" of the Poet in the hands of "the People." Access: a backstage pass to that no man's land of Dylanological real estate between the artist and ourselves. Access: what we—the scholars, the fans, the lunatics—want.

What he, the Living Bob, will not give.

Access. Proximity to the Bobhead. It is a Dylanological obsession. Whole books, like *Encounters With Bob Dylan: If You See Him Say Hello*, offer chronicles of chance meetings and near-meetings between Dylan and cab drivers, secretaries, salesclerks. To see him is something not to be forgotten, a memory handled with care. For instance, considering how many bands Bob has had, Dylanology is surprisingly free of side-man stories. Possibly this owes to the scuttlebutt that Bob has very little to do with his fellow players—for years, supposedly, it was *verboten* to even make eye contact with Bob. There is also a notion of sacred time, that for a musician, playing with Bob Dylan is nothing to speak about idly. Guitarist Steve Ripley, who toured with Dylan in the Eighties, did, however, tell me this story: Apparently, Ripley arrived at the venue at the wrong time for a sound check and found no one around. He was about to go back to his hotel when he saw Dylan, sitting near the stage all by himself. Up to this point, Ripley had exchanged few words with his enigmatic boss. But there was no way to avoid talking now: It was just the two of them.

"I really didn't know what to say to the guy," Ripley recounted. "I mean: He's Bob Dylan. What do you say to Bob Dylan?"

After a long pause, the guitarist finally blurted, "Hi, Bob, hey, how's the family?" whereupon Dylan literally bounded toward the sideman and gave him a big hug.

"Great!" Dylan exclaimed, a giant smile spreading across his craggy face, "Thanks for asking!"

Access.

I suppose it was selfish of me, a typical invasion of hallowed Dylanological space, but I felt I had no choice. At least this is what I'd decided, from a Chevy Blazer, on the road again. I'd been on Bob's tracks for a couple of weeks, trailing him through the Northeast, through Hartford, Connecticut; Mansfield, Massachusetts; Saratoga, New York; Scranton, Pennsylvania; Camden, New Jersey; Columbia, Maryland—everywhere Bob went, I was there, watching The Man in his short black coat and the pants with the honky-tonk stripe up the leg (the same outfit he sang for the Pope in, which was way better than the outpatient's hooded sweat shirt he wore throughout the late Eighties). I was studying the strange half-smile, the playful Chaplin-cum-Elvis-impersonator guitar moves, the sawed-off duck walks, diffident roll of the rheumy eye, the drop of silver sweat poised at the end of his hooked nose, waiting for my chance.

The time had come to apologize, I thought—to apologize to Dylan for wishing he was dead.

I thought it was a memory buried forever in a trunk, but not deep enough, it seems, for there it was, in a 1999 *New Yorker* article about Bob, in the first paragraph, for chrissakes: "In 1978, after the fiasco of *Renaldo and Clara*, Dylan's four-hour art film, Mark Jacobson wrote in the *Village Voice*, 'I wish Bob Dylan died.'"

It was true. There, in the very newspaper where I'd first read of this skinny Jew son of an appliance salesman who'd blown in from the North Country to turn my little Flushing, Queens, world upside down, I had written, "I wish Bob Dylan died. Then Channel 5 would piece together an instant documentary of his life and times, the way they did Hubert [Humphrey], Chaplin, Adolf Hitler. Just the immutable facts . . . seeing all those immutable facts about Elvis made his dying worthwhile. . . ."

Geez, couldn't I at least have left out Hitler? The idea, I guess, was that even Bob dying would have been better than sitting through *Renaldo and Clara* twice. Maybe in 1978 I thought this was some kind of joke.

The incident is well documented. In *No Direction Home—The Life and Music of Bob Dylan*, former *New York Times* folk-music critic Robert Shelton says, "Dylan was most hurt by the reaction from his old neighborhood paper, the *Village Voice*." Bob himself is quoted as saying, "Did you see the firing squad of critics they sent?" Worse yet is the notation in Clinton Heylin's biography, *Bob Dylan: Behind the Shades*. In a chapter titled, "Someone's Got It In for Me," Faridi McFree, one of Dylan's post-Sara girlfriends, reads the *Renaldo and Clara* reviews to Bob over the phone. "It was horrible, absolutely horrible what they said about him, especially in the *Village Voice*."

"Bob," McFree tells Dylan, "they actually really wish you were dead."

But it took the *New Yorker* piece to identify me by name. To point the finger, as Dylan used to say about his early protest songs, at the man in the lonely crowd who was to blame.

I had become Dylanology: I was the man who wished Bob Dylan was dead. What a nightmare. I mean: Bob Dylan was, and remains, my hero. For decades I held on to a letter, signed by Albert Grossman, Dylan's manager, thanking me for my interest, but no, Bob would not be available to be interviewed for the Francis Lewis High School *Patriot*. Once, sometime in the late Sixties, I saw Bob coming out of Manny's Music on 48th Street carrying a white paper bag. Half an hour later, I saw Muhammad Ali, my other lodestone, standing at the same exact spot where I'd seen Dylan. Ali shook my hand. Bob only nodded, but it was enough.

I was there, too, at Forest Hills in 1965, booing Dylan for going electric. Nowadays, there are 20 million ponytailed ex-hipsters claiming to have been at the old 15,000-seat tennis stadium heralding the zeitgeist as "Tombstone Blues" serrated the late-summer air. But really, it was better to have booed. All the real Dylan fans booed. Booing was part of the Dylanological continuum—having expectations shattered, feeling rejected, and then realizing how better, way better, it was to live in this new, bigger world he'd thrust you into.

In retrospect, it seems the ultimate noncompliance that Dylan didn't die taking his Triumph too quick around that curve on Zena Road in Woodstock back in '66. If anyone ever fit the live fast / die young / beautiful corpse trope, it was Bob Dylan. Then, like Rimbaud and James Dean, Dylan could have been one more overromanticized Jim Morrison to sit around watching be a smart mouth in *Don't Look Back*, ranking on poor Donovan and claiming he could hold his breath three times as long as Caruso. Indeed, it makes a good scene, like a *Behind the Music* tale from the crypt: the Bobster, in a steam room, playing rummy with the twin poles of his cross-race pollination-inspiration: Hank Williams (dead at twenty-nine) and Robert Johnson (dead at twenty-seven). Charlie Parker (dead at thirty-four) could sit in, too, if he was in town.

Except Bob Dylan wasn't going for it: this was not his Fate. By whatever confluence of DNA and destiny, he has persisted far beyond the days of his own infallibility. Fifty-nine now, he's had plenty of time to make a nutty movie like *Renaldo and Clara*, be charged with hitting his wife, get born again, make a bunch of inter-mittently inspired records, etc., etc., and have dick-heads like me wish he were dead.

He has lasted long enough for that old-time religion to return. Only yesterday, I was able to sit on the subway, listening to the 1994 version of Dylan creaking through the old folk song "Delia," tears in my eyes at the harsh, ravaged beauty of it all. When he was twenty, he wanted to sound like an old whore singing "House of the Rising Sun," one foot on the platform, the other on the train. Now he'd gotten there. In the end, this was Dylan's true greatness, his spectacular humanity, the keep-on-keeping-on of it all, the adher-ence to the life cycle. At least this was the rap—my rap until that *New Yorker* came through the door.

I mention all this because everyone—everyone I know, anyway—has their own Dylanology. Their own little *chazerei* about how it is between Bob and them. And, like me, they want to tell you all about it.

Could be now or never. Since the 1997 histoplasmosis scare (noted by *New York Post* headline writers as "Bob Dylan Heart Mys-tery"), mortality issues have dominated Dylanological dialogue. How does Bob look, people ask; what's his physical state, his mental state, think he's been drinking? Now, for sure, was the time to be with the Bobster, to follow him around from show to show, to get unashamedly paternal about the guy, not to let the little fucker out of your sight.

It was also very convenient, now that Bob has become an opening act. In the beginning, this was a shock, watching Dylan blast out "Down in the Flood" before 60,000 empty seats at Giants Stadium in 1995, ignored by stray early-bird Grateful Dead fans. But now this seven o'clock starting time is one more Dylanological boon. This way the D fan can easily commandeer a spot in the still-empty first few rows, see Bob's seventeen-song set, be back on the highway (or tucked in bed at the Marriot) by nine, and never hear note one of headliner Phil Lesh.

Bob is like Ali now, lighting the Olympic torch, a (usually) silent Buddha, acknowledging the sweet autumnalness of it all. In current Dylanology the set list is everything, and these days the poet offers mostly a greatest-hits, pre-motorcycle-accident package. You can sit behind where Pablo the sound man lights the candles and burns the sticks of Nag Chompa incense, "a Bob Dylan tradition for the past twenty years," Pablo says, and wonder about it. Wonder if Dylan, the rebel morphed to Sunshine Boy / National Treasure / Beloved Entertainer, has decided to close his show with "Blowin' in the Wind," his corniest signature song, because he thinks we want this showbiz victory lap, this "Forever Young" schmaltz. Or whether he's come to the (painful? joyous?) conclusion that these older tunes, the famous ones of his youth, like "Mr. Tambourine Man," "Don't Think Twice" and "Stuck Inside of Memphis"—not the gospel, not *Time out of Mind*—are really his best, the things he really wants to play so we'll remember him right.

Like Revelations, in seven shows, Bob played seven "Tangled Up in Blue"s, seven "Highway 61"s, seven "Like a Rolling Stone"s, seven "Blowin' in the Wind"s. The Dylanologist, understanding that some around him have been waiting twenty years to hear "It Ain't Me Babe" live, sits patiently, anticipating the "variable" slots, the ones reserved for the special items, the one-offs, the deep rarities. As always, they come: a speed-metal revise of "Drifter's Escape"; a "Long Black Veil," the ultimate murder ballad, never more high and lonesome; a two-night revival of "Tears of Rage"; "Maggie's Farm" (played at Scranton, exactly thirty-five years to the day from the first electric version at Newport, a fact duly noted by attendant tapeheads); an old Stanley Brothers tune; and finally, "Every Grain of Sand."

The "Every Grain of Sand" was especially excellent because that was what the seventy-eight-year-old blue-haired lady in Columbia, Maryland, said she wanted Dylan to play. Leaning on her cane, she said she'd gotten into Bob "about twenty years ago" when her son, who'd been living in the basement, "finally" moved out. Cleaning the place, she found dozens of scratched vinyls under the cigarette-scarred couch. "I always was afraid about what he was doing down there. When I heard this Bob Dylan, I felt a lot better about my son." Then, looking around at the gathering tribes, the old lady smiled and said, "It's so nice that he can draw such a crowd at his age."

"Rainy Day Women #12 and 35" was her favorite Dylan song, the woman said, somewhat surprising for a "churchgoer." But this being the anniversary of her husband's death, she was really hoping Bob would do "Every Grain of Sand," which contains the lyrics "I hear the ancient footsteps like the motion of the sea/Sometimes I turn, there's someone there, other times it's only me" and is described by Michael Gray, in his twenty-five-page chapter on the tune (complete with copious footnotes mentioning Edith Piaf, Frankie Laine, Cain, Abel, St. Matthew, St. Paul, Tony Bennett, William Blake, Allen Ginsberg, Bruno Bettelheim and the Rev. Dr. John Polkinghorne, canon theologian of Liverpool), as a work that is "really about faith vs. doubt."

And, of course, even though Dylan hadn't done "Every Grain of Sand" a single time on the then-thirty-two-date-long tour, he did it that very night at the Merriweather Post Pavilion in Columbia, Maryland. Did it great, too—ethereal, elusive and pure, and not even that far off from the record.

This is how it is with Bob in these latter days, as he makes his fitful rounds of summertime music sheds and second-banana fall apple festivals. He is the gift that keeps on giving, a wish-fulfilling jukebox of high modernism, speaking, as always, in new ways beyond our knowing. Then again, Dylanology has always been a synchronicitous thing: the meaningful coincidence expressed via the mysterium of Bob.

How else to explain the message on the radio driving down the Jersey Turnpike, on the way to the Camden show? The announcer was talking about how then-Governor Christie Whitman was finally going to close Greystone Hospital due to "a series of patient suicides, assaults, unsanitary conditions and understaffing at the 100-year-old facility."

Now, any cub of a Bobcat knows the story of how the first place Dylan went when he came east from Hibbing in February of '61 was

Greystone Hospital in Jersey, to see Woody Guthrie. It says so right
in the liner notes of the first album: Although Bob and Woody were
"separated by thirty years and two generations, they were united by
a love of music . . . and common view of the world." So how do you
figure that after 100 years of understaffing, patient suicides and
who-knows-whatever botched operations, the Governor of New
Jersey picked that exact day to close Greystone?

And how do you figure that Dylan picked that night to play
"Song to Woody," the 1961 tune in which D foretells to Guthrie a
"funny ol' world that's a-comin' along . . ." that is "sick and hungry,
tired and torn, and looks like it's dying hardly before it's been born,"
a heck of a bleak bouquet to lay at the hospital bed of a victim of
Huntington's chorea, even a canny hard traveler like Woody
Guthrie. Quite a vision indeed to behold now, forty years and three
generations on the other side of all that, especially when you're
stuck in traffic, and it's Jersey, too.

Access. If I was going to apologize to Dylan, to somehow erase my
insignificant notation in Dylanological history, "the formation" was
my best chance. It was something new this tour, with Bob and the
boys—Charlie Sexton, Larry Campbell and good ol' Tony Garnier,
in his purple suit, twelve years on the bass. When the set's over, the
band stands there for a minute or so and stares back at the audience.
They don't say anything, only peer off into the cold distance, like a
spaghetti western. Bob keeps his hand on his hip, Bette Davis style.

"Bob!" I shouted from the edge of the stage. "I'm sorry! I'm sorry
I said I wished you died!"

But unlike the cry of the "Judas!" screamer at the Manchester
Free Trade Hall in July of '66, my words did not pierce the din.
Dylan did not turn and call me "a liar," tell me "I don't believe you!"
In Hartford, Scranton, Saratoga, Camden and Columbia, not once
did Bob look my way. Eventually, a friend of mine told me to stop.
My friend, a Dylan hand who knows these things, said if I kept
insisting on apologizing, I'd be on the verge of becoming "a profile," which is what the "Dylan Office," in its well-rumored paranoia
(paranoia being a hardy perennial in all things Dylanological), calls
those who try to get too close, those who too aggressively attempt

to break the plane between Him and us, who want more access than they deserve.

"If Bob wants to forgive you, he probably already has," said my friend.

And I thought of this a couple nights later, driving back toward New York with my wife. We'd thought we would be able to see Bob again that night, which would have made eight straight shows, but the holiday was over. So we headed home, reaching the Holland Tunnel a little after 7 P.M., about the time Dylan would have gone onstage.

"Get a Bob Dylan song on the radio," I said to my wife. This was no doubt a fruitless gesture because maybe thirty-four years ago Murray the K, stone mellow and on FM by then, but with the grease of pastrami still seeping through his veins (but really hip pastrami), said that "Like a Rolling Stone," seven minutes long, was Top Ten. But now there is almost never a Bob Dylan song on New York radio, if you don't count movie tie-ins like "Hurricane" (unplayed live by Bob since 1976).

But then there it was, as we approached the toll plaza, dim at the edges of reception but unmistakable: "Desolation Row," Dylan had revived the song on the current tour, performing it several nights in a row, third in the set list. There was a good chance he was playing the epic tune at that exact moment, on the muddy field of Waterloo Village in north Jersey. When Sinatra got old, he did "My Way": when Elvis was near the end, he did "My Way," too. Bob Dylan does "Desolation Row."

The first time I heard the song was the first time he performed it, the night I booed him at Forest Hills. The *New York Times*, in a review I clipped, called it "a major new composition." Now the "*Titanic* sails at dawn" verse was fading out as we entered the tunnel. Was there absolution in this Cocteau-like visitation? Was this Bob's way of taking the curse off me? Who knew? In my time of Dylanology, it has always been like this. You forget about him for a decade or more, then he's back in your head, suddenly a matter of life and death, again.

Boom!

Amid the crush of CD releases timed to accompany Louis Armstrong's centennial celebration, a two-year event that acknowledges his avowed birthdate in 1900 as well as his true one in 1901, a remarkable oddity has glided in under the radar of many fans. It's an appendage to a collection of 1950s records by Lotte Lenya, the Viennese-born singer and actress whose own centennial in 2000 was strangely neglected. *Lotte Lenya Sings Kurt Weill/The American Theater Songs* includes her robust duet with Armstrong on "Mack the Knife," an uncommon but hardly unknown performance. The curio is a funny eight-and-a-half minute rehearsal tape that allows us to be flies on the wall as Armstrong teaches her to syncopate.

The excerpt begins with a complete run-through of the song, which is persuasive until the very end, when Lenya is supposed to sing, "Now that Mackie's [quarter note rest for rhythmic accent] back in town." She ignores the rest and drags out the last three words for a mile and a half. Armstrong good-naturedly explains to her the jazzy cadence, growling a "boom" to indicate the rest. She laughs and tells him, "That's easy for you." Taking charge, Armstrong informs the producer that there is no need to re-record more than a closing insert, and encourages Lenya ("That's it," "There you go") until she gets it almost right. The irony is delicious: Armstrong cooly coaching Lenya, a near-legendary figure in her own right, on a song her late husband had conceived expressly for her—and she displaying not one iota of prima donna resentment as he spots her take after take. Also amusing is the precise and unchanging pitch with which he repeatedly cues the "boom." The episode reminds us how alien jazz rhythms could be as recently as midcentury. Today, few 10-year-olds would have any difficulty mastering that rest. Thanks largely to Armstrong, we live in a syncopated world.

Armstrong was the most influential, popular, and celebrated jazz musician who ever lived. No one disputes that. But he was also the most bitterly criticized. The Armstrong schism began as early as 1929, before his fame reached anything resembling national dimensions, and it was triggered by his willingness to record and perform Tin Pan Alley songs with—this is what really bugged many of his early antagonists—large bands, which embodied the heresy of the imminent swing era. The argument made no sense, yet stuck around for many years, having been made gospel by Rudi Blesh in his 1946 jazz history *Shining Trumpets*. "Louis Armstrong could conceivably return to jazz tomorrow," he assured readers. "He did it once before, from 1925 to 1928, when he left [Fletcher] Henderson and returned to Chicago." But then, after Earl Hines and Don Redman joined his band, the "quality deteriorate[d] into a sort of sweetness foreign to Louis' nature, one belonging to sweet-swing." For example, "West End Blues," though a "record of great beauty," "narrowly misses banality" because of Hines, and signals Armstrong's descent into "a dark romanticism foreign to jazz."

Reading Blesh, you get the feeling he was determined to protect jazz from the unwashed as well as from swing bands, and that he might have been happy on an island populated by professorial Dixieland addicts and noble savages to satisfy their jones. Perhaps I am unfair. Yet he also wrote that Duke Ellington composed a "*tea dansant* music trapped out with his borrowed effects from jazz, the Impressionists, and the French Romantics." To those who lamented that Ellington had forsaken jazz, Blesh advised, "The Duke has never played it." He could see little difference between "Daybreak Express" and the "theatrical corn" of Ted Lewis. So the hell with unfair.

Armstrong and Ellington were the first major jazz figures subjected to judges who knew better than they what they were supposed to be doing (an arrogance that might appear quaintly eccentric today had it not been embraced so vigorously by the Lincoln Center crowd in the 1990s). Ellington was lambasted for reaching too high, Armstrong for stooping too low. Those who were touched by the latter's genius were offended by his clowning, risqué humor, and acceptance of all the habiliments of pop—never mind that he tailored them to his own tastes. In *Early Jazz* (1969), Gunther Schuller, one of the most perceptive and influential critics of early Armstrong, wrote that "West End Blues" proved "jazz had the potential capacity to compete with the highest order of previously known musical expression." In *The Swing Era* (1989), however, he reported, "our memories are beclouded by recordings of a sixty-three-year-old Louis singing, 'Hello, Dolly!' against a cheap brassy Dixieland sextet."

To which one might shrug: Not my memories, pal. But musical memories are now governed by technology, specifically the accessibility of records, which leads to a kind of critical historicism. Consider the Armstrong myth that dates an overall decline to his wholesale acceptance by the public and his inability to resist commercial blandishments. In the past, even critics sympathetic to late Armstrong were likely to conclude that only when he stepped into the mainstream, in the mid-1930s, did he begin to rely on vocals, beyond his patented scat volleys, and pop songs. The LP generation accepted that because when it came along, the Hot Fives and Sevens were represented on records solely by 36 prime tracks collected on the first three discs of Columbia's four-album series, *The Louis Armstrong Story*, issued in 1951 on LPs and 45s, and kept in catalog for more than 20 years. The only way you could hear the complete works was on European collections.

The story that emerged and hardened into received wisdom is known to every jazz lover and goes like this. Between 1925 and 1928, Armstrong made several dozen records by small studio units known as the Hot Five, Hot Seven, and Savoy Ballroom Five. They are the foundation for jazz's ascension as an art—indeed, for much of what we value highest in jazz and popular music. At those sessions, Armstrong supplanted the marchlike two-beat of the New

Orleans style with a steady and occasionally throbbing four/four; established the imperative of blues tonality; replaced the polyphonic or group approach to improvisation with solo inventions of, in his case anyway, uncanny radiance; and freed the vernacular voice that remains at the center stage of American song. All this is true. The greatness of those records exceeds their influence. We do not pay passive homage to Armstrong's genius, but, rather, lose ourselves in its emotional grandeur, stately tone, earthy comedy, and discriminating rigor.

In 1929, he brought all these strengths to bear on a popular song by Jimmy McHugh and Dorothy Fields, "I Can't Give You Anything But Love." This number was no more compromised by Tin Pan Alley expediency than the songs he had already recorded by such successful songwriters as Spencer Williams ("Basin Street Blues") and Fats Waller ("Squeeze Me"). But their songs were the product of the close-knit world of young African American musicians making headway in jazz and on Broadway. "I Can't Give You Anything But Love" was blues-free white pop. It was also superior to much of the material Armstrong had recorded to that time, and his superb interpretation, in effect, provided a jazz pedigree for a song that would live on as a standard. Still, it generated a simmering pique among the most hidebound of his admirers, who may have astutely surmised that he would no longer belong exclusively to them.

In truth, he never did. Here is where received wisdom was skewed by the vagaries of Columbia Records. Blesh complains that he had abandoned jazz *before* 1925, working with Henderson and an assortment of vaudevillians, including a very mixed bag of blues divas, but ignores the pop records he made between 1925 and 1928, as though they never existed. Until the late 1980s, you could not easily find a complete edition of the Hot Fives and Sevens. But Columbia finally issued a poorly mastered set (a better edition, simultaneously released in England on JSP, can still be ordered online), followed last year by the improved but troublesome *The Complete Hot Five and Hot Seven Recordings*. Today, listeners have no choice but to take them all in—the gold, silver, and lead. In this context, we are no longer blinded by an exhibition of mostly instrumental master-pieces, from "Struttin' with Some Barbecue" and "Potato Head Blues" to "Tight Like This" and "Muggles." Instead, we are treated to a more complicated panorama in which those works alternate with lighter yet almost always earthier pieces intended to entertain.

If you include the spoken raps on "Gut Bucket Blues" and "King of the Zulus," 14 of the first 24 Hot Fives have vocals. On "He Likes It Slow," the Hot Five appears in support of vaudevillians Butterbeans and Susie, and on "Sunset Cafe Stomp" and "Big Butter and Egg Man," Armstrong's guest vocalist is May Alix, a nightclub performer known for her splits (a routine later incorporated into Armstrong's shows when he hired singer-dancer Velma Middleton) and for being so light-skinned that Ellington balked at taking her on tour. Four numbers, including those with Alix, were created by Percy Venable, who staged floor shows at the Sunset Café. One of them, "Irish Black Bottom," begins as "When Irish Eyes Are Smiling," interpolates "Black Bottom" (also a white tune, incidentally) and finds Armstrong singing, "I was born in Ireland—ha ha!—so imagine how I feel." As it is intended to make you laugh, it will never appear on a serious best-of Louis anthology, nor should it. Neither does it becloud one's memories of "Potato Head Blues."

In short, at no time in Armstrong's career—which began with him singing for pennies on New Orleans street corners and progressed to social functions like picnics and funerals that were not covered by the press (alas)—did he devote himself exclusively to a fancied shrine of jazz; at no time was he disinclined to entertain; at no time did he forswear popular material. All the songs he sang were pop or would-be pop. No one wrote tunes, least of all Armstrong, in hope of achieving a cult status. The songs he recorded are jazz classics because he did them. In jazz, the singer makes the song, never the reverse. The most famous of his early vocals is "Heebie Jeebies," which popularized scat; "West End Blues" and "Basin Street Blues," for his soft wordless crooning; and "Hotter Than That," for his virtuoso scat romp. Less talked about is the 1928 "St. James Infirmary," another essential performance, because here for the first time we hear what Armstrong could do with a conventional song, perfectly gauging the high notes and propelling the chorus with rhythmic emotion—three months before the more inventive breakthrough on "I Can't Give You Anything But Love."

Luis Russell played piano on the McHugh-Fields song, and it was Russell's band that Armstrong would front—after he returned from his European sojourn—between 1935 and 1943. Those were the Decca years, which, for me, mark his greatest period as a singer. His voice had a smooth, lustrous, supple quality, richer than in the preceding decade and not as gravelly as in the one to follow, though by the early 60s, it attained another crest—deeper and richer and more authoritative than ever. Perhaps never before or after did his trumpet produce so many gleaming, acrobatic flourishes as in this period—most notably the dazzling and superior remake of "Struttin' With Some Barbecue." The Deccas are still not as widely known as they should be, because they have yet to be properly issued, though with Verve now in possession of the catalog there is hope.

Meanwhile, a company in Andorra, where I suspect copyright laws are more flexible than here, has done the job splendidly on six CDs in two volumes, *The Complete Decca Studio Master Takes 1935–1939* and *The Complete Decca Studio Master Takes 1940–1949* (they are available through the mailorder company Collectors' Choice). With trumpet and voice each at a distinctive peak, Armstrong's creative consistency is stunning. Nobody was singing or playing anything to match his "Love Walked In," "Jubilee," "Thanks a Million," "Swing That Music," "Lyin' to Myself," "My Darling Nellie Gray," "Pennies From Heaven," "Among My Souvenirs," "The Skeleton in the Closet," "Shoe Shine Boy," and dozens more, not least the modern spirituals he put on the map: "When the Saints Go Marching In" and "Shadrach." Some 60 years after they were made, these records sound as fresh and surprising as anything in American music and seem to contain seeds for everything that followed, even hip hop. Consider his rhythmic recitation at an anomalous March 14, 1940, session, which produced "Hep Cats Ball" and the marvelous "You Got Me Voodoo'd." The latter begins with jungly thumping—by Sid Catlett, no less—and a spooky vamp, before Armstrong declaims:

Just like some magic potion,
You fill me with emotion.
You control my very soul.
You've Got Me Voodoo'd.
You knew the goddess Venus
Would start this love between us.
You inspired me with desire.
You've Got Me Voodoo'd.
You knew you had the power
And even picked the hour,
When the full moon was up above.
I was hypnotized when I looked into your eyes:
My heart was filled with love.
Just like the siren Circe,
You've got me at your mercy.
Always yours to have and hold,
Mama, you've Got Me Voodoo'd.

The number is credited to Armstrong, Russell, and Cornelius C. Lawrence, an obscure playwright, actor, and lyricist who also wrote songs with the intriguing titles, "Curfew Time in Harlem" and "Ink Spink Spidely Spoo." Each line of the lyric is the equivalent of two measures, which makes for an AABA song, only without a melody. Louis's trumpet chorus, unlike the proper Prince Robinson clarinet solo that precedes it, uses the rapped rhythm as a starting point before juicing it with melody and taking off on the bridge—a model for what can be done with an intrinsically unmelodic form.

Armstrong always trusted the sound of his own voice, even when no one else did, and often used it with comic authority—on several of his earliest records, the tunes even allow him to boast of his sexual prowess. On the first session as a leader, in November 1925, he used "Gut Bucket Blues" to introduce the fellas (a much imitated gambit, e.g., Jimmie Lunceford's "Rhythm Is Our Business," Andy Kirk's "Git," Slim Gaillard's "Slim's Jam"), letting us know that he was in charge and knew exactly what he was about. Of banjoist Johnny St. Cyr, he chortles, "Everybody in New Orleans can really do that thing." But, in fact, no one in those days could do that thing like Armstrong, and it is likely that had he not come along, jazz would never have become a full-fledged art of universal appeal. Instead, it might have remained a lively regional folk music after the Dixieland fad faded. Even Ellington might have gone a different route, composing theater and dance band music, had Armstrong not awakened his respect for the blues. The confidence we hear in Louis's barking in "Gut Bucket Blues" is not much different from the helpful "boom" he offered Lotte Lenya 30 years later. It wasn't Louis Armstrong who changed. It was us, the people.

KODWO ESHUN

N*E*R*D and the Rise of New Geek Chic

"Girl I feel just like a bird/Though I am just a nerd/I could
fly around this world/With power from this word"
*—"Baby Doll," N*E*R*D*

Archetypes never die. So it is that certain archetypes still stalk the pop cultural landscape like colossal youth: the playa, the thug, the baller, the scrub. A close listen to the production trio/digital rock group N*E*R*D's dazzling debut album *In Search Of . . .* will tune you into a newly resurgent archetype: the black nerd, the hyper-smart and proud of it African-American geek. The smart ass who defies the laws of black cool/ macho by flaunting their love of white music. And sci fi. And comics. *In Search Of . . .* is a manifesto for a new Black Geek Chic. Geek Chic is there in the novels of Paul Beatty and Colson Whitehead. It's there in Elijah Price, Samuel L Jackson's comic art gallerist-supervillain in M Night Shyamalan's film *Unbreakable*. It's OutKast posing in Sherlock Holmes coats and pipes, leaning against library shelves. In the snarky smile Big Boi gives at the end of the Ms Jackson video. It's Kelis talking about science fiction. Its DJ Spooky remixing Steve Reich's City Life one minute, collaborating with architect Bernard Tschumi the next. It's there in the cartoons of Aaron McGruder. In the productions of Dose One/CloudDead.

High school is where the distinctions between clever/unclever, uncool/cool, wuss/macho begin to bite hard. It's the time when teenagers begin policing each other through the intricate hierarchies of peer pressure. The moment when taste becomes a battleground. Its here, in the classroom, that African-Caribbean youth, male especially, fall prey to the assumption that being clever/verbal/scholarly = acting white. Which means internalizing the self-defeating corollary that being stupid/ monosyllabic/illiterate = acting black.

Hip hop, however, reconciles this opposition by putting verbal dexterity and metaphorical cleverness at the service of the insult. Hip hop makes cleverness macho. Part artform, part business and part entertainment, hip hop therefore attracts the clever bullies and the sardonic geeks. Both are deadly enemies yet both are attracted to the power moves it allows. Flash back to the De la Soul video for 1989's single "Me Myself and I." De la Soul, you remember, are being bullied by Kangol-wearing, arm-folding hip hop bigmouths who force their stupid protocols on them. De la Soul's appeal didn't lie in their unrepentant smartness. Nor in their brilliantly hermetic slanguage.

Rather, it stemmed from the trio discovering and explaining how to use hip hop against the bullies who acted like they owned it. "Me Myself and I" and its accompanying video revealed the trio as NERDS who had survived the Playground Wars and Classroom Skirmishes and lived to tell the tale. At a time when white commentators obsessed over hip hop's evergrowing white audience, "Me Myself and I" suggested a much more important preoccupation: hip hop had become a weapon black high school kids wielded to discipline and punish each other.

Sometimes it feels as if the bullies have been winning in hip hop ever since. As Dre 3000 of OutKast said to *Spin* in March: "I don't think black people like change too tough. I think black people like comfort, more than anything. You get them people who be like, 'You're trying to do this for the white people,' or, 'The nigga must be gay' or some shit-all that. Black people aren't into change, period." Post De La, the first sign of the Nerd Chic FightBack came in *The White Boy Shuffle*, ex-poet Paul Beatty's 1996 debut novel. Beatty was especially sharp at capturing the awkwardness of Gunnar Kaufmann, his clever hero, perpetually living at 90 degrees to the rest of the world. "My inability to walk the walk or talk the talk led to a series of almost daily drubbings. In a world where body and spoken language were currency, I was broke as hell. Corporeally mute, I couldn't saunter or bojangle my limbs with rubbery nonchalance."

The White Boy Shuffle is a bildungsroman set in a series of education compounds: Reynier Park, Manischewitz Junior High, Phyllis Wheatley High, El Campesino Real High and Boston University. Kaufmann is a Hip-Nerd, something new under the sun, a teenager who learns how to balance his ultra-sardonic cleverness and poetic attack with basketball skills. He needs all these attributes to negotiate the treacherous terrain of social expectations ready to steer him down a wretched future: "During spring registration I stood in line behind sloe-eyed bangers and listened to kind liberal guidance counselors derail their dreams. 'Buster, I know you want to take Graphic Design, but I'm placing you in Metal Shop. Mr. Buck Smith will know how to handle you, and it'll be a good prerequisite for license plate pressing. You've got to plan for the future, Buster, ol' boy. Can't be too shortsighted, Mr. Brown. Remember, the longest jail sentence starts with one day.'"

Inspired by De la Soul, many hip hop producers such as DC Basehead, Del tha Funkee Homosapien, KMD, Saul Williams, the stable of Anticon producers and Mike Ladd all returned to the psychogeography of NERDishness throughout the 1990s. But N*E*R*D, who called their high school group Surrounded by Idiots (a classic example of sarcastic geek humor) triumphed where these artists only partially succeeded. Partly that's because the N*E*R*D trio of Pharell Williams, the Asian-American Chad Hugo and Shay understand the vicarious thrill of identifying with bullies. They are not superior to bullies. They know that today's geek would become tomorrow's bully, in a flash, if they could. The external battles of the corridors have their parallel but opposite dimension in the psyche.

While the great Mike Ladd and CloudDead are defiant anti-jiggy outsiders, N*E*R*D are insiders as well as outsiders, in love with corporate rap as much as they are ambivalent about it. Adept at playing both ends against the middle, N*E*R*D aren't indie at all. They understand the seduction of the street. *In Search Of . . .* is Stage

2 in the N*E*R*D Plan. Stage 1 was to seduce the bullies of corporate hip hop with their sound. Get them hooked. Stage 2 is now; drawing them into their world. As The Neptunes, producers Williams and Hugo have amped hip hop to delirious levels of sonic thuggishness, with productions such as Noreaga's *Superthug,* (1998) Kelis' *Caught Out There* (1999) and Mystikal's *Shake That Ass* (2000) These singles stomp with a gleeful brutalism that puts the head back into the club banger. They have an intense, headbanging energy that is, nonetheless, worlds away from rap-metal.

On the production of Jay Z's "I Just Wanna Love You (Give to Me)," Williams introduced a beguiling falsetto that insinuated its way through the superior inflections of Jay Z's self-preening-I'm-a-CEO-and you're not-flow. In interviews, Williams explained that his vocal style was modelled on "Sympathy for the Devil"–era Mick Jagger. *In Search Of . . .* expands this fascination with late 60s rock into early 70s post psychedelia. Williams recalled how he "wanted to sing like the guy from (early 70s West Coast country-rock group) America when I was younger and I tried to imitate it on this record." Bone Thugs and Harmony, OutKast and Mos Def have all integrated hip hop flow with harmonies but *In Search Of . . .* goes further, infusing digitally filtered, white country-rock inspired harmonies that MOJO magazine would call Americana, with squidgy AOR keyboards similar to Discovery-era Daft Punk, funk guitar-stabs and battering-ram bass.

These days, hip hop is full of the sonic surprise of white music samples: MOP sampling Foreigner, Jay Z the Annie theme tune, Puffy swallowing Led Zep's Kashmir whole. Partly this harks back to the rock-friendly ethos of hip hop's old school deejays, when Grand Wizard Theodore would spin Rush and Bambaataa would play The Monkees and The Stones. N*E*R*D, however, hardly sample at all; their libidinal electronic funk integrates white rock feel until you can't tell where black music ends and white music begins. Above all, their music plays tricks on you; the signature mood-altering chord changes make each song sound like 3 songs in one. Each track laughs at you with its fake-endings that ambush your attention.

In Search Of... is a lovers' discourse racked by the frankly admitted male need for togetherness and tenderness. Hip hop's emotional armor has gone, replaced by regret (I think I've loved you since high school', Williams sings on "Am I High") forlorn despair ("Stay Together") and the urge for family ("Provider"). Urgent gasps, fervent whimpers and whispered counterpoints form a hormonal percussion and self-doubting commentary. Onomatopeic synths ooh like a girl's bottom being pinched. Self-mocking, puerile interludes set in Princess Ann High School link the album into a songsuite. In the intro to "Baby Doll," Shay orders a woman over the phone. The female operator asks: "What do you look like?" "I'd rather not say." "Sir what d' you look like?" "I'm (pause) 3 feet high. With my afro (pause) I'm 6 feet. Fruit of the looms pulled all the way up to my chest." When Heather, his womandroid arrives, he swoons, "She's purrfect" like the geek he is, and the sound effect evokes 60s sitcoms like *Bewitched*, where witches bamboozle hapless white men.

In Search Of... pulses with a sense of hormonal excitement and psychological confidence that reconciles ruggish thuggish attack with male tenderness, the synthetic syncopation of hip hop with the arrangements of Neil Youngesque country rock. Like OutKast's *Stankonia* and Basement Jaxx's *Remedy*, each song feels like a brand new genre. "Landance" is an unsettling alloy of falsetto swoops and headbanging bass stabs. "Brain" is an electronic stomp set off by a nasal chorus that half mocks and half-pleads. "Truth or Dare" switches abruptly between martial synthesizer stabs and lovelorn harmonies. "Stay Together" fuses its "Raspberry Beret" key stabs with descending harmonies. "Tape You" is an audio-drama of a home-porno session driven by gorgeous tubular synths and false endings. "Rock-Star-Poser" is a rowdy bass banger with Williams hollering at "fucking posers" while "Am I High" has wasted filter-swept vocals drifting over squidgy synths.

It turns out that Williams grew up in Virginia Beach where his family lived near a tribe of Hell's Angels who turned him onto the 70s Southern-fried boogie of Lynyrd Skynyrd. Now the tattooed and bike-riding post–b-boy takes care to be photographed wearing a series of AC/DC, Led Zep and Rush t-shirts. In flaunting the kind of white prog/metal that hip whites shy away from, N*E*R*D have become the latest in a long line of Afrofutrist producers to break the unspoken rule that black artists should only listen to black artists. Partly this rule stems from white hip media; more importantly, it harks back to high school peer pressure, when black kids ruthlessly police each other's tastes.

In this high-pressure environment, liking white rock becomes a guilty secret. Over time, white music comes to evoke the states of mind that hip hop's emotional armor cannot speak: the feelings that dare not speak their name: Sensitivity, seriousness, uncertainty. Maybe all black kids have these anxieties. But only nerds tap into them as a resource. Only nerds turn that love of white music into a secret weapon. Like Gunnar Kaufman's Shakespearean skills and Winston Foshay's love of Battleship Potemkin (From Beatty's second novel *Tuff*) N*E*R*D don't fear white culture. They absorb it and scramble the codes of cool and uncool in the process. Instead of deferring to ghettocentric codes, they follow their fascinations wherever they lead.

"Provider," a gunslinging guitar strummed ballad, exemplifies this heedless mood. Williams sings it as a mutton-chopped Southern Man, a truck-driver "dodging Johnny Law," who wants to provide for his woman. Sung by white rockers, this tale of embattled masculinity would be hokey as all get out. But when Williams scorns the prospect of becoming "another cocaine story," the balls-to-the-wall, cock-rock attitude becomes massively poignant. This mood is deepened when the light-fingered bossanova chorus lifts and yearns for a day when "this'll be over/I'll raise a family/I'll get a job and be a voter" with all the wistfulness of a mirage, acknowledging how much effort these things: family, job, voting, take to achieve.

N*E*R*D is an acronym for No One Ever Really Dies, an acronym that's part spiritual, part scientific as the Intro explains: "We are the dreamers and as long as we dream we will never die. You know why? Because no one ever really dies." Equally though, it's the revenge of the smart kid. *In Search Of* . . . is really the Geek's Return, the pendulum swinging the other way, for the first time since *3 Feet High and Rising*. Its energies stem from revisiting the Taste Wars that mark adolescents so fiercely.

As Williams explains, "I don't mind being called a nerd. We are the people who are proud of being smart, being witty and being clever when everyone else doesn't understand. That's what we do, that's the flag we're raising and waving. If you ever listen to a nerd speak about their experiences in high school, they tell an ill story. They have an ill perspective because of the shit they've been through. You ask the average person, this kind of people that would tease nerds in high school, you ask them what their life is like and they'll give this bullshit, lame boring as story you'll snore to. A nerd is someone who wants to be cool to everybody but its not his fault he's witty and smart and his social skills aren't the best."

Or to put it another way, "The Neptunes are Spiderman, if you will, and N*E*R*D is Peter Parker. Neptunes is what we do and N*E*R*D is what we are." The super-nerd instinctively reaches for Marvel comic parallels because the superhero universe dramatizes the feelings of omnipotence and impotence in one mythical body. The Neptunes are the heroes, invincible, adventurous. N*E*R*D is all too human, assailed by self doubt.

In M. Night Shyamalan's somber movie *Unbreakable*, Samuel L Jackson plays Elijah Price, a figure who believes in the life-changing capacity of comics. He is living proof of that. A victim of a rare brittle bone disorder, sleek yet sinister in black coat, gloves and glass cane, his entire world view is shaped by comics. He runs a specialist comic art gallery and preaches the dialectics of invulnerability as he wheels himself through a hazardous world. Then again, he's the Worm that Turned, a supervillain seething with resentment, laying dynamite, causing fatalities. Empath turned psychopath, Price dramatizes heroism and villainy, trapped in one fragile body.

In Search Of . . . ends on a return to high school where empaths and bullies do battle daily between and within adolescent bodies. Bobby James, sung by Pharell Williams in a sorrowful tone, swathed, swept and distanced by filters, details the tragedy of a teenage 'wuss' who succumbs to drugs to numb the attrition of bullying. Over lachrymose strings and rolling, building, kettle drums, Williams channels this teen despair: "I got pushed at school/I was a wuss/Now my life's a domino that pushers push." Like OutKast's tearful "Toilet Tisha," the harsh tale of a teen suicide, Bobby James replaces hip hop's mandatory callousness with an acute empathy. It fades out on a siren-chorus pleading for the sorrow of the world. Then returns, unexpectedly with Free Design/Stereolab–style baa-baa-baaa harmonies over reversed synths.

In a climate where ghettocentricity is rewarded and applauded, the NERD is a rare and precious bird of paradise. You'll know it when you see it.

CHARLES AARON

Don't Fight the Power

This is a story of shame and guitars, of fame and pianos, of fear and sweatbands getting busy in a fly 280Z (or these days, a PT Cruiser) but forgetting to bring protection. Of sprawling on your bedroom floor, without a car or a clue *how* to get busy, dreaming of guzzling Rémy Martin backstage with your favorite band. Of *being* that favorite band and fiending for ass and adoration so bad that you heave your self-respect out a tour-bus window. Of prom-dancing in itchy polyester with a guy named Snake whose only dream is to join a band that heaves its self-respect out a tour-bus window. Of knowing that he never will, and that you'll probably never see him again, and not caring. It's the timeless, oft-humiliating story of perhaps our most revelatory musical institution—the rock Power Ballad.

Back in the bad-hair days of the 1980s, when Power Ballads were synonymous with Led Zeppelin tribute bands who rocked like Cher on steroids (hello, Whitesnake), most people saw Power Ballads as rock at its most compromised—the moment when macho rockers surrendered all their dignity. But consider for a moment Ozzy Osbourne's epic 1991 honky-tonk ballad, "Mama, I'm Coming Home," rumored to be about his heart-wrenching marriage to wife/Ozzfest matriarch Sharon Osbourne. On the *Live and Loud* concert version, Ozzy wails like a lost, codependent ghetto child on the verge of weeping or busting up giggling. He prefaces the song's guitar solo by weakly shouting, "Show me some tits, man," at the faceless cheap seats. It's a performance so nakedly real that you can't decide whether it's brilliant or god-awful. *That* is the story of the Power Ballad. And it's a story that's still being told every day.

So raise up ya lighters, and come sail away.

1. This Is a Song of Hope

Folks get testy about Power Ballads because they touch the most desperate desires of performers and fans alike—the need to be loved for who you really are versus the need to be loved for who you want to be. The first involves vulnerability—coming clean about romance, homesickness, loss. The second involves ruthless business practice—whose ass do we have to kiss to get paid?

As the primary way that harder rock bands get on primetime radio or MTV, Power Ballads are both embraced (supposedly by girls) and derided as cheesy sellouts (supposedly by boys). Unguarded sentiments that get even football linemen called "fag," "pussy," or "bitch" are foregrounded in Power Ballads, backed by a slow burn of acoustic guitars, grand pianos, and/or strings, swelling to a symphonic group hug with drums and electric guitars (e.g., "Stairway to Heaven"). In hip-hop, where strong black masculinity exerts a powerful control it lacks in real life, death of friends and family has been the driving inspiration/justification for Power Ballads—mournful samples of horns, pianos, strings; a rapper on the verge of tears (Ghostface Killah and RZA spoofed/paid tribute to this "crying" style on the Wu-Tang Clan's *The W*); and videos set at church funerals for maximum hankie effect. Now rappers regularly reach for the Kleenex (Ja Rule's "I Cry" comes to mind). Point being, genre after genre, generation after generation, Power Ballads define artists. Just ask Staind, Eminem, Creed, Train, Coldplay, Incubus, et al.

Vince Neil, singer for '80s glam-punk self-abusers Mötley Crüe, explains: "If you look at most bands, Power Ballads are the songs that you remember. Take [Crüe's strip-club anthem] 'Girls, Girls, Girls.' It's like, yahoo!—you're raising your fist to rock. But with [the gushy Power Ballad] 'Home Sweet Home,' you go, 'Yeah, I was

17 and dating this girl named Tami, and I was holding her hand and lighting a lighter.' It brings up a whole part of your life."

And if history tells us anything, it's that a Power Ballad's lasting emotional impact comes from its absurdly improbable performer. For instance: the virgin-defiling metal marauder who transforms into a tender choir leader, orchestrating a celestial melody; the yelping, pimpish vocalist who overnight begins to croon warmly like Mario Lanza's lost *paisano;* the guitar madman, whose solos are usually the musical equivalent of vehicular manslaughter, who divines the blues with aching care; the bridge-burning roadhog who curls up crying for the comforts of home and hearth; the strung-out satanic dabbler who wants to die for all the world's sins; the deadbeat, 12-stepping dad who wants to save all the children; and worst of all, the aging sleaze who hires a ghostwriter to craft an irresistible ballad dedicated to his *Baywatch*-alumna wife, who leaves him anyway.

Somehow, this train wreck of self-deception produces a story we crave again and again. We love hearing a junkie tramp like Steven Tyler lay down his hard-earned "truth": "Half my life's in books' written pages/Live and learn from fools and from sages." Like gothic romance novels for girls *and* boys, Power Ballads create a momentary general-admission utopia where both performer and audience share their most uncool desires—a refuge where everyone understands everyone else's embarrassing secrets and, although love and freedom are only bad jokes on a bathroom wall, we can still pray for it all to wash away.

So get on your knees. Some hall of famers: Lynyrd Skynyrd, "Simple Man"; Black Sabbath, "Changes"; Aerosmith, "Dream On"; Kiss, "Beth"; Queen, "Bohemian Rhapsody"; Prince, "Purple Rain"; Night Ranger, "Sister Christian"; Poison, "Every Rose Has Its Thorn" and "Something to Believe In"; Guns N' Roses, "November Rain" and "Don't Cry"; Red Hot Chili Peppers, "Under the Bridge"; Ice Cube, "Dead Homiez"; 2Pac, "Dear Mama"; Green Day, "Good Riddance (Time of Your Life)"; Puff Daddy & the Family, "I'll Be Missing You."

Heart's Ann Wilson regrets her band's descent into the '80s soft-ballad abyss ("Glacierlike lost worlds of big synthesizer, everything covered in gel," she says, reflecting on songs like "What About Love?"). But she still understands the appeal of a killer Power Ballad. "Music is a place in the human soul, you know? And the ballad gets right in there . . . I mean, even young boys who are into Kid Rock or something still have their quiet, pensive moments—or so we would hope." If so, they can cue up the Kid's rhinestone-cowboy lament, "Only God Knows Why."

Often, the more unreal the transformation from nihilistic to romantic, the more lighter-inducing the performance. Hair-metal bands of the 1980s—the Crüe, Def Leppard, Poison, Warrant, Faster Pussycat, Cinderella—promoted images of debauched excess and generally lived up to the self-destructive hype. They were also more identified with Power Ballads than any other generation of rockers. "It was the surprise element," says Rhino Records' Emily Cagan, who came of age in Los Angeles' Sunset Strip rock scene and has since produced three compilations of '80s Power Ballads (all respectable sellers). "For girls, these guys rock and talk dirty, but they also have a soft, gooey side. Even though they're going crazy with groupies and drugs, in the songs they're saying, 'Oh, I just wanna settle down and be with that one special person.' And the girl listening is thinking, 'I wish my boyfriend would sing that to me,' with the special lighting and the fan blowing his hair . . . and the guy's wishing *he* could be the singer."

Faerie godfathers Led Zeppelin were the unholiest of terrors, of course, and they channeled the quintessential Power Ballad, "Stairway to Heaven" (which also trademarked the classic Power Ballad song-structure-teasing intro/soaring solo/pounding outro—as well as the iconic double-neck guitar). "Stairway" was so mystically cryptic that teen boys could see it as a call to the Antichrist and 30s-ish housewives could interpret it as a statement of liberation.

This whole goodness/badness duality of rockers and rappers is what pulls us in the deepest. When so-and-so rock jerk trots out his poignant Power Ballad, he's still the same charismatic cartoon who was just ranting about drugs, guns, and oral sex. But he also might be something more.

2. À Chaque Rose, Son Epine

I never thought seriously about Power Ballads until Poison's "Every Rose Has Its Thorn"—it was 1988, she was Belgian, I was lonely, and she could sing all the words in French. The fact that I found this exotically romantic probably says more about me than I want to know. And unfortunately, after one botched one-night stand, it was clear that when she wasn't singing a Power Ballad, her accent was kind of annoying. *C'est la vie.*

Later, I discovered that swooning over corny French crooning had been going on for ages. In the eleventh, twelfth, and thirteenth centuries in southern France and northern Italy, sweet-talkin' hustlers called troubadours kicked tales of courtly love—arguably the original Power Ballads. Later, in the U.S., those rhymes got mixed up with Irish folk songs, African slave chants and blues parables, cowboy songs, dime-novel Wild West myths, Euro classical music, Broadway show tunes, gospel preachers, and buckets of hair-care products. You can see obvious roots of the modern Power Ballad in doo-wop and Elvis' "Love Me Tender," soul testifying from Motown/Stax/Hi Records, Phil Spector's eerie pop echo-chambers, and Bob Dylan's epic folk pastiche.

But Power Ballads first mutated into their current form in the early '70s, when David Bowie, heavy metal, and touchy-feely singer/songwriters all spoke theatrically to bugged-out kids of the post-'60s comedown. Rock stars wanted to say terribly profound things to millions of people, while adopting increasingly jiggy lifestyles. Like Courtney Love today, they were almost proudly full of shit. Which, in its way, was exciting. Rock finally became an institution that people could see for all its awesomely pathetic possibility. Enter the Power Ballad.

In the mid-'70s, when FM stations first tightly formatted their playlists, any band's song that was harder than, say, the Rolling Stones got thrown into late-night stoner rotation. As a result, rock during daylight hours sounded about as threatening as a street fight with Captain & Tennille. As the early punks spit on its grave and stomped off, many hard rock bands figured out how to play and, eventually, hustle the game. As the bicentennial beer bust sloshed on, 1976 became the Year the Power Ballad Broke, and the country's new national anthems were brewing. "Stairway to Heaven," "Free Bird," and "Dream On," all older songs, got a new life. "Dream On" became Aerosmith's first Top 10 hit; studio and live versions of "Free Bird" made the Top 40; and "Stairway," never released as a single, would become possibly the most requested rock radio song of all time. Kiss' "Beth," warbled by drummer Peter Criss, made the pseudo-satanic vaudevillians crossover teenybop icons (their only other Top 10 hit, 1990's "Forever," was also a Power Ballad, co-written by Michael Bolton and featuring Kiss sans makeup). Queen blew up with two Top 15 Power Ballad smashes in '76—"Bohemian Rhapsody" and "Somebody to Love." Breakup screecher "Love Hurts" (an Everly Brothers chestnut) was a Top 10 hit for Scottish bruisers Nazareth. Elton John, who cranked out rockish piano ballads throughout the '70s, now seemed like a Power Ballad prophet, and Elton drummer Nigel Olsson's booming tom fills defined Power Ballad percussion for decades.

But soon a strange situation existed in which many hard rock and metal bands were known mainly for their slow jams. "What rock bands have had to do ever since the '70s to really max out their potential is cross over to Top 40 radio," says Fred Jacobs, the legendary radio programming consultant. "And you're not going to cross over with [Kiss'] 'Detroit Rock City,' but if you put out 'Beth,' you've got a chance." In 1985, responding to the hard rock void on radio, Jacobs developed the 'classic rock' format, which enshrined "Stairway to Heaven," "Free Bird," and "Dream On" as the Power Ballad holy trinity, songs perfectly combining soul-kiss melody, over-the-rainbow lyrics, and head-rush guitar.

During the '80s radio devolution, any band with a rough rep was seen as a pariah, and others became even more desperate to please. As a result, we were assaulted with Journey's cornball opus "Open Arms" and a series of heinous Foreigner wedding songs. Sure, there were stray Power Ballad pleasures—"Purple Rain"; "Sister Christian"; Joan Jett & the Blackhearts' cover of "Crimson and Clover";

the Replacements' "Unsatisfied"; REO Speedwagon's "Keep on Loving You" (yeah, you heard me). But overall, nada.

Then, Aqua Net became young America's favorite drug. Somehow, in 1985, Mötley Crüe's "Home Sweet Home" video—with its signature slow-mo concert footage, so we knew these guys still rocked!—became the first hair-metal Power Ballad aired on MTV. It was so heavily requested that MTV was moved to institute the "Crüe Rule," stating no video could be most-requested for more than three months. In the flick of a fake eyelash, trashy rock became a pop craze. Cynical industry folks signed up every bozo with a guitar and bandana, usually managing to churn out a serviceable Power Ballad. From, say, 1987, with Bon Jovi's fist-pumping "Wanted Dead or Alive," to Extreme's genial "More Than Words" in 1991, the strategy got more and more refined. The songs were often amazing productions (I still have a soft spot for Winger's "Miles Away"), as were many of the videos (grave dude-bonding backstage, on tour buses, and on charter planes), but people started to smell a swindle.

"We were working with this band at MCA called Pretty Boy Floyd," says an industry insider who asked to remain anonymous. "And they were supposed to be the next big something. This was 1990, and we spent at least $100,000 on a video for these guys. They're all dressed in white, everything was white, and they got the big hair going, and it was just one of those moments where you realized, 'Wow, this really sucks. When is this going to be over?'" Then, suddenly, grunge came along, and it was.

3. I'm a Cowboy—on a Steel Horse I Ride

It was a Mississippi night in late 1999, Woodstock fires were still smoldering, and the Family Values Tour was killing us softly with its song. A guy with a roughly shaved head, pierced eyebrow, and acoustic guitar was sitting on the steps of the huge stage. Slowly strumming a head-nod tune, he had a gruff, dazed voice that seemed to float above something unbearably painful. "'Cause inside you're ugly/Ugly like me," he sang, with an almost grunge-like yearn. The song ("Outside") hung in the air until the guy (Staind's Aaron Lewis) was accompanied onstage by none other than Mr. Nookie Puss himself, Limp Bizkit's Fred Durst. Barely joining the chorus, Durst mostly provided comic relief, at one point shouting, "I'm feelin' those lighters!"

But "Outside" cut through Durst's schtick. "I think of it as the 'In the Air Tonight' of alternative rock," says Jacobs. "It sneaked up on people like 'In the Air' did with Phil Collins in the early '80s. People were like, '*He* did *that?*' Good Power Ballads aren't on motion picture soundtracks—you know, the cloying, calculated stuff. The memorable ones come out of nowhere."

Like, say, two of 2001's most memorable singles—Staind's "It's Been Awhile" and Eminem's "Stan." While "Outside" was a ragged dirge that benefited from the Family Values context, "It's Been Awhile" is a nuanced yet full-blown Power Ballad (the Durst-directed video puts the band on wooden stools amid a multitude of candles). After the primal rap-metal/nü-metal onslaught—capped by Slipknot's masked cacophony—"It's Been Awhile" seems like a visitation from Kurt Cobain's lumpy younger brother, quietly asking his peers to ease up on the carnage and listen for a sec.

"Stan" is even more astonishing. The story of an obsessed Slim Shady fan rapped over a sample of Dido's fluttery "Thank You," it masterfully builds and builds and builds to its sad denouement like Jimmy Page himself was on the case. Eminem, the son even a mom could sue, not only feels for the fan but also, shockingly, admits to some responsibility. In the funhouse of Power Ballads, it doesn't get any better than this—a cartoonishly evil protagonist giving his harshest critics teary pause. And when the gay-baiting star performed on the Grammy Awards in February, accompanied by openly gay Elton John (echoing another classic Power Ballad moment when Elton and Axl Rose dueted on "Bohemian Rhapsody" at a London AIDS benefit in Freddie Mercury's honor), the dizziness reached startling heights. As unnerving hip-hop Power Ballads go, I prefer Geto Boys' "Mind Playing Tricks on Me." But for a moment, Eminem (like Aaron Lewis) seemed to recoil from the louder, nastier scene that raised him.

4. Does Anybody Remember Laughter?

On his cockwalk to fame, Warrant's blindingly blond Jani Lane rocked white fringe with glee, titled his band's first album *Dirty Rotten Filthy Stinking Rich*, and joked about gobbling groupie gal pal Bobbi Brown like cherry pie. But for this summer's Glam Slam Metal Jam 2001 at Jones Beach Theater on Long Island, the singer was no carefree libertine.

"I won't bore you with too much of this shit," he moaned, hoisting his acoustic guitar. Dressed in black, hair still bleached but hacked short, bandmates in Ramones and Misfits T-shirts, Lane intro'd Warrant's hugest hit, 1990 prom theme du jour "Heaven." As the sun set over the scrubby beach, couples reflected on virginities lost and mouthed along to the lyrics: "How I love the way you move/And the sparkle in your eyes/There's a color deep inside them/Like a blue suburban sky."

But midway through the song, as the guitar solo subsided, Lane awkwardly stopped short to thank us *"so very fucking much* for singing along, man." His in-your-face humility seemed just a little ... too ... *intense*. Afterward, he spit defiantly: "I'm proud of that song; I don't care what anybody says!"

Why, you ask, is this joker so defensive about the one song that got him into America's pants? Well, even though the '90s alternative rock that marginalized folks like Warrant produced its own share of baldly sentimental Power Ballads (Soundgarden, "Black Hole Sun"; Smashing Pumpkins, "Disarm"; Live, "Lightning Crashes"; Bush, "Glycerine"), many alt-rockers dissed hair-metal's supposedly tacky tactics. Lane, unlike self-assured Glam Slam headliners Poison, is still tormented by some manly shame over his Power Ballad fame. But as rock writer Katherine Turman, a vet of the glam-metal years, points out: "Skynyrd never apologized for 'Free Bird.'"

Savvier '80s metal icons like Poison's Bret Michaels and Skid Row's Sebastian Bach celebrate their songs all day long. To paraphrase a famed Spinal Tap Power Ballad (in D minor, the "saddest of all keys"), if you don't like it, you can lick their love pump.

"People emotionally connect to ballads. I've had stuff go on in my life, as everybody else has, and to express that through a ballad is something I'll do forever," says Bach. "And I'm only 33, so get used to it! I'll be in Vegas when I'm 70 singing [1990's] 'I Remember You,' and that's a high motherfuckin' song, so I better be in shape. I gotta peel out those screams at the end, and it's no easy task. But those are the skills that pay the bills, brother!" Michaels argues that Power Ballads exist beyond trends: "There's no time frame on having a broken heart, or on your best friend dying. Those songs were very personal to us and we did them the way we felt touched in our soul."

Classic Power Ballads aren't easy to write (try suffering through Soul Asylum's "Endless Farewell"), and ones that so massively connect shouldn't be dismissed as simple kitsch. Says Deena Weinstein, author of *Heavy Metal: The Music and Its Culture:* "Think about karaoke. It's mostly these romantic ballads, and it's strongest in Japanese and Korean culture, right? And in those cultures, outwardly dramatic emotional displays are frowned upon, especially for men. And at these metal or hard rock shows, when you hear the crescendo of the ballad, boys are up there singing their little hearts out like romantic idiots. Maybe it's just something we desperately need in this culture, too."

Life is a sketchy gray area—we all screw up, we all wanna stop screwing up. It's not a thorny contradiction, it's a straight fact. That's why Power Ballads—which are so full of conflicted motives and emotions—make so much sense. They're about shattering our illusions of perfection and immortality. When these songs ambush you in the backseat of your parents' car, or after your true love calls you an asshole on a busy sidewalk, or when you're eating chicken wings alone at Chili's, a sense of relief can engulf you. Even if it just means that, for a second, you see how powerless we are to control anything completely.

Most of us crave spiritual kinship, even when we're watching some teenager pass out at Lakewood Civic Auditorium. We crave some experience that allows us to forget the petty, material, self-obsessed grind. What else explains the lighters (except that rock fans smoke a ton of pot)? When we're holding up our Bics in rock amphitheaters or arenas, it's for the same reason we hold up candles in church—we're honoring, or conjuring, a spiritual presence (even if it's the spirit of St. Bonham or St. Van Zant or St. Shakur). Power Ballads are our modern hymns—they bring us down off our pedestal, then try to take us higher. No apologies necessary.

Haiku for Eminem

The Slim LP ruled
It came right out of the blue
You were a cipher

Happy music and
self-loathing and all those words
made for good music

The way you sound black
when you are conversating
but white when you rap?

That is the one thing
people have not acknowledged
this jewel in your crown

It's original
and it obviously has
not hurt your sales, no

You don't get credit
for your answer vocals thing,
the second voice trick

Which Slick Rick did first
but you do such a good job
I cannot complain

Now it's all fear, hate
and allegedly shocking
rhymes full of fake blood

You should have won for
the great Slim Shady LP
not peevish Marshall

But like Russell Crowe
you won for Gladiator
not The Insider

Marshall heard just once
is kind of scary and fun
like a rubber mask

But things like sex and
drugs and rock and roll and joy
are fun more than once

Me myself and I
can't imagine playing it
more than once or twice

RZA wrote a song
about his wife—it was raw
and people complained

You did bad Brando
on that embarrassing song
"Kim," and people clapped

There is no excuse
for your treatment of your wife
aesthetic or no

Why is your version
of "real life" so Hollywood?
Nic Cage, please stand up

Who are these people
who allegedly hate you?
Critics wet their pants

And all the young dudes
buy and memorize your work
the day it comes out

In the New York Times—
the Eminem newsletter
perhaps I should say

They talk about you
daily and on the weekend
maybe once or twice

If you are so tough
why go after Everlast?
He's not so badass

If you are so tough
why don't you snap on black folks?
(Leave Bob Herbert out)

And why 'N Sync, huh?
You think they are equals?
Maybe that's it, yes

Insane Clown Posse?
For this you risk a record?
Please, Marshall, sit down.

JOHN LELAND

It's Only Rhyming Quatrains, But I Like It

In the last days of the Beatles, as things were starting to come apart, the band formed a record label called Zapple. The idea—or lark, really—was to record experimental music and spoken word, starting with the poets who had become the band's friends. The orbits of rock and poetry were pushing at each other: musicians like Bob Dylan or Joni Mitchell were starting to claim the mantle of poets, and the Beats were hanging with rock stars, enjoying a small piece of the reflected adulation. Why not merge the two in one grand goof? It got off to a promising start. Allen Ginsberg, Lawrence Ferlinghetti, Richard Brautigan and Charles Olson put themselves on tape, and Michael McClure, the West Coast poet, volunteered to play his autoharp—a gift from Bob Dylan—behind the verses of a Hell's Angel named Free-wheelin' Frank. But Zapple folded after just two albums, and within a year, the Beatles disbanded.

Paul McCartney, who had been the push behind Zapple, finally invoked his own poetic license earlier this year with the publication of *Blackbird Singing: Poems and Lyrics 1965–1989*. Always considered less writerly than John Lennon, McCartney joins a procession of pop stars who have loosed their song lyrics on the poetry sections of bookstores in recent years. Bob Dylan, Joni Mitchell, Leonard Cohen, Lou Reed, Patti Smith, Suzanne Vega and Robert Hunter of the Grateful Dead have all published big collections of their song

141

lyrics and other writings. A volume of Richard Hell's work is due out in the fall. Henry Rollins, Jewel and Tupac Shakur have published volumes of their poetry.

What does it mean for a select group of pop songwriters, in the wane of their careers, to be repositioned as poets? Norman Mailer once snorted that "if Dylan's a poet, I'm a basketball player." The books are a serious publishing endeavor but an odd one, seeking not an audience or even a lasting imprint—the musicians already have that—but a claim to legitimacy. They revive the old question of how rock or rap lyrics, removed from the roar and theater of the music, fare as poetry. On the cold black and white of the page, do they still sing?

The worst of the fighting has long been settled. Poetry is thriving—on the Internet, in slams and public readings—but for most of us, song lyrics now do the work of modern verse: they organize the truths that rattle around in our skulls. As universities trim their studies of Coleridge or Eliot, English majors read Dylan or Tupac for credit. The lyrics and their supporters have won, if only for outlasting their critics. Of course the lyrics are poetry. No populist definition could exclude the lyrics of rock songs, any more than it could exclude the songs of Sappho or the "hey nonny nonny" nonsense of Shakespeare; any high-culture guardians who would exclude rock have lost the authority to do so. The books of lyrics are the spoils of victory—not an aspirant's claim but a victory lap.

But the value of this victory is questionable. After living so long under these songs' caterwauling sway, I recently spent a month inside the ruminative pages of the printed lyrics, without the alimentary boost of the music. It is a quiet neighborhood, filled with nice finds: the mature lyricism of later Joni Mitchell songs, the economy McCartney hewed to in the Beatles. Yet these seem like dry satisfactions. There are some fine verses in these books, but the power and poetry forged by McCartney, Mitchell and the rest lie in a far more complicated and scurrilous set of connections.

On a brilliant afternoon in the spring, Bob Holman, a poet and believer, piled the books of lyrics on the desk of his TriBeCa loft. An original member of the raucous Nuyorican Poets Café on the Lower

East Side, he has done more than anyone to restore the rattle and dissonance to poetry, the sweaty ambition of performance and rant. He wears rectangular tortoise-shell glasses and has a shock of hair cresting from the top of his head, as if it's pulling him up from above. He jabbed a finger happily at a bridge in McCartney's "When I'm 64":

> *You'll be older too,*
> *And if you say the word—*
> *I could stay with you.*

It was a formal element, a haiku—well, almost—illustrating what Holman thought was wrong with drawing a line between poems and songs, isolating poetry from the stream of popular culture. "We make these distinctions so we have something to talk about other than the poems themselves," he said. He started piling up a second round of poetry books—pamphlets called chapbooks that are sold at slams. "These people are writing great rock 'n' roll poetry," he said, spitting the "hair-flinging anarchy" of rock 'n' roll. He meant this as a compliment, but it was also a recognition of how poetry and pop music have shifted their public roles in the last few decades: how poets are now happy to seek legitimacy in the vulgar swagger of rockers rather than the other way around. The alternative is the quiet cloister of the academy.

Song lyrics have no obligation to work as poetry. Though poetry began in song (lyric poems, for example, were set to the lyre), by now, the two serve different needs. To oversimplify, poems shape the public language—words, meter, what have you—to reveal interior truths. Songs, by contrast, have to unite audiences in collective truths. Great lyrics, even fancy ones, do not necessarily aspire to poetry. For example, John Lennon's song "Give Peace a Chance" scans neatly:

> *Ev'rybody's talking about*
> *Bagism, Shagism, Dragism, Madism, Ragism, Tagism*
> *This-ism, that-ism, is-m, is-m, is-m.*
> *All we are saying is give peace a chance*

But the song's yearnings and remedies are all exterior, and its persuasion lies in melody and timbre; it succeeds as song, not as verse. This is not a lesser victory, just a different one. As Yeats wrote, "We make out of the quarrel with others, rhetoric, but of the quarrel with ourselves, poetry."

Yet nothing prevents songs from taking on this other, interior quarrel. If poetry is, as Leonard Cohen contends, a verdict and not an intention, rock has long extended itself as an opportunity, a soapbox for poets and pseuds. Lou Reed studied with Delmore Schwartz. Cohen and Patti Smith were published poets well before they recorded songs. Richard Hell, then Richard Meyers, ran away from home at age 17 to come to New York and be a poet—a romantic journey, tied as much to vices as verses. "It's interesting how you put that, 'The romance of poetry,' taking for granted that it's about a whole sexy way of life," Hell said in a recent e-mail exchange. As a teenager, he idolized Dylan Thomas; he slid from poetry to what became punk rock, gaining and losing something along the way. "I thought I'd have fun bringing things I'd learned reading and writing poems into music lyrics, but I ended up mostly writing just way more spicy versions of the classic lyric styles."

In the quiet of print, rock lyrics are often less than meets the ear. Rock has always found meaning in nonsense, whether the exuberant whoop of Little Richard's "wop bop a loo bop," or the portentous non sequiturs of the alternative band Pavement:

> *Life is a forklift.*
> *Now my mouth is a forklift,*
> *This I ask: that you serve as a forklift too.*

These puzzlements are diffusely utopian: they promise the existence of another world in which life can be anything and all confusions melt away. Salman Rushdie, in his novel *The Ground Beneath Her Feet*, writes of this vision: "Song shows us a world that is worthy of our yearning, it shows us our selves as they might be, if we were worthy of the world."

The embrace of nonsense and non sequiturs is an inheritance from rural folk music and the blues, which use absurdism to face a capriciously hard world. Dylan adapted this trope for a rock 'n' roll world grappling with Vietnam and the destruction of the civil rights heroes. Applying old truths to a fiercely modern form, he conjured anachronistic landscapes of hard rain and darkness at the break of noon, biblical justice and sorrows. Songs like "Desolation Row" poked at truths using language that was rambling, funny and resolutely poetic, whether sung or sprawled across the pages of Dylan's *Lyrics, 1962–1985*:

> *They're selling postcards of the hanging*
> *They're painting the passports brown*
> *The beauty parlor is filled with sailors*
> *The circus is in town*
> *Here comes the blind commissioner*
> *They've got him in a trance*
> *One hand is tied to the tightrope walker*
> *The other is in his pants*

This was a literary play, evoking one vision of desolation to critique or exorcise another. You didn't have to follow all his allusions; Dylan's power lay in creating mystery, not resolving it. Audiences that once screamed through Beatles shows hung rapt on his words. And after Dylan, it is fair to say, the deluge.

But the import of rock songs often lies in the gaps between the words, inviting the guesswork and reflection and temporary epiphany that are the richest part of listening. The real lyrics to "Louie, Louie," for example, could never signify like the rumor and innuendo. And unlike the words of Cole Porter or Stephen Sondheim or the other pop or cabaret writers compiled in the recent book *Reading Lyrics*, which deliver the same message whether sung or read, the rock songs need the blur of the music to fill in the meaning. Even vacant rock songs—say, "Pretty Vacant" by the Sex Pistols—promise not a vacuity of meaning but a surfeit. It has been a tenet of the rock era that those three-minute songs, pored over by their adherents, carry deeper truths than the institutions around them. This may be a vanity, but it has been a powerful one. The words are just the way in. As Pete Townsend of the Who once said, discussing MTV, "You can speak a language there where nothing you say needs to make sense, but everyone understands you anyway."

The persistence of this shared meaning points to one of the poetic limits of song lyrics. They communicate collectively; they preach to the in crowd. The words to songs, however idiosyncratic, do not direct us to recognize an intelligence independent from and outside our own. Instead, they give novel shape to our points of agreement, what Richard Hell called "the classic lyric styles." Dylan's "Ballad of a Thin Man," for example, about the hopelessly square Mr. Jones, would be lost on its central character. Decades later, when Dylan began writing as a born-again Christian, hectoring his audience—which is to say, moving away from any points of agreement—he ceased to communicate as a songwriter. Poetry is not obliged to these communal ties.

Rock lyrics are by nature overheated and fragmented; they generate more good lines than coherent works. Some of the most compelling believe in revelation or transcendence but stop short of trying to show it (this is perhaps low art's privilege: to defer to a higher art for the details). Lou Reed's "Some Kinda Love," for example, hints at revelation through sexual transgression, walking only as far as the edge without looking over:

> *Put jelly on your shoulder*
> *Let's do what you fear most*
> *That from which you recoil*
> *But still makes your eyes moist*

The lyrics, the jelly, get you halfway there. The music—Reed's flinty voice, the erotic curl of the guitar notes—suggests enough of the rest.

Many of these evocative fragments do not seem so pretty on the page. As poems, even good song lyrics often feel beholden to easy

rhymes or predictable formulas. Taken out of context, these songwriting conventions often feel exposed and mannered. Music is a
soft lyric's best friend, and a lot of the verses here can use the companionship. But there are also some revelations on the pages.
Leonard Cohen, who published his first book of poetry a decade
before his first album, reads as darkly funny on the page, a quiet
smolder in a neatly tailored suit. In a typically corrosive twist on the
cliché of the tormented artist, he writes,

> *I said to Hank Williams, "How lonely does it get?"*
> *Hank Williams hasn't answered yet*
> *but I hear him coughing all night long*
> *a hundred floors above me in the tower of song.*

The biggest surprises are McCartney's. John Lennon's 1964 book
In His Own Write bills its author as "The Writing Beatle!" *Blackbird
Singing* is McCartney's revenge. Instead of mooning about poetic
stuff like misty weather and limpid eyes or reaching for the grand
statements favored by Lennon, McCartney at his best is all business,
compact and plain-spoken. His characters have names, like Lovely
Rita or Father Mackenzie, and perform bold, funny actions: they
came in through the bathroom window or, like Joan in "Maxwell's
Silver Hammer," they got "quizzical, studied pataphysical/Science
in the home," a reference to the Dadaist playwright Alfred Jarry's
science of imaginary solutions. His "Eleanor Rigby," which I find
maudlin as a song, shows its hardness on the page, as flawless a
poem as rock has produced:

> *Father Mackenzie,*
> *Wiping the dirt from his hands as he walks from the grave.*
> *No one was saved.*

McCartney's lyrics are taut and polished; it's nice to have the leisure
to crack them.
     Even on the page, the lyrics do not escape the accidents and tex-
tures of performance. Robert Pinsky, the former poet laureate, has

long argued for the centrality of voice in poetry, whether written or sung. "Poetry, for me, is written with the poet's voice and intended for the reader's voice," he said. "The point for me is not 'the page.' Rather, the test is how beautiful or exciting the language sounds when it is spoken. Great poetry sounds great in any interested reader's voice." Fans constantly give their voice to the lyrics lodged in their heads; the books of lyrics are formal invitations to let-loose—a primal karaoke. Pinsky welcomes the books with the competitive warmth of a poet at a slam. "The cheese department," he said, "should offer many things between Velveeta and an exquisite goat cheese."

So far, publishers seem less eager to enshrine the lyrics of hip-hop, which on record often move too quickly to be counted. Except among the truly committed, there is not much place in the culture now for all-night bullcrit sessions to peel the layers of meaning and nonsense in the lyrics of the Notorious B.I.G. or Eminem. Yet the era's most beguiling, word-drunk songwriting has come from writers like Tupac Shakur, who was killed in 1996. Lauryn Hill, an Ivy Leaguer from New Jersey, laced her rap with a running commentary on how to read her:

> *I treat this like my thesis*
> *Well-written topic*
> *Broken down into pieces*
> *I introduce then produce*
> *Words so profuse*
> *It's abuse how I juice up this beat*
> *Like I'm deuce*

Like the lyricists of the 1960's, hip-hoppers write against a backdrop of social crisis, often exaggerating it with mordant humor. In the early days of N.W.A., Ice Cube introduced himself,

> *I'm expressing with my full capabilities,*
> *And now I'm living in correctional facilities*

This is another wry take on the tortured artist as outlaw, isolated not in Leonard Cohen's tower of song but in Los Angeles's county blues. Rappers have often defended the excessive violence, sexuality, materialism and psychopathology in some lyrics as a kind of journalism, unpretty dispatches from the front. But with their vivid sensationalism and the creative chaos of their language, they function much better as poetry than journalism. The words can be redundant or contradictory—or throwaway, like the formulas Homer used to make his lines scan. The Notorious B.I.G. raps,

> *My life is played out like a Jherri Curl,*
> *I'm ready to die*

How to reconcile the radically divergent tones of the two lines, the dirty-dozens humor of the first, the bleak fatalism of the second? Except maybe to recognize both as survival postures and B.I.G. as running through the various cultural currents flooding his life. The poetry lies in the sum of the two lines, not in their reduction.

If rock or rap lyrics have usurped the role of poetry, it's not very likely that many know enough to miss it. A few years ago, an English professor named David Pichaske asked several groups of people to identify a poem or line from the works of 25 recent Pulitzer Prize–winning poets. Then he asked again, using 25 popular songwriters. The results were exactly as you would expect. The books of lyrics function as souvenirs of this ascendancy.

The collected writings of, say, Patti Smith may not leap off the shelf, but they mark out her place in our public and private lives. For fans squinting toward middle age with their copies of her album *Horses*, the existence of such a book can mean that we haven't outgrown her triumphal squall, even if we're no longer braving the sodden toilets of CBGB to get close to it. If you wanted to put a value on this glow, you might consider Jewel's publishing advance for *A Night Without Armor*, reported to be more than $1 million, compared with the usual $10,000 to $20,000 for books by name poets.

The book's introduction, which cites Jewel's influences, misspells Bukowski.

Rock music has long settled into genteel, adult ambitions. But if the books of song lyrics are intended to breach the canon, they are too late; that battle is over. Writers like Dylan, McCartney, Lennon, Mitchell, Tupac and the rest triumphed by embedding their poetic intelligence in the rhythm and noise and commerce that make up our modern lives. These books distill one part of that intelligence, but they are, as Pete Seeger once described the printed lyrics of folk songs, like a photograph of a bird in flight. They capture the verbs and nouns, but not the power that upended the rules of gravity that existed before.

RJ SMITH

The Many Faces of Korla Pandit

Korla Pandit wandered the West, from big cities to hamlets, throughout his life. Wherever he went, he made the ground beneath his feet seem like the center of a vast turning wheel. However much he was on the move, he let those surrounding him feel they were the ones in motion. People—interesting, glamorous, bizarre people—came to him hoping he'd show them how to get to where he so blissfully stood. They wanted to feel his peace.

He was in his mid seventies when I met him seven years ago. We talked at a coffee shop that no longer exists, in what was the first of many conversations. I was interviewing him about the lounge-music revival, which had led to a modest boost in the old man's career. Soon I became one more neophyte snared by his beatific smile, his mysterious eyes, his strange stories of séances with Marilyn Monroe and how Liberace had stolen his very soul. When you got near Korla Pandit, he took you to some synthetic place.

He came, he explained, from halfway around the world. He had a privileged childhood in New Delhi, where his father, a Brahman, was a government bureaucrat and a friend of Gandhi's. His mother was a French opera singer. Korla was playing the piano at the age of two; by five he was a prodigy, able to perform complicated pieces after hearing them only once. He studied in Europe, then came to the United States when he was 12, and later attended the University of Chicago.

As Korla prepared to leave his family behind and begin the life of a professional musician on the stages of the West, his father gave him a warning: "Son, get your education first. Show business is a dangerous world. You're a hero today and a bum tomorrow." In recounting the story Korla would pause and then add, "Well, he sure knew what he was talking about." Korla came anyway, and he conquered the West, or at least the West Coast, and especially Los Angeles. His TV show, *Adventures in Music with Korla Pandit,* was the first all-music show on television, and Korla was one of the first stars of the medium.

As it happened, I attended the last performance Korla ever gave. It was in 1998 in San Francisco, at a lounge renovated to 1950s vintage called Bimbo's. There were paintings of clowns, and the carpet, banquettes, and walls were as red as tenderloin. A mermaid swam in a large aquarium over the bar. Bimbo's was a lot like Korla himself, an exemplar of a distant time that once embodied suave sexuality but now registered as camp.

Korla's head, swathed as always in an elaborate jeweled turban, hovered above a gorgeous Hammond B3 organ. He played tunes with names like "Trance Dance," "Magnetic Theme," and "Tales of the Underwater Worshippers," songs of an ethereal, light-footed spirituality, songs that evoked faraway places, places he had been, places he had dreamed of.

The concert was a showcase of the oh-so-ironic lounge revival. There were several pop bands on the bill, but nobody had told Korla that. He didn't play a few songs and then get off, the way he was supposed to; he seemed to play every song he knew, many of them tunes that he'd performed on his Los Angeles TV show 50 years earlier. Music poured out of him, and the hipsters in their fezzes and tuxedos and the highball-drinking old-timers got up and danced. Nostalgia and kitsch melted away until all that was left was a man in a turban holding a room in his spell.

When he stopped playing, Korla addressed the crowd in a faltering, accented voice that barely carried to the microphone, offering a cryptic message about the "universal language of music."

"I want to say something to all of you," he said. "Each and every one of you has the right to live on this earth plane in peace and love.

We need each other. And every nation on this earth plane has to tone down and tune in to the supreme intelligence of this universe. We all know something rules." He stared meaningfully, held the mike with the elegance of a permanent entertainer. "I see you tonight. Even in the dark, *I see you.* We have a chance to make this world a better place for everyone. So let's do it. Why not?" Then he offered us his blessing.

In the final years of his life, the wheel had turned again, and Korla Pandit was savoring the renewed interest in his career. He was picking up gigs everywhere from a drive-in movie to the House of Blues, Tim Burton gave him a cameo in his movie *Ed Wood*, and alternative rock bands were declaring him an influence. Korla soaked up all the attention, never tiring of telling the story of his Hindu childhood, of his stardom in the early days of television. New followers flocked to his shows. Old fans rekindled their fervor.

"I was this little Catholic kid, growing up in Seattle, going to church," says Michael Copner, a longtime friend of Korla's. "You'd have to get dressed up in your most uncomfortable suit and tie and go hear the Mass. But I didn't know what it was all about. All I knew was I associated the church organ with heaven. Then I started watching Korla Pandit and thought that somehow the television cameras were getting into heaven, and on rainy afternoons in heaven God must sit around and play the organ. Once I told Korla that, when I was a kid, I saw him on television and thought he was God. And he said, 'You know, you could be right.'"

To scenesters craving a little magic realism in their lives, Korla Pandit became an avatar. One night he was conversing with artist Pat Tierney at the Dresden Room, the holy seat of L.A.'s lounge scene. The pair observed a West Indian patron hitting on a woman. Whether it was because of the man's ineptitude or the woman's displeasure, Korla reacted. "I saw him put a hex on the guy," says Tierney, "He was 14 or so feet away from the man, and after Korla did it, the guy just shot around. He stared at Korla and said, 'You're pretty good.' 'Exactly,' Korla answered."

Korla drove around town in a 1979 Mustang with license plates that read I AM KP. He claimed to be more than 2,000 years old and counseled his young male fans on how to pick up women. "Look at their hands," he explained. "You can tell they're from Venus if their wrists are too small."

A quizzical thing was happening. Hipsters thought they were adopting Korla as a mascot, but really, he was taking them under his wing, holding them in his spell. I was one of the mesmerized: I followed his shows and fell in with the crowd that had befriended him. We'd rent a tour bus, dress up, and scout the last remaining lounges of the San Gabriel Valley and beyond. On a good night Korla would find a decent organ and play.

There was a joke made often in the vicinity of Korla, passed along by any who spent time with him. Everybody who told it seemed to think they were the first to make the crack. The thing about Korla, we'd say, was that while he never spoke on his television show, in person he was hard put to stay quiet. Korla loved to talk, about India and his past and the meaning of life. But for all the talking he did, he kept a secret, one that he protected all his life. Korla Pandit wasn't his real name, and he wasn't Indian at all. He was African American.

Korla Pandit was one of the very first blacks to have his own TV show, and he was certainly the first in Los Angeles. The bargain that he made, with the station and with himself, was that nobody would know. Where better to live this way than in Los Angeles, where people are richly rewarded for conjuring fresh identities out of a half-truth and a pound of hype? He cultivated the public's curiosity, and he fended it off. Instrumental in the project of inventing a 1950s TV swami was his wife, Beryl. Together they created a dazzling fable about an oracular master musician with talent, charm, and supernatural powers. I believe he was all these things; the only thing he wasn't was Indian. When he died, in a hospital room in Sonoma County in 1998, his secret remained intact. Not only did his fans never know the truth, but he never told his two sons. Korla Pandit cast a spell on his followers, then left it behind for his wife and two children and the rest of us to understand.

The Stewart Bridge stood on the periphery of Columbia, Missouri, a leafy college town in the northeast part of the state. Elderly

African Americans point to the place where a rope was tied to the latticework above the railroad tracks and a noose placed around the neck of James T. Scott. Protesting his innocence to the mob that had gathered that day in 1923, Scott was lynched.

Scott held what was, for a black man in Missouri in the early 1920s, a good job: He incinerated the dogs and cats killed in University of Missouri experiments. One day the 14-year-old daughter of a university German professor claimed she had been attacked by a black man near the railroad tracks. Community groups offered a reward, and the local press made a crusade of apprehending the rapist. An anonymous tipster claimed it was Scott, and after his arrest, one local paper demanded he "feel the 'halter draw' in vindication of the law."

A white mob burst into the Boone County Jail, then dragged the beaten and bloodied prisoner through the streets of the city until they came to the spot over the tracks. Their rope was not long enough for the job; the party sent out for a longer cut, and when the girl's father pleaded for Scott's life, they threatened to lynch him, too.

An invisible line stretches from the world of James T. Scott to that of Korla Pandit. I only learned of it through the most idle of encounters. The year after Korla's death I began to frequent an Italian restaurant in West Los Angeles named Carmine's II. There was a big picture of Dean Martin on the brick wall, and the food was nothing special. What brought me to Carmine's was Sir Charles Thompson. Five decades ago Sir Charles was one of the most talented bebop pianists going; he recorded with Charlie Parker and Lucky Thompson and jammed in the clubs on Central Avenue. Styles change, people forget; and there he was, an 81-year-old master playing in a fashion straight out of an airport piano bar for whatever got tossed into a tip jar. If he knew you were listening, Sir Charles would improvise a little something on top.

One evening we started talking between sets, mostly about his early years. He said he had grown up in Columbia, Missouri. Truth was, he couldn't recall much: You spend a life-time improvising, and then in your last days you hold on tight to a handful of riffs learned early.

Still, Sir Charles had two memories of Columbia. One was of another lynching, a murder that led him to flee his home for good and join a New Deal work camp. The other was of a kid in town, an even better piano player, who attended the same segregated school as he did. The kid's name was John Roland Redd, and for a while they were close. Then Sir Charles moved away, and they lost touch. "Later he went to Hollywood and became a famous organist on television," he said. "He used another name, some Turkish title, I guess."

That night when I got home I laid out Korla's albums and studied them: the concealing smile, his eyes holding my gaze. There was no doubt possible. Korla had spent five decades telling the world he was Asian, and the album covers, with the airbrushing, the makeup, the head wrap, presented him as an Indian mystic. Before I spoke to Sir Charles I saw what I wanted to see; I saw what Korla wanted me to see. Studying the albums, I laughed out loud at the audacity of what he'd done. Now the portraits looked radically different. My friend was a black man, and he'd conspired to conceal the fact in the most daring of ways—before adoring mobs.

Since that night at Carmine's I've talked to relatives and acquaintances in the Columbia area who knew John Redd and his family. I have sat in the two-story brick building that is Fred Douglass School, the school that once housed all of Columbia's black children, and interviewed Redd's classmates. I've seen him in his 1932 fifth-grade class photo. I've found references to his father and sister in the black press of the time, seen his birth record and his parents' death certificates.

To consider the life of Korla Pandit—and that's what I will call him because that is who he became—is to consider the weight of wearing a mask for 50 years. It is to grasp the fear of exposure, of a revelation that would have killed his career. One slip and he would have gone from being a mirror of white America's mania for things "exotic" to somebody white America didn't want to face. He would have been revealed as a fraud, and his fans would have never forgiven him. It is to recognize how he had to cut himself off from a black community that he'd grown up in, from a culture that had shaped the musical skills, and the survival skills, that he drew on for the rest of his life.

He bequeathed to his fans a conflicting set of images.

"I have a Native American friend who says he was definitely Mexican American," says Timothy Taylor, an assistant music professor at Columbia University who has written on Pandit.

"I've heard he was Hawaiian. I've heard that he was Filipino," says Michael Copner. "You heard so many stories that they just canceled each other out."

"No, no, no, no," insists Ferdie Furtado, who played organs alongside Korla in a music store in Laguna Hills in the 1980s. "He's from India. Korla Pandit is not an American guy. He is, to be exact, definitely Indian, definitely." Furtado, born in Goa, really is from India.

On his death certificate in the space marked RACE is written WHITE.

It was a given that Korla was larger than life; to hold him to the laws of nature simply wasn't fair, or even the point. Maybe, I tell myself, holding him up to a reporter's scrutiny isn't entirely the point, either. What truth could be more marvelous than the truth Korla conjured every night we were in his presence? Maybe to record the life of a self-created character is to damage the creation. Maybe sometimes biography is an act of assassination.

"He was very Americanized," says humorist Stan Freberg, who worked with Korla in the early '50s at local TV station KTLA. "He was light skinned, about the color of General Colin Powell. To tell you the truth, I think Korla Pandit invented himself."

In 1921 African Americans could walk down Broadway, then as now Columbia's main drag, and buy something from the restaurants and ice cream parlors, but they couldn't consume on the premises. Interracial churches were unheard of. Public institutions were segregated. The Ku Klux Klan was in the middle of a postwar boom. Still, that Columbia was a large college town ameliorated some of the sting of Jim Crow; life there was not as harsh as life in Little Rock or Montgomery. This was the Columbia into which John Roland Redd was born.

Ernest Redd, John's father, was black; Doshia O'Nina Redd, his wife, was of French and black lineage. Their three boys and four girls were light skinned. Ernestine Tapp, a friend of the family in Columbia, recalls going to a movie show with one of the Redd girls: "They tried to make her sit where the white people sat. She had to explain to them that she wasn't white."

The pastor of Second Baptist Church, the largest Baptist church in town, Ernest exerted a huge influence on his children. But right next door to Second Baptist was McKinney Hall, a second-floor dance hall that featured traveling jazz bands. As the Redd children grew up, McKinney began to exert the greater pull. Perhaps it was at McKinney that John first heard Art Tatum play. A legendary piano virtuoso, Tatum became one of his heroes. John's brother, Ernest Jr., called Speck because of his freckles, went on to be a jazz bandleader in Des Moines.

"John Roland was so small, he had to get a little boy's shirt to graduate from high school," says George Brooks, a classmate at Douglass. "He was a fun-loving person. We were all part of the jitterbug generation. One year we went up to play basketball against one of the other high schools. And it was pretty much the whole Douglass school went up there. Afterwards, we were in somebody's house, and there was a piano. And of course, John was attracted to a piano like certain insects are to flowers. He started playing, and it wasn't very long before he had a crowd. And that front-room floor where we were dancing—it broke there in the center. Too much weight! That upright piano was against the wall, and the break was near the center of the room. It was just lucky that the piano didn't turn over. If it had, we wouldn't have had a John Roland."

One by one, most of the Redd family drifted to Southern California. John Redd came in the early '40s. The Los Angeles he encountered was familiar. Defense factories and unions discriminated against African Americans. Restaurants from the Brown Derby to lunch counters didn't serve blacks. Restrictive covenants, which legally barred blacks from living in white neighborhoods, blanketed the city. Even pet cemeteries were segregated according to the race of the pet's owner.

The black novelist Chester Himes migrated to Los Angeles about the same time as John Redd. Himes drew on his experiences in his

1945 novel *If He Hollers Let Him Go:* "It wasn't being refused employment in the plants so much. When I got here practically the only job a Negro could get was service in the white folks' kitchens. But it wasn't that so much. It was the look on the people's faces when you asked them about a job. Most of 'em didn't say right out that they wouldn't hire me. They just looked so goddamned startled that I'd even asked. As if some friendly dog had come in through the door and said. 'I can talk.' It shook me."

John Redd arrived a fully developed jazz pianist able to play barrelhouse, blues, and swing. He was also an accomplished organist. He played keyboards between big-band sets at the seaside dance halls south of L.A., booming clubs that did not let blacks on the dance floor. Many did not let them play onstage, either.

It might just have been a quickly hatched prank, a lark—we may never know—but one day John Redd introduced himself as "Juan Rolondo," a crude Latinization of his first two names. Maybe he got his inspiration from the Mexican family he was living with in Orange County.

He played "Latin" songs in clubs between San Diego and Los Angeles. There was a Latin craze going on; bobby-soxers were craving tunes like "Peanut Vendor" and "Tico Tico." Why not cash in? The white musicians sure were.

There were also practical considerations. You had to join the union to play on a stage in Los Angeles, and through the 1940s the musicians' union practiced Jim Crowism. A white local in Hollywood steered the lucrative film and Hollywood-club jobs to whites, and the black guys hung out at the local on Central Avenue, waiting for calls that came infrequently.

In a town focused on the black-white color line, a Mexican was unaccountable, elusive. Juan Rolondo released a few records and played organ for radio shows, most notably *Chandu the Magician*, a popular drama about a crime-solving mystic who traveled to exotic spots around the world. The Juan Rolondo role had been a boon to Redd, but after the 1943 Zoot Suit Riots, when white sailors and police beat Mexican Americans in the streets, the allure of passing as Mexican must have lost some of its luster.

At some point in the 1940s Redd met Beryl DeBeeson, an attractive, tough-minded blonde who was an airbrusher at Disney's animation studios. Beryl became his confidant and career adviser. The two were married, perhaps in 1948, after a court struck down a state law prohibiting marriages between whites and members of minority groups.

The moment when Korla Pandit was born remains unrecorded. Was this creation a flim-flam meant to last only as long as it took to cash a check? Or was it always going to be a long-term project? A chance to buy the Taj Mahal? I suspect Redd saw Juan Rolondo as a short con and realized Korla Pandit was for the ages. From one angle, he was playing a dangerous game. But from another, he was simply doing what show folk have always done in Hollywood: reinventing himself and saying it was ever so. What we do know is that in 1949 Korla Pandit surfaced as a regular organist on *Hollywood Holiday*, a show broadcast from Tom Breneman's restaurant at Sunset and Vine.

Radio was a paycheck, but in post–World War II L.A., television was getting the big push. A new cultural industry was in ascendance, and surely there was a way for an enterprising, talented musician to ascend with it.

First, though, something had to be done about the way Korla talked. With an "Indian" accent that wasn't all it might have been, Korla cultivated an act in which he said nothing. Men from the East were supposed to be mysterious, were they not? Silence was expedient, but it was strategic as well.

As was the headgear. The turban, strictly speaking, was problematic. Hindus from India, again strictly speaking, do not wear them. Indians who do wear turbans are Sikhs, and they, alas, do not wear jewels in their turbans. Yet to a Hollywood audience desiring an exotic encounter with the Indian "other" but not knowing what that "other" was, showbiz stereotypes were all it expected. Korla, drawing on the same stereotypes, gave the people what they wanted.

He had turquoise, maroon, and burgundy turbans, and each was adorned with a glittering smoky topaz, like an all-seeing third eye. According to his elder son, Shari, the topaz "was supposed to provide the wearer with the ability to psychically or spiritually see the influences which were going on around him. And to sort of balance things, kind of almost be a filter to help protect against unsavory influences."

Those influences were everywhere. "He had times when people would try to run up onstage and loudly expose him for what he wasn't by snatching his turban off," says nephew Ernest Redd. "But Grandmother's side of the family was French, and all the Redd side had beautiful long black hair. He let the hair grow and grow and grow under the turban, so when they snatched it off and thought they were going to find a kinky grade of hair, it just fell out, and they were kind of stunned. It actually came down to his shoulders."

If the turban was chosen to obscure what was African American beneath, it may have had the opposite effect on those who were in the know. Turbans were the favored headgear for a number of black nationalist organizations of the early decades of the 20th century. They were also worn by early-century African American magicians, who wielded a symbolic power that made them quasi-nationalist figures. There was, most famously, the turbaned illusionist known as Black Herman, an Afrocentric pamphleteer who claimed to be descended from Moses and who was an associate of Marcus Garvey and Booker T. Washington. (Another black organ-playing mystic, Herman Blount, aka Sun Ra, was named after Black Herman.)

Hinduism itself had resonance in the 1940s for a generation of blacks who were fighting for their rights. Indian Hindus were using racial equality as an argument against British imperialism; Indian speakers lecturing on their struggle were guests in black churches in Los Angeles throughout the decade. As it happens, one of the more forceful voices for human rights in India was a woman by the name of Madame Vijaya Lakshmi Pandit. Which is to suggest that if Korla was doing everything he could to hide his heritage, he was also proclaiming it to the savvy few who got the message.

Korla Pandit remained nothing more than a fantastic idea until the moment when an émigré from one culture intersected with an exile from another. Sometime in 1949 Korla played organ at the opening of a local furrier. KTLA was broadcasting the event, and the station's founder, Klaus Landsberg, was supervising the shoot. An engineer at heart, Landsberg had an intrinsic understanding of the Hollywood deal. He immediately dangled a TV show in front of Korla and then, almost as an afterthought, told him there was just one catch. If he wanted his own program, he'd also have to play the organ for a puppet show in production called *Time for Beany*.

Hooking up with Landsberg was the break Korla and Beryl had been looking for. The German-born Landsberg had played a role in the first live television broadcast—Hitler's 1936 Olympic Games. Just before the war he had fled the Nazis and landed in the United States, where he was hired by the DuMont network to launch a Los Angeles station. An inventor who could take apart and reassemble a TV camera on the spot, Landsberg built KTLA in his own image and went on to give the world helicopter chases and Roller Derby, Lawrence Welk and Gorgeous George.

"When Paramount wanted to open a TV station here, they asked DuMont who was the best, and they were told Klaus Landsberg," says KTLA newsman Stan Chambers, who has been at the station since its founding. "They didn't know anything about TV, so they just gave Klaus carte blanche. He was the boss. He didn't have to clear it with Paramount or with anybody. He immediately said, 'It's all about the live individual.' We didn't want to run films. He was very much in tune with the live broadcast. Remember, we didn't have videotape back then."

One of Landsberg's most famous feats was the first broadcast of an atomic-bomb explosion. The networks were not interested, so he shot the event himself, convinced that people would watch. Stringing a series of parabolic reflectors from mountaintop to mountaintop between the Nevada Proving Grounds and Los Angeles, Landsberg got the final dish in place moments before the explosion went off. He gave the public its first live glimpse of a mushroom cloud and boosted his station's ratings.

He created spectacle, leaving it to the audience to sort out exactly what it was seeing. Which was fine with Landsberg's turbaned organist. From his very first televised performances, Korla was a sensation. "Korla Pandit was always immaculately groomed," says Stan Freberg. "He was just like Frank Sinatra that way. Imagine, this is a guy sitting in a corner of a small studio at Melrose, just outside the Paramount gate. He'd come sliding in a half hour before airtime in this impeccable double-breasted, dark blue pin-striped suit with a white shirt and French cuffs, beautiful cuff links, three-pointed white hankie in the pocket, and this beautiful turban with a jewel. It was such a waste, because cameramen in T-shirts and tennis shoes are pulling cameras around, and cables are crossing over the top of his organ. It was a strange time."

The show, *Adventures in Music with Korla Pandit*, always began the same way: The numinous light of heaven would fill the screen. Only as seconds passed and the camera drew back would you see that this light was emanating from the jewel in Korla's turban. The camera would pull back a little more, and Korla's face, with its gnostic half smile and ancient countenance, would come into focus. All the while Korla would play his signature song, "Magnetic Theme," and then a selection of numbers from distant lands as his male dancer, Bupesh Guha, and a troupe of gamines willowed among fountains and plywood pillars. His small hands would often play two keyboards at once, a piano and an organ, kindling a music made not for dancing but for easy-chair meditation.

Beryl weighed in heavily on production decisions. She helped design the sets. She oversaw his makeup. She argued with directors over the lighting, insisting that shadows not fall upon Korla's face. "You could tell she was very dominant," says Chambers. "She did a lot of the producing, and she always protected Korla."

Korla never spoke. Everything he communicated came through those slender fingers and that steady gaze. A woman wrote him that she had been planning her suicide when she caught his show and that something in his look stayed her hand. She sent him a grand piano in gratitude. His eyes spoke for him, and this was the essence of his wit. Born at a time when a black man in the South could get whipped for making eye contact with a white woman, Korla Pandit was making dreamy eyes at thousands upon thousands of aproned homemakers, stealing into their dens as they heated their fondue pots.

"That was the day of the intimacy thing. Of evening gowns and people smoking long-stemmed cigarettes and seeking a pleasant romantic mood," says Marty Pasetta, one of Korla's producers. "The women were in awe of him."

He and Beryl bought a big house with a swimming pool in the San Fernando Valley. They were a glamorous couple, turning heads as they dropped in at Hollywood soirees and nightclubs. They partied with Errol Flynn and Bob Hope, and fans would stop Korla on the street. One evening, coming out of a nightclub at Hollywood and Vine, whom should they meet but Duke Ellington, who greeted Korla—or was it John Redd?—with a warm smile of recognition.

He quietly remained a seasoned jazz musician for the rest of his days. When boyhood idol Art Tatum haunted Hollywood's after-hours clubs, Korla would sit in on jam sessions. The nearly blind virtuoso might not have been able to see a face very well, but Tatum had fabled ears, and when Korla would play a few bars, Tatum would greet him by name.

But by necessity Korla sublimated his passion for jazz, erasing from his public performances obvious traces of a music that connoted low-down good times, not to mention black culture. The arrival of a new instrument with few jazz associations helped him greatly. It was his good fortune to have emerged a decade after the invention of the Hammond organ, which generated sounds never before heard.

The soul of the Hammond was its tone wheels, which whirled at various rates. The shape and speed of the spinning wheels produced this new electronic music and in their rotation created what the manufacturer called *vox humana:* the human voice. The warmth of its sound gave the Hammond an uncanny intimacy and Korla one less reason to speak.

Korla was a pioneer of the Hammond, turning an instrument most others were playing like a pipe organ or a piano into a one man rhythm orchestra. He slapped the keys and spanked out percussive drum blasts that were in harmony with the melody; he coaxed outlandish vibrato from the two rows of keys, a tremble of air that stretched from the Los Angeles stage to Persian markets and Moroccan harems.

"His music is so much more creative than any other organist's I've ever heard," says Korla's friend Verne Langdon. "Korla created chords and harmonics that I call purple chords—just *rich* and *deep* and *beautiful*. It would not be unusual to see people crying when he was playing. I was one of them."

Here were the first stirrings of the music that became known as exotica. It started with big bands trying to prolong their existence by grabbing at novelty. Bandleader Tommy Dorsey found an audience for tunes like "Katie Went to Haiti," "Hawaiian War Chant," "Hungarian Rhapsody," and "Song of India," a piece that became one of Korla's staples. Korla told friends that Dorsey would show up at his live shows and pretend to be asleep in the back and then, a week later, play Korla's music for his Hollywood Bowl audience.

Korla implicitly understood the yearnings of a postwar public full of restless soldiers returning home from the Pacific. They sought in backyard luaus, tiki bars, and the music of distant shores a sexuality they denied themselves in their daily lives. Think of Carmen Miranda shaking her fruit with a knowing leer; Korla's music embodied that leer and the sweet perfumed passion fruit lurking beneath the everyday.

Veracity was hardly the point. "I used to laugh when I'd hear the announcer say, 'Now Korla Pandit will play 'Song of India,'" says Larry Bloomfield, who worked at KTLA. "People from India don't know what that song is!"

The love letters piled up, as did the enthusiastic write-ups in *Variety* and *Downbeat*. Somewhere along the way an extraordinary transformation took place. Korla Pandit ceased being a fiction and became every bit as real as any other Hollywood celebrity. There wasn't even a John Redd to conceal anymore. He had tailored his own personality to fit perfectly with the soothsayer he was playing. This was no longer a case of somebody pretending to be something he was not. There had never been a Korla Pandit before, and now, there he was.

He started talking really, really funny. "It was strange. It got to a point he didn't even speak very good English because he had talked that Hinduism or whatchacallit for so long," says nephew Ernest Redd. "When my dad passed away, [Korla] called to talk, and I could not understand him. My mom talked to him in some kind of broken language, and I couldn't understand what either of them were saying. They ended up settling on a jazz musician's hipster talk. It was like pig latin."

The few old schoolmates who ran into him had to pretend they'd never met. He was often seen around town with one of his best friends, the Indian-born actor Sabu, an alliance that brings to mind the "arranged" Hollywood marriage of a closeted gay actor. Black novelist Charles Chesnutt's *The House Behind the Cedars*, about a man who passes for white, has a sentence that could apply to Korla: "Our customs grip us in bands of steel. We become the creatures of our creations."

From slavery right down to this morning, countless African Americans have passed as white because they were evading the lynch mob or wishing for an equal opportunity. The subject has been taboo: Crossing over means denying who you are, means banishing friends and family from your life. You live in a gray zone, and it is the loneliest of places.

Passing for Asian was a little different, because you did not blend into white society. The practice went on long before Korla Pandit first appeared. In the late 1930s, Harlem's *Amsterdam News* reported that a Syracuse University football star named Wilmeth Sidat-Singh was, as a columnist put it, "about as much Hindu as flat-foot floogie." In 1947, around the time that Juan Rolondo was turning into Korla Pandit, the *Los Angeles Tribune*, a lively black newspaper, heralded a stunt pulled by a brown-skinned New York minister. He prepared for a visit through the Deep South by donning a purple turban, affecting "a slightly Swedish accent," and concocting a tale about being a visiting Eastern dignitary. He was doted on and able to eat at white-only restaurants. In Mobile, Alabama, he impishly asked a waiter what would happen if a Negro came to eat. The Negro wouldn't be served, he was told. "I just stroked my chin and ordered my dessert," said the pastor.

When John Redd crossed over, he didn't sever all ties with the world he had known. "It was not top secret," says Ernest. "Among the family we knew what he was doing and very little was said about it. There was times when he would come by, and it was kind of like a sneak visit. He might come at night sometime and be gone before we got up. He had to separate himself from the family to a certain extent. They would go to see him play, but they wouldn't speak to him. They would go to his show and then they would leave, and the family would greet him at a later time."

The situation became even more complicated once Korla's father Ernest Sr., moved to Los Angeles, by the early '50s. Reverend Redd became the pastor of Trinity Baptist Church, a prominent institution in the community. Any night he wanted to, Reverend Redd could come home from the church, switch on the television, and watch his son play the organ, with that strange look in his eyes and that turban on his head. Korla kept in touch with his family, and on occasion he and Beryl scheduled a covert mission to the parents' West Adams home. But even then, detection could not be discounted. Even then, Korla wore the turban. He didn't bring Shari or Koram, his and Beryl's sons.

Having done hundreds of shows for KTLA, Korla thought he was due a larger cut. The organist was a proud man, one not afraid to battle over money he felt he was owed. Korla left KTLA in 1951. Soon he met Louis D. Snader, a real estate developer dabbling in the entertainment business. If Landsberg was the visionary tinkerer, Snader was the tightfisted plodder. Businessmen were overtaking the anything-goes spirit of television's early days. Around the country, local stations were struggling with high production costs, and Snader offered them prepackaged film clips of musical performances by artists like Nat King Cole and Theresa Brewer. Stations could run them between shows or string a few songs together and run them *as* shows. Korla shot a batch of programs for Snader that were sold and aired in different regions of the country. They even aired in Columbia, Missouri.

Then Snader offered Korla a new contract, and pride again was piqued. In the new arrangement Snader would have owned a much bigger piece of the program, including the mail that Korla received. Mail was always a sensitive issue with Korla, perhaps because, as he said, somebody was stealing the gifts that fans sent him. Perhaps he was fearful that a letter would expose him. Korla quit Snader in the middle of shooting a series of performances and moved to San Francisco. With the sets and crew fully prepped, Snader propositioned another keyboardist just beginning to turn heads in Hollywood, a glowing Wisconsin-born youth who went by the stage name of Liberace. Snader filmed a series of programs with his new pianist while Korla brooded in San Francisco. It was the beginning of the Liberace phenomenon.

"You watch Liberace and you think Korla should have been sitting there," Michael Copner says. "It *should* have been him. If Korla had gone along with Snader and they hadn't had the contract dispute, there probably wouldn't have been a Liberace."

Korla often talked about how he'd handed his successor his big break and in weak moments was known to deride Liberace as "a bordello piano player." He also said he cried the day he heard Liberace had died. "Don't know about that for sure," says Copner.

The break with Snader left Korla scrambling for a new venue. There was a television show in San Francisco, followed by another in Los Angeles, and the old programs and Snader clips went into endless reruns. He also broke his silence. On his San Francisco show Korla started speaking to his audience, and though his words were a soothing elixir, to his older fans they broke the spell. "When they had him talk, it ruined the mystique," says producer Marty Pasetta.

And talk Korla did. His show had always leaned toward the spiritual, and in the late '50s he made his philosophy more explicit by crafting a gentle ecumenical theology. Korla began lecturing audiences on the tenets of what he called the Universal Language of Music. The language cited Hindu sacred texts, the Bible, and atomic theory. It was an ethereal concoction that depended on the magnetism of Korla's stagecraft.

"People are cynical because since World War II, they've been under constant bombardment by those who would control their thinking and their lives," he said in an interview. "What I'm trying to communicate is true love and the divine consciousness regardless of religious belief." He exhorted his audience to not judge the world by how it looked. "TV isn't real, it's just light," he explained. "Sound and light vibrations—that's what we are. We reflect light, and that's what determines what 'color' we are." In a 1955 pamphlet Korla elaborated: "Are you looking at life through dark-colored glasses? Remember, we walk by faith, not by sight."

Southern California in the '50s was rife with artists like James Whitney and Oskar Fischinger, who were exploring the spiritual effects of music. At the same time, intellectuals like Alan Watts and Aldous Huxley and figures like L. Ron Hubbard and Jack Parsons were exploring unconventional faiths. Their musings went beyond the suburban interest in exotica, but they were not completely divorced from them, either. All expressed a hunger to see beneath everyday appearances. Once more, Korla's timing was spot on.

He became friends with Paramahansa Yogananda, the spiritual leader of the Self-Realization Fellowship. Yogananda, a true Indian, was a fan and contributed liner notes to one of Korla's albums. He declared once to an audience that Korla embodied his childhood dream of a fusion of Eastern and Western musics. He proclaimed the organist "better looking than Rudolph Valentino." When the spiritual leader died after giving a lecture at the Biltmore Hotel in 1952, Korla played at the funeral.

The spiritual landscape of Southern California in the 1950s was more radiant than the Nevada flats. Korla spoke of wanting to open a string of meditation centers, but short of starting his own religion, it wouldn't be easy getting his message heard. He had no specific religion to sell, no sacred oils or unguents, no holy book, only an experience. He earned enough to live on, and gained one thing more. Nobody—not Liberace or L. Ron Hubbard, not Ed Wood or Art Tatum—ever forged a deeper link with his followers.

As a recording artist, though, Korla never generated hits. He had released albums on the Pasadena-based rhythm-and-blues label

Vita, some with a singer named Jette Satin. In the late '50s he signed with Berkeley's Fantasy label, and over the next decade he put out 14 albums.

So for several decades he traveled, walking by faith, not by sight. He played and prophesied in Safeways and for organ societies, at veterans' retirement homes and in trailer parks. He sold his albums out of the back of his car. In 1967 he and Beryl moved the family to Vancouver to keep their two boys out of the Vietnam War draft but also perhaps to beat back the rising tide of talk that the swami wasn't all he said he was. Korla lived there for a while, raising Afghan hounds, but eventually drifted down to Calistoga or Santa Cruz or Los Angeles, staying with friends, living with girlfriends.

Fear of exposure remained a constant preoccupation, and he tried to limit dangerous encounters. It wasn't always easy: Once, when Korla and a friend were visiting Seattle's Space Needle, a group of Indian tourists appeared on the observation deck. When his companion suggested that they go over and talk, Korla nearly came undone and shot out of the tower.

It must have been a rough comedown from television stardom. Korla railed against Fantasy's bookkeeping practices and was known to spin some improbable conspiracy theories about what had happened to his career. He could get angry. But he also made life hard for himself. Although he had a home and family in Canada—he and Beryl never divorced—Korla chose to wander. In his last years he lived from couch to couch, barely getting by while his health deteriorated. Maybe he stayed away from home because it meant confronting the truth he'd never shared with his children. Or maybe he just liked wandering. I have a hard time thinking of Korla as lonely, and I have never thought to pity him. He always had an appreciative audience, whether he was on a Hollywood stage or at a Ukiah pizzeria.

But more than that, in the years after he left TV he met some of the most fascinating people imaginable. His secret may have severed psychic connections he once shared with his family and friends, but in the '50s and '60s he developed psychic connections few of us ever have. He became friendly with Manly Palmer Hall, the founder of the Philosophical Research Society. The Los Feliz–

based society opened in the 1930s and still functions today. Hall, who died 12 years ago, was a Canadian-born autodidact, a voluminous reader and the author of hundreds of occult books, pamphlets, and articles on everything from Rosicrucianism to Masonic rites. He was also a handsome cipher with many movie friends. "He was a man who seemed like he was 1,000 years old," says cult-film historian Forrest Ackerman, who, as a boy, heard Hall speak. "Not that he was decrepit or anything. You just had the feeling that here was a man who had been around a long, long time." Korla regularly spoke at the society and seems to have derived much of his Hollywood holy man manner from Hall's lecture and television appearances.

Perhaps the most extraordinary person Korla got close to in the '60s and '70s went by the name of, depending on how you knew him, Richard Simonton or Doug Malloy. Born the former, he was interesting enough, an inventor and a businessman who elevated Muzak from a small New York City company into a national corporation. Simonton loved steamboats and invested millions in refurbishing them. He founded the American Theater Organ Society. He was the executor of Harold Lloyd's estate and claimed to have psychic gifts, to converse regularly with an Egyptian spirit.

That was the mundane side of Simonton's life. As his alter ego Doug Malloy, he was a pioneer of modern body piercing. Malloy collected information about various piercing techniques and popularized them through the Gauntlet, a shop in West Hollywood. Like Korla, Malloy wove fables about the origins of his craft; where Korla passed off an organ melody as Egyptian, Malloy devised a nipple-piercing technique and then claimed it was the exact one the Roman centurions had used.

Malloy had a huge house in Toluca Lake, with an indoor garden and a retractable ceiling. There was a church organ in the living room; a spiral staircase led to the downstairs, which featured another organ and a vintage player piano. There was also a fully equipped screening room, and he would invite Korla over to perform and watch silent movies.

Malloy, like Manly Hall and others who crossed paths with Korla, was a professional keeper of secrets, a self-made myth. Such improvisers flourished in a town where people came to reinvent themselves, to "pass" as all manner of things they most certainly were not. Men like these were natural confederates of Korla; perhaps in shared company they were able to relax in the fellowship of true performers. The seer hid, and the hidden saw all.

It was at a memorial for Bela Lugosi, in 1991, that Korla's career was reborn. Lugosi had been a close friend of Manly Hall's and had even been hypnotized by the Los Feliz sage. Korla had an abiding interest as well in hypnosis, and it was at the memorial that he first cast his spell on a new generation.

A young *nuevo* lounge performer named Joe Sehee was also at the wake. Possibly the only roller-skating nightclub singer in Los Angeles, Sehee was assembling a troupe of new and old nightclub acts, including a Frank Sinatra impersonator and schoolbus driver known as Eddie Vegas. Together with Korla they played around town in a chaotic revue that was part tribute to old-school show business and part send-up.

While Southern California had been the home of the 1950s exotica craze, by the early '90s the region's tiki bars and Alpine restaurants were falling to pieces, like ancient ruins. They provided the appropriate backdrop for what was the start of the lounge revival.

The Dresden Room was a favored haunt, but perhaps the most sacred site was Kelbo's in West Los Angeles. Kelbo's was a world within a world, filled with blowfish, carved gods, flaming drinks. In a round room, beneath a giant coconut shell, Korla and Sehee performed weekly. By the end of the decade the film *Swingers* and the swing-dance fad had, for a moment, turned lounge into mass culture, but the Kelbo's scene was artier, more twisted—it was talent night at the René Magritte lounge. Folks in their twenties and thirties got their first taste of Korla's organ stylings and wondered how anything so cool could have been on television in their parents' heyday.

Throughout his last years Korla hitched his Hammond to this traveling circus, but he also kept his distance. If there was a trade wind blowing irony his way, it never touched him. His sons thought the scene was beneath him, but Korla seemed happy to have the new audience. He kept a bemused outlook, even when he played in a run-down Azusa drive-in. Fans honked their car horns in tribute, would-be exotic dancers writhed in a makeshift mosh pit, while on the stage Korla projected a surreal obliviousness. To the list of all the miracles he performed throughout his life this one should be added: Even when playing with a roller-skating crooner, even when bowling-shirted hepcats a quarter his age were swooning at his feet, even then, Korla Pandit maintained a stately dignity.

To reach the British Columbia town of Sechelt from Vancouver, you take a ferry that scoots around green peninsulas usually crowned with huge gray clouds. Part suburb, part sleepy seaside village, Sechelt was where Korla's son Shari lived with Beryl.

It was two years ago, and I'd already spoken to them on the phone, never quite finding the right moment to mention what I'd learned about Columbia. I'd hoped to see them and tell them at the proper time.

During our phone conversation Beryl expressed what I took to be anxiety concerning my questions about Korla's music career. "I don't see why anybody cares," she said. But Shari enthusiastically answered questions about his dad, telling stories of the boy who left India at the age of five.

In Sechelt, Beryl was polite but declined to continue the conversation. Shari, though, agreed to meet me at a coffeehouse popular with local musicians. There, for several hours, he filled in what information he could about his father.

Had he ever met any of his father's family? "We were his family," he replied.

"I have to tell you, my mother was a little nervous about me talking to you," he went on. "She has a little paranoia from her professional past. She was always kind of the watchdog of the family."

Long ago, he explained, there had been others who had come with questions about Korla, and she had refused to cooperate.

"Somebody once wrote a thing about my dad," Shari said. And then he did a strange thing. He broke into the cartoonish dialect whites use when they stereotype black speech. "*'Oh, his pappy was a black minister from Mississippi,'*" he said, his face lighting up. "There's been some really wild excursions."

I told him Sir Charles's story. "It's not true," he said, rolling his eyes. "Lawdy lawd, ah swear it's not true."

There was no mistaking how much of Korla there was in Shari: At the age of 51 he had the same delicate eyes, the same smooth skin. And there he was, mocking African Americans. The Hindus believe in a great wheel that spins slowly and balances scores left unsettled: They call it karma.

Later I reached one of Korla's sisters, who lived in Los Angeles. She told me that his children had never been told about their father's lineage. Korla, she said, never told the boys that they had aunts, uncles, cousins, and grandparents living in the same city. Although she didn't understand the decision, she respected it and wouldn't say more.

After I'd gotten home from Vancouver, I wrote Beryl a letter. Wasn't it time, I wrote, to celebrate one of the first African American entertainers to appear on television? She never wrote back. I then called her. She was furious.

"I was offended by your letter, because I wouldn't marry anyone of that type," she said. She fell silent. Before I could formulate something to say, she added, "I wish you would go doodle on somebody else's life."

Shari died of cancer last December. In the spring I spoke briefly to his younger brother, John (who had changed his name from Koram). Shari had shared my questions with him, and now John was as angry as his mother. "Frankly, it sounds like a crock," he said. "It pisses me off because it's fucking not true. I must have heard stuff like that a dozen times. Somebody saying, 'Oh, I knew him in San Bernardino when he was working there.' Somebody else saying, 'Oh, I knew him back in Chicago.' I don't believe it."

John's voice suddenly got sharper. "I wouldn't be interested in discussing things along your lines," he said. "How would you feel if somebody told you they had a different history of your whole life?"

In 1933 Langston Hughes published "Rejuvenation Through Joy," a short story about a messianic tyro who lights up Manhattan society. He is the great Eugene Lesche, protean lecturer, philosopher, seer, master of the esoteric. He becomes famous for pulling wealthy white folks out of their lassitude. Lesche addresses a ballroom of society women, relishing their attention. "Look at the Indians! Look at the Negroes! They know how to move from the feet up, from the head down. Their centers live. . . . They do not mood and brood. No! They live through motion, through movement, through music, through joy!"

Lesche buys a mansion in Westchester, turns it into a colony for his followers. With his lofty talk and the jazz bands he uses to illustrate the essence of the human spirit, Lesche has the swells in the palm of his hand. They, too, get what they want; the music lifts them up—until jealousy destroys all, and the great Lesche is revealed as the ultimate scoundrel: a black man passing.

Korla Pandit never suffered the fate of Lesche. Nor were his last days anything like those of Sir Charles Thompson, playing standards for tips at an Italian restaurant. He was somebody who didn't exist who lived far more fully than the pastor's son who did exist ever might have. He kept playing on and savored his audiences, big and tiny, whether they were devotees who remembered the KTLA days or young hipsters wrestling with the secret syntax of the Universal Language of Music. If you choose to, you can read his story this way: A life can't be described, labeled, summed up. It can only be performed.

I saw him once without his turban. It was at his last recording date. The Federal Building in Oklahoma City had just been bombed, and the public was in an anti-Arab mood. Korla, not taking the chance of having someone mistake him for an Islamic terrorist, had left the head wrap at home.

He entered the tiny Hollywood studio wearing polyester slacks and Nikes, his unbelievably lustrous jet-black hair flowing from crown to collar. The session had been hastily assembled; the rented Hammond B3 was still on a dolly. He grappled all day with an old Ventures song, "Diamond Head," but the stars were not in his favor. The engineer accidentally erased good takes. Feedback shrieked when Korla just brushed against the organ, and his elaborate toggle-switch tricks were spitting up what sounded like lava erupting out of a volcano. Numerous takes yielded nothing. It was a hundred degrees in the small room, and the whole session was going down the drain.

A couple of girls in skirts arrived, and Korla's mood lightened. Then, while we silently waited for an indication that he was ready to record again, Korla leaned over the keys. There was no erupting lava, no feedback. He stared past the sheet music and summoned a dance tune from 60 years ago. It was a big-band number called "Tuxedo Junction," and Korla played it with a crisp, deft touch, with a jauntiness that had us imagining dances nobody knows how to do anymore. This wasn't exotica. It was a groove he might have heard in 1940 at a jam session back home in Columbia. It was the sweetest sound he would make that day. The tape was not rolling.

Days of the Nü

Keith Metzger.

Even at 16, the guy looked like middle management at Radio Shack. His hair was pederast red, his skin was albino white and punctuating the two was every nerd's special project: My First Mustache. Keith, with whom I shared third period art class, was a very nice guy, but he was also the kind of guy who might have been too nice. He might have married the first girl he slept with. He might have taken the fall for getting caught with a sheet of acid in college. But all this niceness, this middle-class low expectation, is tempered by one thing in my remembrance of him:

Keith Metzger was a full-on metalhead.

A hesher. A dude. A burnout. And he was the first smart metalhead I ever met. He was the first among us to eschew the brainy Rush for being something not very metal at all, and also the first to embrace the signpost of grunge in Soundgarden. (This was in the very late 1980s.) And even still, even after he had started to notice girls—or, scratch that, notice something and turn ambiguously sexual—he still loved Iron Maiden. At the end of each school day, like some weird Mister Rogers in reverse, he would hang up the jacket and tie our school required and put on his oversize acid-washed denim jacket, meticulously arranged with buttons of his favorite bands, and emblazoned on the back with a lurid, full-size patch of a Maiden album cover.

We let him run with it. Most of us in third period art, by then having moved on to more adult tastes in postmodern sensations like

the Smiths or the Inspiral Carpets, secretly thought Keith's obsessions were beneath him—kid stuff. But we also knew that there was
no rule that said he couldn't indulge, either. One of the things the
Jesuits tried to hammer into our heads day after day was tolerance,
and in this rare instance of teenage civility, we practiced what they
preached. He was not punched in the nuts; he was not Maced with
shaving cream.

Thinking back on it now, I finally see what Keith saw in metal,
what it had to offer him: drama and escape, the promise of unreality,
of black-and-white good and evil and all the simplicity of human
motivation that childhood seems to promise and never delivers.
There was true bombast and emotion in the metal Keith listened to,
his Walkman blaring it as he set up lighting rigs for the school's
upcoming production of "Brigadoon." Keith's metal was of the
Dennis DeYoung Styx variety—a little Dungeons & Dragons, a little glam rock and also a little . . . Fosse. He wanted what everyone
wanted out of music back then: escape from the mundane fates he
secretly knew would one day befall each and every one of us.

And, yes, back then, in the late '80s, metal was strictly for nerds or
trash, and often did the twain meet, and to paraphrase Spinal Tap,
oh, how they danced. This was before nü metal, before the mooks
took over with a thunderous cry of *"Nerds!!!"* and threw the Keith
Metzgers of the world, the Dave Mustaines, the Rush fans out of the
game, against the wall and into the nearest Creed or Matchbox 20
show.

Since its inception, metal has maintained an uncomfortable coexis-
tence of mooks and nerds. Even way back in the early '70s, when
rock critic Lester Bangs coined the term to describe bands like
Black Sabbath, there had always been an audience overlap between
people who liked scumbag bands because they themselves were
scumbags and people who liked scumbag bands because they offered
the same comic-book elements of fantasy and escape that prog-rock
bands like Yes did. Basically, if you were a white male disenchanted—or, conversely, enchanted but didn't want to figure out
why—with the pansification of rock, with glam-era David Bowie on

one end of the spectrum and sweet baby James Taylor on the other, metal had lots to offer.

As the '70s morphed into the '80s, though, metal eventually embraced a sort of sublimated pansy element to its pantheon of disguise, and this is what we called the era of the hair band. Hair bands—the most notorious of which were Ratt and Poison and, the big daddy of them all, Guns N' Roses—copped a look and sound from glam, but swore the makeup was only there because it got them more pussy. True metalheads saw right through this, though, and this is where the metal underground started in earnest, giving way to the atomic splits and microgenre branding that now characterizes almost every form of popular (and nonpopular) music today.

Death metal. Speed metal. Christian metal. All of these, each one a punk rock unto itself, were formed in reaction against something that was going on in the broader pop world of metal proper during the '80s. And with the push-and-pull broadening of metal's horizons, other elements were brought into the mix: punk, post-punk, hip-hop, goth, industrial and so on. All of this got to the point where, if you wanted to speak to the metal masses, if you wanted to make true metal for the people, your language had to speak to all these factions.

The first result of this was a band like Metallica, who worked their way from indie obscurity to become both the thinking man's metal band and music to date-rape and burn stuff to. It's easy to forget now, what with drummer Lars Ulrich turning himself into the ultimate cyber-narc with his cred-stripping Napster debacle, but Metallica really are the U2 of metal; they've seen it all, done it all and probably ruined themselves twice. Remove Metallica another rock generation or two, add the "renaissance metal" feel that was the rhetoric of grunge and you've got the first wave of nü metal: Rage Against the Machine, Korn, Limp Bizkit.

First, a qualifier: What is nü metal? In reality, nü metal barely exists—in fact, nothingness is a popular theme among nü metal bands. Not to put too fine a point on it, but if it chug-a-chugs with the big hairy guitars, makes a stop-starty sound over and over, yarls or does the ninth-grade Satan death scream (alternating with busting a Caucasoid rhyme from time to time) and has some wack DJ scratching and interjecting his best Chuck D "Yyyeah!" every so often, it's probably nü metal.

For some time after Kurt Cobain and before the Wu-Tang Clan, the metal world woke up with a massive headache from the sickly-sweet pop tendencies of grunge and realized that right under their noses, directly in their bright blue-light ray, not men but *total fucking pussies* were in their domain. And what's more, dude, Judas Priest frontman Rob Halford was a fuckin' homo!

No more.

Enter nü metal, that genre of bands who have distilled their shared history and now wide-ranging influences into a white-hot form that doubles as aggravated assault, intent on expressing one emotion: anger.

But at what?

Honestly, dude? It's totally obvious: yer fucken mom and dad. Or so it seems. What else could incite the blinding rage about . . . well, nothing that so informs the nü-est of nü metal?

And so, to prove my hypothesis—that the whole world has gone c-r-a-z-y that this shit is actually in the mainstream now—I did what no one in America over 13 years of age has the patience (or time) to do: I sat down for a good hard listen to the country's most popular nü metal albums, poring over the cover art, getting that nasty head-phone sweat over my ears and, perhaps most important, perusing the lyric sheets.

Boy, is my sense of irony tired.

In the absence of Nirvana—and just about every other good band that, for one reason or another, imploded and failed to produce decent singles during the latter half of the '90s—nü metal has done well with the seemingly always-fledgling modern rock radio format. This, in a lot of cases, might cause some of the bands mentioned here to be identified as the new sound of what was called alternative music.

But make no mistake: There is nothing alternative about it. You can't swing a dead freshman these days without running into this sub-Bizkit band or that one. In fact, the influence of Limp Bizkit throughout just about all of modern rock these days is nothing short of epidemic; it's not even worth quibbling over what exactly lead singer Fred Durst and the boys are angry about. Take one listen to their last record, one look at MTV News, and it's obvious what's pissing off Durst: playa-hatas, charges of inciting riots, attorney bills, and bitchy pop starlets. In so many ways, Durst is not a whit different from Puffy Combs.

What's far more interesting—and telling about what makes these bands resonate with the kids—is looking into what the lesser bands are on about, what's propelling these more or less anonymous working bands, each one more angsty than the other, onto the charts for their brief spell.

What would my high school friend Keith make of the fact that the umlaut in nü was not in tribute to the glammy days of metal yore but, of all things, irony? (Irony had not played too well in metal prior to, say, 1998, unless it was the punk-metal Anthrax.) What would he make of the fact that Durst, definitely the biggest star in the nü metal world, tried to *rap?*

And what about all the anger? Could Keith's well-adjusted—if admittedly somewhat closeted—mind have handled that? Who or what can incite such anger? Beyond that, if kids today are supposed to be so smart and media-savvy, why can't they see through all this showbiz rage and know that they're being played by bad poets, overweight DJs and clueless hessians? As the Minutemen, an angular punk band that very well may have made the world ready for Primus, a zany, thrashing funk band that arguably could have paved the way for the Bizkit, would have asked, What makes a man start fires?

When it comes to cover art, the influence of the movie "Se7en" on nü metal cannot be underestimated; so much of the imagery—be it CD packaging or videos or promotional material—depicts a rustic world of science and higher learning gone horribly awry. Using calm colors and clinical typefaces, the imagery of nü metal tells us that there's a new face to the rock gore endemic to metal since its birth; where Gene Simmons of Kiss once spit blood and fire, nü metal swells and hemorrhages internally, trading the horror movie for the museum of medical oddities, where alien emotion matches up perfectly with alien body parts.

So much of nü metal all but quotes the greats of goth and industrial, and it doesn't even know it. That deep, dark, satanic yarl? We used to call that Scraping Foetus Off the Wheel. The dust-blown trench coat pose with the imposing guitar arpeggiation? The Mission UK.

Also, there are very few proper nouns in the lyrics. Nü metal avoids specifics like a politician who knows he's not saying anything anyway; why indict someone who might be listening? Time was, metal lyrics were divided into two distinct camps: Comic Book Blood 'n' Guts (images of hell, war, apocalypse and so on) or Comic Book Goodtime Poo-Say (Mötley Crüe, Poison et al.).

In nü metal, it's all . . . he said, she said, you, me and, ad infinitum, I. It's not a far cry from the singer/songwriter histrionics of the '70s, only all the other cultural signifiers try to point out what big balls this stuff has. If you're not convinced that this is the case, well, you're on to something.

> *"Why does it feel like night today?*
> *Something in here's not right today*
> *Why am I so uptight today? Paranoia's all I got left"*

This is not the text of a rejected ad for Prozac or Ativan; instead, this is how the debut album by Southern California quartet Linkin Park begins. On paper, these words seem earnest, dejected and desperate; on record, the overall attempt is to make them sear with blame. On paper, it sounds like the first day at a community college poetry workshop; on record, there's bloody spit shooting out with the words, a lunging forward of the torso, a complete bodily manifestation of disgust and rage, catharsis and breakdown.

At the same time, something in the delivery is just a little too WWF, a little too hot rod. You get the sense that the whole thing is all for show.

And that would make Linkin Park emblematic of nü metal bands everywhere—they're a bunch of kids looking for a pass because they're screwed up, trying to trade in dysfunction for cool points. They're the sound of the Ritalin generation, all Eminem cadences laid over soaring choruses and hackneyed scratching; it's all so derivative, so by numbers, so strangely—underneath it all—eager to please that, like so many other times during my days spent listening to nü metal records, I feel ill at ease. Not because I was being rocked out of my skull but because—there's no nice way to say this—I'm embarrassed for them.

I'm not sure what this music is, but it's pretty fair to say that it's not rock 'n' roll. I mean, insofar as rock 'n' roll is a pose, maybe it is that, but nothing else. The horrible truth about nü metal is that it's all a pose. It's like watching a 9-year-old smoking a cigarette: awful, but so stupid you can only hope he learns something from it.

Things don't get any better with the single off their album—at No. 5 on the Billboard modern rock chart after 27 weeks. (The album is platinum.) "One Step Closer" would have you believe, with its refrain of "one step closer to the edge and I'm about to break," that it's some nod to Grandmaster Flash's "The Message," some paean to a modern world where people no longer count.

Wrong. Scratch the surface, and the song depicts the same kind of garden-variety high school psychodrama you usually get from a good episode of "Boston Public": "I find the answers aren't so clear/Wish I could find a way to disappear." To hear Linkin Park tell it, these boys don't need to *rock*—they need some Paxil.

Papa Roach, a Northern California band that has been around in some incarnation since 1993 and whose 15 minutes seem to be up—a consequence of their overtly pretty-boy looks, perhaps, and the instant MTV overexposure that such a thing can cause—struck a pose even more vulnerable than Linkin Park's camp-counselor-friendly antics. In "Broken Home," we find our hero going through the darkest hours of his parent's divorce: "I'm stuck in between my parents/I wish I had someone to talk to." What follows is some major riffage, followed by a curdling scream of *"Bro-Kan-Hohm!"*

It's hard to tell if Papa Roach are masters at trivializing what's easily one of the hardest things a kid can ever face, or if they just happen to be great at pastiche, at playing for cheap sentiment. Either way, as the song plays out, you can almost see the e-mails scroll across the bottom of the "Total Request Live" screen: "Carson, what's up? This is Scott from Champaign, what up dawg?!!! Can you play Papa Roach's 'Broken Home'? My parents fight and stuff, and like, Papa Roach are off the heezy. Thanx!"

I said it before, I'll say it again: I'm not sure what this is, but it's not rock 'n' roll.

Record companies have found a way to make the nü metal bands—save for a handful of industry-committed titans like Bizkit—as faceless and replaceable as they have made the hip-hop artists; if you don't believe me, in six months check for most of the names mentioned in this piece in cutout bins everywhere: Disturbed, Papa Roach and so on. To say nothing of the likes of Crazy Town, Incubus or Staind.

But if nü metal takes so many cues from hip-hop, hasn't anyone in its camp noticed how much the mainstream has squashed the life out of hip-hop? Hasn't anyone noticed how replaceable St. Louis rapper Nelly is? What makes these nü bands think that the same won't be true for them? Certainly no prevailing sense of originality; nü metal bands revel in their uniform sound and look (one interchangeable white boy in dreads or white G, one classic pot-smoking hessian, one S/M—or Manson—freak and the fat "ethnic" DJ). To most kids, one group is as good as the other.

The bands don't seem to get it, because a grandstanding pose that passes for something extreme or rebellious is still lingua franca for these bands. Check out this gem, from Fear Factory's "Shock":

> *"I will be the power urge*
> *Shock to the system*
> *Electrified, amplified*
> *Shock to the system."*

Dude, I got a shocker for you: You are the system. And you're as expected as rain. At this point, in a mass landscape of boy bands and pop stars, a hibernating underground that seems to at long last know better than to play the Man's game and significant exceptions like the post-grunge Creed, the milky Matchbox 20 and stalwarts like U2, nü metal bands are the only thing passing for mainstream rock music today.

But the record business is playing these kids instead of demo tapes. As Fear Factory would say, "Deeper into this abyss/Weighted down and sinking fast." They probably didn't have the music industry in mind, but it works. They're screwed.

Where my man Keith relished the fantasy that metal once provided, Fear Factory and their kin make a huuuuge deal out of shouting over and over again, *"This Is Reality!"*—in much the same way that my other man, Beavis, revealed to the world a few years back that he was Cornholio. Both claims have equal reservoirs of believability.

Here's another shocker: Women fare as well in nü metal as they do in its metal antecedents and gangsta rap. Which is to say, not very well at all. For all its props to hip-hop, the boyz of the nü don't give love to the ladies at all. Even where a guy like Tupac Shakur would try to make restitution for all his years of "bitch" this and "ho" that by making a nice song about his mama every once in a while, women are portrayed in nü metal as alternately "insane," "fucked up" or some other such nonsense. Everybody's doing it for the nookie, which, in the music of the Bizkit and their acolytes, appears to be little more than a strangely disembodied box to be displayed and humiliated at every opportunity.

That's why Kittie—a quartet of ladies just out of their teens who pummel and scrape with the best of them—makes my heart soar with glee. On their debut "Spit," the band brings a feminine touch to the mook revolution, and far from pansying it up with melody and harmony, the gals instead take their flair for drama and make something distinctly darker. (If only because the ninth-grade Satan death scream coming from a pretty girl—shades of Linda Blair abound in the music of Kittie—is that much scarier.)

Kittie, when it all comes down, are incredibly close to being a proper goth band. The dyed hair, the lipstick, the paleness—each member looks like a different side of the actress Fairuza Balk—will take you right back to that band you saw open for goth band Sisters of Mercy back in '88, right before you went preppy.

Still, even the ladies can't help using the nü as an airing ground for their most pedestrian residual adolescent angst, something that's seemingly beneath their abilities. Songs like "Do You Think I'm a Whore" and their single from a few months back, "Brackish," revel in a confounding game of low self-esteem, blame throwing and empty profanity that seems to be part and parcel of nü metal. The only thing separating Kittie from those girls that television host Maury Povich is always sending to boot camp is a record contract.

Disturbed, a Chicago quartet, is one of the newer entries on the mook mosh pile, and we can tell the band is serious because the singer is bald. These guys mean business. On "Voices"—a single that just dropped off the modern rock Top 20 chart—the boys squeeze sub-Metallica riffage into a funky little package that'd make the Red Hot Chili Peppers seem puny. "So, what's up . . . I'm gonna make you do some freaky shit now/Insane, you're gonna die when you listen to me" is how my favorite part goes, and it'd be—hey!—disturbing if it, like, made any sense at all. By and large, the syntax of nü metal is a mess.

With song after song about uncertainty and confusion, after a while it becomes pretty clear that this isn't rock music, this is panty-waist bullshit about some dude's *feelings*. Was this really what Woodstock '99 was about? The confusion over how to be a man, over how to act in a schizoid society?

Puh-leeze.

In so much of nü metal, there's a nasal whine that on first listen seems to hark back to our most wonderful exemplars of insurgency down through the rock age: Bob Dylan, Johnny Rotten, Hank Williams Sr. But where these guys had something of a real bite back there where the nasal drip does ever flow, when Fred Durst does it, it's a minstrelsy of sorts: He's dying to create the old rock drama, the kind that really did make you wanna break stuff, instead of just a mutually agreed-upon soundtrack to break stuff to.

But here's the rub: It's not their fault. Can you really blame nü metal bands for cluelessly pumping up a rage that has no center? Can you truly fault them for living entirely without reference points? I don't know.

The guys in Papa Roach or Linkin Park grew up in a time when—we must admit this now, as hard as it might be—rock was groping around for a new relevance, and only finding it intermittently. Instead, it usually found gimmicks, and that's why Durst is famously as schooled in the work of Madonna and *Licensed to Ill*–era Beastie Boys as he is in the Red Hot Chili Peppers and Poison. The poor sonuvabitch, like the rest of his generation, had to take it where he could get it.

But I do know this: We should not blame Marilyn Manson for nü metal, nor should we poke the finger at the Beasties, Rage, the Peppers, NIN or even the Wu. Instead, maybe we should blame Glenn Frey, as well as every other piece-of-shit rock star who disappointed these kids in the '80s when they were so desperately needed. Because of such an oversight, all these kids make the music such a broken house of blues might dictate: confused, enraged and laden with a self-pity that, if you're not careful, you just might mistake for sincerity.

These kids aren't just faking the funk; they're faking the rock. And it's hard to tell which is worse.

ERIK DAVIS

Only a Northern Song

When he wasn't writing about hobbits, J.R.R. Tolkien studied Northern European languages at Oxford, and the most important thing he did as a scholar was to transform our experience of the old Anglo-Saxon poem *Beowulf*. Before Tolkien, academics treated the work as a linguistic ruin, historically useful but too full of stupid monsters to count as literature. In contrast, Tolkien not only argued that *Beowulf* was a fully realized work of imagination, but that the poem's power derived precisely from the presence of the monsters. Tolkien pointed out that, unlike the baddies in Homer, where even an asshole cyclops like Polyphemus could still be the son of a glorious god like Poseidon, the monsters of the Northern imagination were irredeemably horrible—a chaotic, almost Lovecraftian crew that would, at the end of time, gobble up men, the gods, and the cosmos itself. The fact that the monsters were destined to win the ultimate battle explains the peculiar melancholic power of the Northern heroes, who fought with courage but without hope.

Something of this imagination is still alive and kicking, at least in black metal, a thoroughly globalized music that nonetheless comes mainly from the land of the ice and snow. The glory days of Scandinavian black metal began over a decade ago, when Oslo gloomsters like Mayhem, Emperor, DarkThrone, and Burzum hoisted the Satanic banners nicked from '80s bands like Venom and Bathory over the ever mutating engines of extreme riffage. While embracing the postmodern nihilism of death metal, with its speed, atonal aggression, and growled, unintelligible lyrics, Norwegian black metalers also tuned into the more spectral energies of, well, evil. Cookie Monster was still on the mic, but now he was wearing corpse paint.

In terms of Tolkien's reading of *Beowulf,* you could say that black metalers identified with the monsters of chaos—the most obvious and available one being Satan. But as the scene mushroomed across the North, many bands shifted their allegiance from the enemy of God to His pagan predecessors, especially Odin and Thor. In other words, the groups didn't just identify with the monsters, they also wore the grim mask of the Northern warrior. By combining bummer vibes with righteous gloom, the subgenre's evil pose could become as extreme as its sound, leading to a dark aesthetic so fantastically over-the-top that it neutralizes all attempts at satire from the get-go. It's easy to make fun of the Scorpions, but where do you start, for example, with a Finnish band that calls itself Impaled Nazarene?

Writing in the esoteric journal *Aorta,* the Austrian occultist Kadmon calls black metal "a werewolf romanticism." Obviously, this sort of mythic indulgence can go south fast: Black metal has played a role in the recent resurgence of Germanic pagan fascism, and racism continues to dog the fringes of the subculture. But the more lasting outcome of this romanticism is inclusive, at least musically speaking. Because once black metal opened the door to romanticism, it could not prevent the Gothic from waltzing in, spoiling the Viking gruff with absinthe and lace. Though genre-splicing is an endless game with metal, a lot of music now marketed as black metal embraces gloomy melodies, epic keyboards, female vocals, Hammer-film ambience, neomedieval acoustic guitars, even flutes. Though often "progressive" in feel, these steps are really moves toward accessibility, or at least listenability—in other words, pop.

That's why the German label Angelstar was wise to subtitle its recent two-CD *Blessed by the Night* compilation as "dark metal" rather than black. Like the Nuclear Blast compilation series *Beauty in Darkness,* the Angelstar discs highlight the more hummable wing of the music. The first cut, by the Americans Aesma Daaeva, shows how far we have come from the Beelzebub bop of the early Oslo scene: A superbly trained female voice chants "O Death" over a classical guitar, whose arpeggios are soon overtaken by mild blast-beats and keyboards lifted from the first *Halloween* movie. Songs like Tristania's "Beyond the Veil" and Vintersorg's "Svälivinter" feature wailing Valkyries, Renaissance pluckings, and thoroughly gendered duets of beauty and the beast. Both metal and Goth have long had classical fixations, and their fused drive toward the operatic reaches its apex in the contribution by Therion, a glorious slice of pomp that not only sounds like it's from *Carmina Burana* but actually is from *Carmina Burana*.

Blessed by the Night still features plenty of gut-shrieks, Satan chants, and mispronunciations of "Samhain." Satyricon serves up an admirable death metal bass-drum blur, memorably characterized by the Heavy Metal FAQ lodged at www.anus.com as "an undulating wall of sound that conditions listeners to act out the diabolical bidding of the bands and their master, Satan." In their cut "Fallen Skin Dimensions," the Austrian act Third Moon present a perfect blend of conventional tunesmithery and nihilistic mess, pushing their syncopated beats and witchy melodies to the edge of incoherence. And Dimmu Borgir, a band popular enough to have garnered a nomination for the Norwegian equivalent of a Grammy, bring an appealing trollish swing to their relatively blistering "Moonchild Domain." Chords slide by like broken slabs of ice, while evil elven keyboards play eighth-note melodies that skitter around like dolls in a mad Santa's shop.

In some ways, the mainstreaming of black metal resembles the transformation of the Klingons on *Star Trek:* Originally barbaric and one-dimensional bad guys, they grow sympathetic as we learn of their myths, their rituals, their women. From a commercial point of view, this makes perfect sense, though it's precisely this kind of accommodation to conventionally human taste that extreme metal has long attempted to purge through its sonic nihilism. "True" black metalheads bemoan even the snarling likes of Dimmu Borgir, and most of *Blessed by the Night* would make them gag.

And you can't really fault them. It's tough to go velvet while still getting medieval on your ass, and much of *Blessed by the Night* resembles Enigma on steroids. The return of glossy rock drums is an abject failure, the keyboards often sound like they were lifted from old video games, and the cut-rate Dead Can Dance moves lack that band's flare for exotica. On the other hand, if you allow yourself a little of that old suspension of disbelief, this eclectic and emotionally dramatic music has plenty of room for marvels. In "View From Nihil," the latest Mayhem singer sounds like Mark E. Smith channeling Beckett on a drill sergeant's megaphone, while the Swedish band Otyg digs so deep into their folk roots they sound like Danzig playing a hoedown for dwarves. Still, most of these bands simply do not have the chops or the taste to back up their lofty aspirations. They fall flat, like Lucifer stubbing his toe on the gates of hell.

One blackish metal band that has amassed enough D&D hit points to risk such adventures is the Swedish group Opeth, which has built up a small but fanatical cult since their wrenching 1994 debut, *Orchid*. Avoiding the cornier trappings of Goth metal and the Satanic hordes, Opeth still paint on an epic canvas, sounding at times like black metal's answer to '70s King Crimson. Restless with moods and melodic lines, their impressively long songs flow and unfold over shifting blocks of rhythmic ice. But even their wankier passages remain rooted to the riff—which gets Opeth's mastermind, Mikael Åkerfeldt, a golden star in my prog rock book. He has also perfected the dynamic tension that has driven many of the most expressive metal bands since Led Zeppelin: the interplay of quiet and crude, of shivering acoustic passages and brutal electric squalls. In fact, Opeth's "blackness" lies less in the music then in Åkerfeldt's morbid lyric obsessions (death, despair, misery) and tonsil-shredding vocals, which he nonetheless varies with what has become, over the course of five albums, an increasingly convincing "clean" voice. Lately, he's even been willing to slip in ballads about—eek!—girls.

The new *Blackwater Park* continues to open up Opeth's sound. Producer Steve Wilson, who fronts a pop-prog act called Porcupine Tree that manages to be both off-kilter and straight ahead, fills out Opeth's sound with shinier riffs, nifty vocal filters, and the occasional electronic blurp. Despite delightful eruptions of atonality and old-school prog moves, many songs here are more repetitious and conventionally structured, and so wear their length less justifiably than on 1999's amazing *Still Life*. Still, you would be remiss to call *Blackwater Park* "pop," even in the sense that *Blessed by the Night* is pop. While the 11-minute "The Drapery Falls" starts out with catchy choruses and lots of acoustic strumming, the tune gets twisted after the five-minute mark, with ice-cave vocals, crazy Frippertronics, and manic beats from the two Uruguayans named Martin who back up Åkerfeldt and guitarist Peter Lindfren on bass and drums.

Despite lyrics about coffins, crypts, and drapery, Opeth's Romantic spirit manifests itself less in Gothic trappings than in the strange vulnerability with which Åkerfeldt presents bleak and blasted emotions. Åkerfeldt's melancholy is now as believable as his rage, and the album's strongest passages are generally the mellow ones. After twisting and turning through a fistful of angry riffs, "The Leper Affinity" ends with the man on the grand piano, tinkling out rainy-day ruminations that simply drift away to a diminished end. Even his "evil" vocals don't communicate Viking fury so much as the desperation and weakness with which we submit finally to anger and despair, like a trapped animal or the "derelict child" mentioned in "The Funeral Portrait." In essence, Åkerfeldt does for the black metal bad guy what John Gardner did for Beowulf's foe in his book *Grendel:* He gets inside the monster to reveal its sad confusion, its helpless knowledge that it will, in the end, be swallowed up by the very darkness that fills its sinews with might.

Walking on Thin Ice

Platinum and gold. The walls of Courtyard Management's office are lined with discs commemorating prodigious feats of unit-shifting in far-flung territories of the globe. Located in the somnolent Oxfordshire village of Sutton Courtenay, Courtyard is nerve centre for one of the world's most successful groups. But all previous triumphs (*Kid A* winning the Grammy for Best Alternative Album, the anointing of *OK Computer* as 'Best Album of All Time' by the readers of *Q*) surely pale next to the ultimate accolade: making it onto the cover of *The Wire*.

Seriously, though: maybe your first thought on picking up this issue was 'whatthefuck?!,' and maybe that's an understandable reaction. After all, Radiohead are a group who have chalked up multi-platinum sales in 50 countries. I haven't done the maths (I'm not that crazy), but it does strike me as perfectly conceivable that the total career sales of every single other artist featured in this current issue, totted up, still might not match the global sales of *OK Computer*, Radiohead's biggest selling album to date. And there is a potent argument that a group with this kind of commercial heft and such a degree of mainstream consensus of praise behind them simply has no place on the front cover of a magazine known for championing mavericks and margin-dwellers.

But Radiohead, I will argue, have earned it. Consider the facts: late last year, three albums rejuvenated the moribund concept of 'post-rock', Sigur Rós's *Agætis Byrjún*, Godspeed You Black

Emperor!'s *Lift Yr Skinny Fists Like Antennas To Heaven*, and
Radiohead's *Kid A*. All three tampered with post-rock's increasingly proforma formula in significant ways: Godspeed! bringing
political angst to this generally abstract and dispassionate genre;
Sigur Rós adding human songfulness to what's usually instrumental mood music; *Kid A* doing a bit of both. But only one of this
'post-rock reborn!' triumvirate entered the UK and US album
charts at Number One. Now its sister-release *Amnesiac*—drawn
from the same sessions as *Kid A*; indeed at one point the two
records were set to be a double album—has repeated this extraordinary feat.

What's fascinating, and unprecedented, is just how Radiohead
pulled off this swerve from the path seemingly mapped out for them
(*OK Computer* had left them only a step away from becoming the
biggest rock outfit on the planet). For whether it's Autechre-ish
glitchtronic contraptions like "Pull/Pulk Revolving Doors," the
'Scott Walker scored by Penderecki' balladry of "How To Disappear Completely," the Spirit Of Eden/On Land vapourscape of
"Treefingers," the Faust-meets-Mingus interstellar overdrive of
"The National Anthem," the samples of computer compositions by
Paul Lansky on "Idioteque," or the thick orchestral haze on "Dollars & Cents," reminiscent of the arrangements on Alice Coltrane's
early 70s albums such as *Universal Consciousness*, Radiohead are currently operating as mainstream ambassadors for many of the musical innovators this magazine cherishes.

Asked to ponder this mystery, Thom Yorke—Radiohead's singer
and by all accounts its aesthetic tillerman—shrugs it off as simply
not that remarkable. "Maybe we just took some sort of left turn," he
muses. Relaxed and healthy looking, he barely resembles the gaunt,
ghostfaced figure that appears in the *OK Computer* world tour documentary *Meeting People Is Easy*, harrowed by the endless grind of
interviews/meet and greets/photoshoots/soundchecks/ligs. Nor is
he the prickly, blood-from-a-stone interviewee of legend. There are
moments, though, where it occurs to me that 'genial, laidback,
unassuming' might just be another shield: a more sly strategy of
self-protection than the 'fools not gladly suffered' persona of old.

'Downplay everything' seems to be the new Radiohead media relations policy—the canny pre-emptive disarming of any accusations of autohype or delusions of avant grandeur. So Yorke suggests that *Kid A* was "not as much of a radical gesture as some said." And guitarist/multiinstrumentalist Jonny Greenwood, speaking by phone from Spain a few days later, claims Radiohead just picked up where they had left off on *OK Computer*. "With us, it's never going to be a case of 'let's tear up the blueprint and start from scratch.' When the *Kid A* reviews came out accusing of us being wilfully difficult, I was like, 'If that was true, we'd have done a much better job of it.' It's not that challenging—everything's still four minutes long, it's melodic."

Such self-effacing professions of modest ambition are rather at odds with the impression given by Radiohead in the press blitz around *Kid A* last autumn, which painted a picture of a group almost tearing itself to bits in the struggle to achieve total aesthetic renewal. Yorke spoke of how he had even contemplated changing their name in order to make a break with Radiohead's past recordings, towards which he felt utter alienation. Instead of self-destruction, Radiohead eventually settled on self-deconstruction: discarding or tampering with the two elements most celebrated by fans and critics alike: their guitar sound, and Yorke's singing and lyrics. *Kid A* is largely devoid of guitars (Jonny Greenwood preferring to play the Ondes Martenot (an early electronic instrument that dates back to 1928), arrange a string orchestra, even play the recorder). And *Amnesiac's* slight-return to rock is not going to get the fans transcribing fret fingerings and posting 'guitar tabs' up on their Webzines, as they did with *OK Computer*. As for Yorke's singing, on *Kid A/Amnesiac*, studio technology and unusual vocal technique are both applied to dyslexify his already oblique, fragmented words. Yorke has said he will never allow the lyrics to be printed and that listeners are expressly not meant to focus on them.

Radiohead's 'not such a radical shift really' line is also belied by Yorke's evident glee at the way *Kid A* upset his 'peers' in the Britrock aristocracy. The album was clearly taken as some kind of stinging reproach by a number of underachieving and deeply compromised Britpopsters, including accusations of "cowardice" from Oasis.

"We've obviously riled them in some way," agrees Yorke. Perhaps the Gallagher brothers' broadside is related to Britpop's core ideology of 'make it big at any cost,' a rhetoric of shooting for the charts which denigrated older indie rock idealism as defeatist, obscurantist, even elitist. Not only did *Kid A* resurrect a different concept of ambition—artistic growth as opposed to sales bloat—but it interfered with Radiohead fulfilling their 'proper' destiny: becoming a front rank, U2-sized megagroup.

A brief history of Radiohead: how they got here from there. Formed in Oxford by five schoolfriends—Thom Yorke, brothers Jonny and Colin Greenwood, Phil Selway and Ed O'Brien—the group first grabbed attention in 1992 with "Creep," a single that got nowhere on its first release in Britain, but became a massive hit in post-Nirvana America when modern rock radio programmers picked up on it. In many ways, the 'Grunge ballad' sound of "Creep" and its lyrical stance (maladjustment and ressentiment akin to the outcast protagonist of "Smells Like Teen Spirit") made Radiohead an English equivalent to Nirvana. The two groups had similar influences and idols (Pixies, REM, Sonic Youth), were fuelled by similar distaste for the phony, and faced similar accusations of wallowing in misery. But the crucial word there is 'English': you can imagine Kurt Cobain, if he'd chosen to live, probably going the unplugged troubadour route, stripping down his sound to let his plaintive songs stand naked and alone, folky and forlorn. You could never imagine him doing a *Kid A*, plunging deeper into studio science. Therein lies the vast, enduring gulf between American and British ideas of rock.

By 1995's *The Bends*, the English art rock element was starting to come to the fore. Pop musicians and movie stars started turning up to their shows; stoners and lapsed ravers turned onto the sheer drug-conducive luxuriance of their sound. But it was 1997's *OK Computer* that really transformed Radiohead into the rock group it was, OK for electronica headz to dig. It was also the album where Yorke and Co started to complicate the anthemic qualities of their earlier music in earnest, by deep immersion in such avant staples as Miles Davis's *Bitches Brew*.

A sort of semi-concept album about technology and alienation, *OK Computer*'s sheer magnitude—of sound, thematics, aspiration—served time on Britpop, replacing its laddish anti-intellectualism and vacant hedonism with the glamor of literacy and angst. Noel and Liam are right to feel goaded: Radiohead are the Anti-Oasis, and *OK Computer*'s massive popular success, eclipsing the Gallagher brothers' cocaine-blighted/bloated *Be Here Now*, announced the closure of an entire era of Britrock. Yet touring and promoting the album for much of 1998 convinced Yorke that it was still too mired in rock tradition, too epic. "'It was still pressing all the correct buttons," he says. When *Q*'s readership infamously voted *OK Computer* the Best Album of All Time (an error of passion perhaps, but certainly preferable to the usual pantheon of *Pet Sounds/Revolver/Astral Weeks/London Calling*), Radiohead had become rock icons in the most old fashioned sense—the singer as seer, oracle, figurehead, spokesperson.

"I tell you what's really ridiculous, going into a bookshop and there's all these books about yourself," Yorke says of the multiple cut and paste Radiohead biographies that came out in *Computer*'s wake. "In a way, it feels like you're already dead. So you've got a kind of license to start again."

Worn out by the experiences documented on *Meeting People Is Easy* (like touring America's infamous 'shed circuit' of 10,000-capacity, corporate-sponsored venues) and the self-consciousness feedback syndrome induced by being over-interviewed and reading pseudopsychoanalytical interpretations of his work ("People presume everything you write is completely personal . . . it feels weird, like someone walking over your grave"), Yorke spiralled into a black period of confusion and creative block. "Melodies became an embarrassment to me," he told an interviewer last year; he hated the lyrics he was coming up with. Even the sound of his voice made Yorke nauseous. "It did my head in that whatever I did with my voice, it had that particular set of associations. And there were lots of similar bands coming out at the time, and that made it even worse. I couldn't stand the sound of me even more." Embarking on the fraught, spasmodic sessions for *Kid A/Amnesiac*, he "got really into the idea of my voice being another one of the instruments, rather than this precious, focus thing all the time."

This instrumentalisation of the lead singer was just one facet of a total deconstruction of Radiohead as rock group, instigated by Yorke. As guitarist Ed O'Brien put it, the members had to learn "how to be a participant in a song without playing a note." In a sense, every member took on the role of Brian Eno in Roxy Music: a non-musician producer/catalyst, abandoning their designated instrumental function and grappling with unfamiliar sound-genera-tion devices as if they were toys, with a childlike wonder and joy. "It's not about being a guitarist in a rock band, it's about having an instrument in front of you and you're really excited by it," says Yorke. "It's like with Jonny playing Ondes Martenot on . . . just about everything! We couldn't stop him! We had to beg him to play guitar on 'Morning Bell.'"

Greenwood says the Ondes Martenot obsession dates back to hearing it used in Olivier Messaien's Turangalîla Symphony when he was 15. "I spent years reading all these descriptions of them, I couldn't even find a photograph, and then two years ago I finally got hold of one, and they're fantastic. The best way to describe it is a very accurate Theremin that you have far more control of. The most famous use of the Martenot is the *Star Trek* theme, and it sounds like a woman singing. When it's played well, you can really emulate the voice. I get annoyed with electronic instruments because I reckon the Martenot is a bit of a peak."

With producer and "sixth member" Nigel Godrich gradually coming round to the new approach, Radiohead embarked upon all kinds of Eno-esque oblique strategies: working on dozens of songs at once; moving on to something different as soon as it got boring or blocked; splitting into two groups engaged in different activities. "It's like you're dabbling, but at the same time, when something really comes off, it's all down on tape," says Yorke. "Nigel's really into the idea of capturing a performance, even if we're doing pure electronic stuff. So it's never like we just program stuff and let it run. There always had to be something else going on, processing in real-time."

Another model was Holger Czukay's jam/slice/splice productions for Can. "Dollars & Cents," one of *Amnesiac*'s highlights, was edited down from an 11 minute improvisation. "It was incredibly boring," laughs Yorke, "but it's that Holger thing of chop-chop-chop, making what seems like drivel into something coherent." Then orchestral strings—arranged by Greenwood and recorded in Dorchester Abbey—"were added to give it a sort of authority."

No strangers to the studio craft of overdubbing and effects, on *Kid A/Amnesiac* Radiohead finally and utterly abandoned the performance model of rock recording and went fully into concocting sonic fictions using the mixing desk as instrument. Answering a fan's query on Radiohead's Web forum, Greenwood talked about being obsessed with "the whole artifice of recording. I see it like this: a voice into a microphone onto a tape, onto your CD, through your speakers is all as illusory and fake as any synthesizer—it doesn't put Thom in your front room. But one is perceived as 'real,' the other somehow 'unreal' . . . It's the same with guitars versus samplers. It was just freeing to discard the notion of acoustic sounds being truer." Speaking on the phone, Greenwood says the idea was influenced by reading Michael Chanan's 1995 meditation on recording, *Repeated Takes*. "The more concerts we do, the more dissatisfied we get with trying to reproduce the live sound on a record. In a way, it can't be done, and that's a relief really, when you accept that, and recording just becomes a different thing."

The most striking departures from the real-time three-guitar group sound are pieces like *Kid A*'s title track (with its exquisitely wistful music-box chime and melted-candle Yorke vocal, it's worthy of Curd Duca or Boards Of Canada) and *Amnesiac*'s "Like Spinning Plates," whose dissassociated drift reminds me of Robert Wyatt's *Rock Bottom* updated for the IDM era. "Plates" is partly built from an earlier song called "I Will" played backwards. Says Yorke, "We'd turned the tape around, and I was in another room, heard the vocal melody coming backwards, and thought, 'That's miles better than the right way round,' then spent the rest of the night trying to learn the melody."

Although some have accused Radiohead of jumping on the electronica bandwagon, Yorke says his interest in Aphex-type music actually predates the group's 1993 debut *Pablo Honey*. "When the Warp thing was first happening, I was really into things like Sweet Exorcist's 'Per Clonk.' It sounded really amazing coming out an enormous PA system. All that Warp stuff made the bassbins blow with their turbo sounds." Studying art and English at Exeter University in the early 90s, he even participated in a Techno-influenced rock group called Flickernoise as a sideline from Radiohead, but found working with sequencers too frustrating. After the *OK Computer* tour, though, utterly burned on music containing guitars and singing, Yorke bought the entire Warp back catalogue and started ordering obscure IDM records via the internet. For a long while during the *Kid A* sessions, he was totally uninterested in melody, just into exploring texture and rhythm. The result was tracks like *Kid A*'s "Idioteque," which sounds like a PiL/"Death Disco"–style twist on two-step Garage, but is actually "an attempt to capture that exploding beat sound where you're at the club and the PA's so loud, you know it's doing damage." On *Amnesiac*, the dirty 808 bass of "Pull/Pulk Revolving Doors" invites you to reimagine Yorke's mid–80s adolescence—not pining indoors to REM's *Murmur* and The Smiths' *Hatful Of Hollow*, but spraying graf and breakdancing in deserted shopping centres alongside LFO.

All this mixing-up sounds very post-rock—unsurprisingly, a banner behind which Greenwood, ever so courteously, declines to rally. More tellingly, it's also very post-punk: the Lydon-esque rhetoric of leaving rock for dead ("I never wanted to be in a fucking rock group," Yorke told *Spin*), the post-Eno/dub embrace of the studio, the forays into electronics, black dance rhythm, jazz. Radiohead are possibly the very last of a generation of groups formatively influenced by the 1979–81 moment. Too young (all are in their early thirties) to have experienced Joy Division, Magazine, etc as they actually happened, they encountered it through the time-honoured "older brother syndrome." (Or, in the case of Jonny and bassist Colin Greenwood, an older sister.)

Greenwood's guitar sound—more audible on *Amnesiac*, which has a couple of Smiths-y tunes but is nothing like the "back to normal

Radiohead business" it was touted as—is firmly in the postblues, non-riff lineage that runs from Tom Verlaine through Will Sergeant/Johnny Marr/Terry Bickers: that plangent dazzle-ripple-chime. "Our guitars are more clitoris substitutes than phallus ones—we stroke them in a nicer, gentler way," Greenwood once said; when I bring this up, he says he nicked the line from Slowdive, another Thames Valley group. "I think guitars are over-idolized as instruments. All the guitarists I've ever liked have had the Bernard Sumner approach. It's about not practicing. I like what Tom Waits said about only ever picking up an instrument if he's going to write a song."

Radiohead's very name comes from an obscure song by Talking Heads, whose Eno-produced 1979 LP *Remain In Light* was a life-changing event for Yorke, both musically and lyrically. "I'd listened to it endlessly but never looked at the words," he recalls, "and when I finally did, it really freaked me out. When they made that record, they had no real songs, just wrote it all as they went along. [David] Byrne turned up with pages and pages, and just picked stuff up and threw bits in all the time. And that's exactly how I approached *Kid A* . . . Jerry Harrison, their keyboard player, turned up to one of our gigs, just walked into the dressing room. Poor chap, after we realized who he was, he got grilled for hours on *Remain In Light*—'Are they any loops or did you just play it all?' And they played it all, even though it sounds like tape-loops. Do you know the story about 'Overload'? They'd read about Joy Division for the first time in *NME*, thought 'That sounds interesting,' and decided to do a tune based on what they thought Joy Division would be like, never having heard them."

Two other things about Radiohead also strike me as very post-punk. First is their quiet but steadfast insistence on "total control," which recalls PiL's (largely rhetorical) notion of itself as a "communications company" using a major label's marketing muscle but essentially remaining autonomous. In Radiohead's case, "total control" encompasses not just the license to indulge themselves that underpins *OK Computer, Kid A* and *Amnesiac*, but a host of other aspects: the way they've kept their operational base outside London; the obsessive attention to detail that goes into their artwork (*Amnesiac* comes encased as a hardback library book, complete with much-stamped slip; inside, there are lavish color plate illustrations by Yorke's alter ego Tchocky and university pal Stanley Donwood); the group's Website (also designed by Donwood), via which Radiohead maintain direct contact with its fans. Shrugging off the PiL analogy ("We could never do a record on a par with *Metal Box*, let alone *Flowers Of Romance* . . . and I'm no Lydon: I can't keep up the attitude!"), Yorke likes to stress that their independence within the corporate mainstream is precarious, dependent on the massive success of *OK Computer.* Greenwood admits, "We are a little fascistic in how and where our music is heard, but then we can be. If we were struggling, I'm sure we'd sell our music to anybody just to carry on."

The other spirit of 79 quality is Radiohead's relentless bleakness, an alienation that is never entirely private, sourced merely in individual neurosis. Reversing the old post-punk dictum, one might describe it as "the political is personal." Yorke has described *Kid A/Amnesiac* as being about "bearing witness." The things witnessed range from the connivings of politicians (*Amnesiac*'s "You And Whose Army?" is about British Prime Minister Tony Blair, based on direct encounters that came about through Yorke's involvement in the Jubilee 2000 campaign to write off Third World Debt), to a wider sense of the world becoming ever more overcontrolled, and at the same time out of control.

You can pick up this feeling from the lyrics: oblique images of running out of future, Darwinian dog eat dog struggle, cannibalism, an emotional "Ice Age coming" (an unwitting echo of Margaret Drabble's novel *The Ice Age*, a counterpart to punk in British literature which captured a mid-70s moment of malaise and crisis in the UK). More than the words, though, it's audible as a certain tenor, even timbre, of voice. "You And Whose Army?" offers words of defiance in a voice that sounds like all the fight has been kicked out of it (which is why it works in 2001, where an update of "Stand Down Margaret" would seem facile). Yorke is literally voicing (rather than articulating) contemporary feelings of dislocation, dispossession, numbness, impotence, paralysis; widely felt impulses to withdraw and disengage that are perfectly logical, dispirited responses to the bankruptcy of Centrist politics, which ensure that everyone remains equally disenchanted and aggrieved.

"It's all so part of the fabric of everything, even the artwork," Yorke says, referring to the recurring, Art Brut–ish schizo-scrawled motifs of Grim Reapers and Weeping Bears. "I couldn't really say it directly so much, but it's there—the feeling of being a spectator and not being able to take part. I was really conscious of not wanting to use a sledgehammer to bang people over the head with it. It's pretty difficult to put into songs. In a way you have to wait until it's a personal issue or experience." In June 1999, the attempt to deliver Jubilee 2000's "Drop The Debt" petition to the G8 summit in Cologne was when it became personal. The petition's presenters, a group which included Yorke and U2's Bono, were outwitted by the G8 politicians, who denied them their desired photo opportunity in front of the conference's building. "We were made to walk down the back streets, and it was fucking surreal—we had these German military police escorting us down a tiny pedestrian shopping street, we're carrying this fucking banner, surrounded by bemused shoppers."

Playing off Greenwood's love of Polish composer Penderecki, you could describe *Kid A/Amnesiac* as a Threnody For The Victims Of Globalisation. Yorke says that spending three years in the UK after a lot of time touring abroad was a big influence: reading newspapers, noticing the discrepancy between mainstream pop culture and what was going on "out there." Three members of the group read Naomi Klein's anti-corporate bestseller *No Logo*, and at one point it was rumoured that *No Logo* would be the album title. Talking about the upsurge of antiglobalization dissent, Yorke defends the movement from charges of ideological incoherence and being merely reactive. "That's how it's always dismissed in the mainstream media, but that's because it's this coalition of disparate interest groups who are all pissed off because they've been disenfranchised by politicians who are only listening to corporate lobby groups or unelected bodies like Davos [*i.e.*: the World Economic Forum]. It's not based on the old left/right politics, it's not really even an anti-capitalist thing . . . It's something far deeper than that: 'Who do you serve?' It's a new form of dissent, a new politics, and the point is that the most important political issues of the day have been taken out of the political arena. They're being discussed by lobby groups paid for, or composed of, ex-members of corporations. And they spend a lot of effort trying to exclude the public, because it's inconvenient."

Yorke cuts himself short with a self-deprecating "I could go on like this forever, but I don't know what the fuck I'm talking about really!" He's fully aware of music fans' traditional scepticism and low tolerance for popstars who speak out (see Sting and the rain-forest), and conscious of the contradictions of Radiohead as dissi-dents bankrolled by Parlophone/EMI/Time/Warner/AOL. "We're screaming hypocrites. No, we are!" He also acknowledges that plat-inum-in–50-territories Radiohead are arguably the hip face of glob-alization. Recalling Coca-Cola sponsored MTV events they played in Mexico and Thailand back when "Creep" was a heavy-rotation video, he says, "It was a weird feeling, because you are right at the sharp end of the sexy, sassy, MTV eye-candy lifestyle thing that they're trying to sell to the rest of the world, make them aspire to. It's fair enough to question it. Unfortunately, if you're interested in actually being heard, you have to work within the system." He slips into a comedy Nazi accent: "Zey haff Kontrol!"

If Radiohead are a love-or-hate proposition—and they do seem to induce violently polarized responses—a lot of it is down to Thom Yorke's voice, the dolorousness that is its natural tone-and-texture. "Miserabilist," "whinging," "tortured": these are the kind of adjec-tives hurled by the hostile. Fans, in contrast, tend to talk of "beauti-ful sadness." This split response is reminiscent of how Morrissey divided listeners in 1983 into those who found his voice nectar to the ear or grating as nails on a blackboard. The parallel is apposite. That 1983 feeling is a lot like 2001: mainstream pop sounds relent-lessly glossy and upful. The conditions that made The Smiths (or REM, in Reagan's America) necessary as a counterweight to the likes of Wham! have returned.

The anguished timbre may be an acquired taste, but Yorke is an amazing singer. What's especially impressive about *Kid A/Amnesiac* is the way he operates as an ensemble player, another color in the group's palette. Bored with all the standard tricks of vocal emoting, Yorke decided to interface voice and technology and develop what he's called "a grammar of noises." The first two tracks on *Kid A*, "Everything In Its Right Place" and the title track, are especially striking in this respect, almost a declaration of intent: the words drastically processed in order to thwart the standard rock-listener mechanism of identify-and-interpret (the very mode of trad rock deep-and-meaningfulness that *OK Computer* had dramatically revived).

"The real problem I had was with the 'identify' bit," says Yorke. "Even now, most interviews you do, there's a constant subtext: 'Is this you?' By using other voices, I guess it was a way of saying, 'obviously it isn't me'." Turning the voice into an instrumental texture, Other-izing it via effects, allowed Yorke "to sing things I wouldn't normally sing. On *"Kid A,"* the lyrics are absolutely brutal and horrible and I wouldn't be able to sing them straight. But talking them and having them vocodered through Johnny's Ondes Martenot, so that I wasn't even responsible for the melody . . . that was great, it felt like you're not answerable to this thing."

Another vocal treatment Yorke resorted to was the Autotuner—most famous from Cher's "Believe", but widely used in contemporary R&B as an intermittent glister of posthuman perfect pitch added to particular lines or words. "We used Autotuner on *Amnesiac* twice. On 'Pakt Like Sardines,' I wasn't particularly out of tune, but if you really turn up the Autotuner so it's dead in pitch, it makes it go slightly . . . "—he makes a nasal, depersonalized sound. "There's also this trick you can do, which we did on both 'Pakt' and 'Pull/Pulk Revolving Doors,' where you give the machine a key and then you just talk into it. It desperately tries to search for the music in your speech, and produces notes at random. If you've assigned it a key, you've got music."

Elsewhere, Radiohead's "vocal science" bypassed state of the art digitalia for antiquarian technology and the sort of ad hoc boffinry

redolent of John Lennon and George Martin's techniques at Abbey
Road during the late Beatles era (Yorke confesses that *Revolution In
the Head,* Ian MacDonald's book detailing the recording of every single Beatles song, was "my bedside reading all through the sessions
for the albums"). On "You And Whose Army?" the muzzy vocal—
which sounds like Morrissey sliding into a Temazepam coma—was
an attempt to recapture the soft, warm, proto-doowop sound of 40s
harmony group The Ink Spots. "We hired all these old ribbon
microphones, but it didn't work because you need all the other gear,
like the old tape recorders. So what we ended up using is an eggbox!
And because it's on the vocal mic, and the whole band's playing at the
same time, everything on the track goes through this eggbox."

Radiohead also used a device called the Palm Speaker on "You
and Whose Army?," creating a halo of hazy reverberance around
Yorke's vocal. "The Palm Speaker is something else that Monsieur
Martenot invented, to go with the Ondes," explains Greenwood.
"It's a bit like a harp with a speaker in the middle of it. The strings
are tuned to all 12 semitones of an octave, and when you play a note
in tune, it resonates that specific string and it creates this weird kind
of echo that's only on those pitches."

On *Kid A/Amnesiac,* Yorke performed his vocals knowing the kind
of spatiality it would be moving through: the effects are always "live,"
audible to him through headphones. "Nigel Godrich is very into this
idea that if you're going to do something weird with a track, you
make it weird there and then, rather than doing it in the mix afterwards, because the effect changes the way people play. They'll play
to it. And that's really inspiring, because it's like having a new instrument. If you've got an incredibly cool reverb or something on your
voice, suddenly you're really excited about what you're doing again."

The vocal tricknology on *Kid A* was perhaps the most offputting
aspect for many listeners, prompting accusations of emotional withdrawal and a refusal to connect with the audience, or the absurd,
frequently heard charge, "there are no tunes on the album" (actually, almost every track is structured like a song, and hauntingly
melodic). The mixed response *Kid A* garnered in the UK revealed
how the Britpop era has weakened the rock audience's (or more

likely, the rock media's) ability to handle anything not blatantly sing-
along. At its lowliest—Oasis—Britpop was barely more than ampli-
fied busking, disregarding the studio's sound sculpting potential and
relegating rhythm to a menial timekeeping role. Call it the new
philistinism: as Greenwood commented acidly circa *Kid A's* release,
"people basically want their hands held through 12 'Mull Of Kin-
tyres.'"

Surprisingly, the more trad-rock America gave *Kid A* an almost
uniformly rapturous reception, with two exceptions. One was author
Nick Hornby, in his *New Yorker* rock column, who complained,
absurdly, that the album was simply too demanding for adults
exhausted by work/parenting, and accused critics who raved about
Kid A of thinking like 16-year-olds. The other was Howard Hampton in the *New York Times*, who dredged up that hoary old "it's just
like the mid–70s again" scare tactic, a scenario in which Radiohead
are the new Pink Floyd and it's high time we had another punk rock.

The Pink Floyd analogy has dogged Radiohead since *The Bends*.
And there are parallels, for sure: the concept album flavor of *OK Computer*; the lavish artwork (there's a secret booklet concealed inside *Kid
A's* CD case); their obsessive attention to track-sequencing the
albums to work as wholes; even the fact that both groups came from
Oxbridge towns. Despite a dearth of real sonic similarity, Radiohead
are often described by journalists as Floyd-influenced, which Greenwood fears may have stemmed from interview comments "from about
five years ago, when I heard *Meddle* for the first time and liked half of
it. And I felt a bit ripped off, because when I was at school, the popular post-punk myth was that Floyd were rubbish."

I'm hardly a fan of that group post–Syd Barrett, but it's worth at
least querying why "Pink Floyd" is such an enduringly potent insult,
such an instantly discrediting reference point. Johnny Rotten may
have famously scrawled "I Hate" on his Pink Floyd T-shirt (but why
did he own one in the first place, I always wonder?), yet of all the
pre–1976 dinosaurs, Waters & Co were arguably the least decadent,
corrupt, and aesthetically bankrupt. 1975's *Wish You Were Here* contains anti-record biz sentiments that anticipate punk; *Animals* and
The Wall are as bleakly no-escapist and apocalyptic in their view of

modern society as anything from the post-punk vanguard. At one point in the mid-70s, Floyd even planned making an entire album using household implements, a gambit that would have surpassed in advance PiL's *Flowers Of Romance*, ATV's *Vibing Up The Senile Man*, Nurse With Wound . . . not to mention Matt Herbert.

There's a case for arguing that 1977-style three-chord punk was just a back-to-basics blip in the continuum of UK art rock, and that 'Progressive' pretty much resumed in the form of post-punk, albeit shaped by some new sonic prohibitions/inhibitions. Before 1977, figures like Eno and Wyatt collaborated with Prog types like Robert Fripp and even Phil Collins. After punk, some of those early 70s art rockers fitted the new rules of cool (Eno producing Devo, No Wave, Talking Heads; Wyatt playing with Scritti and recording for Rough Trade).

Perhaps the Pink Floyd comparison has less to do with any real stylistic parallels and more to do with the vein of inverted snobbery that runs through British rock culture, one symptom of which is an abiding discomfort with the notion of "art rock" itself. "Too fucking middle class, that's our problem!" says Yorke. Radiohead met at the same Abingdon public school, where several members had classical music training of varying kinds; most went on to university (Cambridge, in Colin Greenwood's case). But what are their qualifications in the university of real life? What right do they have to "moan" about anything? How can such polite, well-educated, well brought-up, diligent, meticulous young men be "rock 'n' roll"?

One of the things I like about Radiohead, though, is that they seem comfortable with their middle classness: not proud, conscious of the issue of privilege, but at the same time not adopting 'Mockney' accents or concealing the fact that they are widely read (*Amnesiac*'s title, for instance, was inspired by a passage Yorke read in a book about Gnosticism). Even the fact that Greenwood went AWOL from the original interview at Courtyard's office in order to watch the first day of cricket at Lords seems, perversely, part of their authenticity.

"People distrust learning, don't they?" muses Greenwood. "There's all these stories of Miles Davis going to the Juilliard academy and poring over classical scores in the library. That side of

Miles is glossed over a bit in favor of the living on the edge stuff. But it just makes me love him even more, the idea of him wanting to get musical inspiration from everything and everywhere." For his part Yorke attacks what he calls "the noble savage idea of creativity" as "a really destructive myth" and "a trap" for the artist.

"At one point, I started to believe that if you sit down and analyze what you're doing, worry about it, then you're not being your true self. But, for instance, Mark E Smith is not a noble savage—he's a fucking intellectual. With us, though, there's this suspicion of calculation all the way through what we do. Where does this come from, the idea that if you sit down and think about something you can't be emotional in any way? Maybe it's some sort of punk hangup."

"Sometimes, I think they're right about us," muses Yorke. "Sometimes we do over-think things." He thinks that's why accusations of humorlessness are often directed at Radiohead, despite the fact that in interviews they're perfectly witty. "People used to throw that at The Smiths all the time, but Morrissey obviously had a sense of humor. Even something as dark as 'How Soon Is Now' has a quippy element." Imputing humor-deficiency is one of the classic levelling weapons in the arsenal of English anti-intellectualism, used to deflate anything radical ("bloody humorless feminists") or pretentious and arty. "How dare Radiohead take themselves so seriously?" is the subtext of much of the animus against *Kid A/Amnesiac*: witness the *NME* album review that began with the words, "The unbearable heaviness of being Radiohead." But it's precisely the group's reinvocation of art rock earnestness, their refusal of levity and frivolousness, that is actually dissident within pop culture right now, pervaded as it is with post-*Loaded* bluff blokey cheer, heterosexualized camp (from Robbie Williams to the current rash of 80s nostalgia TV), and "won't get fooled again" cynicism that aims to trivialize intensity or vision-quest of any kind. Yorke says he can understand the demand for light entertainment, though. "The reason people are so into escaping is there's a fucking lot to escape from," he concludes. "In a way, the last thing anyone needs is someone rubbing salt in the wounds, which is sort of what we're doing."

Strokes Thread

Maybe I've led a hopelessly retro existence, but they don't really sound all that much MORE like the velvets, television, or (especially) the stooges than hundreds of tiny little indie bands I've heard over the years. Tons of bands have been mining that vein of ny rock for years—albeit most of them more ramones/dolls influenced than television-influenced.

What sets The Strokes apart from the generic-nyc-'76 bands is how BRITISH they sound. I hear Morrissey and Ian Curtis and even Jarvis Cocker & Damon Albarn in the vocals as much as Lou or Verlaine. And their "posh" background—that's so ENGLISH! I'm sure they were all huge Brit Pop fans. They dress EXACTLY like Menswear in Converse all-stars—another NME "saviour of rock"—or any number of those "new wave of new wave" bands of a few years ago. The fact that they embody, to NME et al, some sort of mythic ideal of what a New York band should be is mystifying.

I really like them, by the way. It's so nice to have a rock n roll band to argue about again.

— FRITZ (fritzalias57@hotmail.com
<mailto:fritzalias57@hotmail.com>),
August 16, 2001.

I think it's important to separate the "Strokes as Band" phenomenon from the "What it Means that People Like Them" phenomenon. As

I've said before, I don't think the band will wind up much of any-where, and my guess is that "The Modern Age" will wind up much like "(I'm) Stranded" or "Where's Captain Kirk"—an old single to be pulled out and loved (or anthologized 20 years from now along with 20 soundalike tracks by bands called the Rubs and the Caresses or the Aneurysms and the Cardiac Arrests).

But—and I suppose you've heard me say this before—I really think people's excitement over them (even if it is still limited mainly to a set of tastemakers and critics) represents a reaction to the prevailing tone of music over the past 5–7 years: we've been soaked in futurism, an unprecedented emphasis on arrangement and "sound," a pull toward sparkly studio amazements that are meant to feel like something much more than just people playing music. All of that's been *great*, in my opinion, but I think it's essentially led people to forget what the old mode of playing was like, so much so that the slightest reminder (the Strokes) suddenly seems like a revelation—and for those young enough not to have much memory of that mode, even more so.

None of which is to say that the Strokes are particularly *good* at this. But I bought that single and spent the rest of the day listening to it over and over, and I had to stop to ask myself why—and the answer was that I was in the mood to hear something come from that particular place. Not the Strokes, not something so devoid of its own innovation—but I *do* want to hear some really fresh brilliant bands come out of the "faithful recording of people playing specific instruments" vein, and I think it's going to happen soon.

Sorry to restate My Overarching Theory of What Will Happen, but it's my honest answer to the question.

— NITSUH (nta@alias.edu
<mailto:nta@alias.edu>),
August 16, 2001.

I hadn't even heard of The Strokes until I started lurking about ILM, so their media blitz can't be reaching all quarters (then again, I am pretty much a hermit these days). So, out of curiosity, I read Tom's piece on NYLPM and downloaded "The Modern Age" through less than legal means. (I think they're probably doing okay, so I don't feel too guilty.) The one thing I *was* struck by was just how much this guys voice does sound like Lou Reeds; I didn't mind it, but it was kind of disarming. But I agree with Tom that there's nothing "important" about them (and important is a pissant word anyway as he mentions), any more than there was about the Blues Explosion. (I'd hesitate to say it, but I think Pussy Galore *may be* "important." But they also wouldn't rate an NME cover today.) It's safe, and by that I mean comforting in the way that reading a book you loved in HS five or ten years later is comforting on some level. If it leads a teenage kid to appreciate the VU or Television or even the NY Dolls, then I'm all for it. But I think growed ups might be a little embarrassed gushing about something so retro.

— JESS (dubalias@hotmail.com
<mailto:dubalias@hotmail.com>),
August 16, 2001.

Does anybody know specifically where all this Strokes hype originated from? Is there a Ground Zero? (Is there ever a Ground Zero?)

— DAVID (daver@alias.org
<mailto:daver@alias.org>),
August 16, 2001.

I think Ground Zero for the Strokes hype probably physically resides at the Mercury Lounge, as the fellow who booked them there and the Bowery Ballroom (thus allowing people to see them) is now their manager. Also, they have, and have had, several lawyers, publicists, etc . . . since right after they started. Also I apologize for using the word "important" in my last entry on this thread to describe a band. I agree it is a poor word to use in such a context. It implies alot more than what I wanted to mean, which is simply that said "important" bands were often the basis of what dozens of other "unimportant" bands put out in the years following. Basically, that means while the strokes are unimportant now (cause they're entirely derivative), when a million kids in Ohio start copying them (and not consciously copying the older stuff), then the strokes will suddenly become important.

— H A N S (hansalias@hotmail.com
<mailto:hansalias@hotmail.com>),
August 16, 2001.

"Basically, that means while the strokes are unimportant now (cause they're entirely derivative), when a million kids in Ohio start copying them (and not consciously copying the older stuff), then the strokes will suddenly become important."

I had to reread this a few times before I realized I basically agree with it (cuz I'm friggin tired today, sheesh). It's probably the best use to the word important, since "importance" is only ever bestowed in retrospect and seems to follow Eno's Velvets dictum of "sold no copies, but everyone who heard them formed a band." People have been covering this axis (Velvets/Stooges/Dolls/Television/Ramones) for decades. There are whole labels devoted to it (Sympathy For The Record Industry, Estrus, anyone?); I guarantee you drive to any major American city and you'll find at least one, if not a handful, of bands "exploring" this retro/trash/garage sound. It's never going away, and I suppose its popularity will wax and wane based on the popularity of bands like The Strokes. It can be a lot of fun, but nothing to assume is going to spearhead any sort of rock revival. (Wasn't there a similar what's the hub bub, bub? a few years ago about Jonathan Fire Eater?, and then boom boom shake the room, where are they now?) My question is why do the Japanese do this sound so much better than most Americans? Guitar Wolf is about the only band I've enjoyed in this idiom in the last five or six years ... "Jet Generation" gives me an ice cream headache everytime I listen to it. (Which is a plus.)

— J E S S (dubalias@hotmail.com
<mailto:dubalias@hotmail.com>),
August 16, 2001.

I don't see how the Strokes are remotely like "garage rock" as I understand it, other than the fact that they are pleasingly inept on their instruments.

Garage rock is originally by 60's american bands who were inspired by british invasion bands who were inspired by american blues and r&b, it is not '01 american bands who were inspired by american bands of the mid–70's who inspire british rock writers to cream their jeans.

— F R I T Z   (fritzalias@hotmail.com
<mailto:fritzalias@hotmail.com>),
August 16, 2001.

I'm slightly with Fritz on this one, in the following sense: I don't think people who are actually *into* the Strokes are into them in the garage sense. I get the feeling that they're liked as a pop band, basically, albeit one with a bit more swagger than's been the norm in recent years.

I mean, these are songs—structurally and melodically—that one could essentially imagine a more rudimentary version of Belle and Sebastian playing.

— N I T S U H   (nta@alias.edu
<mailto:nta@alias.edu>),
August 16, 2001.

"*I think Ground Zero for the Strokes hype probably physically resides at the Mercury Lounge, as the fellow who booked them there and the Bowery Ballroom (thus allowing people to see them) is now their manager. Also, they have, and have had, several lawyers, publicists, etc . . . since right after they started.*"

This is pretty well correct, although they were together as a band—with, for a time, a different manager who they left despite being under contract with her and who actually booked the band's first Mercury Lounge appearance—for a couple of years before anyone paid notice. And those lawyers, publicists were hired right after that new manager, Ryan Gentles, came on board. His contacts got them to Geoff Travis at Rough Trade and the (near?) unanimous hype started from there.

Key to their appeal, as well, I think is that like Oasis they not only return a guitar-bass-drums setup with familiar consensus-building roots to rock but they act and, arguably first and foremost desire to, be rock stars in all of the elegantly wasted, groupie-shagging conotations. Reading the press from their first UK tour one learns that not only do they rock, but they get drunk, start fights, make boasts—like Oasis did, like Proper Rock Stars should. They photograph pretty well, too. It makes the press' job pretty easy. Outside of that much maligned n,-metal or hip-hop we have to go "Behind the Scenes" for this type of personality and decadence these days—Travis and Coldplay are hardly cutting it in these departments, are they?

This is also one of the characteristics that they share with the Dandy Warhols and the neo-garage bands: fetishizing the attitudes as well as the sounds of the past. VH1 is reportedly negotiating a second season of "Bands on the Run," to feature more established bands and—surprise, surprise—in a brilliant stroke (heh) on the station's part, they are, acc. to Buddyhead and others, rumored to be considering the Strokes, Dandys, BRMC, the Warlocks, and Brian Jonestown Massacre.

And, as always, Nitsuh seems to speak a lot of truth. His career trajectory, in the U.S. at least, seems as if it will be the band's fate.

As for the music, we're looking—more specifically on the Post-Punk Canon thread—at the trees, but I think most veteran critics may be pleased as punch with the forest: Pop music being inspired by Lou Reed and Television! Finally! Some of these writers, whether they've known it or not, have probably waited a long time to be able to back a band such as the Strokes.

— SCOTT P. (scott@alias.net
<mailto:scott@alias.net>),
August 16, 2001.

Wait: before I catch shit for that statement, let me clarify. I'm not actually trying to draw that comparison, which would be a tad ridiculous. I just mean that underneath the stylistic references, they're a pop band playing pop songs, and I think the people who are enjoying them are enjoying *that* more so than they're enjoying the very muted touch of swaggering New York late–70s attitude. I'd even guess that there's a bit of perceived irony going on, a sort of "Well, why not?"

— NITSUH (nta@alias.edu
<mailto:nta@alias.edu>),
August 16, 2001.

Constant Sorrow

The Long Road of Ralph Stanley

Looked at from the world's point of view, it was a triumphant day for Ralph Stanley. Looked at from his own, it was a long wait to sing three songs. He hadn't slept well—"I must've turned over a hundred times"—partly because his two-year-old grandson was in the hospital back home, in Virginia, with pneumonia, and partly because no normal person could sleep in New York. His description of the hotel where he and his wife, Jimmi, were staying made it sound like an S.R.O. in Hell's Kitchen. (In fact, it was the aggressively fashionable Hudson, on West Fifty-eighth Street.) And Carnegie Hall's Dressing Room D, where he'd been hanging out behind a closed door since one-thirty in the afternoon for an evening performance, had just about everything a man didn't need: an upright piano, plates of fruit and cold cuts, and air-conditioning that wouldn't go off.

Stanley had come here during a hot spell in June as the culminating attraction of a sold-out concert featuring music on the best-selling soundtrack album from the film "O Brother, Where Art Thou?," for which he had joined such roots-music loyalists as the late John Hartford, Emmylou Harris, Gillian Welch and David Rawlings, the Cox Family, and three sweet-and-sour-voiced little girls from Tennessee called the Peasall Sisters. Since May of last year, when these people were last onstage together, at Nashville's Ryman Auditorium, they had had occasion to reflect on the truisms about mortality and mutability in the songs they sing. Just a few days before the Carnegie Hall concert, Hartford had died of cancer. Several months earlier, the fiddler Willard Cox had broken his back in a car wreck; tonight he was playing in a wheelchair.

As the concert began, Stanley changed into his stage clothes, remarking—not without a certain sly satisfaction—that they made him look like "an undertaker": black suit with a blacker stripe; black shirt; busy tie in muted red; and a tiepin with a tiny clockface. His physical presence is not commanding. He's a short, owlish-looking man with wire-rimmed glasses and tightly curled, meticulously styled gray hair; when he's not playing the banjo, he often does his hell-harrowing singing with his hands in his pockets. And since he had come here only to sing and not perform with his own band, he had left his custom-made Stanleytone five-string and his trademark white Stetson at home. He stood in the wings with Jimmi, listening to the others, until it was time for him to go on and close the show. A few performers respectfully approached him, but he glad-handed no one. At last, he squared his shoulders and strode onto the stage to a standing ovation.

Backed by a few of the evening's other performers, he sang three of his strongest, most death-haunted songs. (Probably half of the two thousand or so numbers that he has recorded involve lonesome graves, cold dark shrouds, murders, dying parents—also dying children, siblings, sweethearts, and Saviours—and the prospective glories of Heaven.) His first song, "Oh Death," was an unaccompanied solo on the ancient theme of bargaining with the Reaper to "spare me over till another year." Next came "Man of Constant Sorrow." With its insistent, chugging rhythm, as much blues as blue-grass, and its weird, angular melody, it has been his signature number for more than fifty years. He closed the program with "Angel Band," a song that he first recorded in 1955 with his late brother, Carter. "My latest sun is sinking fast," it begins. "My race is nearly run." The performance was Ralph Stanley at his present-day best: his well-aged tenor voice strong and hard, its edge unblunted, as he navigated the turns and ornaments that he learned as a boy, singing in a Primitive Baptist church. He had performed these songs thousands of times over half a century, but, as usual, he changed a few nuances. In "Angel Band," when he got to "whose blood now cleanses from all sin/And gives me victory," his voice leaped up a clarion-call fifth on the word "me."

Ever since the death of Bill Monroe, the putative father of bluegrass, in 1996, Ralph Stanley has been the supreme icon of authenticity in American vernacular music. He is neither the last nor the oldest of the mountain-music patriarchs: Earl Scruggs, who is the prototypical bluegrass banjo player, and served as an early model for Stanley, has just released his first album since 1984, "Earl Scruggs and Friends." But Scruggs hasn't performed much in the past quarter century; Stanley, who is slightly younger, continues to do more than a hundred shows a year. Even when he was in his twenties, Stanley's voice—hard, piercing, with a touch of raspiness—made him sound like a scary old man. Today, he sounds even scarier, and he has begun appealing to an audience far beyond the usual bluegrass circuit of summer festivals, college-town coffeehouses, and school and firehouse gigs throughout the rural South.

Stanley has striven for commercial success ever since 1946, when he and Carter started out as the Stanley Brothers. But since he's ultimately selling his own rugged unworldliness, he also needs to keep the culture of getting and spending at a distance. After his brother died, in 1966, he deliberately turned backward and inward. He cultivated his own conservative musical instincts—soon, for instance, he began featuring stark a-cappella gospel quartets—and, over the years, he has kept as close as a touring musician can to the primal landscape of his childhood: Virginia's Clinch Mountain region. For years, he has listened to few recordings but his own—if he's in the mood for Nashville-type country, he chooses George Jones—and his duets with such admirers as Bob Dylan and Lucinda Williams suggest that these better-known musicians want to touch the source of an almost mystical purity. Unlike Monroe, who occasionally hired urban college types, Stanley won't take on a musician who's not from the Southern mountains. "With all due respect," he told me, "I don't think Northern city boys have got the natural . . . you know. I like to have a man in my band that talks like me. I just like to keep it down simple."

Stanley often begins the ritual opening speech at his shows with "a big old howdy" and a promise to deliver "that old-time, mountain-style, what-they-call-bluegrass music." This bumpy formulation is an attempt to draw a fine distinction: the most revered performer in bluegrass isn't sure that the term fits him. The name originated with Monroe, a Kentuckian who boosterishly called his band the Blue Grass Boys. Ralph Stanley's music sounds, superficially, like Monroe's, but to a musician of Stanley's generation "bluegrass" still feels like a brand name. He generally refers to what he plays as "my kind of music," or, if you press him, "just that old-time mountain music."

In fact, mountain music was never that simple. By the time fiddlers, banjo players, and singers from the Southern Appalachians began to be recorded, in the nineteen-twenties, they had already synthesized influences as diverse as ballads and dance tunes from the British Isles; blue notes, the banjo, and rocking polyrhythms from Africa; ragtime tunes and Victorian parlor songs. Twentieth-century technology, which allowed the music to travel independently of the musicians, only encouraged such exchanges. Stanley, who was born in 1927, remembers when his parents got their first radio—a battery-powered model, as they had no electricity—and when he first heard the Grand Ole Opry broadcasts from Nashville. Well before the advent of bluegrass, mountain music had already become a media-disseminated entertainment.

The band that Monroe formed in 1945 inspired a revolution. For all of bluegrass's traditional roots, it is a recent—even modernist—form, only a few years younger than bebop. Unlike ensemble-oriented old-time mountain bands, Monroe's group allowed individual musicians to play jazz-like, semi-improvised solos, and ornate obbligatos behind the singing. To complement his own hopped-up, asymmetrical mandolin and his bluesy, androgynous tenor voice, Monroe picked a team of virtuosos—notably Scruggs, who had perfected an intricate system of three-finger picking that produced a dense, high-speed flow of notes, like a twanging tommy gun. From that day to this, almost every bluegrass band has been a variation of Monroe's: Scruggs-style banjo, fiddle, mandolin, rhythm guitar, and bass, with sometimes a lead guitar or a dobro, and a repertoire of retooled folk, gospel, and love-gone-wrong songs.

Bluegrass might be described as meta-mountain music—self-referential and driven by an anxiety that the old ways of life, and the music that went with them, are vanishing. Monroe's "Uncle Pen" is the best-known example of a favorite bluegrass trope: an uptempo fiddle showpiece about an old fiddler and the tunes he used to play. Song after song tells the same story of uprootedness and alienation; the genre's locus classicus is the Stanley Brothers' version of "Rank Strangers." "I wandered again to my home in the mountains/Where in youth's early dawn I was happy and free/I looked for my friends, but I never could find them / I found they were all rank strangers to me." "Rank Strangers" reflects the hard times that drove people away from the mountains of Virginia, West Virginia, Kentucky, and Tennessee after the Second World War. These new urban workers made up an appreciable part of the bluegrass audience; for them, Stanley's "Man of Constant Sorrow" ("I bid farewell to old Kentucky, the state where I was born and raised") was both a nostalgic reminder of home and a bitter anthem of loss. "I've saw it when we'd play the bars and things up in Ohio—Dayton and Columbus and Cincinnati and through there," George Shuffler, who was the Stanley Brothers' lead guitarist, told me. "That was where all the people migrated to get out of the coal mines. I've saw 'em raise the roof when Ralph would start into that thing."

Stanley has known that feeling of exile. In 1951, he and Carter briefly took jobs at the Ford plant in Detroit. "That was a pretty miserable ten weeks for me," he said, fifty years later. "I was a truck-pan welder, spot welder. I was working night shift, about three until twelve or something. I got homesick. I thought they's something better to do than punch a clock. So I quit and went home."

Stanley still lives in a remote area of southwestern Virginia, between the towns of Coeburn and McClure, just a few miles from where he grew up. The country looks much the same as it did when he was a boy, except for some flattened hilltops that the coal companies once strip-mined, where cattle now graze. You're getting close when you hit a crossroads with a Kwik Stop, a Freewill Baptist church, and a sign that reads "Jesus Is the Answerer and Finisher of Our Faith."

Stanley's house is a large, elegant, one-story gray stone rambler on a gentle rise; a section of his thirty-five-acre property near the road is marked off with a gentleman farmer's white fences. Stanley's son and lead singer, Ralph II—his father and his bandmates call him Two—lives in a small white trailer next door with his wife, Kristi. When I pulled into the driveway one morning, I was greeted by Two's German shepherd, Harley. Stanley, dressed for company in slacks and a sports shirt, ignored Harley's tail-wagging. "I'm kinda mad at him," he said. "He goes after the horses. So I don't fool with him much." He showed off his palomino, Angel, who was about to foal, and his John Deere Gator, a six-wheel all-terrain vehicle that he'd wanted for several years, but which now sat unused in a shed. "I bet it hasn't got more than fifteen miles on it," he said. (A few months later, he sold the thing.) Stanley clearly loved this place, but he also seemed at a distance from it—perhaps the consequence of spending most of his life on a tour bus, heading from one town to the next to sing about his home in the mountains.

In the kitchen, something smelled good: Stanley, who likes to cook, had some beans on the stove. He led me into the reddest living room I've ever seen: an acre of red carpet, a plush red sofa, red curtains pulled open to reveal a manicured lawn. The floor-to-ceiling picture window and the meticulous housekeeping made the room seem like a diorama; ceramic dogs here and there, a white ceramic pillar with a cupid holding a cornucopia of roses, a display case with china angels, china birds, and a china Jesus. The only thing that looked out of place was the banjo case on the floor. Jimmi Stanley came in to say hello, chatted about the weather and her allergies, and offered us coffee. Stanley has small hands, and it was hard not to stare at his fingers: they curl away from the thumb, which made me wonder how he still managed to play banjo as strongly as he does. As we talked he drummed his fingers on a glass-topped table.

In conversation, Stanley has his set pieces: The road-not-taken story about his once having to choose between spending five dollars on either a brood sow or his first banjo; the there-but-for-the-grace-of-God story of a drunk who shot and killed one of his lead singers, Roy Lee Centers, who sounded uncannily like Carter. "Roy went to a party, and of course they all got drunk," Stanley said. "Roy's little boy was with him. He was about eight or nine years old at that time, maybe ten. And the tale the little boy told, this fella drove Roy home and he changed routes a little bit. Roy said, 'Where you going?' The fella said, 'I'm gonna take you up this road here and kill you.' He took him up there, got him out, and said, 'I'm gonna silence that beautiful voice forever,' and shot him right in the mouth. Then he turned around and took the butt of the gun and beat him all to pieces."

Stanley walked me briskly through his childhood: the period when he worked in his father's sawmill; his early thoughts of being a veterinarian; his father's leaving the family when Ralph was thirteen. From that time on, he said, "we didn't see too much of him." Stanley began taking music seriously as a teen-ager, singing brother-act harmonies with Carter, who played guitar; they sometimes performed for donations outside the Clinchfield Coal Company on paydays. He did a short stretch in the Army, just after the war ended. Then he and Carter formed a band with a mandolinist, Pee Wee Lambert, and a fiddler, Leslie Keith. Before long, they'd landed the midday spot on "Farm and Fun Time" on WCYB, in Bristol, on the Virginia-Tennessee border, fifty miles from home. Even then, the shy and taciturn Ralph let his older, taller, more outgoing brother do most of the talking and lead singing. "Carter would've just as soon called the President as he would've called me," Stanley said. "He was a good mixer, a lot more forward than I am. Easier to get acquainted with."

At first, Stanley played banjo in the archaic clawhammer style that his mother had taught him: a clip-clopping sound produced by a downstroke of the index fingernail, followed by the thumb playing accents on the fifth string. He had also mastered the smoother two-finger style, in which the index finger picks upward. But, in the forties, a few banjo players—mainly in North Carolina—were refining a more complex three-finger style, attacking the strings in repeating sequences called "rolls"; on fast tunes, an overpowering technician like Earl Scruggs could unleash as many as fifteen notes per second. "I believe the first person I heard do that was a man by the name of Hoke Jenkins," Stanley said. "He was playing it on the radio somewhere. And I thought I needed to be doing it that way. There was just more of a drive to it. Then I heard Earl Scruggs with Bill Monroe on the Grand Ole Opry. I could tell they was using three fingers. But I never could copy anybody. When I found out there was a sort of a roll, I wanted to just play it the way I felt it, and I didn't want to hear them anymore. I guess I still don't have it right. Earl Scruggs probably knows a little bit more about music. I'd say he's more polished, you know." When I asked Steve Sparkman, a Stanley disciple who now plays the more difficult banjo parts with the Clinch Mountain Boys, to characterize the difference between the two masters, he said, "Ralph took the drive and put more drive in. You might say overdrive. Just *wham!* Keep that forward roll jammin'."

Stanley's other contribution to the band's sound, his raw, yearning tenor voice, was even more distinctive. He sang lead mostly on the old-time songs—"Little Maggie," "Pretty Polly," "Man of Constant Sorrow." On the others, he sang high harmony to Carter's lower, smoother-textured melody. Perhaps the most dramatic moment in all the Stanley Brothers' hundreds of recordings occurs in the chorus of "Rank Strangers." After Carter sings the verse, Ralph enters with the words "Everybody I met/Seemed to be a rank stranger" in a voice that stabs like an icepick. He raised the tension in the Stanley Brothers' music to the nearly unbearable: singing above Carter's melody, he would hang on a dissonant note in anticipation of the chord that was about to arrive. Over time, these harmonies became wilder, more edgy and attention-getting—a separate drama that didn't cozy up to the melody but defied it before an ultimate reconciliation. "Every lead singer that sings with me will say I'm hard to sing with," Stanley said. "I hardly ever sing the same verse exactly the same way."

Initially, the Stanley Brothers so admired Monroe that they annoyed him by copying his sound. Their maniacally up-tempo 1948 recording of "Molly and Tenbrooks" was an almost note-for-note version of what Monroe was playing on his radio broadcasts, and when Columbia signed the Stanleys, later that year, Monroe left the label in protest. But the feud, such as it was, was short-lived. In 1951, Carter briefly became a Blue Grass Boy. And at one point both Stanleys did a few gigs with Monroe. "The last night I played with him, Bill said that he would like to have me join him and call it Bill Monroe and the Stanley Brothers," Stanley said. "But I just never did like to work for anybody." In later years, Stanley and Monroe sang together at festivals, where they indulged in the blue-grass world's mode of friendly rivalry: how high could they push the key before somebody's voice cracked? "After the shows," Stanley said, "we personalized. We'd talk about music, we'd talk about farming. Bill cut his hay with a horse-drawn mowing machine. He was an old-timer."

In contrast to Monroe, who was something of a martinet (he recruited band members to work on his farm when they weren't playing), the Stanley Brothers had a complementary partnership. Carter, who was the principal songwriter, had a gift for the country-style objective correlative—"For years they've been dead / The fields have turned brown"—while Ralph played the fiery instrumentals. Carter did the talking onstage, while the more retiring Ralph did most of the booking and the business. Musically, Carter was the progressive and Ralph the traditionalist. "Carter believed in searching a little bit, and I never did," Stanley said. Everyone who knew Carter was struck by his sharp intelligence, and George Shuffler likes to remember him laughing and throwing his head back so far that you could see his gold tooth. John Cohen, a member of the New Lost City Ramblers, saw a different man. "Carter was so deep into himself," Cohen recalled. "I think it was this huge drinking thing that he had. You couldn't get to where he was."

When Carter died of liver disease, at the age of forty-one, Shuffler was in the hospital waiting room with Ralph. "When the nurse came in and told us," Shuffler recalled, "Ralph was just as limp as a string." Monroe flew to Bristol and was driven up the icy mountain roads to sing at Carter's funeral. (Thirty years later, when Monroe died, Stanley went to Nashville to "sing over Bill," as he put it.) Carter's death made Stanley think, briefly, about quitting music. "He had a hard time in his heart knowing what to do," Ricky Skaggs, who played mandolin for Stanley in the early seventies, told me. "But Ralph had a desire to keep the Stanley Brothers sound alive. And he didn't know any other trade. He didn't have anything else to do."

Stanley said, "I knew that I had one or the other of two ways to go: up or down. I wanted to go up."

Last spring, on a Thursday night in Berkeley, California, I caught up with Ralph Stanley and the Clinch Mountain Boys. They were in the middle of a two-week tour. Freight & Salvage, a large coffeehouse on a side street near the university, has been a regular stop of theirs since the seventies, and both the Thursday and Friday shows were sold out. The band likes the West Coast: the audiences are knowledgeable and enthusiastic, and they tend to have more money than folks in the Deep South; on a tour like this, the band members who have solo CDs and tapes to sell can make fifteen hundred dollars above their usual wages. The audience was a typical folk-music crowd: faculty, grad students, a couple of Sikhs with beards and turbans, a biker in a Merle Haggard cap, an alert-looking young woman with a T-shirt that read "Got Banjo?" Median age: forty. Percentage wearing glasses: fifty. Randy Campbell, an agent who books the band on the West Coast, calls this sort of venue "the Church of Ralph Stanley."

The Clinch Mountain Boys are a seven-member repertory company. The fiddler, James Price, is so magisterially large that he looks as if he were holding a kid-size Suzuki violin. Price doubles as the comedian—Stanley, of course, is the straight man—and he does convincing onstage impressions of Johnny Cash and Willie Nelson (as well as a convincing offstage impression of Ralph Stanley). The lead guitarist, James Alan Shelton, has mastered George Shuffler's "cross-picking" technique, a wrist-twisting approximation of the three-finger banjo style; he's also the road manager. Steve Sparkman plays Stanley's old banjo pieces, such as "Hard Times" and "Clinch Mountain Backstep." The mandolinist, John Rigsby, can fill in singing either Carter-like lead or Ralph-like tenor, as the occasion demands.

Jack Cooke, who was once Bill Monroe's lead singer, has been Stanley's bass player for thirty-one years. He's a source of manic energy despite an arthritic hip and the open-heart surgery he had a couple of years ago. On the band's bus, he'll burst into a Little Richard song or deliver dire prophecies about the environment and the Bush Administration. (Like Stanley, he's a lifelong Democrat.)

Ralph Stanley II, who is twenty-two years old, has been the band's lead singer since he was sixteen. Two started riding the Stanley bus as a boy, and when he couldn't come along he'd play his favorite Stanley Brothers album and his favorite Ralph Stanley album each night on his bedside boom box. "I'd listen to every song on both them records," he told me. "They's twenty on one, twelve on the other. And then I'd go to sleep." With his beard and aviator sunglasses, Two looks like a video-ready young Nashville star. Longtime fans used to roll their eyes about him—his voice hadn't finished changing when he first took the job—but he's become a warm, moving singer, who combines the soulfulness of his Uncle Carter with the more anguished mainstream country style of his hero Keith Whitley, who sang lead with Stanley in the seventies.

Onstage that Thursday night in Berkeley, the band locked into the usual sweetly aching harmonies and headlong rhythms: the heavy bass that brings the words "bull fiddle" to mind, the woody acoustic guitars, the bell-toned jack-hammering of the twin banjos, the keening and skittering fiddle. But Stanley sounded hoarse, and he looked as if he were having trouble keeping his eyes open. On "Man of Constant Sorrow" he strained to hit the top notes, and later apologized to the crowd: "We left Virginia last Wednesday, and we've been playing for eight nights straight. I tell you, that works on you." He joked about his age and his problems remembering new songs: "'Doc, it seems like I can't remember anything anymore.' 'How long have you been that way?' 'What way?'" Then he took out his glasses and a piece of paper, and sang "Daddy's Wildwood Flower," a ghost story in which Mama dies and Daddy, with the help of "God's mighty power," summons her back by playing her favorite song on his guitar.

On Saturday morning, the bus, a standard-issue country-star Silver Eagle with "Dr. Ralph Stanley & His Clinch Mountain Boys" painted on its sides, took to the road again: a show in Palo Alto, an all-night run to Los Angeles, a last gig in Tempe, Arizona. On the way, the band members talked cuisine ("You ever eat that swordfish? I don't like that worth a shit"), football, music, and women. James Price read a motivational book by an ex-N.F.L. player; James Shelton read Seymour Hersh's *Dark Side of Camelot*. But mostly the musicians dozed in their seats or looked out the windows. Stanley seldom said a word. "This must get rough on him," I said to Shelton. "It's all he knows," Shelton said.

In Tempe, the bus pulled up to a flat-roofed building in a dicey neighborhood, next to an adult bookstore. Price looked out the window and said, "Regular hole in the wall." Stanley shook his head and said, "It ain't even that." But Nita's Hideaway, as the place was called, turned out to be far better than it looked: an ironic simulacrum of the sort of bar that George Shuffler calls a "skull orchard," with black velvet paintings (J.F.K., a squatting cowboy with a lariat, bullfighters, galleons, a charioteer), a pool table, and comfortable easy chairs in a side room. It was the natural habitat of Stanley's newest admirers—the tattooed, the pierced, the dreadlocked, and the shaven-headed—who have discovered him either through "O Brother, Where Art Thou?" or through certifiably cool music stars (Yoakam, Welch, Dylan) who have certified him as even cooler. Yoakam has gone as far as to call him an "archangel."

Ricky Skaggs had suggested to me that Stanley now transcends bluegrass. "He's become like an old African," Skaggs said, "a world-music person." Stanley's best performances involve you so deeply that any sense of a particular genre gets lost, the way the book, the page, and finally the words disappear in a great work of literature. A few other American musicians have had this gift: Armstrong, Ellington, Bill Monroe, Merle Haggard, James Brown, Howlin' Wolf. Despite bluegrass's mystique of mountain purity and Afro-Druidic roots—what Monroe called its "ancient tones"—there's nothing inherently special about it. Good bluegrass—like good blues, good jazz, and good rock and roll—is sweet and sad, wild and sexy. Mediocre bluegrass, which you can hear at any festival from a dozen perfectly competent parking-lot bands, is among the most wearisome music on the planet; the more it tries to stretch its parameters—with arty lyrics or bebop licks—the more evident its limitations become. Ralph Stanley understood that the way to go was to simplify, intensify, countrify. As Steve Sparkman explained it to me, "Take a little block about that big and put everything in it and keep it there. Ralph's been the king of that."

At Nita's, Stanley played the two best sets I heard him do. Sometimes fatigue or irritation revs him up more than a good night's rest, and maybe a long day of travelling to a hip hellhole did the trick. He delivered violently intense versions of "Pretty Polly" and "Little Maggie"; his two-banjo breaks with Sparkman had an unaccustomed aggressiveness; and his shamelessly over-the-top harmonies seemed to defy anybody who'd ever dared call him what he calls himself—"an old hillbilly." As he does now at every show, he sang "Oh Death"—it has become his greatest hit—and the whole bar fell silent. When he got to "I come to take the soul," he executed a semi-yodelled upward turn on the last word that gave me chills. After two weeks on the road, Stanley's voice was shot, but he didn't apologize; he was overdriving it the way a rock-and-roll guitarist overdrives an amplifier into grainy distortion, and he seemed to be revelling in the rawness. The crowd at Nita's might not have been able to tell you—as the crowd at Freight & Salvage probably could—the name of everyone who had been a Clinch Mountain Boy in 1958, but they understood the truest secret of Ralph Stanley's appeal: a bedrock punkishness, a righteous lack of ease in this world, a refusal to comfort or be comforted.

From the beginning of his career, Stanley, like almost every country performer from Roy Acuff to George Jones, has sung mini-dramas of sin and redemption—"Are You Afraid to Die?," "My Sinful Past," "Cry from the Cross," "When I Wake Up to Sleep No More." Fifteen years ago, he wrote a song titled "I'll Answer the Call." Yet, until last summer, it was only words. "I went to this country church," Stanley told me, "and I heard this man preach, name's Ezra Junior Davis. After we left the church house, two ladies were going to be baptized. The Clinch River runs by there, and I thought that river was pretty—pretty shade trees. From then on, I could *see* that river. Well, one Saturday night I couldn't sleep much—worried, had that on my mind—and I got up about four-thirty and called Brother Junior and told him I wanted to be baptized there in the Clinch River that day."

Stanley took me to a graveyard near his old home, at the top of Smith Ridge. "There's Grandpa right here," he said, "and Grandma on the other side of that tree. My mother. And there's Carter"—he pointed to a mausoleum. Next to it was an identical mausoleum with two names and dates of birth carved on it—"Me and Jimmi's resting place someday." From below came a sound that might have been a woodpecker or an idling chain saw. I asked Stanley about a gravestone with a Harley-Davidson carved on it. A father and son, distant cousins on his mother's side, he guessed; they'd both died of drug overdoses. "You see that little bitty house over there, painted white on this end?" Stanley said. "That's the house my mother and I had. The old one burned that used to set there, where I was raised, and I built that little house for her." He pointed to another house. "Carter built that little yellow one. My first cousin lives there now." What about those houses, over to the left? "That's some of their son-in-laws, daughters, and so forth. It's all family down here."

The next day, a rainy Sunday morning, Stanley and I got into his Lincoln Town Car and drove over to Grundy. The Hale Creek Primitive Baptist Church, just outside town, was a new, plain white building, across the road from a rocky stream, a picnic pavilion, and a futuristic-looking power transfer station. Nearby stood the original log church, now in disrepair. Inside, rows of padded benches faced a table that had a display of artificial flowers and a box of tissues. Stanley's "brothers and sisters," as the members call themselves, were mostly around his age. He greeted them in the group's ritual embrace—a handshake, then a hug—and chatted about coon hunting, about which relative was in the hospital, about the grand-kids.

The service began when one woman, then two, started singing amid the chitchat. (Primitive Baptists allow no instruments in church, and sing only in unison.) Gradually, everyone joined in, but I could hardly hear Stanley: he's so used to leading other singers and obeying his own instincts that he finds it hard to follow the turns in the melodies. Several elders felt inspired to stand and preach. One prayed aloud for "the little children on drugs and alcohol"; another pointed to a window and said, with tears on his face, "All these rain-drops, and I see them being taken away, one by one. And each one has a meaning."

Brother Junior, a well-barbered young man with wire-rimmed glasses, began to preach in an unprepossessing mumble, but soon he was singing a King James–like cadence in a scorching tenor that would have shone in any bluegrass band. Men and women wept; some rushed up to shake his hand and hug him. Stanley watched and listened.

After the service ended, the brothers and sisters remained stand-ing to sing one more song: "Happy Birthday." Today, Brother Ralph turned seventy-four. He had momentarily forgotten all about it. But he smiled like a good sport at all the fuss over him—spared over, as the song says, till another year.

England's Oldest Hitmakers

In the beginning the ideal pop tune was as simple and irreducible as an egg, and once it had entered your head you couldn't drive it out with any device short of frontal lobotomy. It had to be so in the early days of the entertainment industry (pop songwriting got going sometime between the 1830s and the 1870s, but the business was just approaching adolescence in the early 20th century) because there was no radio and few could afford gramophones. People heard pop tunes at shows—revues, pantomimes, operettas—and reproduced and communicated them by singing or whistling. Technology has since made whistlability optional; these days the only musical form that lives and dies solely on the basis of its mnemonic adhesion is the advertising jingle. The mammoth 106-track Bear Family compendium *Round the Town*, on which the earliest recording was made February 7, 1901, includes tunes so elemental that they've survived, if only through some intermediary agency. "Daisy Bell," for example, a hit for Katie Lawrence in 1893, we know from Hal the computer in *2001: A Space Odyssey* (I had actually heard it "sung" by a demonstration computer two years before the movie came out).

Music hall was, roughly, the British counterpart to the American institution of vaudeville. Acts toured constantly, appearing on stacked bills in theaters all over the country, singers and comedians alternating with magicians, trapeze artists, dramatic monologuists,

"eccentric" dancers, and animal acts. All classes and all segments of
the population attended these shows, if not always at the same
venues. Although they waned after World War II, both institutions
took a very long time to die. In America the form survived longer
than the content—as recently as the 1970s, James Brown was touring with a revue that included ingenue singers, comedians, and a
fashion show.

In Britain the music itself lingered on. Some of the monuments
on this package, whose narrative thread runs through the late '20s,
kept performing into the '60s and found themselves sharing bills
with Cliff Richard and the Shadows. But by then the stuff had
apparently been woven into the double helix of British pop. The
Kinks, once they were done inventing heavy metal, reverted to a
music-hall default setting, brilliantly updated; the Beatles invoked
music hall on any pretext; even the Rolling Stones gave it the occasional whirl (e.g., "Something Happened to Me Yesterday"). Meanwhile, "Henry the Eighth," a major hit for Harry Champion in
1911, was a major hit for Herman's Hermits in 1965, and years later
you still couldn't get away from it—on school buses and at summer
camp it was as inevitable and pestilential as "99 Bottles of Beer on
the Wall." As if it were a dormant virus seeking a population that
hadn't been immunized, it was released as a single only in America.

The selection here is not an impartial X ray of the genre.
Notably—and wisely—it omits the sentimental morbidity, the dying
mothers and dead babies bathed in a golden syrup that would send
any contemporary human racing for a purgative. Neither does it
dwell much on romance, also a subject usually glued shut with tears
and sugar; patriotic themes, too, are thankfully limited. Instead it
throws every kind of novelty at the listener, like so many dead cats
over a fence. Music hall is best remembered for its novelties. If novelty is defined (as the current *Britannica* entry has it) as a type of
song designed to sound unlike anything else on the charts at the
time, then music hall, a culture of novelties, was something of an
oxymoron. Then again, since its musical range and character were
kept purposely narrow (simple, catchy, buoyant, major-key), its novelties were primarily verbal. Songs capitalized on vogue expressions,

on recent inventions, on current events—although without much trenchant satire of the sort that could spark discontent—and worked 10,000 variations on the comedy of marital strife. Accents, mostly cockney but occasionally northern, were deployed for comic effect. Enunciation was generally crisp. Rhymes fell into place like billiard balls in the pocket.

Actually, the performers were themselves the novelties, each embodying some character type, at once broad and singular. At this remove it's hard to say whether Mark Sheridan was parodying an identifiable stock figure with his monocle, flaring coat, high-water bell-bottoms, and ruthlessly cylindrical top hat, or whether he just put together an eccentric outfit of his own devising (his song "I Do Like to Be Beside the Seaside" sticks in the mind like gum on a shoe, in any case). George Formby, father of an identically named and more famous son, is photographed looking like a failed Paul McCartney after a long bout of the grippe, and playing what might be a ping-pong paddle as if it were a guitar. The very fetching Happy Fanny Fields escaped from America, where she was one of a zillion "Dutch" (that is, German-accented) comedians, to London, where she cornered the market. Phil Ray clipped his lines as if doing so would save him money, and his extraordinary band played catch-up with the resulting jagged tempo. The perkily boyish Vesta Tilley and the commanding Ella Shields were male impersonators, the latter's deep voice particularly convincing. The rubber-faced Dan Leno, a household name in his day, was one of a number of performers here for whom a mere snatch of song sufficed to lead into a spoken comedy routine, which regrettably doesn't translate all that well into contemporary laffs. Marie Lloyd, buxom and toothy, was also a huge star, and you can understand why—she exuded a jolly, earthy, carefree sexuality, so much so that the stiff Americans couldn't handle her (she "traveled openly" with a jockey who was not her husband, for one thing, and for this was held at Ellis Island until her promoters bribed her way out).

There was quite a bit of traffic between the continents before the first World War. The Brits sent over Vesta Victoria, who was forever being comically jilted, and Alice Lloyd, Marie's younger sister, who was harmless and had a voice like a nine-year-old. The Americans countered with ragtime and blackface and the big hit of 1904, "Under the Anheuser Busch" (the lyrics had to be altered in Blighty, the indigenes not yet having been reduced to drinking Budweiser). The ragtime here is mostly courtesy of Irving Berlin, but the blackface is thoroughly English—aside from the pro forma insertion of a few *n*- and *c*-words, the songs are grave, dignified, and free of any attempt at dialect or accent. Then there was Pete Hampton, a bona fide black American who went over and stayed. His 1904 rendition of "Bill Bailey Won't You Please Come Home" is a forceful reminder of that song's ragtime backbone for anyone who grew up in the days when it was the standard number eked out on TV variety shows by comedians, jugglers, barflies, Broadway hustlers, and anybody else who couldn't sing.

This box set is a mixed blessing, in my life at least. It is awe-inspiring, to a degree, to hear voices warbling across the span of a century, knowing just how much business lies in the stretch between their breath and yours. Some of the tunes are quite memorable, some of them so memorable and so relentlessly peppy that you'd be inclined to hire a contractor to remove them from your waking and sleeping consciousness. I might find myself singing some of them, like Charles Coborn's "The Man Who Broke the Bank at Monte Carlo," although my affection for it owes something to the memory of hearing it sung in the sleigh-ride scene of Orson Welles's *The Magnificent Ambersons*. The two songs I unreservedly love are anomalous: Nat Travers's "He's Moved in a Bigger House Now" and Billy Bennett's "She Was Poor, but She Was Honest" are the two numbers in the set that draw blood. A few months ago a letter writer to the *Times* reproached those rockist sorts who have distorted history in favor of old murder ballads while disregarding the genius of Jerome Kern. I plead no contest. The Travers and Bennett numbers, which were recorded in 1929 and 1930, respectively, are the only two songs I can imagine being sung in a deadfall in Limehouse by cutpurses and harlots. Their humor is harsh, their accompaniment skeletal, and "She Was Poor" is even in a minor key. But of course the cutpurses and harlots of Limehouse in 1910 or 1930 would have gone for the dead-baby numbers, no question; crooks have always been notoriously sentimental. These are the only two songs that could be sung today without too much ironic framing— not because innocence has been lost, but because it's become an alibi. The veneer of innocence now just looks sick and guilty. The rest of the songs, with their unguarded smiles and tears and buoyant major-key airs, wave faintly at us from a psychological past as remote as Troy.

GEOFFREY O'BRIEN

Seven Years in the Life

On a summer afternoon in 1964 I went to a neighborhood movie theater to see the Beatles in *A Hard Day's Night*. It was less than a year since John F. Kennedy had been assassinated. Kennedy's death, and its aftermath of ceremonial grief and unscheduled violence, had if nothing else given younger observers an inkling of what it meant to be part of an immense audience. We had been brought together in horrified spectatorship, and the sense of shared spectatorship outlasted the horror. The period of private shock and public mourning seemed to go on forever, yet it was only a matter of weeks before the phenomenally swift rise of a pop group from Liverpool became so pervasive a concern that Kennedy seemed already relegated to an archaic period in which the Beatles had not existed. The New York DJs who promised their listeners "all Beatles all the time" were not so much shaping as reflecting an emergence that seemed almost an eruption of collective will. The Beatles had come, as if on occult summons, to drive away darkness and embody public desire on a scale not previously imagined.

Before the Christmas recess—just as "I Want to Hold Your Hand" was finally breaking through to a US market that had resisted earlier releases by the Beatles—girls in my tenth-grade class began coming to school with Beatles albums and pictures of individual Beatles, discussing in tones appropriate to a secret religion the relative attractions of John or Paul or Ringo or even the underappreciated George. A month or so later the Beatles arrived in New

York to appear on *The Ed Sullivan Show* and were duly ratified as the show-business wonder of the age. Everybody liked them, from the Queen of England and *The New York Times* on down.

Even bystanders with no emotional or generational stake in the Beatles could appreciate the adrenaline rush of computing just how much this particular success story surpassed all previous ones in terms of money and media and market penetration. It was all moving too fast even for the so-called professionals. The Beatles were such a fresh product that those looking for ways to exploit it—from Ed Sullivan to the aging news photographers and press agents who seemed holdovers from the Walter Winchell era—stood revealed as anachronisms as they flanked a group who moved and thought too fast for them.*

And what was the product? Four young men who seemed more alive than their handlers and more knowing than their fans; aware of their own capacity to please more or less everybody, yet apparently savoring among themselves a joke too rich for the general public; professional in so unobtrusive a fashion that it looked like inspired amateurism. The songs had no preambles or buildups: the opening phrase—"Well, she was just seventeen" or "Close your eyes and I'll kiss you"—was a plunge into movement, a celebration of its own anthemic impetus. Sheer enthusiasm, yet tempered by a suggestion of knowledge held in reserve, a distancing that was cool without malice. When you looked at them they looked back; when they were interviewed, it was the interviewers who ended up on the spot.

That the Beatles excited young girls—mobs of them—made them an unavoidable subject of interest for young boys, even if the boys might have preferred more familiar local products like Dion and the Belmonts or Freddy Cannon to a group that was foreign and long-haired and too cute not to be a little androgynous. The near-riots that accompanied the Beatles' arrival in New York, bringing about something like martial law in the vicinity of the Warwick Hotel, were an

---

¹Or so it seemed at the time. The anachronisms worried about it, of course, all the way to the bank, while the Beatles ultimately did their own computing to figure out just how badly they had been shortchanged by the industry pros.

epic demonstration of nascent female desire. The spectacle was not tender but warlike. The oscillation between glassy-eyed entrancement and emotional explosion, the screams that sounded like chants and bouts of weeping that were like acts of aggression, the aura of impending upheaval that promised the breaking down of doors and the shattering of glass: this was love that could tear apart its object.

Idols who needed to be protected under armed guard from their own worshippers acquired even greater fascination, especially when they carried themselves with such cool comic grace. To become involved with the Beatles, even as a fan among millions of others, carried with it the possibility of meddling with ferocious energies. Spectatorship here became participation. There were no longer to be any bystanders, only sharers. We were all going to give way to the temptation not just to gawk at the girl in Ed Sullivan's audience—the one who repeatedly bounced straight up out of her seat during "All My Loving" as if pulled by a radar-controlled anti-gravity device—but to become her.

I emerged from *A Hard Day's Night* as from a conversion experience. Having walked into the theater as a solitary observer with more or less random musical tastes, I came out as a member of a generation, sharing a common repertoire with a sea of contemporaries. The four albums already released by the Beatles would soon be known down to every hesitation, every intake of breath; even the moments of flawed pitch and vocal exhaustion could be savored as part of what amounted to an emotional continuum, an almost embarrassingly comforting sonic environment summed up, naturally, in a Beatles lyric:

> *There's a place*
> *Where I can go*
> *When I feel low . . .*
> *And it's my mind,*
> *And there's no time.*

Listening to Beatles records turned out to be an excellent cure for too much thinking. It was even better that the sense of refreshment was shared by so many others; the world became, with very little effort, a more companionable place. Effortlessness—the effortlessness of, say, the Beatles leaping with goofy freedom around a meadow in *A Hard Day's Night*—began to seem a fundamental value. That's what they were there for: to have fun, and allow us to watch them having it. That this was a myth—that even *A Hard Day's Night*, with its evocation of the impossible pressure and isolation of the Beatles as hostages of their fame, acknowledged it as a myth— mattered, curiously, not at all. The converted choose the leap into faith over rational argument. It was enough to believe that they were taking over the world on our behalf.

A few weeks later, at dusk in a suburban park, I sat with old friends as one of our number, a girl who had learned guitar in emulation of Joan Baez, led us in song. She had never found much of an audience for her folksinging, but she won our enthusiastic admiration for having mastered the chord changes of all the songs in *A Hard Day's Night*. We sang for hours. If we had sung together before the songs had probably been those of Woody Guthrie or the New Lost City Ramblers, mementos of a legendary folk past. This time there was the altogether different sensation of participating in a new venture, a world-changing enterprise that indiscriminately mingled aesthetic, social, and sexual possibilities.

An illusion of intimacy, of companionship, made the Beatles characters in everyone's private drama. We thought we knew them, or more precisely, and eerily, thought that they knew us. We imagined a give-and-take of communication between the singers in their sealed-off dome and the rest of us listening in on their every thought and musical reverie. It is hard to remember now how familiarly people came to speak of the Beatles toward the end of the Sixties, as if they were close associates whose reactions and shifts of thought could be gauged intuitively. They were the invisible guests at the party, or the relatives whose momentary absence provided an occasion to dissect their temperament and proclivities.

That intimacy owed everything to an intimate knowledge of every record they had made, every facial variation gleaned from movies and countless photographs. The knowledge was not necessarily sought; it was merely unavoidable. The knowledge became complex when the Beatles' rapid public evolution (they were after all releasing an album every six months or so, laying down tracks in a couple of weeks in between the tours and the interviews and the press conferences) turned their cozily monolithic identity into a maze of alternate personas. Which John were we talking about, which Paul? Each song had its own personality, further elaborated or distorted by each of its listeners. Many came to feel that the Beatles enjoyed some kind of privileged wisdom—the evidence was their capacity to extend their impossible string of successes while continuing to find new styles, new techniques, new personalities—but what exactly might it consist of? The songs were bulletins, necessarily cryptic, always surprising, from within their hermetic dome at the center of the world, the seat of cultural power.

Outside the dome, millions of internalized Johns and Pauls and Georges and Ringos stalked the globe. What had at first seemed a harmonious surface dissolved gradually into its components, to reveal a chaos of conflicting impulses. Then, all too often, came the recriminations, the absurd discussions of what the Beatles ought to do with their money or how they had failed to make proper use of their potential political influence, as if they owed a debt for having been placed in a position of odd and untenable centrality. All that energy, all that authority: toward what end might it not have been harnessed?

At the end of the seven-year run, after the group finally broke up, the fragments of those songs and images would continue to intersect with the scenes of one's own life, so that the miseries of high school love were permanently imbued with the strains of "No Reply" and "I'm a Loser," and a hundred varieties of psychic fracturing acquired a common soundtrack stitched together from "She Said She Said" ("I know what it's like to be dead") or the tornadolike crescendo in the middle of "A Day in the Life." Only that unnaturally close identification could account for the way in which the breakup of the Beatles functioned as a token for every frustrated wish or curdled aspiration of the era. Their seven fat years went from a point where everything was possible—haircuts, love affairs, initiatives toward world peace—to a point where only silence remained open for exploration.

All of this long since settled into material for biographies and made-for-TV biopics. Even as the newly released CD of their number one hits breaks all previous sales records, the number of books on the Beatles begins to approach the plateau where Jesus, Shakespeare, Lincoln, and Napoleon enjoy their bibliographic afterlife. If *The Beatles Anthology* has any claim, it is as "The Beatles' Own Story," an oral history patched together from past and present interviews, with the ghost of John Lennon sitting in for an impossible reunion at which all the old anecdotes are told one more time, and occasion is provided for a last word in edgewise about everything from LSD and the Maharishi to Allen Klein and the corporate misfortunes of Apple.

The book, which reads something like a *Rolling Stone* interview that unaccountably goes on for hundreds of pages, is heavy enough to challenge the carrying capacity of some coffee tables and is spread over multicolored page layouts that seem like dutifully hard-to-read tributes to the golden age of psychedelia. It is the final installment of a protracted multimedia project whose most interesting component was a six-CD compilation of outtakes, alternates, and rarities released under the same title in 1995.

Those rarities—from a crude tape of McCartney, Lennon, and Harrison performing Buddy Holly's "That'll Be the Day" in Liverpool in 1958 to John Lennon's original 1968 recording of "Across the Universe" without Phil Spector's subsequently added orchestral excrescences—were revealing and often moving, and left no question at all that the Beatles were no mirage. Indeed, even the most minor differences in some of the alternate versions served the valuable function of making audible again songs whose impact had worn away through overexposure. In the print-version *Anthology*, the Beatles are limited to words, words whose frequent banality and inadequacy only increase one's admiration for the expressiveness of their art. People who can make things like *With the Beatles* or *Rubber Soul* or *The White Album* should not really be required also to comment on what they have done.

The most interesting words come early. Before *Love Me Do* and
Beatlemania and the first American tour, the Beatles actually lived in
the same world as the rest of us, and it is their memories of that
world—from Liverpool to Hamburg to the dance clubs of northern
England—that are the most suggestive. The earliest memories are
most often of a generalized boredom and sense of deprivation. A
postwar Liverpool barely out of the rationing card era, with bomb-
sites for parks (Paul recalls "going down the bombie" to play) and
not much in the way of excitement, figures mostly as the blank
backdrop against which movies and music (almost exclusively American) could make themselves felt all the more powerfully. "We were
just desperate to get anything," George remarks. "Whatever film
came out, we'd try to see it. Whatever record was being played,
we'd try to listen to, because there was very little of anything. . . .
You couldn't even get a cup of sugar, let alone a rock'n'roll record."

Fitfully a secret history of childhood music takes form: Paul listening to his pianist father play "Lullaby of the Leaves" and "Stairway to Paradise," George discovering Hoagy Carmichael songs and
Josh White's "One Meatball," and Ringo (the most unassuming and
therefore often the most eloquent speaker here) recalling his
moment of illumination:

> My first musical memory was when I was about eight: Gene
> Autry singing "South of the Border." That was the first time I
> really got shivers down my backbone, as they say. He had his
> three compadres singing, "Ai, ai, ai, ai," and it was just a thrill
> to me. Gene Autry has been my hero ever since.

Only John—indifferent to folk ("college students with big scarfs
and a pint of beer in their hands singing in la-di-da voices") and jazz
("it's always the same, and all they do is drink pints of beer")—seems
to have reserved his enthusiasm until the advent of Elvis and Jerry
Lee Lewis and Little Richard: "It was Elvis who really got me out of
Liverpool. Once I heard it and got into it, that was life, there was no
other thing." If one can imagine Paul playing piano for local wed-
dings and dances, George driving a bus like his old man, and Ringo

perhaps falling into the life of crime his teenage gang exploits seemed to promise, it is inconceivable that John could have settled into any of the choices he was being offered in his youth.

None of them ever did much except prepare themselves to be the Beatles. Their youths were devoid of incident (at least of incident that anyone cared to write into the record) and largely of education. John, the eldest, had a bit of art school training, but for all of them real education consisted more of repeated exposure to Carl Perkins, Chuck Berry, and Frank Tashlin's Cinemascope rock'n'roll extravaganza *The Girl Can't Help It*. On the British side, they steeped themselves in the surreal BBC radio comedy *The Goon Show*—echoes of Spike Milligan and Peter Sellers's non sequiturs are an abiding presence in their work—and in the skiffle band craze of the late Fifties (a renewal of old-fashioned jug band styles) they found a point of entry into the world of actual bands and actual gigs.

"I would often sag off school for the afternoon," writes Paul, "and John would get off art college, and we would sit down with our two guitars and plonk away." Along with the younger George, they formed a band that played skiffle, country, and rock, and played local dances, and after some changes in personnel officially became, around 1960, the Beatles, in allusion to the "beat music" that was England's term for what was left of a rock'n'roll at that point almost moribund. Hard up for jobs, they found themselves in Hamburg, in a series of Reeperbahn beer joints, and by their own account were pretty much forced to become adequate musicians by the discipline of eight-hour sets and demanding, unruly audiences. Amid the amiable chaos of whores, gangsters, and endless amphetaminefueled jamming—"it was pretty vicious," remarks Ringo, who joined the group during this period, "but on the other hand the hookers loved us"—they transformed themselves into an anarchic rock band, "wild men in leather suits." Back in the UK they blew away the local competition: "There were all these acts going 'dum de dum' and suddenly we'd come on, jumping and stomping," in George's account. "In those days, when we were rocking on, becoming popular in the little clubs where there was no big deal about The Beatles, it was fun."

Once the group gets back to England, the days of "sagging off" and "plonking away" are numbered. As their ascent swiftly takes shape—within a year of a Decca executive dismissing them with the comment that "guitar groups are on the way out" they have dropped the "wild man" act and are already awash in Beatlemania—the reminiscences have less and less to do with anything other than the day-to-day business of recording and performing. Once within the universe of EMI, life becomes something of a controlled experiment, with the Beatles subjected to unfamiliar sorts of corporate oversight:

> PAUL: . . . We weren't even allowed into the control room, then. It was Us and Them. They had white shirts and ties in the control room, they were grown-ups. In the corridors and back rooms there were guys in full-length lab coats, maintenance men and engineers, and then there was us, the tradesmen. . . . We gradually became the workmen who took over the factory.

If they took over, though, it was at the cost of working at a killing pace, churning out songs, touring and making public appearances as instructed, keeping the merchandise coming. It can of course be wondered whether this forced production didn't have a positive effect on their work, simply because the work they were then turning out—everything from "Love Me Do" and "Please Please Me" to *Rubber Soul* was produced virtually without a break from performing or recording—could hardly be improved.

It is the paradox of such a life that it precludes the sort of experience on which art usually nurtures itself. The latter-day reminiscences evoke the crew members on a prolonged interstellar flight, thrown back on each other and on their increasingly abstract memories of Earth, and livening the journey with whatever drugs or therapies promise something like the terrestrial environment they have left behind. In this context marijuana and LSD are not passing episodes but central events, the true subject matter of the later Beatles records. In the inner storms of the bubble world, dreams and private portents take the place of the comings and goings of a street life that has become remote.

The isolation becomes glaring in, say, Paul's recollections of 1967: "I've got memories of bombing around London to all the clubs and the shops. . . . It always seemed to be sunny and we wore the far-out clothes and the far-out little sunglasses. The rest of it was just music." One can be sure that the "bombing around" took place within a well-protected perimeter. It is around this time that we find the Beatles pondering the possibility of buying a Greek island in order to build four separate residences linked by tunnels to a central dome, like something out of *Dr. No* or *Modesty Blaise*, with John commenting blithely that "I'm not worried about the political situation in Greece, as long as it doesn't affect us. I don't care if the government is all fascist, or communist. . . . They're all as bad as here."

The conviction grows that the Beatles are in no better position than anyone else to get a clear view of their own career. "The moral of the story," says George, "is that if you accept the high points you're going to have to go through the lows. . . . So, basically, it's all good." They know what it was to have been a Beatle, but not really—or only by inference—what it all looked like to everybody else. This leads to odd distortions in tone, as if after all they had not really grasped the singularity of their fate. From inside the rocket was not necessarily the best vantage point for charting its trajectory.

Paul's comments on how certain famous songs actually got to be written are amiably vague: "'Oh, you can drive my car.' What is it? What's he doing? Is he offering a job as a chauffeur, or what? And then it became much more ambiguous, which we liked." As much in the dark as the rest of us as to the ultimate significance of what they were doing, the Beatles were all the more free to follow their usually impeccable instincts. So if John Lennon chose to describe "Rain" as "a song I wrote about people moaning about the weather all the time," and Paul sees the lyrics of "A Day in the Life" as "a little poetic jumble that sounded nice," it confirms the inadvisability of seeking enlightenment other than by just listening to the records. (John, again: "What does it really mean, 'I am the eggman'? It could have been the pudding basin, for all I care.") The band doesn't know, they just write them.

In the end it was not the music that wore out but the drama, the personalities, the weight of expectation and identity. By the time the Beatles felt obliged to make exhortations like "all you need is love" and "you know it's gonna be all right," it was already time to bail out. How nice it would be to clear away the mass of history and personal association and just hear the records for the notes and words. Sometimes it's necessary to wait twenty years to be able to hear it again, the formal beauty that begins as far back as "Ask Me Why" and "There's a Place" and is sustained for years without ever settling into formula. Nothing really explains how or why musicians who spent years jamming on "Be Bop a Lula" and "Long Tall Sally" turned to writing songs like "Not a Second Time" and "If I Fell" and "Things We Said Today," so altogether different in structure and harmony. Before the addition of all the sitars and tape loops and symphony orchestras, before the lyrical turn toward eggmen and floating downstream, Lennon and McCartney (and, on occasion, Harrison) were already making musical objects of such elegant simplicity, such unhectoring emotional force, that if they had quit after *Help!* (their last "conventional" album) the work would still persist.

Paul McCartney recollects that when the Beatles heard the first playbacks at EMI it was the first time they'd really heard what they sounded like: "Oh, that sounds just like a record! Let's do this again and again and again!" The workmen taking over the factory were also the children taking over the playroom, determined to find effects that no one had thought of pulling out of the drawer before. They went from being performers to being songwriters, but didn't make the final leap until they became makers of records. Beyond all echoes of yesterday's mythologized excitement, the records— whether "The Night Before" or "Drive My Car" or "I'm Only Sleeping" or any of the dozens of others—lose nothing of a beauty so singular it might almost be called underrated.

MONICA KENDRICK

Gimme Shelter

It would be nice to always be able to present the album or concert review as a completely self-contained unit, a nice symmetrical form independent of what went on outside its frame of reference. For instance: I'm in love with the Japanese psych band Acid Mothers Temple, especially after seeing them play in Chicago twice in one weekend last month, and I wanted to write a concise and shapely love letter that had to do with the rupturing, unreassuring nature of the true psychedelic experience. The evening after the second show, at Reckless Records, I went home and got about halfway through such a piece, then went to bed. When I woke up, the World Trade Center was imploding. I suppose a real professional would have been able to finish the essay more or less on schedule—but to me it would've seemed like crossing a line between "professional" and "living in a complete vacuum."

I've never had much luck with tuning out so-called extraneous information—which is why I feel compelled to point out that psychedelia in its original conception was about letting the world rush in, not about tuning it out. But what has passed for the psychedelic aesthetic for some time now is the antithesis of the original, a sort of laid-back multicolor malaise that borders on terminal. In college, I oh-so wanted to be a hippie, but I couldn't reconcile myself to so much music that sounded so oddly boneless—like a drowsing cat picked up off the couch—or to all of the plain old sitting around that contemporary American hippies seem to do an awful lot of.

Surely, I thought, there must be more to counterculture than oodly guitar solos, Frisbee, veggie dogs, and the endless contemplation of hydraulic bongs.

So I reluctantly left the grass gazers and fell in with a crowd fond of grinding No-Doz into a powder and snorting it, but that wasn't satisfying for long either. There it was—I couldn't really pledge allegiance to any subculture with music that ever got familiar enough to breed contempt, be it polite honky blues or three-chord punk. It was the weird stuff, that which would never consent to be mere background music, that rang my bell, and my unreconstructed metalhead reptile brain needed volume and edge: I'll probably believe till I die that Sonic Youth's *Bad Moon Rising* is a better trip album than anything by the Doors, and that Keiji Haino makes more accurate religious music than, say, those Gregorian chants some people like to use when coming down. On the other hand, I defy any knee-jerk hater of boomer rock to keep standing upright in the face of, say, the version of "Set the Controls for the Heart of the Sun" that I found on one of my dad's 1970 Pink Floyd bootlegs, or to deny outright that Don Van Vliet was not a fantasist at all but a gritty realist. What does all of this righteous noise have in common? Maybe it's best encapsulated on another dark-psych favorite of mine, the Velvet Underground's *White Light/ White Heat:* "And then my mind split open . . ." SCREEEEEEEECH. Rupture as rapture.

Acid Mothers Temple—more properly known as Acid Mothers Temple & the Melting Paraiso U.F.O.—are the pinnacle of this kind of psychedelia. A loose collective of wandering souls who come together in various configurations to play, led by the monster guitarist Makoto Kawabata, they're ferocious and funny, deeply weird and musically brilliant. At the Hideout, tiny androgynous-looking keyboardist Cotton Casino manned her wired rig as if it were the bridge of an out-of-control spaceship, seemingly oblivious to everything else; bassist Atsushi Tsuyama let loose an unearthly bastardization of throat singing, in a giggly cross between Japanese, English, and maybe Venusian. They spent a healthy portion of the set sending their impressive hair flailing in all directions, but then they'd plunge unexpectedly into eerie and lovely melody inspired by Tsuyama's love of southern France's Occitanian folk music or possibly by the Incredible String Band or vintage Fairport Convention. In hindsight, it occurs to me that what they were doing was exploring myriad ways to translate into music the beauty of flight: sometimes as natural and soft as a bird, sometimes as high-tech and searingly loud as the Concorde.

On Tuesday morning, the shit hit the fan, and I probably should have forgotten all about music. For a while I think I did. Reality and unreality mingled. For a few minutes I was on two phone lines at once—one with my former fiancé, who lives in New York, and the other with my editor, trying to fix a flawed metaphor. When I sat down to write, all I could summon about Acid Mothers Temple was a mental picture of them stranded at O'Hare. I wondered what they must be making of all this, and then I projected on them all these notions of mine about epiphany. I'd gotten such a moment of clarity from them, and now I felt it twisted into grotesquerie by epiphany's evil twin—a moment of sheer horror. I had many moments that day that were hopefully as close as I'll ever get to that, as I envisioned the attack from various perspectives (most disturbing of all probably that of passengers on the doomed planes). Epiphany can be rendered in music, but horror cannot, because it's a form of chaos, and music is an act over which the musician can't help but retain some measure of control. No musician, I am fairly sure, has ever made music that can effectively express annihilation.

By nature, neither epiphany nor horror can last, and something must come after—provided there is an "after." How do we come to terms with those fiery crashes now burned into our brains? Candle lighting and flag waving don't in themselves add up to soul-searching, and neither does music, inherently, but at least it has more potential. But what kind of music? As helpless as we all feel, I find that I have less patience than ever for sitting around, be it in pleasant lethargy or depressed numbness. But I do have renewed appreciation for the cultivation of comfort—which is often simply a more urgent form of sitting around. We've been cajoled to please resume the pursuit of the banal and the pleasurable, and hey, it sorta works, however briefly. Among my guilty pleasures are comfort food (I've fattened up the Little Debbie ledgers as well as some, um, personal assets in the past month), comfort vices (smoke 'em if ya got 'em), comfort lit (if the British are so keen on supporting us, can't J.K. Rowling write a little faster?), and certainly comfort music.

On a long train ride to New York a couple weeks ago, one of the first CDs I instinctively reached for was Spacemen 3's Sound of Confusion, and once in, at no point did it make anything other than perfect sense. Cofounder Jason Pierce, aka Jason Spaceman, has always made a point of straining toward the sky; his melancholy hymns and dirgey grinding seemed to me as relevant to the current zeitgeist as Bono's preachy sincerity suddenly does to other, ordinarily sensible members of my profession.

In Spiritualized, Pierce's post–Spacemen 3 band, these efforts have only intensified. The group has actually pursued the record for "highest show on earth," playing 1,136 feet up in Toronto's CN Tower in 1997 and at Windows on the World, the restaurant on the 107th floor of One World Trade Center, in 1998. The group's new fourth album, *Let It Come Down*, is a cathedral of a record, huge and yet delicate, heavily ornamented—and engineered out the wazoo. It's been picked apart and reassembled and reanalyzed down to the teeniest decay wave—and that's all before the choir and the police sirens get overdubbed. "I'm just trying to find a peace of mind," Pierce mutters on "Out of Sight," a sort of neo-latter-day–Pink Floyd number. But "gravity just keeps on keeping me down."

But as the Handsome Family sings about the soaring towers of the Cologne Cathedral (where "every one of us is swept away like bread crumbs"), *Let It Come Down* brings only limited comfort. As a singer, Pierce is a bit too stiff to pull off anything resembling real soul, and his arrangements are getting more and more by-the-book. Though he's still passable when he's trying to climb Jacob's ladder, it's the more intimate tunes, like "I Didn't Mean to Hurt You" and "Stop Your Crying," that stand out the most.

In times of trauma, a little pinch of opiate for the masses can come in very handy. But sooner or later it's time for real spiritualizing, which comes by opening the mind rather than trying to cushion it; for the raw pseudoviolence of epiphany, which reveals a place where reassurance may no longer be possible or plausible or even desirable, where the bright lights of the soul are presented rather than merely described. We need to feel gravity's pull, good and hard, to remind ourselves of the sensation of liftoff—of the reason we risk crashing in the first place.

GREIL MARCUS

Days Between Stations: Kelly Hogan

SEPTEMBER 20—I had no problem playing Kelly Hogan's *Because It Feel Good* over and over in the days after the attacks on New York and Washington, D.C. It was sitting in the CD player. I'd stumbled on it the week before. It sounded OK. It wasn't as if I cared if I heard anything else. I was taking a break from the television, scared that I'd miss something. Hoping I'd miss something.

Hogan has a past; doesn't everybody? If you want her life story you can look it up. Maybe on a better day you'll run into her and she'll tell you hers and you can tell her yours.

On *Because It Feel Good* Hogan is a torch singer. That doesn't mean she comes off like the Statue of Liberty, though the image comes to mind. The Statue of Liberty might have been taken out, too; it might be taken out tomorrow. But in a way the metaphors the times force on music are always apt, can always tell you something if you let them. What is a torch singer but someone appearing in front of other people—maybe standing tall, maybe slumping, maybe sitting in a chair—and testifying that the worst life has to offer can't kill her? Or hasn't yet? You might hear endurance; you might hear triumph; you might hear a death waiting just off stage, suicide in one tune, murder in another, the end of the world in a third. "Our love will last til the end of time" means that time can come to an end.

As Hogan sings you are hearing a woman who sounds as if she can say anything, even if she also sounds as if she's holding back at least half of what she has to say. Half of herself: she might need it someday. That's the feeling on "(You Don't Know) The First Thing About Blue." She takes you all the way into the song in an instant. She calls back the mystical nowhere Paula Frazer explored a few years back with her band Tarnation—a nowhere you knew had to be somewhere on Route 66, though now it might as well be in some downtown New York City bar. Has everything changed? Has nothing changed? If history is made at night, does that mean history can really change the heart? Hogan merely comes down the stairs of the song, quietly, slowly, with a slow, quiet menace. She seems almost to regret the fact that the person she's singing to will never learn, will make the same mistakes again and again and again.

An echoed, chiming guitar comes in behind her, taking the story into the past, letting the singer walk past it into the future. "You say you'll cry if you lose my loving," she comes back to say. "You say you just don't know . . . what you'll do. Believe me, baby, you ain't seen nothing—" Hogan lets the last line go into the air like smoke, just as she's already caressed "you'll do" into a melodic curve so sensual it's as if for a second she's forgotten who she's singing to or why.

In its lack of any need to press, any need to make sure you get the point or appreciate how good the singer is, the number radiates out across the album. It gives weight even to "No, Bobby Don't," formally a 1950s teen sob that could have been sung by anyone from Bette Midler to Rosie and the Originals (not only does the guitar play those "Angel Baby" triplets, the strings do). But after "(You Don't Know) The First Thing About Blue," the number takes on the displacement of the teen-dream auditions early in David Lynch's *Mulholland Drive*, where sophisticated, tough-as-nails stars dress up in chiffon to lip-synch Connie Stevens' 1960 "Sixteen Reasons" and Linda Scott's 1961 "I've Told Every Little Star." In the movie, in the beginning, when the movie seems like a regular story with different characters, just like, you know, life, you nevertheless sense that there's something off here, that the pieces don't fit together: that there's more happening, more at stake, than you can put into words. It's the same with Hogan.

By the end of *Because It Feel Good*, this little ditty has faded into the plain desperation of Charlie Rich's "Stay," into the simple terror of Randy Newman's "Living without You." As with a 1960s soul singer, there's a stillness in each note. If you've heard the songs before, you probably won't remember where.

The torch singer wears her heart on her sleeve. Today on Hogan it looks good, like a dress she's had for years, that simply didn't look right until now, when something in the air brought it into style. Up against the facts of life it's the smallest thing in the world, but you pick up the pieces one by one.

A Long, Strange Trip

One of the great rock and roll singers stood on the stage with his arms crossed. He uncrossed them and crossed them again. He yawned. Then he sang a verse of one of his songs, "Don't Slander Me." His once-mighty voice was thin and couldn't quite reach all the notes. He turned his back on the audience between verses. He looked beat. It was 1993, and Roky Erickson and his backing band were performing at the Austin Music Awards. When they played his biggest song, "You're Gonna Miss Me," a piece of proto-punk rock that had once been an anthem of mid-sixties teen attitude, it sounded like a rehearsal for retirement. Roky, with his long black hair and thick beard, didn't look happy. He wasn't. He was a diagnosed schizophrenic who hadn't taken any anti-psychotic medicine in several years and who would go home that night to a house where he kept half a dozen radios, TVs, and stereos blasting noise to drown out the voices in his head. It really hadn't been his idea to be onstage that night. He hadn't won anything, and he hadn't made an album in more than a decade. He might as well have had a sign around his neck: "Sixties Nostalgia Act." But he had said yes when his friends asked him to sing. They were well intentioned—they wanted to give Roky and the crowd a feeling for what had once been, back when psychedelia was young and Roky was a sign of something else entirely.

Back then, in 1966, Roky (pronounced "Rocky") was a teenage rebel with an electric guitar. He had a sweet, round face and a buzz-saw voice, and sometimes he'd shake his head and scream like a banshee, which drove the kids crazy. He wrote hopeful, yearning melodies like his hero Buddy Holly, who had died only a few years earlier. He and his group, the 13th Floor Elevators, were the best rock and roll band in Texas. Indeed, they were the first psychedelic group ever, and they changed the sound of rock, influencing everyone from Janis Joplin and Billy Gibbons to the Grateful Dead. They sold more than 100,000 records, had a hit song, and appeared on *American Bandstand.* They had everything that other seminal bands of the era, like the Doors, had: vision, great musicians, and in Roky, star power.

And then he went crazy and the band broke up. At 22, Buddy Holly was dead; at 22, Roky Erickson was in an insane asylum. Drugs, excess, schizophrenia: Roky was a casualty of the times. He got out and made more music, but he always found himself back in some kind of trouble. "Roky's story is a descent into Dante's inferno," says Bill Bentley, a senior vice president of publicity at Warner Bros. Records, who grew up in Houston, saw the Elevators, and became a friend of Roky's. "I've never seen such brilliance accompanied by such a fall, where every wrong thing that could happen happened." In spite of this, or maybe because of it, over the years Roky kept getting rediscovered by musicians and fans, and he became a cult star, as much for his bizarre life as for his sublime, ferocious music. (In the mid-nineties an Englishman published a fanzine called *Roky Erickson and the Secret of the Universe.*) "Some artists are able to cut right through everything and *get* you," says punk rock icon Henry Rollins. "Brian Wilson, Sam Cooke, Roky Erickson. His voice, lyrics, and then the man himself—a sweet, likable guy who is so mysterious and obviously a genius."

Everyone who meets Roky comes away with a story that is both funny and horrifying. Mine came when I first interviewed him, in 1984, during one of his periods of decline. I was a cub rock writer, and he had been one of my heroes ever since I'd heard "You're Gonna Miss Me," two and a half minutes of prehistoric garage-rock fury. Roky had long straggly hair, long nails curling out of nicotine-stained fingers, and deep creases in his forehead. After we started our interview that afternoon, he pulled the cellophane from a cigarette pack out of his shirt pocket to reveal a bee crawling around inside.

He examined it briefly, returned it to his pocket, and continued, rambling on many subjects, making connections between things that weren't the least bit connected. He said he was the rock messiah. He said he was flattered at being called the first punk rocker but pointed out that true punk was a song by fictional characters Doug and Bob McKenzie of the television show *SCTV.* He said he had a new song called "I Love the Sound of a Severed Head When It's Bouncing Down the Staircase." At one point he started talking about Satan. "The devil is the person who commands the opposite place of God," he said. "Satan wants to crucify Jesus. I kind of like Jesus. Jesus got crucified, died for our sins. Satan was an angel who was kicked out of heaven. His name was Little Michael, Little Michael Hall . . ." I stopped taking notes and looked at Roky, waiting for a wink, a chuckle, a pause—anything. He ignored me. "I'm Satan and the devil is the devil," he went on. "You always want to be the stranger in the woods, the angel Paul . . ." Yes, I had heard him correctly, and either I was the Dark Lord or Roky was pulling my leg. He was obviously more in control than I had given him credit for, and all afternoon he did what he has done all his life: He danced along the line between the lucid and the scatterbrained. Perhaps, I thought, he's crazy. Perhaps he's pretending. Perhaps he's both.

I saw him occasionally over the next decade and a half, but Roky became more and more reclusive, and stories about him got more dire. During most of the nineties, he lived alone in the sonic chaos of his blaring appliances. His teeth had rotted to nubs, and he was in constant pain from oral infections. As the decade wound down, he wouldn't open the door to anyone but his mother, Evelyn Erickson, who had been caring for him. Many friends were afraid he might die. But then last year, in a tense and sometimes bitter struggle, Roky's youngest brother, Sumner, went to court and wrestled control away from their mother, moving 54-year-old Roky to his home in Pittsburgh. Roky was back on anti-psychotic medicine. He got new teeth. He was alive.

It seemed like a good time to try to contact Roky again, to try to properly tell his story. All previous attempts have gotten lost in the swirl of fact, myth, and outright lies that make up the Roky Erickson legend. (Expect other attempts too: a Hollywood movie, a documentary, and a book on Roky and the Elevators are all in the works.) So this summer I flew to Pittsburgh and spent three days with him. Seventeen years after my first interview, he was not nearly as effusive, often letting long stretches of time go by without saying anything. Conversation with Roky is always a Zen experience, and sometimes one hand does all the clapping. He is especially reticent about his past, with good reason. For most of us the past is another country; for Roky it's another planet. He looks better than he has in years—his beard is trimmed, his hair is short, and because of his dentures, he's not afraid to smile. Roky used to look like Rasputin; now he looks like Jimmy Stewart's dotty Uncle Billy in *It's a Wonderful Life*. He is sweet and eager to please, and he marches around his brother's house like a toddler might—slowly, back straight, arms out. Emotionally, Roky is still a boy, and he often tests his boundaries with Sumner.

Roky and I took a lot of drives and watched a lot of cartoons, and I became, for a short time, one of his minders, part of a long line of people over the years who have been drawn to him. Such people inevitably want to take care of him, to shield him from himself and his demons, and so they try to fashion Roky according to the image they have in their heads. They create their own versions of him. And though they try to save him, sometimes they do him harm. Throughout his life he has fought the law, doctors, the music industry, and his own schizophrenia. But some of his toughest battles have been with friends and family who, in order to maintain their versions—who he was, what he needed, what he didn't—became fiercely protective and downright manipulative. It's tempting to point to one villain or another in Roky's life story, but most of the people around him have wanted to help him. They meant well—they just had their own ideas about who their favorite rock eccentric should be. "Everybody in this story has good intentions," says Evelyn, whose intentions have been the best of all. "But you know what they say about the road to hell."

In 1983 Evelyn shot a home video of her son playing songs. It opened with Roky singing, "For you, I'd do anything for you . . ."

while the video camera focused on a portrait of Evelyn as a young woman. She had black hair, red lips, and fair skin and looked like Elizabeth Taylor. The camera stayed on the painting, then panned to Roky, who stopped halfway through the first chorus. "Like it?" he asked the camera in a high drawl. Evelyn's voice told him that what he had sung was just a test run. Now they'd do the real one. Then she said, "You want to comb your hair real quick?" Roky had flowing locks, a mustache, long sideburns, and eyebrows that almost met over kind, sad eyes. His bright red-orange shirt and orange pants looked like they came from Goodwill. He did the song again (this time the camera stayed on him the whole time) and then sang nine more. Several times the camera came back to the portrait. After each song he asked some variation of "How about that one?" And Evelyn said some variation of "Good."

Evelyn has been Roky's director for most of his life, his first influence and the one who made him the great and fragile artist he is. She's artistic, iconoclastic, and self-absorbed. She's also the one who is most to blame for Roky's current condition, say several people close to him, who half-jokingly call her Develyn. Evelyn didn't set out to be a Svengali. She was a high school cheerleader in Dallas who married her high school sweetheart, Roger Erickson, in 1944. Their first son, Roger Kynard Erickson, Jr., was born July 15, 1947. He was called Roky because of the first two letters of his first two names. Soon the Ericksons moved to Austin, where Roger, a civil engineer and an architect, designed and built their home on Arthur Lane in South Austin. Evelyn put Roky in piano lessons at age four. A few years later, she was taking guitar lessons and then running home to teach him. Evelyn had a strong voice and sang with the University of Texas Opera Workshop. She won an Arthur Godfrey talent contest in 1957, singing the aria of *La Traviata*. The next year she even released a single of "O Holy Night" on a local label. Around that time Roky, with younger brothers Mikel and Don, made his public debut, singing "Mother Dear" to Evelyn on a local TV show called *Woman's World*. She sang in an Episcopal church choir, and Roky and his brothers (Ben was born in 1959 and Sumner in 1962) sang in a Baptist one. The Ericksons were devout believers, and Evelyn says that when Roky had a broken leg, her prayer group healed him.

They weren't your typical fifties American family. When I told Evelyn that they seemed quite eccentric, she replied whimsically, "I'd prefer to call us 'eclectic.'" Now in her seventies, Evelyn has bright eyes and a pixielike smile. "I just thought we were being creative," she said with a laugh. George Kinney, a boyhood friend of Roky's and now an Austin musician, remembers how the neighborhood kids loved to go to the Ericksons', where the rules weren't as strict as those at other homes. Another friend remembers no rules at all: "The Erickson house was often a mess—clothes everywhere, kids running amok, and Evelyn would be painting a mural across the living room wall." Dad was a brilliant architect but a workaholic and a hard drinker who was rarely home. "Roky feared his father," says Kinney. "We *all* feared his father. He was real sarcastic. Very disapproving of Evelyn's liberal way of raising the kids." Kinney remembers Roger coming home in the wee hours one night when he and Roky, who were growing their hair long because of the Beatles, were awake and reading comic books. Roky's father called his son out and cut his hair.

Comics were a big part of Roky's life—superheroes like the Fantastic Four and horror comics—as were scary movies. "He was a weirdo," says Kinney, "but a gentle one. Real funny, popular with girls, good-looking. Not part of the crowd." Roky loved rock and roll. His favorite was Buddy Holly, but he liked the way Little Richard and James Brown screamed, and he'd play Brown's records and wail along. Then he heard Bob Dylan, and by 1965 Roky and George were playing guitars down on the Drag, the section of Guadalupe Street that borders UT, a tip jar at their feet. They started hanging out with college kids and early hippies. They discovered marijuana. "He started getting his confidence," recalls Kinney. "We were all stumbling around, trying to find what we wanted to do. He found his spot." Roky wanted to play music. He left high school three weeks shy of his 1965 graduation—whether he dropped out or was kicked out is unclear, though Evelyn says he was booted for having long hair. Soon he joined the Spades, a local group. They recorded and released one of his songs, "You're Gonna Miss Me." In retrospect, that wild, muffled 45 was one of the first punk-rock singles.

Roky now found himself part of the budding counterculture and music scene at UT. Rock bands and folkies were writing songs, smoking marijuana (which was illegal—possession was a felony and a joint could get you twenty years), and taking psychedelics like LSD and peyote, which were still legal. Roky fell in with a pushy intellectual named Tommy Hall who loved LSD and saw it as the foundation of a new philosophy. Hall couldn't play an instrument, but he picked up the jug, a staple of many folk bands of the day, and recruited a band, stealing Roky from the Spades with the promise of a supergroup with a super philosophy: truer living through chemicals. They called themselves the 13th Floor Elevators. "If you want to get to the thirteenth floor," Roky once explained, "ride our elevator."

Roky wrote most of the music, but Tommy, five years older, wrote the words and set the group's tone. Hall saw the Elevators as missionaries, and he insisted they take acid—only the best—before every show, although sometimes they played on other hallucinogens such as DMT or mescaline. "Tommy manipulated the band, and especially Roky, with LSD," says musician Tary Owens. Hall was the teacher and Roky the child, and the Elevators quickly became the most popular band in Austin, drawing hundreds of people to clubs like the Jade Room. Nobody had ever seen a group like this. They proselytized about freeing your mind while other bands sang about cars and girls; they wrote their own songs when others were playing "Louie, Louie"; they made a weird *ticka-ticka-ticka* sound (it was the jug); and they were fronted by a white teenager who screamed like James Brown. "He was the most electric performer I've ever seen, and that includes Hendrix," says Bill Bentley, then a Houston high school kid who would see the band at clubs like La Maison. "He was possessed, so vivid and mesmerizing. His voice was so sharp and cutting—sometimes he'd get lost in his screams." Roky would cock his head to the right and shake it as he screamed. In early 1966 the group recorded a new version of "You're Gonna

Miss Me" for Contact, a small Houston label. Contact then sold it to International Artists (IA), another small Houston label, which released it that spring. The song became a regional hit.

It was hard to be a hippie in Texas in 1966, especially a popular one. The police were not happy about this gang of longhaired rock stars and began shadowing the group after members were busted for pot. "The police declared war on the Elevators in Texas," IA's Lelan Rogers (country star Kenny Rogers' brother) once told rock writer Jon Savage. Cops would search the band's equipment before and after shows. In Baytown the police dismantled the group's gear in the parking lot looking for drugs, and local kids had to lend the musicians their amps. "The police thought people like Roky were out to take over the government and corrupt their children," says Roky's high school friend Terry Moore, now a Lake Tahoe real estate broker. The Elevators eventually lucked out on the pot arrest. They could have gone to prison, but because of a judge's error, all went free or were put on probation.

In August the Elevators went to San Francisco, where they found another fledgling counterculture. The Texans carried a mystique with them—they were loud, they'd been busted, and wildest of all, they played on LSD. Bands like the Grateful Dead (who formed shortly after the Elevators played their first San Francisco gig) *took* LSD, but they didn't *play* on it. These hard-edged Texans blew into town and blew people's minds. They were *psychedelic*. They were the first to use the term, and soon Bay Area bands were following their lead. When "You're Gonna Miss Me" peaked at number 55 on the *Billboard* pop singles chart, IA called the band back to Texas to do an album, which they recorded in eight hours. *The Psychedelic Sounds of the 13th Floor Elevators* came out in November, with a bright psychedelic cover and Hall's rambling acid manifesto on the back: "Recently, it has become possible for man to chemically alter his mental state and thus alter his point of view. . . ."

The record was a hit, and the group began working on a follow-up, *Easter Everywhere*, a kind of LSD concept record. Roky conceptualized freely, ingesting whatever pills others offered him, sometimes without asking what they were. "He had to live up to his status as the weird psychedelic mutant," remembers Kinney. Roky started getting more and more paranoid. At a November 1967 concert in Houston, he was afraid to walk onstage because he didn't want people to see the third eye in the middle of his forehead. By then the band's singular live show had degenerated into feedback and druggy jamming. When Bentley saw them in 1968, Roky stood with his back to the audience, singing a different song from what his bandmates were playing. "It was heartbreaking," Bentley says. "I thought, 'It's over. How did *that* happen?'"

The Elevators scrambled to make a third album for IA, even though they had problems with the label and complained that they had never made any money beyond a weekly $50 salary. Roky was in and out of clarity. "He was a vegetable," says bassist Ronnie Leatherman, who still plays music in Kerrville. Roky sang on only a handful of songs on the record, which was called *Bull of the Woods*. The band played a disastrous show at the just-opened HemisFair in San Antonio and Roky limped home. "He was all wired up and talking gibberish," says Evelyn. "I had to worry about his effect on my other four kids." She hired a psychiatrist, who put Roky on anti-psychotic drugs that left him in a stupor. She hired another doctor to take him off those drugs. Roky entered a private hospital in Houston, but two weeks later Hall helped him escape, and the two hitchhiked to California. Roky was free, but it was the end of the Elevators.

At a New Year's Eve, 1968, show at the famous Winterland, Roky's friend Terry Moore, who was in San Francisco to check out the legendary scene and score some good acid, saw Roky and George Kinney, who needed a ride back to Austin. It was hard to say no to Roky. "Everybody treated him like a god," says Moore. "Nobody would say, 'Roky, you need to straighten up.'" The three of them, plus three others, loaded into a VW Bug and headed home. Roky was in bad shape—unshaven, without shoes, and incoherent; apparently he'd been doing a lot of speed. In Arizona they broke out the LSD. Terry held out his hand and began passing it around. "I said, 'Roky, want some?' He grabbed a handful and put it in his mouth—took at least ten hits, and this was good acid." Soon Roky was holding one arm and hitting himself with it, yelling, "Get out, bad spirit!" Roky's friends dropped him off in El Paso, and he found his way back to Evelyn, freaked out and covered with sores.

In February 1969 Roky was busted for marijuana possession and eventually sent to the Austin State Hospital to be examined. He was diagnosed with "schizophrenia acute, undifferentiated" and put on the anti-psychotic drug Haldol. In May he escaped with the help of his girlfriend Dana Gaines. (She was not surprised to learn that a week before another girl had tried the same thing but she and Roky had been caught.) The police arrested Roky three months later. The best way out of a two-years-to-life sentence was to convince the judge that he was insane. Roky looked and acted crazy enough, and Dr. David Wade testified that Roky was hopeless—"a classic example of a schizophrenic reaction, a mental illness, mixed with drugs." He was ruled insane and therefore innocent of possession. Six years later Roky would claim that he had faked the whole thing; he seemed to enjoy keeping people guessing.

Because Roky had a habit of escaping minimum-security joints, he was sent to Rusk State Hospital, a facility that housed the criminally insane in East Texas. After several years of gobbling massive amounts of LSD, speed, and any other drugs someone might offer, he was given shock treatment and massive amounts of Thorazine, a drug used to sedate psychotics. Roky later told drummer Freddie Krc how terribly he was treated: "I was in there with people who'd chopped up people with a butcher knife, and they treated *me* worse because I had long hair."

The hair was cut. Evelyn visited, often bringing one of her other sons. She recorded Roky doing some of the songs he was writing— love songs and religious poems. Kinney began smuggling pages out, which he published as a book called *Openers*. Roky started a band, the Missing Links, with a couple of other inmates—a black guy who would perform with his face painted white and a redneck with long sideburns—and played at the hospital, rodeos, and a nearby college. Though he was doing well enough, his "open" sentence meant that unless someone proved he didn't belong there, he could stay in Rusk for the rest of his life. In 1970 Roky's brother Mike hired attorney

Jim Simons to get him out, and Simons finally got Roky a trial in 1972. The Austin courtroom was packed. By now Roky was something of a cause célèbre, the closest thing Austin had to a rock star but also a symbol of the counterculture. The jury came back in less than fifteen minutes. Roky was not a danger to himself or others, they said, and he was discharged from Rusk, "sanity restored."

But free Roky was confused Roky. "He didn't know where to grasp onto life again," says Kinney. "He depended on the largesse of friends." Once, when Moore saw Roky walking and gave him a ride, his friend didn't seem to recognize him and kept saying the CIA was watching him. Roky tried to get the band back together, and they even played a handful of shows. But things weren't the same, says writer Joe Kahn, who was hanging out with the group at the time and who now writes for the *Boston Globe:* "There was a lot of simmering frustration and bitterness at how they'd been ripped off by International Artists." (Roky, remembers Kahn, was oblivious to the problem.) Soon Roky and Dana Gaines got married. At first he was taking his meds and was happy. Soon, though, he went through a violent period. Dana recalls, "Out of the blue, he would go into rages. I was black and blue." She says that he once attacked her in her sleep. Roky would also take out a copy of *Openers* and cross out "Jesus" in his religious poems and write in "Satan." After nine months he stopped attacking his wife, and around then he had an affair with a woman named Renee Bayer that produced his first child, a girl named Spring, in 1974.

From 1973 to roughly 1982, Roky bounced back and forth between Austin and the Bay Area. He played with a band called the Aliens and recorded a couple of stunning new songs, "Starry Eyes" and "Two Headed Dog (Red Temple Prayer)," with Doug Sahm. The songs would become two of his best known and would roadmap the way he wrote for the next decade—a singular mixture of angelic love songs and demonic rock. "Starry Eyes" sounded like a Buddy Holly gem, while "Red Temple Prayer" was a ferocious slab of hard-edged guitar. Roky's new kick was that he was an alien from Mars; he claimed he had the legal documents to prove it and that

"You're Gonna Miss Me" really meant "You are gonna miss a Martian E." He was writing songs about ghosts, vampires, and beasts. Perhaps they were a reaction to the hell of Rusk State Hospital or perhaps he just wanted to shock people. Even though his new songs had titles like "I Walked With a Zombie," his melodies were still gorgeous, sometimes with a fifties-era innocence. A friend of his once asked him where his melodies came from. He paused, then said, "The very best ones are sent from heaven by Buddy Holly. The rest take the better part of an afternoon to rip off."

Roky signed a management and publishing contract and seemed to be getting his life in order. But in 1979 Dana, who was tired of Roky not taking his medicine and worried about how his antics were affecting their three-year-old son, Jegar, drove Roky from San Francisco to Austin and left him with Evelyn. Roky was soon discovered by local punk rockers, and he played with avant-weirdos the Re*Cords and then the new-wave band the Explosives. In 1980 he made his first full solo album (its title is a bunch of runic symbols) for CBS in England, where he had a devoted following. He was taking his medicine again, though producer Stu Cook later told an interviewer that Roky didn't like how it made him shake and wobble. "Roky would often say that he'd rather be nuts . . . than the way he felt," said Cook. As soon as Roky started feeling better, he'd go off the medicine and start taking speed and any other drugs his friends gave him. Divorced from Dana, he married a former bartender named Holly Patton, with whom he had a daughter named Cydne in 1984.

But Holly left too, and Roky wound up living with friends. Roky was always surrounded by friends. One of them was Jack Ortman, a fan who had been collecting everything ever written about Roky. In 1986 Ortman released the first of four volumes of Roky scrapbooks—it had more than three hundred pages, a sign of how vast Roky's influence was. Though CBS rejected a second album, small labels in the U.S. and Europe were releasing various studio and live bootleg albums, many recorded and released by Roky's friends. In 1987 Roky played his last full show, at Austin's Ritz Theater, and it too was eventually released as a live album. At the end of the show you can hear Roky calling out to his audience, "Thank you! Thank you! I really enjoyed the show! Thank you for playing tonight!" Inscrutable and lovable, he was a full-blown cult hero.

But there wasn't much money coming in to support Roky or Evelyn, who had been separated from her husband since 1979 and who had power of attorney over her son. She'd cash his Social Security mental-disability checks and give him $20 every other day for food and cigarettes. She moved him to federally subsidized housing in Del Valle, southeast of Austin. Roky shared a mailbox with two other tenants, including a friend of his. Roky would collect the mail for all three and take it to his friend, who would distribute it. When the friend moved out, Roky continued to collect the mail for all three addresses. Around Christmas a new tenant figured out why she wasn't getting any mail and called the police, who found it unopened and tacked on the wall near Roky's front door. Though Roky had clearly not intended to steal her mail, he had committed a federal offense, and this time he was sent to a federal mental institution in Missouri. He eventually wound up back in the Austin State Hospital, where he was given therapy and medicine for sixty days and then released. Roky immediately stopped taking his meds, and visitors to his home would walk in on a bunch of TVs, radios, stereos, and police scanners blaring white noise. Roky called the noisemakers his "electronic friends" for hiding the voices in his head.

As the nineties began it seemed like Roky would finally get some of the recognition he deserved and the money he was owed. On Halloween, 1990, *Where the Pyramid Meets the Eye* was released by Sire—a nineteen-track compilation of Roky's songs done by rock stars he had influenced, such as REM and ZZ Top. Several trusts were set up to organize Roky's finances. Attorneys hired by Evelyn, working pro bono, began a ten-year battle to get back royalties from International Artists; they claimed that though the band had sold many records, members had never received any royalties from label owner Lelan Rogers (who would soon sell the Elevators catalog to Charly Records in England, meaning the attorneys would now have to go after them). Roky began playing in public again at the urging of his friends, first at birthday parties and then at the Austin Music

Awards. Unfortunately, he played the same four songs at every appearance. During one performance, when Roky forgot the words to one of his songs, Bill Bentley says, "I realized that he had no business being up there, and I might have helped push him up there."

Roky made it through the past decade because of a steady group of minders who, along with his mother, took care of him. They'd go to his house, marvel at the noise and mess (in the wake of his mail bust, Roky had become obsessed with getting mail, writing away for every free catalog he could get), take him out to dinner, drive him around, hang out at Evelyn's—the one place Roky would relax—and marvel at his resilient way of seeing the world. Once, on an election day, Roky, Casey Monahan (the director of the Texas Music Office), and Butthole Surfers drummer King Coffey were driving around when Coffey asked Roky if he had voted. "I'm voting right now," he replied. Most of his minders were music business veterans like Monahan, musicians Owens and Coffey, freelance journalist Rob Patterson, and Emperor Jones label owner Craig Stewart. All seemed to see in Roky qualities that made them fall in love with rock and roll in the first place. As Monahan says, "He's a guy who's been screwed so many times but still looks at the world with an innocence completely at odds with his experience."

In 1993 Monahan, with help from Roky's brother Sumner, began collecting all of Roky's songs and poems; two years later they were published as *Openers 2*. Monahan also got Roky back in the studio again, for the first time in a decade, to record six old songs that were combined with five that were already recorded; the result was *All That May Do My Rhyme*. Roky's voice wasn't as strong as it once was, but it's a gorgeous album and one on which you can hear his true genius—his love songs. Roky's melodies will break your heart, from the luminous "Starry Eyes" to the soulful "You Don't Love Me Yet." Sumner played tuba on the album and was getting more and more involved in Roky's life. Like his brother, Sumner had been a teen prodigy, though he had followed a different path. He started playing the tuba in junior high school and was asked to join the prestigious Andre Previn–led Pittsburgh Symphony Orchestra when he was only eighteen.

Sumner wanted his brother back on medication, but Evelyn wouldn't hear of it and neither would Roky. They didn't trust doctors. Evelyn thought Roky's friends were the best medicine he could have, and she distrusted anti-psychotic drugs. She told me that Haldol, which Roky had taken in 1968, gave him the shakes and made him walk like a zombie. "You have to be careful," she says. "These psychotropic drugs should be monitored very seriously. If they're going to treat your mind, they should look at your whole body. Look at all the people who've died because of drugs." Evelyn's antipathy to prescription drugs comes partly from Roky's experience with hallucinogens. Evelyn and Roky didn't seem to trust dentists either. Roky's teeth were rotting in his gums, and he was in a lot of pain, but still, remembers Patterson, "He'd say, 'I'm not going to the dentist!' And Evelyn would say, 'Roky, if you don't want to go to the dentist, that's okay.'" Evelyn often said that what Roky needed was more people praying for him.

But Roky's minders think there was more to her refusal. "It was to protect her relationship with Roky," says Owens, "to protect her control over his life." There was a degree of madness behind her method, says Monahan: "Every woman Roky has ever been close to was ostracized by Evelyn. The only way for her to keep control was no girlfriend, no prescription drugs, no therapy. She seems to gain her identity from being his caretaker." Warner Bros. Records executive Bentley disagrees. "I never saw the dark side of Evelyn," he says. "She tried to cure Roky in so many ways, according to her belief. She might have loved him too much. He was her oldest, the most talented. He was a star, a little God-like creature."

Besides, Bentley says, picking on Evelyn misses an important point. "It's easy to say Evelyn told him not to take his meds," he says. "I think Roky *liked* the nothingness of his life. There was too much gigging and practicing." Roky is the king of the lollygaggers, and even as he has attracted people to him, bringing out their best— a sense of wonder, a nurturing instinct, a rush of gratitude that gentle weirdos like him walk among us—he has allowed them to take advantage of him, to turn him on, prop him up, trumpet his resurrection and their place alongside him. Roky, who is smarter, stronger, and more aware than anyone gives him credit for, is his own worst enemy: relentlessly passive. As his old friend Kinney says, looking back on Roky's life, "Sometimes I think he just didn't want to get a job, and he's pulled it off beautifully."

Last year Sumner decided enough was enough: Roky had a disease and he needed treatment. Sumner was angry that his 52-year-old brother, who was then living in a small federally subsidized apartment in South Austin, hadn't been seen by a doctor in ten years. In January of this year, Sumner applied for guardianship. In May a psychiatrist who had visited Roky filed a report with a Travis County court saying that abscesses in Roky's teeth were in danger of infecting his brain. Soon after, Roky was admitted to Shoal Creek Hospital, where he got two weeks of medical, dental, and psychological exams. Again he was diagnosed with schizophrenia, "a biological, genetic illness," says his doctor, William Privitera, that was probably waiting to happen in 1969, "though perhaps it got sped up by drug use." He was put on Zyprexa, one of a newer breed of anti-psychotics, by Privitera, who says it doesn't have the side effects of the older medications like Haldol: "It helps him think more clearly, it reduces his auditory hallucinations, helps with his attention, and reduces his agitation." Though Evelyn says Roky was anxious to leave the hospital, other family members saw immediate progress. "He shook my hand and asked about my kids," says his brother Mike. "He'd never done that before."

Evelyn visited Roky in the hospital every day. He asked her to cut his hair, which had grown into a massive dreadlock, and she did. She knew that the doctors were against her. "Theirs is an unhealthy, enmeshed relationship," says Privitera. "It's difficult to tell where she stops and he starts. We need to give Roky an opportunity to come into his own—to see what life without Mom can be." At the June 11 guardianship hearing. Evelyn voiced her distrust of Roky's medicine. "I would rather see the psychologists use methods more humane, more holistic, like yoga," she said. The judge thought more drastic action was needed and made Sumner Roky's guardian. Sumner felt he had to get Roky out of Austin, and nine days later they flew to Pittsburgh.

Once when he was a young boy, Sumner sat in the living room on Arthur Lane and listened to his big brother practice. Later he'd visit him in the insane asylum. Now he leaves him cheerful Post-it notes in his kitchen—"Dear Roky: Good Mornin'! I hope you had a good rest. Here's your 8 AM med." He plans to raise $1 million through a new trust so that he can eventually buy his brother a home in Austin and support him for the rest of his life. "If a hundred thousand people each give ten dollars, there's a million," he says confidently. On the wall just around the corner from the kitchen is a drawing Roky made of Tubby the Tuba when he was a boy, years before Sumner was born. Sumner is convinced Roky had something to do with him hearing his calling. On the mantelpiece is a sculpture of a beautiful woman, done by the famous artist Charles Umlauf, an Erickson family friend. The woman is Evelyn.

"Roky looks good," his rather taciturn father, Roger, says one evening. Roger, who designed Sumner's ultramodern home, lives next door yet doesn't see Roky much. Neither Roky nor Sumner seem particularly close to him. Indeed, Roky looks to Sumner for all things parental, asking him for permission like a child, sometimes testing his authority. Sumner, fifteen years younger, is patient and fair. Mostly Roky likes to watch the Cartoon Network and ride around in their dad's big blue New Yorker with the radio tuned to his favorite Top 40 station (Roky hasn't driven in years, terrified of getting stopped by the police). Roky is eating well, though he probably smokes a pack a day, dragging deeply on each one, exhaling, and almost immediately inhaling again. He doesn't drink or do any kind of illicit drugs. He loves ice cream. He loves his new teeth and is no longer ashamed of his smile. (Evelyn says she had wanted to get Roky's teeth fixed in 1994 with a root canal and caps, trying to save what teeth Roky had left, but the procedure was too expensive, so she never did it.) Sumner says that after years of not seeming to be interested in women, Roky is eyeballing them again. He likes going to talk to "this lady" who is helping him relax—Kay Miller, a new-age psychophysical therapist and Sumner's "mentor" of twelve years who is seeing Roky thrice weekly. The only thing Roky doesn't like is the tuba playing. "How about we go to your hotel and watch TV?" he said to me one afternoon when it was time for Sumner to practice.

On one of our drives, I asked Roky what he missed most about Austin and he said, "I miss my mother." He hasn't talked to her since a phone call on his birthday in July; Sumner says she tried to talk Roky out of taking his meds, so Sumner began blocking her calls. Sumner is just as determined as Evelyn was to have things his way, by his rules, and that means no contact with Mother. Without Evelyn, Roky's past six months have been a paradigm shift as drastic as the one he was forced to undergo in 1969, when he went from living on LSD to living on Thorazine.

And though Sumner is kind to Roky, his way is not all sweetness and light. He is extremely bitter about Evelyn and vowed long ago never to return to her house—his childhood home—again. "Sumner is so wonderful," says Roky's ex-wife Dana, "but I hate it that he's got this anger inside him." Indeed, it borders on hatred, as strong as Roky's love. It's a sign of how upset Sumner is, how hard he's pulling in his direction, that he doesn't realize how irrational he sometimes sounds when he talks about Evelyn. "Every time he brings up his mother to me, he talks about what a horrible person she is," says Monahan. "He wants everyone to know what a better job he is doing with Roky. He saved his brother's life—why isn't that enough?" Not everyone is happy with the way Sumner has gone about it. Dana worries that Sumner's mentor, Miller, a woman in her seventies like Evelyn, will shift Roky's dependency and become another Evelyn. Then there's the money: attorneys hired by Evelyn finally reached a settlement with Charly (the company that bought the rights to Roky's material from IA) that would have put more than $100,000 in Roky's trust, but Sumner, the new guardian, has held up the deal for months so that he and his attorneys can scrutinize it further. And there are complaints that for too long Sumner has kept Roky away from his home, Austin, and his son, Jegar, who lives there (Spring lives in Houston and Cydne in Williamsport, Pennsylvania).

And, of course, Evelyn. At some point Roky will finally return to Evelyn's world in Austin—"We're taking it a day at a time," said Sumner in October. "It could be two months, it could be eight"—

and Sumner will go back to Pittsburgh and Sumner's version of
Roky will meet Evelyn's. She is still angry and hurt over the way
Sumner and the state took Roky away, and she filed a 75-page com-
plaint with the Board of Medical Examiners about the whole affair.
When I told her that Roky said he missed her, she said she missed
him too. She was dismayed when I told her he was smoking a lot. "I
had him down to ten cigarettes a day," she says. "This worries me.
The drugs cause you to overeat and oversmoke." She's concerned
about Roky getting diabetes. She fills her days practicing the piano
and doing yoga. Ever the iconoclast, she marched in an October
anti-war demonstration and got her picture in the paper. She sings
at church and at an open mike every once in a while with a little jazz
band, doing a couple of old songs. On one such evening I was
reminded again of Roky's debt to her when I noticed how she
cocked her head to the right as she sang "September Song," just like
she must have done fifty years ago when her son mimicked her
every move. She didn't shake it, though; that was Roky's idea.

One night I asked Roky if he felt like playing the guitar. "Oh, no,"
he said. But then he drawled, "I also play organ a lot." My ears
perked up; it was in the vicinity of such logic that the real Roky
emerged. So you do play guitar some? "Yeah, just not in public." Do
you think you ever will? "I don't really think so," he said, laughing
nervously. "I hope not." Are you writing any songs? "Sometimes I
write. I've got some ideas in my head right now." For songs? "Uh-
huh." Are they going to be different? "I don't know." Then, after a
pause, he asked, "Where are we?" He was changing the subject. But
I had become one of those well-intentioned meddlers and I pushed
him, saying I hoped he'd write and perform again. "Uh-huh," he
responded warily. Then I said how a lot of people would *love* to see
him play again. Roky was silent. He was not going to be led somewhere he didn't want to go. It was creepy how easy it was to take
advantage of Roky's childlike nature and humbling how firm he was
in rejecting me. He was testing his limits, trying, it seemed, to come
up with a version of himself he can live with.

KELEFA SANNEH

Gettin' Paid

*Jay-Z, criminal culture, and
the rise of corporate rap*

Earlier this year, VH1, the music-video channel, broadcast a television series called "Bands on the Run." Four rock groups were sent on tour, competing to see which one could sell the most merchandise; the winner would get a hundred thousand dollars' worth of new equipment, fifty thousand dollars in cash, a VH1-financed video, and a showcase concert with industry executives. The bands weren't very good, but the animosity of the competition was entertaining. In one episode, a group called Soulcracker started a grassroots smear campaign, telling fans that a victory for the rival group Flickerstick would be a victory for "corporate rock." It was an absurd claim—both bands were, after all, angling for a corporate contract, on a corporate television show—and the insult backfired: Flickerstick demanded an apology, and got one. The next week, Flickerstick won the competition.

What's funny about the insult is how old-fashioned it seems. The term "corporate rock" is a relic of the nineteen-seventies, popularized by critics who felt that the big record companies had coöpted a rebellious, authentic genre for mass consumption. In 1978, the rock journalist Lester Bangs wrote, "The music business today still must be recognized as *by definition* an enemy, if not the most crucial enemy, of music and the people who try to perform it honestly." Over the past ten years, though, "corporate rock" has been upstaged by "corporate rap," which has emerged as the country's new music. Rappers are responsible for three of the country's ten most popular albums, and the Recording Industry Association of America estimates that last year rap music generated more than $1.8 billion in sales, accounting for 12.9 percent of all music purchases; it has surpassed country music as the nation's second most popular genre, after rock and roll. The obscure rap record labels Fo' Reel and Hypnotize Minds have teamed up with the media conglomerates Vivendi Universal and Sony, respectively, and have found millions of customers. Rappers, with a few notable exceptions, are black men, but their listeners are not: About seventy percent of the people who buy rap albums are white, and an increasingly large percentage are female. "Hip-hop," once a noun, has become an adjective, constantly invoked, if rarely defined; people talk about hip-hop fashion and hip-hop novels, hip-hop movies and hip-hop basketball. Like rock and roll in the nineteen-sixties, hip-hop is both a movement and a marketing ploy, and the word is used to describe almost anything that's supposed to appeal to young people.

What's most unexpected about this boom is the reaction of the rappers themselves, who rose to prominence as icons of rebellion and authenticity. They have not only accepted corporate rap but embraced it. Like Frank Sinatra before them, they are chairmen of the board: *Fortune* put the rapper Master P on its cover in 1999, after he branched out into film production, sports management, and fashion, and today's biggest rap acts, from OutKast to Snoop Dogg, are diversifying, leveraging their popularity to create their own companies. Eminem may deliver antisocial lyrics, but as a businessman he's a model citizen, an entrepreneur who recently put his solo career on hold so he could build up his new imprint, Shady Records.

The greatest of the corporate rappers is Jay-Z, a thirty-one-year-old tycoon from the Bedford-Stuyvesant section of Brooklyn. He has all the necessary credentials: a record label (Roc-A-Fella Records), a clothing company (Rocawear), a production house

(Roc-A-Fella Films). What's more, he has the right sensibility: non-chalant, devious, witty. He has put out five successful albums in five years—the only rapper to have done so—starting with *Reasonable Doubt*, his début, in 1996, and he's sold more than eleven million records. Many rappers have made money, and lots of it, but none have rapped so eloquently about making money, or about the lure of wealth and ambition. Jay-Z has succeeded by treating hip-hop above all as a corporate enterprise, by embracing ruthless profes-sionalism as his guiding aesthetic. As he once put it, "What y'all about to witness is big business, kid."

I met Jay-Z for the first time this spring, in Los Angeles. He was in town for the Soul Train Music Awards (he'd been named male entertainer of the year), and I spent a day watching him rehearse and shop for sneakers at a nearby mall. There was a constant pro-cession of well-wishers and autograph-seekers, and he greeted most of them wordlessly, with faint smiles and loose handclasps. Jay-Z is not flamboyant in the way that rappers are expected to be flamboy-ant. He doesn't have a gimmick, or an outlandish persona, or an especially fancy wardrobe. He usually wears a T-shirt and jeans, invariably made by Rocawear. He's tall and lanky. His hair is shaved barbershop-close, and there is the hint of a goatee on his chin. Dia-mond earrings and a diamond pendant are the only indications of his fortune and, indirectly, his fame.

Jay-Z was born Shawn Corey Carter in 1969. He grew up in the Marcy City Housing Projects, a forbidding bastion in Bedford-Stuyvesant; he has turned the project name into a hip-hop brand name. (At a recent concert in Washington, D.C., he was introduced with the words "Marcy projects, y'all!") He was the youngest of four children, two boys and two girls, and was brought up by his mother, Gloria; his father left the family when Jay-Z was eleven. Jay-Z is among the few rappers who memorize rhymes without committing them to paper, but he says that as a kid he always kept a green note-book with him. "I used to write in it every day, at my mom's house, banging on the table and saying my raps," he says. When an older neighbor called Big Jaz got a record deal, Jay-Z left George Westinghouse Technical High School to become his sidekick. "He took me to London, and I was, like, 'People pay you? To make raps? Oh, shit!'" After a few years, when it was clear that Big Jaz would never become a major rap star, Jay-Z left him to tour with Big Daddy Kane, a popular rapper whose career was beginning to decline.

Jay-Z returned to Brooklyn, where, he says, he spent his early twenties selling crack cocaine. He is vague about the specifics. "I was running the streets," he told me, and that's about as far as he would go. In song, he's more forthcoming:

> *I took trips with so much shit in the whip that if the cops pulled us over, the dog would get sick.*

In 1995, after Jay-Z was shot at from six feet away, he decided to give rapping another try. A producer named Clark Kent introduced him to Damon Dash, a Harlem entrepreneur who had contacts in the rap industry, but no one was interested in signing Jay-Z. His old songs were considered too "sophisticated," he told me. "You had to really like rap to be, like, 'This dude's clever: the way he's using his words, the way he tackles his subjects—that's different.'" So Jay-Z and Dash, along with a silent partner, Kareem (Biggs) Burke, formed Roc-A-Fella Records, to put out Jay-Z's music themselves. Roc-A-Fella eventually struck a distribution deal with Priority Records (which it later left for Island/Def Jam) and issued Jay-Z's first album, *Reasonable Doubt*, in 1996. A cheerful, filthy love song called "Ain't No Nigga" became his first hit; it also launched the career of Foxy Brown, who rapped as Jay-Z's girlfriend.

Reasonable Doubt is filled with rhymes as smooth as the hustlers Jay-Z sings about, and even the grittiest (or most exuberant) song suggests the poise and strength of a shrewd businessman. The first thing you notice listening to the album is the high, nasal voice, steely and precise; the enunciation is clear, and Jay-Z moves over each syllable lightly. The words pour out so effortlessly that rhyme and rhythm seem almost like an afterthought. His style is suggestive rather than declamatory; instead of shouting threats of murder, he sighs, "Believe you me, son, I hate to do it just as bad as you hate to see it done."

"Reasonable Doubt" sold more than half a million copies, but in order to cross over to the pop audience Jay-Z needed catchier tunes. Rap songs are a combination of rhyming and "beats"—heavily rhythmic tracks built from synthetic sounds, live instrumental music, and samples of other songs. In 1997, Jay-Z tried to find a more beat-driven sound; the result was a disappointing album called *In My Lifetime, Vol. 1* ("I wish I could have nailed that one," he says now) that sampled eighties rock songs such as "You Belong to the City" and "I Know What Boys Like." Then, in 1998, he bought an unlikely beat from a veteran producer named Mark 45 King, which added a heavy bass line to "It's the Hard-Knock Life," from the musical "Annie." Jay-Z slowed down his delivery to match the tempo, and the result was the crossover hit "Hard Knock Life (Ghetto Anthem)":

> *I'm a be on top, whether I perform or not. I went from lukewarm to hot, sleeping on futons and cots to king-size dream machines.*

An accompanying album, *Vol. 2 . . . Hard Knock Life*, sold more than five million copies and made Jay-Z rap's biggest star.

Jay-Z has made two albums since. *Vol. 3 . . . Life and Times of S. Carter*, was released in 1999, and *The Dynasty: Roc La Familia (2000–)*, a showcase for other artists on Jay-Z's record label, was released last October. Since his first album, Jay-Z has simplified his intricate rhyme style: His lyrics have become less tightly constructed, and less descriptive—an approach that appeals to mainstream fans, who buy hip-hop for the beats, not the words. He explains by affecting the pinched voice of a casual, presumably white listener: "I'm from West Motherfuck. I don't know what they're talking about. But the music is good." When I asked him if he thought the transformation was an improvement, he responded with an unsentimental comparison to Michael Jordan. "In his early days, Jordan was rocking a cradle, cranking it, all crazy, but he wasn't winning championships," Jay-Z said. "And then, later in his career, he just had a fadeaway jump shot, and they won six titles. Which was the better Jordan? I don't know."

In an earlier era, a rapper might have been tempted to ignore mainstream listeners, or to pretend to, but for Jay-Z sound business practice trumps artistic ambition. Still, no one wants to watch a man make jump shots forever—not even perfectly executed fadeaway jump shots—and so Jay-Z has to find a way to keep people interested, including aficionados. On *The Dynasty*, he rapped about a girlfriend's miscarriage, and he and one of his protégés, Beanie Sigel, have written a pair of songs that berate their deadbeat dads. Songs such as these convincingly convey personal desperation, but they suggest a professional desperation as well.

In the beginning, hip-hop wasn't "about" anything at all: It was invented not by rappers but by disk jockeys. In 1973, a Jamaican immigrant in the Bronx who called himself DJ Kool Herc popularized the art of manipulating two turntables at once, so he could repeat his favorite drum patterns over and over. The jumpy music that resulted was given the name hip-hop. D.j.s who performed regularly in parks or clubs or roller rinks began hiring m.c.s to extoll their skills to the crowd, drawing on the African-American tradition of street-corner rhyming. In the studios, when the first hip-hop records were made, d.j.s were sometimes replaced by live bands, and the m.c., or rapper, became central to the music. In 1979, a group of dilettantes called the Sugarhill Gang released a song called "Rapper's Delight," and it became a hit. "Hip-hop" had become "rap music."

The first generation of stars were cartoonish figures from New York City—Kurtis Blow, Whodini, Run DMC, the Fat Boys, the Beastie Boys, and LL Cool J. They had whimsical names and wore whimsical clothes, and their records were filled with whimsical boasts. Run DMC proclaimed itself "the big, bad wolf in your neighborhood—not bad meaning bad, but bad meaning good." Then, in 1988, Public Enemy, a Long Island collective, released an album entitled *It Takes a Nation of Millions to Hold Us Back*. The group presented itself as a paramilitary outfit agitating for black power, and, just as the Beatles established the idea that pop songs could be art, Public Enemy established the idea that hip-hop could be politics.

Hip-hop has an insatiable appetite for new characters and new stories, and Public Enemy was soon overshadowed by a West Coast counterpart, NWA (or Niggaz with Attitude). NWA had a different arsenal of slogans—"Fuck tha Police" instead of Public Enemy's "Fight the Power"—which were delivered in first-person tales of crime and sex influenced by nineteen-eighties storytellers like Too $hort, Slick Rick, Kool G Rap, and Ice-T (who named himself after the pulp novelist and ex-pimp Iceberg Slim). A new term was coined to describe this foulmouthed genre: gangsta rap. And yet, for anyone who follows hip-hop closely, "gangsta rap" isn't a very useful term; over the past ten years, it has come to denote any rapper who talks about gunplay in the first person—and this includes almost every one.

Rappers may emulate businessmen these days, but they are still linked to crime and violence. The story of corporate rap starts with the murder of two of the most popular rappers of the nineteen-nineties: In September of 1996, in Las Vegas, Tupac Shakur (who recorded as 2pac) was shot and killed, and six months later, in Los Angeles, Christopher Wallace, better known as the Notorious B.I.G. (or Biggie Smalls) was shot and killed; neither case has been solved. Shakur and the Notorious B.I.G. followed NWA, putting NWA's thuggish imagery to more personal use. On albums such as *Me Against the World* and *All Eyez on Me*, Shakur turned his life into an epic tale of self-sacrifice. Biggie was a superior stylist and a great narrator; he told his life story in a series of morbid jokes and pointed anecdotes. Both Biggie and Shakur celebrated money, but mainly they celebrated themselves, and you got the sense that they might have rapped for nothing, if they'd had to. The two had once been friends, but they had become embroiled in a seemingly baseless feud—it involved a mugging and, of course, a woman—when Shakur was killed.

The Notorious B.I.G. was a protégé of Sean (Puffy) Combs, a music executive who moonlighted as a rapper under the name Puff Daddy. In the summer of 1997, Combs initiated hip-hop's big-money boom with a eulogy for Biggie called "I'll Be Missing You," in which he rapped over "Every Breath You Take," the eighties chestnut by the Police. "I'll Be Missing You," which became the most popular song of the summer, seemed to be the paradigmatic story of hip-hop: a flashy businessman mourning a slain thug.

Most people thought of Puffy and Biggie as opposites—the executive and the thug, the businessman and the artist, the pop star and the rapper—but Jay-Z's insight was to seize upon the avarice that united them. Rappers had long suggested that the music industry wasn't much different from the drug world (as Biggie put it, "If I wasn't in the rap game / I'd probably have a ki, knee-deep in the crack game"); now Jay-Z conflated Biggie's eloquent thug and Puffy's smooth executive to create the image of an utterly mercenary man who just happens to rap. In an industry characterized by pumped-up personae, it reminded the listener that rapping is nothing more or less than a job. And in the wake of two murders, that seemed like good news—and good business.

Still, it is tempting to believe that rappers are the deadliest rich people in the country, forever guzzling champagne and spilling blood, and the arrests that have accompanied hip-hop's mainstream success have only reinforced this perception. In 1999, Combs was charged with beating a record executive with a chair, a telephone, and a champagne bottle (hip-hop has a weakness for leaden symbolism). The charges were later dropped. Recently, Combs stood trial for weapons and bribery charges in connection with a 1999 night-club shooting. (He was acquitted, but his protégé Shyne was convicted of assault, reckless endangerment, and gun possession, and was sentenced to ten years in prison.) Three weeks before the Combs shooting, Jay-Z was arrested for the stabbing of Lance (Un) Rivera, a record executive (and former friend) whom the rapper reportedly suspected of pirating his new album before its official release date. (The trial is scheduled to start next month.) In April, Jay-Z was arrested again; police said that his bodyguard had been found outside a night club with an unlicensed Glock 9-mm. semiautomatic.

Earlier this year, it was reported that New York police were "profiling" rappers, and last month the Senate held hearings on "media violence," focusing on the world of hip-hop. Hip-hop is a particularly easy target for cops and senators, because rappers make their living by telling stories that sound like autobiography, and they do so in lyrics that are spoken, not sung. Six months before his most recent arrest, Jay-Z seems to have predicted it in rhyme, right down to the kind of gun:

> *See me with a bodyguard? That means police is watching. And I*
> *only use his waist just to keep my Glock in. But*
> *when shit goes down, you know who's doing the popping.*

Life rarely imitates art that faithfully, but the convergence of rap and rap sheet is so common in hip-hop that it was barely noted even by Jay-Z's most vigilant fans.

To a casual listener, it may not be immediately obvious what makes one rapper better than another. But, like the generation of fans who dissected Bob Dylan's lyrics and debated the merits of various bootleg recordings, rap fans pore over arcana in magazines and squabble about literary prowess online. On one hip-hop Web site, visitors recently debated "What is the hottest metaphor or simile ever written?" From the beginning, Jay-Z was admired for the quality of his verse. He compared his rhymes to luxury goods, as a way of flattering his listeners' powers of discernment:

> *Time to separate*
> *the pros from the cons, the platinum from the bronze,*
> *that butter-soft shit from that leather on the Fonz.*

Much attention has been paid to rap's content—the prevalence of words like "nigga" and "bitch," the forthright treatment of sex and violence—but surprisingly little to the construction of the lyrics. And yet success in hip-hop has as much to do with style as with content. For much of the nineteen-eighties, rap was bound by strict metric conventions: Each line had four beats, with the stress on the second and the fourth, and each verse was a series of couplets. Run DMC perfected doggerel in 1984 ("Cool chief rocker, I don't drink vodka / But keep a microphone inside my locker"), and by 1988 the rhyme virtuoso Rakim had stretched the rules with tricky alliteration and run-on lines ("Music mixed mellow maintains to make / melodies for m.c.s, motivates the breaks").

Jay-Z's lyrics, on the other hand, sound like everyday speech. He throws in conversational tics—a little laugh in the middle of a line, or a pause, as if he were thinking something through—to heighten the effect. This style creates a sense of intimacy, which is undermined by a chilly sensibility, a frankly avaricious way of looking at the world, and an aversion to sentiment. In his best songs, Jay-Z exploits this contradiction by telling stories that balance a C.E.O.'s suave self-confidence with a memoirist's introspection, using unpredictable rhyme schemes to keep the listener off balance. "D'evils," from *Reasonable Doubt*, begins with a criminal's monologue:

> *The shit is wicked on these mean streets—none of my*
> *friends speak, we all tryna win. But then again,*
> *maybe it's for the best, though, 'cause when they seeing too*
> *much, you know they tryna get you touched. Whoever said*
> *illegal was the easy way out couldn't understand the*
> *mechanics and the workings of the underworld. Granted,*
> *nine to five is how you survive—I ain't tryna survive,*
> *I'm tryna live it to the limit and love it a lot.*
> *Life ills poison my body, and used to say, "Fuck*
> *mic skills!" I never prayed to God, I prayed to Gotti. . . .*
> *It gets dangerous, money and power is changing us,*
> *and now we're lethal, infected with d'evils.*

"D'evils" (the title is pronounced "da evils") is a song about money and power, and it describes a world in which ambition is the root of all evil (and all success), a world where the criminal ethic— "We all tryna win"—sounds a lot like a capitalist code. In the second verse, we find a young hustler kidnapping a young mother, desperate to locate her lover, who has, it seems, betrayed him in a business deal. The hustler pays her to squeal, and there's an implication of violence—"my hand around her collar"—suggesting that he might be literally stuffing her mouth full of bills: "About his whereabouts I wasn't convinced. / I kept feeding her money till her shit started to make sense." It's a sardonic joke about the rap industry, which feeds its stars money and power in exchange for a convincing story. Jay-Z aspires to the hustler's merciless attitude, but, as a rapper, he also resembles the kidnapped girlfriend, squealing for cash. Part of what makes "D'evils" compelling is this sense that Jay-Z's persona—his professionalism—might be at odds with his profession. The first verse described d'evils as a criminal compunction; now it seems more like a narrative compunction—a disease that makes you talk too much.

If Jay-Z's skill accounts for his reputation, and his practical approach to marketing his skill accounts for his success, then his ability to sense what his audience wants to hear before his audience senses it—to tell stories that don't just demand belief but inspire it—accounts for his longevity. A few times a year, there's a meeting in the Def Jam offices to decide what the next Jay-Z single and music video will be. Last year, after the release of *Vol. 3 . . . Life and Times of S. Carter*, none of the executives could decide what single to release. The obvious choice was "Things That You Do," because it featured the pop singer Mariah Carey, but Kevin Liles, the president of Def Jam, thought it was "too mainstream." Then support started building for "Big Pimpin'," an unlikely candidate—its beat sounded North African, and it lacked a sung hook, which is generally considered essential for a hip-hop single. Liles, a convivial, round-faced man, and an energetic storyteller, recalled the conversation: "Jay said, 'It's a movement: This is how you big pimp.' I said, 'I don't know, Jay.' He said, 'Nah, we gotta do a video. We gotta show people what big pimping is all about. Let's make the movement.' So I said, 'Let's go, let's do it.' And the rest is history." The "movement" they created was this: Jay-Z on an enormous yacht somewhere warm, drinking champagne with women in swimsuits, and rapping about a life of sex and cash. As he put it:

> *On a canopy my stamina be*
> *enough for Pamela Anderson Lee.*

MTV, "Jam of the Week."
Made my money quick then back to the streets.

The video cemented Jay-Z's reputation as hip-hop's smoothest hustler, and "big pimpin'" became slang for living large; Jay-Z even made a follow-up song, "Parking Lot Pimpin'."

Expensive cars, yachts, champagne, and jewelry are everywhere in contemporary rap songs and videos. While hip-hop was once attacked for what was perceived as political rage, it has now given critics a different sin to excoriate: greed, or "bling bling" (after a song that asked, "What kinda nigga got diamonds that'll—bling!—blind ya?"). Last year, *Newsweek* ran a cover story that announced, "Welcome to the bling-bling generation." Hip-hop, the article claimed, had become "a Frankenstein's monster—with fifty thousand dollars worth of white gold draped over its neck pegs." (In fact, this characterization is inaccurate: most major rappers disdain white gold, considering it inferior to platinum.) Ever since the Sugarhill Gang rhymed about having "more money than a sucker could ever spend," it's been clear that hip-hop isn't an ascetic culture, and in the late nineteen-nineties it became more infatuated than ever with earning power and spending habits.

"When everybody else was doing gold," Jay-Z says, "I was, like, 'I want something platinum.' And then seeing the whole world switch—the whole world, you know what I'm saying? For a kid from Marcy? No one can take that away from me." In hip-hop, achievement comes down to style: life style, musical style, rhyme style. Jay-Z has moved out of the Marcy projects and into a penthouse apartment in Fort Lee, New Jersey (rich rappers inevitably move to the suburbs, for safety and privacy), which has a view of the Manhattan skyline and a private screening room. Roc-A-Fella Films has made a distribution deal with Miramax, and Rocawear, available at Macy's, among other places, has replaced Phat Farm and Fubu as New York's most visible brand. Jay-Z's latest hit, "I Just Wanna Love U (Give It 2 Me)," was a champagne-fuelled celebration song inspired by a birthday party for Kimora Simmons, the wife of Def Jam's co-founder Russell Simmons. But, despite all his big-money rhymes and real-life wealth, Jay-Z has never once described what champagne tastes like. His is the pleasure of a man obsessed with status (he recently called himself a "status-tician"), rather than the simpler pleasure of a hedonist.

Hippies and punk rockers used to talk about artists "selling out," chasing money at the expense of art. As the years passed, rockers got not only older but richer, and their newfound wealth was, inevitably, a bit of an embarrassment, or, at any rate, an absurdity: a rich society guy in late middle age singing about being a "Street Fighting Man." Rappers, on the other hand, don't sell out; they "fall off"—that is, they lose their artistic credibility and their financial viability at the same time. Punks (and their descendants in the world of underground rock) were afraid that big audiences and big money would ruin their subculture of authenticity, but in hip-hop success is a form of validation—a rapper's riches are proof that he's good at what he does. Platinum jewelry and platinum plaques are metaphors for artistic achievement, not just commercial success. It's hard to imagine a major rapper refusing to make a video at the height of his career, the way Pearl Jam did. In hip-hop, stories are either convincing or they're not; when a rapper loses his power to convince, it's usually a failure not of authenticity but of rhetoric. Jay-Z will be a master criminal and a brilliant business mind and a great rapper until people stop believing him.

Jay-Z's recent arrests have given him new material. He has even made a music video, for a song called "Guilty Until Proven Innocent," loosely based on the stabbing of Lance (Un) Rivera, in which he takes the witness stand, delivers a defiant defense, and celebrates his acquittal. But on a spring morning in a Manhattan courthouse, where Jay-Z was attending a scheduling hearing in the Rivera case, the discrepancy between Jay-Z the rapper and Shawn Carter the defendant couldn't have been clearer: Being on trial mainly means keeping your mouth shut, in the courtroom and outside it, and that's exactly what Jay-Z did.

I arrived just in time to see Jay-Z sprinting up the steps to meet one of his lawyers, Murray Richman. It was the first time I'd seen him without a flock of handlers and bodyguards and managers and friends trailing him. I passed through the metal detector with Jay-Z and Richman, and as we got to the elevators Jay-Z turned around and looked at me, not quite smiling. "What's going on?" he said.

It was not a day of high legal drama. The court date was a mere formality—a request for a postponement. There were only half a dozen other people in the courtroom; no reporters, no fans.

Jay-Z sat alone at a small desk before the bench, dressed in a Rocawear T-shirt and Rocawear jeans. The hearing took almost no time: The lawyers stepped forward and murmured to the judge. The judge murmured back, one hand over the microphone. Richman smiled broadly and said, "Thank you so much." The postponement had been granted, and Jay-Z strode out of the courtroom. A few weeks later, a publicist from Def Jam called me. She told me that for "legal reasons" Jay-Z wouldn't talk to me anymore.

As Jay-Z's lawyers would be the first to tell you, rapping about crime doesn't make you a great criminal. By the same token, rapping about money doesn't make you a great businessman. Jay-Z is a part owner of Rocawear and Roc-A-Fella Films, but Damon Dash takes most of the meetings himself. "If I gotta bring Jay, that mean we got a problem," he says. Jay-Z is more actively involved in Roc-A-Fella Records, which he intends to establish as hip-hop's ruling family. In recent years, realizing, perhaps, that his own career won't last forever, he has been shilling for Roc-A-Fella at every turn. "Y'all niggas truly ain't ready for this dynasty thing / Y'all thinking Blake Carrington, I'm thinking more like Ming," he rapped in a recent song. And yet he has had a rough time with his protégés: Amil, a young female rapper, left the Roc-A-Fella stable shortly after releasing a poorly received début album last year, and Memphis Bleek, a Marcy-projects alumnus, hasn't quite found his own style or marketing niche. Jay-Z's most promising protégé is Beanie Sigel, a hard-bitten twenty-seven-year-old, who is as forthcoming as Jay-Z is guarded. "My style is crack houses in South Philly," Beanie says. "That's where most of my life was written."

The first time I heard *The Reason*, Beanie Sigel's new album, I was sitting in an S.U.V. that was hazy with marijuana smoke. Half a dozen of Beanie's friends and handlers were nodding their heads in unison, and Beanie himself was rapping along, offering running commentary: "Yo, we in church right now—this one make you get the Holy Ghost." His first album had been uneven, but *The Reason* is one of the year's best, full of verses knotted with syllables:

> *Crack topic: back block it, thirty-one long blacktop it, you can't stop it, Gat top it, black Mack, black Glock it, blast rocket, sit your faggot-ass on your back pocket.*

Sitting in a deserted pool hall in Chelsea later that night, Beanie recalled the day that a friend of a friend got him an audition with Jay-Z. "Meeting Jay was like meeting the perfect hustler," he said. "It was like being a young kid on the block, when a dude drive up in a big Caddy and throw you the keys, like, 'Park the car, shorty.' It was like meeting that guy."

Along with most of his hip-hop contemporaries, Beanie Sigel has internalized the rules of corporate rap—he explained to me that you have to have a "good marketing plan" when you're "selling your product," whether it's music or crack. And yet he doesn't come across like a C.E.O. If Jay-Z is a salesman, then Beanie Sigel is a product, a charismatic hustler who senses that part of his appeal is his roughness (he described himself as "all edges, all the way around, three-sixty"), a slick talker whose style emphasizes wordplay over plain speech. (He even answered some of my questions in rhyme.)

The new corporate rapper is intensely self-aware. Eminem has rhymed, with seeming amusement, about being a "commodity." One of rap's new stars calls himself Ludacris. Even Master P has recognized this changing atmosphere: His own career has slowed down, and his empire has fallen apart, but he's found new success through his son, an eleven-year-old rap star named Lil' Romeo. Maybe, after four years of corporate rap, the obsession with businessmen is turning into an obsession with products.

Fifteen years ago, a rapper might have called himself a "microphone controller" or a "rhyme animal"—epithets that called attention to lyrical skill. Today, rappers distract listeners from the fact that there's any rapping going on at all, claiming to be pimps and thugs and cocaine dealers and businessmen and leaders and commodities. "Where I'm from, it wasn't cool to be a rapper," Beanie Sigel told me. "If you was a rapper, you was a sucker, straight up. So I kept it under my hat. I'd say, 'Nah, man, I ain't no rapper.'"

Beanie Sigel's disavowal of rapping reminded me of something I'd heard before. Later that night, I pulled out his first album and confirmed a hunch: There's a moment early on when Beanie tries to get rid of a fan by sneering, "I ain't no fucking rapper," as if he wished it were true. You can hear the same ambivalence in Jay-Z's willingness to sacrifice complex rhymes for a good beat, in his insistence that "without rap I was crazy straight," and in his half-serious threats of retirement: "Back to Shawn Carter the hustler, Jay-Z is dead." The success of corporate rap has inspired a kind of self-loathing among rappers, who have begun to suspect that rapping itself is beneath them; if the hip-hop boom is drawing to a close, it can't be said that the rappers didn't see it coming.

It would be somehow fitting if rappers, who made d.j.s obsolete, ended by talking themselves into obsolescence, unable to compete with their own tall tales. You get the feeling that some rappers envy Shakur and the Notorious B.I.G., who were killed mid-act, immortalized in character. Jay-Z has been talking about retirement ever since he released his first album, which he also claimed would be his last. He wasn't planning to be a rapper all his life, and he certainly wasn't planning to stay in the game long enough to fall off. He said that, having established himself as the consummate smooth criminal, he would move on—back, perhaps, to the streets. Like a gangster looking for one last big score, or a corporate boss angling for a lucrative buyout, he dreamed of quitting while he was ahead, of getting out before he was pushed out. That's what the sound of "Big Pimpin'" is—a celebration before the falloff.

Rapping as a means to a financial end: This is the narrative of the era of corporate hip-hop. Strangely, it's kept hip-hop interesting and exciting, because it has forced rappers to find new ways to talk about themselves, new ways to tell their stories. But for Jay-Z it poses a question: If you're so good, why are you still rapping? As he prepares to release his sixth album in six years, he sounds apologetic. "Can't leave rap alone, the game needs me," he explains in his new single, and it's true, for now. It won't be true forever.

The Moon Looks Down and Laughs

The wonderful, horrible jazz life of Anita O'Day

> *"Now, why do we ignore the melody?"*
>
> —Thelonius Monk

The horses are running in the second race, but the dude in the panama hat and snakeskin boots is staring down his nose at this old white lady in owlish sunglasses, an acid-washed jean jacket, and a champagne supernova hairstyle. She is leveling a mesh-gloved hand, Queen Mumlike, at the middle of his chest. "Huh?"

"Isthisthesecondsetyet?" Her speech is garbled. She appears simultaneously keyed up, pissed off, happy, and disoriented. She waves her Hollywood Park Official Program at the televised stat screens: "Is-this-the-second-set yet?"

"You mean the second . . . race?" the guy echoes, frowning at the people around him.

"Yeah, race! Oh, sorry, I can't talk too good!" She lowers her sunglasses to flash her green eyes, showing a radiant grin of perfect white teeth—a showbiz smile—as her words spill out like a purring machine gun. "Yes, the race! The race! I forgot the word for a sec. Canyouseeit? Has—"

"You mean the one now?" the dude says. "I'm not here f'that."

"Huh? Then whatthehellareya here for, bub?" the lady snaps, mis-understanding, before stalking off in a determined, high-stepping bird walk. Vic, her stolid companion with Aqua Velva hair and rose-tinted aviator sunglasses whom she calls "Kid" (he is 71) shrugs resignedly, as if to say, *There's nothing I can do.* "Damn, there's no such thing as an innocent bystander!" the dude marvels to no one, blinking rapidly. "I mean, what the hell was that? That was damn rude!" I step up and put my hand on his shoulder: "Hey, you can tell your grandkids about that. She's considered the greatest living white female jazz singer."

Which only makes the poor soul look more befuddled. Later, jazz historian Will Friedwald, who has written extensively on the subject he simply calls "O'Day," will correct me: "She's the greatest living jazz singer. Period."

In the 1959 film the *Gene Krupa Story*, a sultry moll (Susan Oliver) sidles up to a tuxedoed Krupa (Sal Mineo) brooding at a smoke-choked bar. Fake Krupa nods tiredly over to a canary in a corner singing "Memories of You" with the house band: "Who's the snakecharmer?"

Moll shrugs. "Anita O'Day. Not bad—if you like talent."

This is the between-set video-projection part of the evening at the Atlas Supper Club, on the edge of L.A.'s Koreatown. The clips play the "Then" Anita on a retractable screen over the small stage; the "Now" Anita sits in the dark with her lemon and hot water and receives her public from a back booth. "Howareya?" she fires off with a bullish, Edward G. Robinson cackle to anyone within earshot. "Are ya enjoyin' the soundies?" Boomer couples approach the 81-year-old jazz diva, but all they can muster is "My [mother/father] says 'Hi'!" It's the old timers who have the stories: They saw her at the height of her Swing-era fame—with the Gene Krupa Orchestra in '43 at the Oriental Theater; or solo, when she played the Hula Hut in Phoenix two hours before the joint burned down; or an El Segundo strip dump in '54 when Lenny Bruce and his mother were the MCs, right after she was released from Termi-

nal Island and her career was in a shambles for not the first (and not
the last) time. And the tiny blonde woman with the big voice returns
their adulation with loud, random exclamations like, "When I sing I
just forget the melody! And if I screw it up I just do it again a little
different, y'know? That's jazz!" or "I didn't come to Hollywood to
sing or be in the pictures, I came to play the horses!"

This is why a good portion of the jazz and swing aficionados
present tonight revere Anita O'Day: They know the dynamic perfection of her art is so radically different from her unvarnished personality. They know she was once the poor Irish thrush with the
Dickensian childhood—and the hard-boiled, streetwise attitude to
match—who took Louis Armstrong's trumpet sound, gospel singer
Mildred Bailey's emphasis of consonants over vowels (as do most
singers), Billie Holiday's fashion of shaping and flatting notes, Ella
Fitzgerald's sly, tightly controlled scatting and even actress Martha
Raye's way of presenting her body when she sang, and produced a
peerless hybrid that revolutionized jazz singing. It was the '40s
O'Day who really swung—literally giving women singers in her
wake their own voices, elevating them from their status as dolled-
up, Big Band tchotchkes to competitive vocal instrumentalists. It
was the O'Day of the '50s and '60s whose eccentric phrasings, light-
ning-fast scatting, and uncanny sense of time provided a vocal
bridge between Big Band and Bebop. Yet O'Day herself will deny
up and down, loudly and emphatically, that she has any voice or
vocal chops. She'll tell you that she doesn't care about the past. That
she is not even a singer, bub.

Which is probably the reason for the youthful faces at her shows
lately—a fascinating palate of worshipful gay men, obsessive jazz-
heads, and *Swingers*-weaned hipsters. They recognize that there's a
difference between today's idols and those, like O'Day, who have
been there, done that—and survived. They've grown weary of
media-molded musical "heroes" who spend the years 19 through 23
becoming multimillionaires; in her day O'Day earned $7.50 each
from "Let Me Off Uptown" and "Thanks for the Boogie Ride," the
first of the hits she sang that fattened Krupa's pocketbook. They have
a headache from the *Behind the Music*–fed aura of excess and come to

see the lady once referred to as the "Jezebel of Jazz"—the hip, danger-tinged yang to labelmate Ella Fitzgerald's proper, refined yin.

Admittedly, many of them are fans of what jazz critics consider to be her finest hour: her Verve/heroin period (1952–1962), where all her personal tragedies and abuses intertwined with her evolution from "canary" to jazz singer and embossed her voice with a breathtaking worldliness. And they've surely seen the filmed image that made her an international sensation: her performance at the 1958 Newport Jazz Festival, shot by fashion and advertising photographer Bert Stern for the documentary *Jazz On A Summer's Day*. Released this year on DVD, *Jazz* is generally considered the first feature-length concert film, the spiritual godfather to films like *Monterey Pop* and *Woodstock*. In this respect, Anita O'Day at Newport '58 was to the beat generation what Hendrix at Woodstock would be to the hippies 11 years later. When a new print of *Jazz* was screened at New York's Lincoln Center in 1997, the handbill (and even reviews of the film) chose the indelible image of O'Day's sensual grimace as she stood before the microphone, wearing a wide-brimmed black cartwheel hat that a journalist once referred to as having "possibly every feather from one ostrich on its brim." In the film, looking like a très hep lampshade in a long black dress (one reporter called it "junkie's black"), trademark white party gloves, and soon-to-be-immortal hat, she ascends the steps to the stage to polite—if not indifferent—applause. She is a woman surrounded: the lethargic, beer- and sun-lulled audience to her front, pianist Joe Masters (with whom she was having an affair at the time), bassist Eldee Young, and drummer John Poole at her back— she begins to weave a spell that will eventually leave them all twirling on her finger.

As Poole's tom-toms ooze steadily out of the heat, O'Day at first appears to be engaging in a mating dance with the mike stand. (Dick Cavett once observed, did any singer so completely hold sway over microphones as she?) Her first words float in from nowhere: "Noo-oo-oo-ooooo gal-maaaidd-has-got-a-shaaade-on-Sweet Geooor-gia Brown . . ." She shifts, tilting her head with one glove raised: "Theeeyyy all-sigh-and-wah-nah-dieeee/For Sweeeeeet Gee-oh-gia

Brown/I'll tell ya why—I don't liiieeee..." Pause, smirk.
"... Much!" She bobs her head like a pigeon, bouncing on the balls
of her feet: "TWO. LEFT. FEET./Oh! SO neat!" This sinewy intro
lasts a full two minutes—O'Day reducing her voice to barely a peep
and the music threatening to peter out completely. Then, like saying achtung, she is off: "IT's/been-SAID-she/KNOCKS/them-
dead/WHEN SHE la-ah-ands/in tooo-ooown..." Leaning her
head almost out of frame, she starts the note away from the mike,
bringing it gradually back, slicing the air in half:
"... eeeeEEEEEET Geeeor-GAH Bro-owwn..." She curls her
lips—pronouncing the last word "Braun" and dropping her voice
low—and her famous teeth, which seem to jut out of her mouth at a
120-degree angle, make her look like she is engaged in some devil-
ish private joke. The singer admitted as much later in her 1981
autobiography *High Times, Hard Times.* "The fact that I looked so
together after all the horrendous things [people had] read about me
caught [the public's] imagination." By Newport '58, her heroin rep
caused George Wein and the other festival organizers to defer from
putting her on Saturday night's bill, opting instead for the more
sedate 2:30 PM slot the next day. Despite the fact that she says she
was "higher than a kite" that very performance (at that time, three
quarters of her quartet were users), she may have seen Newport '58
as a chance to make the latest in her series of "comebacks." But to
watch the performance a few times—even to watch O'Day watch
it—it's easy to see how she might have seen it as a chance to stick it
to the rich, Eisenhower-numbed "moldy figs" in the audience and
standing in the wings measuring her. Through this lens, it becomes
the afternoon jazz-set-as-flaming-Viking-funeral—the Beatles
would put most of them out of work in four years anyway. And she
wore the appropriate colors.

Twenty feet away, shooting with a long-lensed still camera on a
specially built platform, Bert Stern, who admits he knew virtually
nothing about jazz before he made the film, was caught completely
off guard by the force of her performance—especially when she
launched into the standard "Tea for Two" from her Krupa days.
"O'Day is so perfectly in time that one imagines she must have been

conceived and born on the beat," Will Friedwald later wrote. "'Tea for Two' reveals that her relationship with time is so solid that she can completely trust it—she doesn't have to hug it constantly for fear that it will get away from her." She stands as still as a lamppost, hands clasped together mock-ladylike, as the words literally whirrrr out of her mouth in metric precision: "Picturemeuponyourknee-andteafortwoandtwoforteaandcan'tyousee howhappywecanbeeyee!/ There'snobodynearustoseeorhearusnofriendsorrelationsonweekends orvacationswon'thaveitknownthatwe own-a—telephone, deaahh!" By this time she has suspended all pretenses toward the melody, using the syllables to navigate the chord structure underneath it, spinning them like tops around the frisky beat: "CAN'T-you-SEE-how-HAP-py-WE-can-BEE-EEE-EE-EEE." It's cubistic gib-berish—expertly, joyously constructed. The crowd begins to take to its feet. Then comes her scatting: She moves the mike stand over a few feet, fires off a line, then moves the stand over again, spits another line, touches her hat, looks over her shoulder, begins to spar back and forth with the combo, splicing in a mocking, childlike melody, then holding up her gloved hands, opening and closing them like little white birds—"ee-ee-ee-ee-ee-ee"—her face wincing in ecstasy. She spreads her arms wide and sings the song like a paint-ing: "We three-ee-ee-eee-eee-eeeee." As applause washes over the stage, she is gone. Afterward, the gossip columnist Walter Winchell, a man not usually known for his progressive taste in music, raptur-ously proclaimed her the "Queen of Jazz Singers."

❧

Jazz belongs in the basement!

—O'Dayism

"Where have all the great jazz singers gone?" the late jazz critic Leonard Feather mourned in his last *L.A. Times* essay. "The era produced five major influences: Billie Holliday, Mildred Bailey, Sarah Vaughan, Ella Fitzgerald, and Anita O'Day." That was 1993; since then, only Anita O'Day survives the five women named, and at one time even that was up for debate. In 1996, while President Clin-

ton was awarding her (in absentia) the prestigious $20,000 Jazz
Masters Fellowship in Washington, D.C., O'Day—whose singing
style inspired everyone from Bette Midler to the ubiquitous Diana
Krall—was strapped to a hospital bed diagnosed with permanent
alcoholic dementia, blood poisoning, staph infections, pneumonia,
cancer, and every other malady under the sun. "I was told she would
likely die," said then-manager Alan Eichler. "There was no way she
could live because all her organs were shot from years of abuse."

Nowadays, the blessing of survival—of living, say, Billie Holiday's
life and inexplicably outlasting everyone and everything around
her—sometimes looms like a curse. (It's driven home by the Atlas
handbill advertising her under the "Jezebel of Jazz" moniker—one
she always despised.) It's the result of the paradox that has licked at
this unapologetic woman's heels: her unique style of singing versus a
life that reads like a rap sheet. Born one Anita Belle Colton in
Chicago on October 18, 1919, the daughter of a mother who
referred to her as "excess baggage" and a charming, alcoholic
roustabout of a father who would eventually remarry 11 more times,
O'Day began singing and dancing when she was five. Her first public performance at age 12 singing, "Is It True What They Say About
Dixie?" was for coins thrown on a dance floor. From 14 to 16, she
hitchhiked around the Midwest as a professional dance contestant in
the grim, exploitative world of Depression-era "walkathons," smoking reefer in the back of broken-down dance halls and seedy ball-
rooms in places like Muskegon, Racine, and Kankakee. "You're in
this big auditorium and everybody's sitting around on these bleach-
ers," she recalls. "Ten thousand, twenty-five thousand people a
night! Not too bad for business, right? They'd start ya out with
walking around the floor. They'd start out with fifty couples and in
two weeks there would be twenty, then usually end up with three.
Sometimes you'd drag your partner. We'd get a 15-minute break
every hour to sell or wash up or eat—they fed us seven meals a day.
The finish line was when the last three couples were on the floor,
then they'd have a race and then whoever falls out . . . the winner
gets 10% of the door." She had the endurance for the jazz life
beaten into her early on—walkathons could go up to 500 hours

(nearly a month) and one of Anita's favorite stories is the dance where she claims to have covered 4,656 miles in 2,328 hours.

She began wandering the taverns of Chicago's notorious Uptown district—and got yanked out by the truant officers in the process. Changed her name to "O'Day" to: (a) avoid "the Man"; and (b) because it was pig-Latin for "Dough . . . and I wanted to make some of it!" First drink (a Pink Lady) at age 16. Began dancing and performing in Chicago taverns as a part of scantily-clad chorus girl revues, where she was required to drink with the customers (and developed her lifelong flirtation with libations). At 19 moved into a "musician's hotel" on Wilson Street, essentially a hardcore street-character flophouse replete with gamblers, hookers, and chorus girls; here she played poker and jammed with the jazzbos, hanging out in the 22/7 bar downstairs "trying to drink up all the cognac in the place." She was hired in 1939 by *Down Beat* magazine's Carl Con to be the house singer at the Offbeat, an informal jam session space in the basement of his Three Deuces club. At the Offbeat, in particular, appeared some giants of 20th century jazz: Art Tatum, Baby Dodds, Leon "Bix" Beiderbecke, Lil Armstrong, Chick Webb, Eddie Condon, The Dorsey Brothers, and this uptight cat from the Bloody Maxwell section of town, Benny Goodman. By 1935, Goodman had inaugurated a dance craze based on 4/4 time that was at the peak of its popularity, partly due to a young, frenetic new drummer with wavy black hair named Gene Krupa. When Krupa split to form his own formidable Big Band and hired O'Day (replacing incumbent canary Irene Daye) along with bantam-sized trumpeter Roy Eldridge, she was already a hardened veteran of show business.

From the beginning her throat was different in the most literal sense: Like Art Tatum's half-blindness or Django Reinhardt's paralyzed fingers, O'Day took an abject handicap—a careless dentist clipped off a seven-year-old Anita's uvula—and worked around it, first, as she says, by listening to records not just for the vocals but to pick out each individual instrument, isolate it, and then use her voice to repeat it. "I never felt I really knew a record until I could sing all of the solos: the trumpets, the trombones, the reeds, and the rhythm!" she explains. Her vibratoless tones (the uvula allows for vibrato) freed her to toy with the phrasing of the lyrics—"love," elongated as "looooooove" by any other torcher, was transformed by O'Day into the skittering "la-ah-ah-ah-ah-ah-ve." This way she could ignore the melody, offer up her own paraphrases and scat around the song like a boomerang—every note, it seemed, was a radical chord change—always landing back in the palm of the band by the end of the song. "The most important thing," she is fond of saying, "is to never lose the story!"

Until Krupa's bogus drug bust in late 1942, the O'Day/Eldridge/ Krupa combo stirred up the wartime masses, starting in '41 with "Let Me Off Uptown" and O'Day's heated interracial banter with Eldridge—she encourages him to "blow" one of the most raucous, soaring trumpet solos in jazz history. On the hits they recorded— "Thanks for the Boogie Ride," "Opus One," "Boogie Blues," "Skylark," "Drum Boogie," "And That's What You Think," "Georgia on My Mind," "Stop! The Red Light's On," "Chickety Chick," "The Walls Keep Talking"—O'Day, according to Big Band historian George Simon, "came on strong, full of fire, with an either-you-like-me-or-you-don't-but-if-you-don't-it's-your-loss attitude." From the outset, especially in her insistence on wearing the derby-jacket-and-shirt uniform of the Krupa orchestra instead of a frilly gown, she was signaling that she was no mere canary. (To drive home this point, she once even threatened to measure her Krupa bandmates' dicks on the tour bus—all 15 of them.) Not an easy path this, considering that she, like many other women fronting big bands of the day, got little sympathy—and at times outright hostility—from the testosterone-dominated bandstand. Not only could O'Day outperform, outdrink, and outlast them, she could play poker with them in the belly of a DC–3 and, upon hearing that ice forming on the wings would force the entire orchestra to abandon the plane via parachute, have the presence of mind to stuff the "oh-day" she had won from them into her bra. As jazz writer Don Gold bemusedly opined—perhaps referring to the persistent rumors surrounding her sexual preference—"Anita O'Day is a woman . . . but for many years, Anita was unwilling to accept it."

⟨☙⟩

Lord, jazz is wonderful!
From A to Z, Anita to Zoot,
Hot, cool or funky,
Dizzy or Bunky,
It's a boot!

—from "Jazz," unpublished
poem written for Anita O'Day
by Sammy Davis Jr. (1956)

Arguably her bravest creative hour was when she bailed on Big Band. From 1941 to 1945 she had topped over 22 critic's polls from *Metronome* to *Esquire*—joining the ranks of Helen Forrest, Betty Roche, Peggy Lee, and her idol, Billie Holiday—not to mention a run of hits that would make her the godmother of a whole singing style at age 28. Yet by 1949, the godmother herself had almost completely dropped off the commercial map. After recovering from a nervous breakdown brought on by her exhaustive half-decade of touring (where she spent two weeks hiding in a closet), she took small club jobs for $200 per week, two shows nightly. She recorded only 25 commercial sides in six years—primarily for a group of smaller, more obscure labels like Gem, London, and Signature, the latter owned by Lindy's restaurant heir Bob Thiele. The ten tracks she recorded for Thiele's label were particularly diverse: the demented hot jive of "Hi Ho Trailus Bootwhip," the cool exotica of "Magualena," the jaunty prefeminism of "I Told Ya I Love Ya, Now Get Out," and "Ace in the Hole," a randy detailing of New York's Old Tenderloin district.

It was the beginning of a pattern for her: She became more innovative during the periods where her career seemed mired in straits. She had always been hinting at a more complex style of singing than allowed her—spontaneous yet cool—breaking out of the rhythm-and-novelty vein of Big Band and hinting at the individualism that would explode in the next decade as Bebop. When she met one of its harbingers, Charles "Yardbird" Parker, in Chicago in 1954, it was sitting in the back of a car waiting to score drugs; the gentle, troubled giant wolfing down three roast chickens told her: "You come from the same branch of the tree as I do when it comes to time." (Eight months later he was dead at 34.) She took Bird's cryptic comment as "the highest compliment." Both had been booted offstage early in their careers for their revolutionary sense of "time" (she by CBS bandleader Raymond Scott, he by Count Basie drummer Jo Jones). Both had also received their share of criticism from the mainstream jazz press too: One West Coast jazz writer disparagingly referred to her as "that O'Day woman" and went on to complain that "she sings out of tune and has a funny sense of time." One critic characterized her sound as "strangulated," while *Metronome's* Barry Ulanov famously advised that "Anita O'Day should clear her throat." To this day critics seem to prefer the sacred scatting of Ella Fitzgerald or Sarah Vaughan to O'Day's harder-edged sparring, declaring it—as Gary Giddins does in his book *Rhythm-a-ning: Jazz Tradition and Innovation*—often "riddled with clichés."

By the '50s, like so many other songbirds from the Swing Era, O'Day attempted to grapple with its death throes by recording mostly inconsequential pop or novelty tunes. "O'Day, Oh Dear" was the headline of a March 1951 article in *Melody Maker*, which when she first went solo in 1947 dubbed her "the greatest of all American vocalists working regularly with bands, white or colored." Now, it lamented that she was relying on piffle like "Yeh Boo," a cover of Patti Page's "Tennessee Waltz" (actually a hit), the nursery rhyme "Mairzy Doats," the mock-calypso of "Jamaica Mon" and her vanguard takes on "How High the Moon" and "Vaya Con Dios," later pop hits for Les Paul and Mary Ford. Ironically, her "bust" period had also launched itself, and she joined Parker and her old boss Krupa as tabloid fodder for yellow rags like *Confidential* or *Hush-Hush*. Her favorite headline, she says, followed an incident where the Long Beach police arrested her onstage for heroin she wasn't even holding (or using). "It said: 'Bars for O'Day, Not Music!'" she laughs. "It was like war was declared! Before, my hair was all done up and I was 'Miss O'Day.' Then, when they busted me it became 'Get in the car, A-neee-tah!'" Her mother died while she was incarcerated on Terminal Island, but O'Day was not permitted to attend the out-of-state funeral. (Her father was decapitated in Wisconsin a decade later.) She had her second nervous breakdown at Terminal Island—after which she was kicked down to Dorm D with the psychotics for giving another inmate an orange while on kitchen detail. When she was released, on February 5, 1954, she and her new drummer John Poole, whom she liked because "he always played on the downbeat," consciously and deliberately began playing a darker, more complex style of jazz. Listening to the O'Day of this period now, you can hear the effects of Terminal Island in her voice: anger, hurt, a directionless sense of rage and betrayal are hidden in her subtle inflections, her ability to amplify the sadness or joy of lyrics while maintaining a cool musician's head, and her stubborn determination to remain in the realm of the unusual and the unexpected.

This time also, she quite consciously and deliberately began to shoot heroin.

⚬⚬⚬

You haven't had a hard life. The only bad thing that happened to you was that you got on dope, and you did that to yourself.

—singer Trilby Hailey to
Anita O'Day (1980)

En route to another day at the Hollywood Park Racetrack, O'Day's friend Vic—he of the rose-tinted sunglasses and Aqua Velva 'do—rides in the back seat of her car, shaking his head silently. Anita and I are in the front, screaming at each other:

"You're confusing me!"

"You're confusing *me!*"

I have asked her two questions. I understand that this is inevitable; every writer who has ever faced off with O'Day knows that it can be a frequently bruising and humbling experience. She exposes my eager-to-please niceties ("Ya know, you smile way too much, kid!"), foils my attempts to pull away to a neutral, objective distance ("Stop starin' at me from over there!"), and even challenges my journalism school vocabulary (she pokes you with the Glove when she forgets a word: "What do they call it? What am I thinkin'? That word? C'mon, you're the writer!"). When you think you'll catch her off guard by mentioning the deep, acidic divots in her personal and professional life—like the 1999 death of Poole, her drummer and friend of thirty years, from congestive heart failure—she dismisses it with a wave, as if the man were a mere curio: "Ah, whatever. He carried the suitcases, drove the car, got the plane tickets, the hotel rooms, hired the musicians . . . that was the past."

Then, after a long silence, she'll point the Glove out the window at a random intersection. "Right there, Washington and La Brea, that's where I used to come down here to cop. I also used to go down to Western Avenue—even Temple Street, John [Poole] and me. One time we came down here and ran into Miles Davis!" She lets out a laugh. "He was waiting for our guy!" I ask her how she remembers so clearly after all these years. "Oh! Well, when ya came down here to score, you wouldn't remember the street names, you'd remember the landmarks, right? 'Turn left at the Greek restaurant, make a right at the yellow house by the gas station' and de-de-doo-da-da. That kinda thing. That ways, when they stopped ya, you wouldn't be able to give them the address of where your [connection] was, because, man, all you knew were buildings!"

They first met in Oakland during the war. Poole, a deeply religious Krupa disciple, was in the Navy and approached her with a snare drum for her to sign. O'Day had a few drinks in her that night and blew him off. It was six years after the war, at the Club Starlite, a strip joint just south of L.A., when she actually heard him. "He was in the house band," she remembers. "I said to the MC, 'Where's the band?' 'Behind the curtain,' she says. I said, 'I'd like to meet [that drummer]; he can't see the girls dance, but he catches every bop . . . the girls don't know what they're doin' but they do a kick or somethin' and he'd be right in there: bop-bop!' . . . and I said, 'I want that drummer!'" Musically, she was fascinated by him—he wasn't the world's greatest drummer, she wrote later, but he had fast wrists and good ideas: "He came at me with the suggestion that we pick up the tempos of the jump tunes so the ballads would have more impact." Critics began taking notice; Bill Brown of the *Los*

Angeles Daily News wrote that "Anita . . . has got a new sound and it's better than anything she's ever done in the past. The girl is hitting fantastic notes and demonstrating a control that is hard to believe . . . She has a hushed, almost reverential delivery that scores!" O'Day even took to singing with her back to her audiences—a trope she learned from Miles Davis.

By this time she had also become, by her own admission, "a falling-down drunk" and was drawn to Poole for another significance: He never touched alcohol. She later found out why—it was another religion besides his Christianity. When he finally agreed to fix her, she says she found that doing heroin made her feel like "I didn't need booze anymore." Soon they were sharing needles along with the downbeat, canvassing the U.S. like a jazzbo Bonnie and Clyde, eating mostly cereal and canned milk for breakfast, roadside-diner food for dinner. They broke down in tiny towns in Wyoming or Michigan, trying to cop while they were sick from the need; tried to kick in countless methadone clinics, occasionally harassed by the police—in Kansas City they were led handcuffed through the crowded lunchtime crowds of the Andrew Jackson Hotel. "Everyone assumed we were lovers," O'Day later explained. "[My second husband] Carl Hoff even called me 'Mrs. Poole.' We loved one another dearly but we weren't in love. What could we do? Explain it was dope instead of sex?" But she didn't touch alcohol for eight years.

During this time, she met another important man in her life. O'Day had actually known Norman Granz since the '40s through his famous Jazz at the Philharmonic concerts in L.A., programs that had featured Billie Holiday, Gene Krupa, and Ella Fitzgerald (but, oddly, not her). Granz stood up for his talent—he once threatened to sue U.S. Customs for harassing the spotless Miss Ella—and he was, above all, a businessman who could deal with intemperate artists. Wunderkind arranger Buddy Bregman helmed *Anita*, the inaugural release on Granz's label, which he had just rechristened Verve. Recorded in December 1955 in three days of sessions at the old Capitol building on Melrose where Frank Sinatra had once worked, *Anita* is generally considered a masterpiece of jazz self-reinvention. For the first time, a magazine—*The New Yorker* no less—referred to her as a "jazz singer." The cover—a murky, melancholy, hand-tinted picture of O'Day perched on a rock, head resting in the crook of a tree—said it all: A mature woman had emerged from oblivion and was reintroducing herself, scars and all. From the crisp opening salvo of Bregman's horn section in "You're The Top" to the almost classical leanings of the 1931 ballad "Beautiful Love"—O'Day's grainy, bittersweet delivery was a perfect foil to Bregman's lush, buttery arrangements—she sounded fully empowered again. She could be peppy and ballsy on "Who Cares?" and "As Long As I Live," wise yet vulnerable on the ballads "Time After Time" and "No Moon at All." As for her definitive treatment of "Honeysuckle Rose," *The New Yorker* said simply: "Here is a jazz vocal that is just about perfect."

Subsequently, O'Day's Verve albums were not just scattershot collections of hits and filler but shimmering, elegant, meticulously constructed song cycles that mixed pop sensibilities with the highest jazz aspirations—every bit the equal of Sinatra's comeback albums with the Nelson Riddle Orchestra. Her formidable vocal chops could handle the difficult arrangers Granz paired her with: Bregman, Russ Garcia, Billy May, Johnny Mandel, Marty Paich, Ralph Burns, Bill Holman, Jimmy Giuffre, and Gary MacFarland. Although, in typical jazz musician's style, she defers the credit of song choice to Granz, she had a hand in picking a majority of her tunes, showing a talent for bringing in quirky or obscure material—like *Anita*'s English wartime ballad "A Nightingale Sings in Berkeley Square," which became one of her trademarks, the kiddie-pop hit "Mr. Sandman" and the proto-feminist anthem "Peel Me A Grape" (*Time For Two*), "The Moon Looks Down and Laughs," and "If the Moon Turns Green" (*Travellin' Light*), which her own arranger had never heard of—not to mention the theme song to the "Orphan Annie" radio show and the decidedly non-jazz "Hurray for Hollywood" (Cool Heat). *All The Sad Young Men* (1961) is practically a concept album of superb-yet-marginalized composers.

In the studio, she worked like the musician she was now respected as: reading scores, working out her arrangements with her musicians and musical directors, and outlining her own ideas for songs. As usual, she didn't suffer fools gladly: "I like my musicians to stimulate me," she once told the *Christian Science Monitor:* "I like [them] to fill in the spots, 'play in the hole' in other words. If there's an empty spot, a piano player can ripple out a few chords—'da ba do ba,' get it? I detest—and please underline this—*detest* somebody that sees a job and waits for somebody else to do it." At Verve, Granz paired the Jezebel with superlative accompanists, including Latin jazz vibraphonist Cal Tjader, pianist Jimmy Rowles, saxophonists Ben Webster and Budd Johnson, and drummer Mel Lewis—not to mention members of Woody Herman's Herd, Dizzy Gillespie's Big Band, and an inspired 1956 reunion with Krupa and Roy Eldridge. *Anita Sings the Most* (1957), in particular, was recorded live in one thrilling 6 AM session after she had already done three club sets (the last of which began two and a half hours earlier) before facing off with the intimidating, dexterous fingers of pianist Oscar Peterson. "All were unrehearsed arrangements," marveled the *LA Weekly's* Jonny Whiteside years later. "Many of the tunes were nailed in one take, the entire set mind-bendingly perfect." Peterson's playing is so hyper-aggressive that it's been widely speculated that he was trying to throw off O'Day for her "recording-studio shenanigans." (Appropriately, they tangle and rip-roar throughout "You Turned the Tables On Me.") O'Day and fiery, pugnacious arranger Billy May—both holdovers of the days—had some legendary battle royales while recording their twin tributes to Cole Porter and Rodgers & Hart. Not surprisingly, having finally listened to them, O'Day considers the May albums her finest achievements.

Ten years earlier she was earning less than the average band instrumentalist: anywhere from $50 to $75 a week, of which she paid $10 in hotel expenses, $12–$15 for meals, $5 for the hairdresser, and up to $3 for various other expenses. In the '50s she started earning $100,000 per album on Verve. (She still had to pay anywhere from $5,000 to $8,000—including overtime for union session men—out of her own pocket for studio time.) She bought three Jaguars, one for herself, one for Poole, and one for a piano player friend of hers—"I needed my buddies to drink with, and they didn't have cars!" she says now. "We used to go racing them down Hollywood Boulevard!" She had always loved the track, particularly the Santa Anita in Arcadia. "I used to place all my bets with a runner right from the bar," she says exuberantly. "All day I'm drinkin' and drinkin' and placin' bets, and la-da-da-te-da, every one's a winner! So everybody starts watchin' same horses I pick, right, and the runner is coming in and out of the bar with about fifty different bets for the same horse!" Most of it, of course, went to heroin, the Sisyphus and the Rock of O'Day's Verve years. Even though she could be a perfectionist at working out a song in session, she rarely ever stayed to hear her playbacks. All of the arrangers who were interviewed for Mosaic's nine-CD *The Complete Anita O'Day* on Verve/Clef sing a single keynote about her: "A real space case," "one crazy lady" but also "a true original" and "nothing but a professional" in the studio. She just simply had to leave after her takes so she could keep herself from getting deathly ill for 24 more hours. She overdosed twice: once in '58 before a gig (she made it, barely) and again in '66— in a bathroom stall of the American Guild of Variety Artists in Los Angeles. The first time, someone other than Poole, who always knew what he was doing, fixed her; she fixed herself the second time—after which she was declared dead at the Beverly Hills Emergency Hospital. Her psychiatric report, dated 3/8/66, reads: "Drinking heavily unknown quantities of whiskey, wine, and beer daily, eating and sleeping poor, moving from place to place until on the day of admission finding herself without money or lodging . . . She admits, 'I drink because I'm depressed,' but denies suicidal intentions or attempt . . . She firmly denies [her near-death episode] being self-inflicted."

When she went to Hawaii to kick it cold turkey in 1966, she had exactly sixty cents in her purse.

❧

> *For my love's a sickness*
> *There's no physician, what could be to tell me to use*
> *No liquid or pills I'm sure ever did or will cure*
> *A woman alone with the blues.*
>
> —from *All the Sad Young Men* (1961)

By the 1970s, after the closing of many top jazz clubs and the ebb of record company interest, the jazz-vocal crossover fever reached often bizarre proportions: Ella Fitzgerald was doing rock 'n' roll and country albums, Peggy Lee and Sarah Vaughan were doing Beatles songs, and Ethel Merman was doing disco. "Anita was doing Anita," says Alan Eichler, who met her and Poole in 1976 and would be her manager/publicist for the next 22 years. "She's not a careerist. I've dealt with so many people who really work their careers, very conscious and careful of making all the right moves and talking to all the right people and kissing all the right asses. Anita never cared about any of that—she went her own way." Her career—now smack-free—had picked up a bit through the Japanese discovering her when *Jazz On A Summer's Day* opened there in the early '60s. She was still playing small clubs, not making top money, but she did a little better when she played the jazz festivals at home or abroad. She had just started Emily Records, her own label (named after her dog, a Yorkshire terrier, whose paw print was its logo). Besides some albums in Japan, however, she hadn't recorded for a major record label since Verve in the mid-'60s.

Eichler introduced O'Day to a new audience that eventually would help O'Day expand upon her success abroad—namely the young, trendy, cabaret–hardcore gay audiences of the mid-'70s Greenwich Village and West Hollywood. From there it seemed the strange irony that had dogged her whole life was working in reverse: Other female singers were falling apart while she was on the mend—and singing better than ever. Chris Connor, one of O'Day's disciples who (along with June Christy) followed her as the vocalist in Stan Kenton's orchestra, was booked to follow her at a club called Marty's in New York but, due to health problems, couldn't finish her run; O'Day came back and finished out Connor's two-week engagement. Marty's was where the renaissance started: Harry Reasoner came in and wanted to profile her on *60 Minutes* (she had never heard of it—or him); Rex Reed came in and did a full page feature in the *Daily News;* Tom Snyder put her on the *Tomorrow* show; and *Dick Cavett* had her on for two nights, where she gamely attempted to teach the dainty-boned Nebraskan the rudiments of Jazz Vocal.

By the time the rights to her 1981 autobiography had been purchased by producer Karen Kramer, wife of film director Stanley (*It's A*

Mad Mad Mad Mad World, Judgement at Nuremberg), O'Day was living in a 43-foot trailer in the desert town of Hemet in the San Jacinto
Valley, near Palm Springs. Unfortunately, the combination of O'Day's
drinking and personality had developed into a vicious circle: "I had to
fight with everyone to hire her because she was getting the reputation
of being difficult," says Eichler. "The jobs were getting more scarce
because she was drinking more because she was bored." Her interviews had been growing more bizarre: Will Friedwald recalls a Syracuse friend who went to interview the singer for the college
newspaper "in the worst place possible for that task: a bar." O'Day
wound up leaving with a gentleman she just met—and the cub
reporter without his story. On a joint photo shoot with blues pianist
Hadda Brooks for *Venice* magazine, O'Day threw the photographer
out of her apartment, accusing the hapless woman of stealing her
pearls. ("I had to beg Anita to let her back in to get her equipment,"
remembers Eichler. "She was drunk; the pearls were in her drawer.")
But Eichler says he first realized something was seriously wrong at
the opening night of O'Day's former Verve-mate Margaret Whiting's
1995 comeback at the Cinegrill in Hollywood. "We were at one table
together in front, and Anita was taking prescription cough syrup as
well as drinking," he remembers with peculiar detachment. "Margaret is onstage in the middle of a quiet ballad and Anita is talking
loud, things like 'How much longer is this gonna be? When is this
gonna be over? When she going to be finished?' The whole room
could hear her. I didn't know what was going to happen next ... I
kept saying, 'Anita, pretend you're going to the ladies' room and just
get up quietly and go out—it'll be over soon!'" Somehow they managed to get to the end of the show. "The lights came up and Anita
went to stand up and I was trying to get her out of there—Don Heckman from the *LA Times* was at the next table, and Anita fell right on
top of him. Literally, on top of him. J.D. Kessler, who runs the Cinegrill, told me he didn't ever want to see her in the club again."

The closest Kramer came to launching the good ship O'Day to
film was when she arranged a meeting with her former agent,
William Morris Agency czar Norman Brokaw. After bringing
O'Day in from Hemet, Kramer went to her hotel to find that

O'Day had left for breakfast and had never returned. "I was livid," she recalls. "I rushed back to the Agency. Norman had flowers and candy and everything set up just beautifully—as it turns out, he had a huge crush on her when he was a young man in the Army—and I sat there with him and I could see him growing gradually insulted." As it turned out, O'Day had gotten so drunk at breakfast that her manager had to bring her back to her hotel room. "I had a fit," says Kramer. "I said, 'We've lost a major, major opportunity! The head of the William Morris Agency was going to take over this project out of his absolute worship of you!' She said, 'Baby, we'll just do it again'. . . I told her, 'Anita, you get one shot with that kind of power! We could have made this happen and we blew it!'" A few years later, Kramer tried to bring up the project with Brokaw again but he wouldn't even hear of it. Says Kramer matter-of-factly: "He hardly speaks to me today."

Kramer admits she still loved O'Day despite it being "absolutely heartbreaking" that her film project had fizzled. She, along with O'Day's other friends, employees, protectors, and fire-snuffers, had become companions as well as spectators to the arc of this strange woman's life—downward or upward. Now, it seemed there was a dangerous lull developing—she knew how to sing but not to pass the time. She didn't even have music in her trailer. "She would stay in [there] and not do much, drink and not eat," says Kramer. "The man next door to her—who didn't smoke or drink or have any vices whatsoever—would call me and let me know how she was doing." The neighbor, Gary Weiner, a 53-year-old construction contractor and classical-music fan, recalls: "She once told me that she gets all this adulation from people who come to see her shows—but in the end she goes home to a lonely hotel room. Life can be disappointing for her when she's not onstage."

Then one day, she disappeared.

⌬

> *No moon at all*
> *What a night*
> *Even lightning bugs have dimmed their light*

Stars have disappeared from sight
And there's no moon at all . . .

—from *Anita* (1956)

In the high desert of California near Palm Springs—where the sun shines for 11 months out of the year—there's a beauty salon called Didi's. Walk inside and on the wall you'll find a signed picture: "To Helen, my favorite hairdresser in the whole world! Love, Anita O'Day." (Helen herself laughs: "I kicked her out of my salon I don't know how many times . . . I think that's why we hit it off so well.") When O'Day failed to show up at the salon the day after Thanksgiving 1996, Helen was immediately alarmed. "I called her trailer and there was no answer," she says. "After work I went over, and she wasn't there . . . [The park manager] had closed her door and her driver was out of town." Helen found out that O'Day had been taken to Hemet Hospital; the day before she had gotten drunk, tripped over her dog and fallen down the steps of her trailer. That morning at 5 AM, Gary Weiner, her tetotalling neighbor with whom she had spent Thanksgiving, was awoken by a call from O'Day who was in terrible pain. In L.A., Kramer received a call from Weiner: "She's broken her arm, badly, and she's not doing very well." When Kramer drove to Hemet, she found O'Day "sort of out of it; she was in pain, but her arm was in a sling and they had bandaged her cuts and abrasions. I remember going into her room and sitting with her and telling her, 'Anita, you've broken your arm because of your drinking' . . . and she says, 'I know, I have to stop doing that, don't I?'" A nerve in her arm had been damaged in the fall and they needed to install a rod; she also had to be transferred to the detoxification wing of nearby Yoma Linda Hospital, after which she would need nursing-home care for at least a month. It wasn't the first time O'Day had detoxed—or tried to, as the Hemet doctors remembered dealing with her ten years before—and she was prepared for it. But when Kramer got back to L.A. the next night, she again received a phone call from Weiner. "He said, 'She's been transferred again' . . . Somebody had come in the middle of the night and taken her to Los Angeles."

They found her—ten days later—at Queen of Angels Hospital in Hollywood, almost near death. "She couldn't even open her eyes and they didn't give her 24 hours," Kramer says quietly. Because of her feistiness, and because she was not very happy with what was happening to her, she had been heavily sedated. Kramer confronted the hospital staff: "I said, 'My God, do you understand that we're trying to get her off this stuff and not back on it? All that was wrong with this woman was that she broke her arm.'" They told Kramer she had no authority—and the ones who did weren't returning her calls. "So I stayed there, and every hour on the hour, I took her hand and said, 'Anita, you're not gonna die, you're gonna live . . . you've gotta fight, you've been close to death before and you've gotta come back, you've fought before and come back, there must be a reason why you've decided to continue to fight and I believe you can hear me'—I didn't know if she could hear me or not, of course, but I couldn't let this happen to her. And so Gary and I would take turns staying [with her]; I finally had to go because I had responsibilities at home [but] I would call the nurses, and say, 'Please go in there every hour and tell her she's going to live.'"

Once her fans and friends began showing up at her bedside, they learned O'Day had had a little stopover before landing in Queen of Angels. "She had been taken to some nursing home, a terrible place," says Kramer, who later visited the dilapidated facility in Hollywood. "They didn't pay any attention to her—just dumped her and left her there. During that time she developed a blood disorder . . . They moved her [to Queen of Angels] because they were terrified that they would be held responsible for her death." O'Day had become emaciated and dehydrated—her body already compromised from the severe reaction to alcohol withdrawal. "When I walked into that room, I wouldn't have known her if I would've known it was her in the bed," says Weiner, his voice betraying a touch of emotion. "She was just this shriveled up little woman in a fetal position. I had no way of knowing if she even knew I was there. She simply couldn't communicate."

O'Day's favorite hairdresser also came up from Hemet. "Karen called me and says, 'Helen, you gotta come see her. They've taken her

teeth out, she's only ninety pounds, *they have her in diapers.*' I said,
'You gotta be kidding me.' We got there and I walked into the room
and I looked at the bed and I thought, 'This is not Anita O'Day'
. . . Her lips were all cracked and bleeding. Her tongue was bleeding
[and] real big. She couldn't talk but I could read her lips: 'It's about
f—ing time you're here.'" Helen laughs nervously. "She looked like a
different person: She couldn't walk. She couldn't get out of bed. She
couldn't feed herself. She couldn't lift her arm. Her hair I don't think
had ever been washed. It was matted so bad that I had to just take my
scissors and just cut it to the scalp. The smell—it smelled so bad . . .
[But] I couldn't get over her mouth, I could not get over the fact that
her tongue was so large and bleeding. The nurses didn't know anything. They said, 'You'll have to talk to her doctor,' and they kept asking me if I was a relative and I said, 'No, I'm just her hairdresser.' I
said, 'She doesn't have family.'" Helen sighs. "I really didn't give her a
week; the doctors didn't either. I didn't think I was ever going to see
her again. I left there crying. I said goodbye without really saying
goodbye, you know? I put my arms around her after I had cleaned her
mouth out; she said, or sort of mouthed, 'You'll be back?' and I said,
'I'll be back next week.' Of course I didn't think there would be a next
week. But I came back each week after and she was doing a little better . . . She couldn't walk for three or four more weeks, but I could
start understanding what she was saying.

"She said, 'I've beat it before and I'll beat it again.' And I believed
her."

⟨❧⟩

How to survive the loss of a love.

—handwriting on anonymous scrap
of paper left on Anita O'Day's
table at her last Atlas performance

On May 17, 1998, at the Jazz Bakery in Los Angeles, Anita Belle
Colton O'Day made her first public appearance since her accident.
"She refused to coast," wrote the *LA Times*'s Don Heckman, the
same man whom she had fallen on in a stupor at the Cinegrill two

and a half years earlier. "[She is] singing the only way she seems to know how—full out, never hesitating to try for the offbeat line and the odd note in the harmony."

She had lost everything again: In the months she was incapacitated, most of what was in her trailer—her career memorabilia, her appliances, her dishes, her clothes, her TV, her bike, her pictures, her dog—and even her car passed through different hands while she was being transferred from hospital to nursing home and back again. She had to relearn how to walk and eat. She even got her voice back—not slowly, but all at once: "I decided I wanted to walk and I walked!" she says. "Same with the singin,' ya dig?" She even had to buy her own albums to relearn her songs. Her arm had been reduced to a shriveled, paralyzed claw from numerous operations to correct the horrific missetting of the bone that occurred, most certainly, when her treatment was interrupted. "We never did understand how she was moved," is all Kramer, for one, will say. "It's still a major mystery."

But Anita O'Day has once again cleared her throat: She has a new combo, a new lawyer, a new driver, and a new manager who, in a 12-month long contract, pays her rent at Bethany Towers, an assisted-living complex in the heart of old Hollywood that was once actress Mary Pickford's home. In 1998 she rerecorded "God Bless the Child" (made famous by her idol Billie Holiday) with Sweetback, the band that backs up Nigerian chanteuse Sade. She has her eye on an empty star on the Hollywood Walk of Fame—the one right next to the woman who first influenced her, Martha Raye. She has a lot of new friends—all of whom she calls "kid" and treats with her peculiar mix of aloofness and affection, like she's saying: "Thank you for loving me for who I am because you know I have to be grand, you know I have to be what I am." The old ones like Gary or Karen or Helen always tack on an appendix after their interviews: "Say 'hi' to Anita from me, and please tell me when she's playing next." Knowing what they know about how her illness was handled and how she was advised to handle it after she recovered—by attempting to sue several of the hospitals for malpractice—meant that the blonder, healthier, peppier, cleaner, and sober Anita was still

Anita. Only ten times more human because they saw now that she was scared. This is probably why, when you drop O'Day off after spending a day with her—after watching her buzz around like Macy Gray on Benzedrine, creating chaos wherever she goes, insisting on picking up literally every penny on the ground she sees, slamming the Glove on the car seat and yelling at you ("All you do is ask me questions about the past! I'm tryin' to get on with it!")—she stops and turns to you and says, "I guess I'm never going to see you again, am I?"

I cannot speak for the others who come to see her at her last show at the Atlas before she starts practicing for her upcoming Japanese tour (!!). I can only say that I wanted to see the woman who time simply could not kill—because people like this go out only when they say so. What she's lost in her voice and her intonation, the mobility of her arm and hand, the way she really has to fight to exact the vocal calisthenics she is known for—nowhere is this more evident than when her performance reels from the past are played. They, particularly the *Jazz on a Summer's Day* performance, still have an undeniable power and always get a strong reception from the audience. But they also underscore the fact that O'Day is competing with her own past acumen that—due to the inevitables of time and age—dictate that when she mounts the stage again for her second set, she will have to overcome the fact that the Then Anita is the one who set the standard, and the Now Anita is struggling to match up. Right now she's trying. She blew the first few lines of "Sweet Georgia Brown" by singing "Honeysuckle Rose"—twice—during the first set. During the next set, she will sing "Old Devil Moon," a song she hasn't done live in years. But now, with the performance-reel images washing over her face, she turns to her bassist Jim Dejulio: "I don't think I can do it tonight." It sounds uncomfortably like an apology. Dejulio, a jovial, hyperkinetic man who once played alongside Sinatra and marveled at how the Chairman had fallen apart during his last four years while O'Day continues to create havoc at race tracks, looks at her agape: "Are you kiddin' me?! I gave up an important gig to come here tonight! You're playing that damn song!" It is delivered affectionately—but Italian-affectionate.

Then a funny thing happens. O'Day does not become angry, offended, or divalike. She says, "Okay, kid." Her musicians—per her request made to the *Christian Science Monitor* nearly a half-century ago—are challenging her. That's it. That's all she asks.

When she has sung the second set, no two people in the club will remember it the same way—like a delicate purse-snatching or an extremities-tickling fender bender. They hear her strain for the chords, yes, and they hear her trail off when she forgets lyrics; sometimes she just can't hit the note and replaces the lost line with a joke ("You're such a good audience, you won't notice when we screw it up!"). But when she hits "Old Devil Moon" she will practically lunge for the microphone and sing the shit out of the song. She demands solos from her men ("Not loud! Just brisk!"), holding the mike directly at their instruments, pumping her arms like a shrunken Rock 'Em–Sock 'Em robot. She no longer wears a glove onstage, and directs the band with her frozen hand like it is a graceful baton—even blowing drummer Jack LaCompte a kiss. As her vocal lines hang and sway like an easy hammock, dropping into a cascade of tiny, staccato peaks and valleys ("broum-broum-broum-a-deedle-doodle-doobie-doo, yeah!"), men's hands appear on the backless backs of women and pregnant glances and heated moments are exchanged all over the room. They'll smell sea breeze though it's sweaty, grimy Koreatown. They'll swear they are under pinpoint starlight even though they're indoors. They'll catch an old timer in rose-tinted aviator sunglasses and an Aqua Velva hairstyle, sitting in her shadow by the stage, his face a frozen smile of rebounded ecstasy. (Later, when asked, he won't remember what he was thinking.) Guided by O'Day, they'll all forget the melody—their version of the standards for the ones that she spins out of her battered, abused, celebrated throat. When each tune is done, she leans into the spotlight conspiratorially and reminds them they will never get it back: "You'll never hear that version again!"

But that's all still to happen. Her goblet of lemon and water sits on the piano, her microphone rests on a stool, her young apple-cheeked driver waits by the stage to help her climb the stairs. Onstage, Marty Harris, her one millionth piano player, is crowing

in his basso hipster croon: "Laaaa-dies and gentle-men, please welcome Missss . . ." Anita O'Day studies her crowd, blinking, tapping
her long fingernails, eyes wide open, simultaneously imperious and
vulnerable as a dove. Finally, she eases herself out of the booth and
struggles up. A young couple calls out to her from a table:

"Hey! Hi, Anita! How are you!"

"The best!" she barks as she walks by. The couple laughs. The
host, leaning by his podium, nods, "She's so great. She's a trip." Up
on the screen. Then Anita kicks her legs and does a twirl while
seductively singing "Thanks for the Boogie Ride!" to—in another
moment of exquisite O'Day irony—a gawking motorcycle cop in a
Smokey the Bear hat. Now O'Day, meanwhile, begins to feel the
familiar ache in her ankle that probably brings her all the way back
to the sadistic, mocking announcements of the '30s Walkathons,
when she and her partner would take turns sleeping while dancing,
leaning on each other, trying not to be struck out of the race—if
only in hopes of surviving to the next: *Now one more plucky little girl,*
Miss Anita O'Day, has fallen by the wayside! But, in tribute to her spirit,
the remaining contestants will pass, one by one, to bid adieu to a girl whose
courage and fortitude only they can appreciate. So dig not into your pockets,
but in your hearts, and let's hear the silver ring as it hits the floor! It will
be her only buffer against cold and hunger!

Moving toward the stage, reaching her hands out to the kid, she
shakes it off.

That Same Lonesome Blood

"All them old Depression people, babe,
I know they took a heavy load.
All their children, my kin folks and cousins,
still walking down Tobacco Road.
They still talk about Hank Williams,
they're clinging unto his fame.
I'm of the same race,
I'm from the same place,
Got the same lonesome blood in my veins."

—Steve Young, "Long Way to Hollywood"

When I found Steve Young, I had been heartsick a while, and he was singing songs that told stories about a world I knew. It's a world where you go somewhere and aren't sure how you feel about it, where you feel the past pushing you away and pulling you back, where you cover sad feelings with crooked smiles and bitter words, where you make tough choices and always pay the price for them. But it was his voice, a voice full of grief and anger and tenderness all fighting to be heard at once, that captured me and made those songs and their rhymes and rhythms often feel more real than the rest of my life.

Until I was eight, I'd lay on my mother's bed on Saturday nights and fall asleep to the muffled voices of the *Grand Ole Opry*. Mama would take charge of the radio as the last shots of *Gunsmoke* were fired. The radio dramas were my favorites, but soon the distinctive sounds of the *Opry* filled the space between us until her world was my world and her stars were my stars. And for a time, there next to my mama, with my father in his study working on the next day's sermon, and only the voices of Hank Snow, Ernest Tubb, and, her favorite, Faron Young, around us, I felt soothed and safe.

I was a child full of fears: The Dark. Water. Elevators. Carnival Rides. Flying. My Father. Finding My Father Dead. Mama was my protector. She was a big woman, five feet, seven inches and fleshy enough to call herself big boned. She had the high cheekbones of the Cherokee, who had married into her mother's family, and she could hide her emotions in a mask as stoic as bluegrass music, but there was a hint of moody sensuality about her and mischievousness in her smile. Her eyes, like her hair, were dark brown, though I remember them as more distant than colored. One of twelve children, she had grown up in the hills near the Tennessee River. Their house had neither electricity nor plumbing and had never been painted. It was all bedrooms across the front, three of them with two beds each, and a kitchen in the back. She had gone to the one-room Doe Creek School for grade school and then walked four miles to Scotts Hill for high school. She'd found her way out of the hills when my father, a Methodist minister, had preached a revival near her home. At sixteen, she left home to become his wife. She taught herself most of what she needed to know by watching and reading, and she lied about her education and age to make a better fit with my father, who was college educated and ten years older. They moved through a string of rural "circuits" of three and four churches with names like Campground, Church Grove, and Palestine. My sister, Kaye, ten years my senior, often had to hear the same sermon four times on a Sunday. But by the time I was born my father was serving single churches in the small towns of Western Kentucky.

In 1954 we moved to our first brick house, a four-bedroom Tudor that stood next to a matching church on a bluff in Hickman, Kentucky, that overlooked the Mississippi River. We were used to finding our place in farm towns. What we weren't used to were the plantation airs of Hickman: the colonial houses, the big cars, the fur stoles. This was cotton country, and the large farms that filled the river bottoms made it seem like the Mississippi Delta. A few families controlled most of the rich land and sat atop a class structure that was mostly poor people, black and white. We were part of the small middle class, but much of the local aristocracy attended our church, and our lives straddled the class lines of the town. For my mother, Hickman was both an alluring and foreboding place. Closer to her dreams of the good life than she had ever expected to be, she drank in the elegance of that sleepy river town and turned off the *Opry*. Hickman was a place too grand for country music.

She rose every morning at five and worked most of the day cleaning the house. In the afternoons, she often attended one kind of churchwomen's meeting or another. She sometimes gave the devotional at these gatherings, mixing our family stories with inspirational readings and biblical passages: "If you will permit me," she would say, "I would like to tell you of some suffering in the lives of the Eason family." That was her transition to a discussion of the role of God's will in preserving my father's life during a recent surgery. "You say that was all in the skill of the doctors? I say God still has work for him to do."

She worried a lot about having the right thing to wear, though she and my father argued regularly over her spending, and she lied about some of it to keep the fights manageable. "Why, Lester," she would say, "I have had that old dress for years." There was never any real resolution to these arguments. Daddy couldn't make the budget balance, and Mama couldn't stop dressing up her insecurities. Her life—our life—was orchestrated to avoid criticism about our clothes, our car, our grammar, our manners, our intelligence, the state of our souls. There was a correct way to do everything, and no matter how public the situation, she would ridicule you for breaking one of her rules. But she could be very funny, even about the pretenses. Our best times were when she would tell the old stories about growing up poor and isolated. She would laugh until tears filled her eyes, and I, not really understanding the stories but loving the laughter, would roll on the floor beside her.

My attachment to Mama became my humiliation as I approached adolescence. One minute I wanted nothing more than to be away from her forever, and the next I was running back for comfort. She didn't help much, clutching to me as her confidant and folding me into her fears and anxieties. Mama saw all sorts of little aches and pains as indications of some greater, undetected illness. She took a hundred aspirin tablets a week, often went to bed before dark, and visited doctors continually. Her self-absorption gave me some room, but it was her deceitfulness with my father, and my implication in it as I aged, that finally pulled us apart and helped me enter his world. A turning point came at the end of my freshman year when I wanted a sport coat for a spring banquet. Daddy was a solitary man who wrote poetry and loved to fish and hunt. I still feared him, and Mama often intervened for me. He said we couldn't afford the coat, but Mama told me to charge it to her anyway. I wore it to the banquet and to church on Easter as well. When I left the church, I shook hands with my father. He looked at the coat, and he held my hand longer than usual. I was afraid. I looked up at him, expecting anger. But his face wasn't angry; it was disappointed. He never mentioned the coat, but I always remembered it. During my high school years we became close. He came to all of my basketball games, even when he was too sick to do so. And after each game we would sit up late into the night and analyze plays. I helped him around the church and started thinking that I might follow in his footsteps and become a minister.

Mama started listening to country music again when I was in high school. By this time we had moved on to another Tudor in Newbern, a farm town just over the Tennessee state line. My father's heart had been damaged by a combination of rheumatic fever and a boyhood shooting accident, and his health had worsened yearly as he reached his fifties. By my junior year it had reached the crisis stage. One Saturday afternoon during this time, I found my parents in the family room, cuddling on the couch and watching the *Flatt and Scruggs Show*. For as long as I could remember they had divided the house between them, creating a distance far greater than the sum of the rooms that separated them. It was a rare moment of intimacy. Every Saturday afternoon for more than a year, they watched a string of syndicated shows out of Nashville—*Flatt and Scruggs*, the *Wilburn Brothers*, *Porter Wagoner*. I saw those country music shows only out of the corners of my eyes. My parents never encouraged me to watch. Perhaps it was just our family dynamic—we always seemed more able to do things in twos than in threes. But I took the new Saturday ritual to be an act of resignation on their part, and one they didn't want for me. It was as if they were saying, "David, this music is fine for country people, but where you are going, it will just be a burden." I had my own music by then anyway. My friends and I ridiculed the country stations that surrounded us and listened to urban rock 'n' roll: WHBQ out of Memphis by day and WLS out of Chicago by night. Still, our tastes were always closer to country than we imagined. We liked Bobby Bare's "Detroit City," though we didn't understand that it was a homesick country song. It was pop music to us, just like Patsy Cline's "She's Got You," my best friend's favorite song in 1962. And riding on the bus to basketball games, we sang all of the hits, often going from the Beach Boys' "Fun, Fun, Fun" to Leroy Van Dyke's "Walk on By": "Just walk on by, wait on the corner/I love you but we're strangers when we meet." We understood that Van Dyke was a little country and added some extra twang to show that we weren't. But it was a bad act.

Daddy died the following fall from congestive heart failure, and Mama moved us into a public housing project. She had gotten hooked on tranquilizers during his illness. Often she took them in doses large enough to make her balance unsteady and her speech slurred, and, sometimes, they would keep her almost comatose for days. She was in and out of psychiatric hospitals, but nothing offered lasting relief. Daddy had had a leg amputated earlier in the summer, and Mama's situation had worsened. I devoted more time to looking after him, and when he died, I had never felt so alone. I wish I could say that I'd worried for her, too. I suppose I did, but mostly I just thought about getting away. Shortly before his death, Daddy had found about a thousand dollars in unpaid bills, and it

seemed to my sister that he had never been the same after that dis-
covery. To me, it was just one more thing to hold against her. Mama
continued to deteriorate. I was called out of school to take her home
after police in a neighboring town found her swerving down the
street in her car. And we left one of her sisters' homes at Thanksgiving in a fury after some medicines were discovered missing. I slept
fitfully, fearful some nights that she might kill us both. That always
seemed less likely in the morning, but it was hard to know what was
possible and what was imaginary. On the night the Beatles played
The Ed Sullivan Show, I came home from church to find Mama hys-
terical. I waited for the doctor to come while the Beatles sang "I Saw
Her Standing There."

A few days after graduation in 1964, I took a bus to Nashville. I
stayed at the James Robertson Hotel on Seventh Avenue, two short
blocks from the Ryman Auditorium, home of the *Grand Ole Opry*,
but I never walked those blocks, never thought about the *Opry*. I was
going the other way, to a theater on Church Street, where I was
learning to be a door-to-door book salesman. Somehow I lasted the
summer, and by the end I had sold enough dictionaries to prove I
would always be able to support myself. I sold books for three sum-
mers on the porches of country people in Georgia, South Carolina,
and North Carolina. I made enough money to keep myself in cars
and clothes, and to pay my expenses at Lambuth College, a
Methodist school in Jackson, Tennessee. I gave up on being a minister for a while and tried to be a fun-loving college boy. But I was
running on sadness and anger, and the props couldn't hide it. I
started drinking and didn't handle alcohol well from the start. I had
a string of moving violations, and when I transferred to Memphis
State for a year, I was expelled from a dormitory for having a beer in
my room.

I found a voice for my rebellion in folk music. Over Thanksgiving
of my freshman year, I went to New York as part of a United
Nations seminar. On the last night there, a group of us went to a
Village folk club. We really didn't know what we were looking for,
but we ended up at the Gaslight Café, where John Hammond and

Phil Ochs were playing. I was swept away by Ochs. Within days I had his album *All the News That's Fit to Sing*, and by the end of the year I had a large stack of folk records. I loved the protest songs, but I was fighting so many personal devils that I found my true home in Bob Dylan's new electric music, where the songs focused on resentment, betrayal, and the absurdity of life.

I went home as little as possible. Mama pulled herself together for a bit and went to work. She took the only jobs that were offered, first as a maid, and then as a cook on a river tugboat. That took some courage, and she was proud of herself. She bought a second set of china and a mink stole to celebrate. She got married again, to a river man who had come back from World War II a broken alcoholic. He was a mechanic, and they bought a service station in a neighboring town, but he couldn't stay straight long enough to make it work. Soon Mama was back on the river again and then, after a while, back on the pills.

After graduating from college I revived the idea of going to seminary and attended Southern Methodist University. In a single act I was trying to stay out of Vietnam and to find something worth living for, but I didn't have enough faith to be there and left school after a year. Before I could be drafted, however, Nixon instituted the lottery, and I received a high number. I was visiting a friend in Watertown, New York, on the day the numbers were drawn. I was aimless and had met a woman there whom I liked, so I looked for a job. I ended up working as a copy editor and reporter for the local newspaper, the Watertown *Daily Times*. That's where I was when I found country music again.

Watertown was a few miles from an Army base, Camp Drum, which, in those days, functioned as a training site for reserve troops. I was working on a story on the summer bar scene and was making the rounds checking out the soldiers' haunts: strip clubs, dance spots, country joints. I was in the Clock Grill, just off the town square. The Clock was the only black bar, and it had a jukebox full of soul tunes. There was, however, one song by country music's only successful black singer, Charley Pride, called "Is Anybody Going to San Antone?" I played it repeatedly for an hour or so that afternoon and returned a couple of times later just to listen to it some more. It's about getting away ("any place is all right as long as I/forget I've ever known you"), but in my imagination the singer was going home. That was the kind of song I needed, one that went in two directions at once. I wanted to be right where I was, as far away from Mama as I could get, but some part of me that I didn't understand wanted nothing more than to return home.

I had a profound, if contradictory, case of homesickness, and it would follow me for twenty years through Illinois, Wisconsin, and Utah. I bounced back and forth between newspapers and graduate school before earning a doctorate and settling into life as a journalism professor. I worked hard to master the social and intellectual ways of the academy, but I lived another life as well, a life on the run from all that felt false in the one I had chosen. I was a hard drinker, and my favorite spots were the taverns and honky-tonks of working people, where no one knew of my degrees and where country music was usually on the jukeboxes: the Atomic Grill in Watertown, the Poor & Hungry Café in Memphis, Midland's in Carbondale, Illinois, Axel's on Oakland and Tony's on South Second in Milwaukee, and Junior's in Salt Lake City.

In the early '70s I was living in Memphis, working at the *Commercial Appeal*, and listening to a lot of Merle Haggard and Tom T. Hall when a friend came from Austin with an album by Waylon Jennings. The rock vitality in that "outlaw" country music caught me for a while and gave me a new group of singer-songwriters whose songs sustained me for years: Billy Joe Shaver, Rodney Crowell, Guy Clark, Townes Van Zandt, and, my favorite, Steve Young.

Young was the only one of the group not from Texas. He had grown up in Alabama and in the '60s had headed to the West Coast, where he had been a part of the L.A. folk-rock scene. He recorded two albums in California—*Rock, Salt, and Nails* on A&M and *Seven Bridges Road* on Reprise—before moving to Nashville. In the mid-'70s he made *Honky Tonk Man* on Mountain Railroad before signing with RCA for two albums. He had songs on albums by Waylon Jennings and Hank Williams Jr., and played on Jennings's *Honky Tonk Heroes* as well. He is probably best known for the song "Seven

Bridges Road," which has been covered by the Eagles and many other artists, most recently Dolly Parton. Some of his early work is available in reissue, but most of it is now out of print. A collection, *Lonesome, Ornery, and Mean*, on Raven documents his work from the '60s and '70s.

I first started listening to Steve Young in 1975 in Carbondale. I had moved there from Memphis a couple of years earlier to work on a doctorate. It was an unseasonably spring-like day in late February when I found one of his albums at a JC Penney. I had just bought Emmylou Harris's first solo album and was heading out the door, when I stopped to look in the bargain bin. There among the discounted albums was a lime-green cover with a photo of a young woman walking across a bridge. The sign on the bridge read SEVEN BRIDGES ROAD. The pastels and photo suggested the soft rock style popular with the singer-songwriters of the time, but when I surveyed the list of songs, I discovered that the singer had written "Lonesome, Ornery, and Mean," a song with some grit that I knew from Waylon Jennings. The back cover was dense with lyrics and had a candid photo of a young man and a woman holding a baby. Their eyes downcast, the couple contradicted the breezy style on the front.

I took the album to the trailer I was sharing with Barbara, the woman I would marry in a few months. We pointed the speakers toward the open door and sat on the steps in the sun. We drank some beer and marveled at the power in Young's voice. The album was sad, full of songs about the desire to straighten out a life that was out of control. Many of them conveyed a deep longing for home. Sometimes this longing was sweetly told, as in "Seven Bridges Road":

> *Sometimes there is a part of me has to turn away*
> *and go, running*
> *like a child*
> *beneath warm stars down the Seven Bridges Road.*

But most often it was told more resentfully, as in "Montgomery in the Rain":

I know I look funny to you all honey,
but I'm just one
who was once from here and now who's come back again.
And I ain't asking for nothing but my song
and a cemetery wind.

For the next thirteen years Barbara and I would listen to that album thousands of times. When we got married, we made up our own ceremony, but it would have been better to have used Steve Young songs; he was far nearer to our core. Barbara was a strong woman who had suffered losses early—a mother to cancer, a daughter to a harsh custody battle, and a husband to a motorcycle accident. For a long time, we tried hard to make up for what the other had lost. We were the best of companions, but underneath it all we were wedded to a sense of loss. To keep the feeling tied to something tangible, we attached that loss to our love for the South and then headed the other direction, first north and then west.

I took a position at the University of Wisconsin-Milwaukee after graduate school. We had been there a year when we got a call from Mama in the summer of 1977, asking us to visit. She was changing her life, she said, getting a divorce, losing weight, and going back to work. She would be home in early August and wanted us to come then. I had stopped going home five years earlier, after I had found her so doped up she was unable to recognize me, but I agreed to make the trip.

On the night before we were to leave, I received a call. Mama had been found dead, and the police suspected murder. It turned out she had died from a heart attack, but it was a day or so before police figured out she had not been killed. They assumed the worst, I discovered, because they had answered so many domestic disturbance calls at the house. We had a small service at the funeral home in Hickman. The music was recorded, old hymns as indistinct as elevator music. The funeral director popped the 8-track in and out of the recorder without much skill, leaving the drag of the tape to scar any illusion of musical presence. The old minister, a friend of the family, didn't know what to say about the last years of Mama's life; his words ended with the year my father died. My sister and I conspired in our own way to blot out those same hard years. We turned back the clock and buried her as Nelle Eason in the plot beside our father.

We cleaned out her place, a little ranch house on a quiet street where she had been the last white person in the neighborhood. Though her background told her to move, she had seemed content enough to stay there. Inside, there wasn't much left from our child-hoods: some photos, odd furniture, and a few figurines, though all had one kind of chip or another. The old cedar chest had our family mementos—baby books, graduation programs, birthday cards. There was also a big box of yellowed magazine and newspaper arti-cles. Some described national events, V-E Day, V-J Day, the Kennedy assassination, but most offered tips on how to live a life: how to raise children, throw parties, meet strangers, write letters, give talks, wear scarves, arrange tables, make punch, fix hair. Noth-ing in that house seemed as personal as that box of sad clippings.

I thought I'd gotten a head start on the grief with all that distance I had put between us, but I was wrong. I drank more and looked for solace in my records. I found my greatest comfort in a new album Steve Young had recorded on RCA. The album was titled *Renegade Picker*, and it portrayed him as one of country's new breed of out-laws. It was a dark collection of country songs full of guitars inspired by Southern rock. I played the album all winter, though it was hardly a collection of songs most people would call comforting. *Renegade Picker* describes a world where people are tortured by love, punished by memories, and burdened with an insatiable longing for home. Young is a distinctive stylist with a well-developed sense of drama. He could take a song like John D. Loudermilk's "Tobacco Road," with its story of growing up poor, and universalize it until there seemed no way for anyone to escape: "Tobacco Road, I hate you 'cause you're filthy/But I love you 'cause you are home." The building of such intolerable tensions was part of the music's greatest appeal. Country music, I reasoned, was a music of lines, the ones you can't cross, the ones you must cross, but most of all the ones you just have to walk.

Living with a liar
Is a hard ol' way to go
And laughing just to keep from crying
Ain't no way to grow old.

Barbara liked Young's version of Guy Clark's "Broken Hearted People," but sometimes the music was too much for her. On the night we found out about Mama's death, I had sat alone and played repeatedly "Home Sweet Home (Revisited)" by Rodney Crowell. It's a song Young would introduce live as one he should have written. "Home Sweet Home" describes the decay of a family in a series of powerful images—a rotting house, a watch that won't run, an abandoned car: "Tomorrow has no home sweet homes./Look what they have done to mine."

Barbara had heard the song for months, when one summer night she yelled over the sound of the stereo, "If you play that one more time, I'm leaving!" I played it less frequently, and she accepted that as not playing it at all. We made a lot of compromises like that, but we also had an intense love, and celebrated it in music. Two of our favorites were on Steve Young albums: "Light of My Life" and Townes Van Zandt's "No Place to Fall," the title song on Young's second RCA album.

Milwaukee was a tough, cold, working-class city, and it took us a while to take to it. But we loved its anonymity, sturdy turn-of-the-century architecture, and mix of ethnic groups. Still, we pined for the South. It was home for us in a powerful way that didn't seem to diminish. In the spring we would visit Biloxi or Charleston or New Orleans or Savannah. We always drove, and the trip itself—out of the cold, across the flatlands of the Midwest to a softer, greener place—was our best ritual.

Steve Young came to Milwaukee regularly in the '70s to play at the Blue River coffeehouse. Without a band, he was more the folk troubadour than the guitar-driven renegade picker. He mixed his own songs with Appalachian ballads, old country tunes, and an occasional rock song. The sets varied in intensity. Sometimes he looked as if he had just awakened, but he reached for a deeper level of emotion whenever it was obvious that people knew his songs. It was wonderful to feel that requesting "Long Way to Hollywood" actually made the show better. Mostly though, the crowds were small and random in a way particular to folk clubs—first dates, visitors from downtown hotels, assorted walk-ins. Young, in turn, was often distant, protective, self-absorbed. But we always stayed to the end. Though the club would be virtually empty, the aura of the albums was so powerful that I never was able to introduce myself and tell him how much his music meant to me. But I would talk about the shows for days. I longed to see him with a band or even just in a better setting. Milwaukee, I rationalized, must surely be a dead spot between livelier venues in Chicago and Madison.

Young disappeared for a year or so in the late '70s. When he returned in the summer of 1980, Barbara and I helped informally with the publicity for the event. The show, in a new venue, had a bigger audience, and we were pleased. This time, with the help of a reporter friend, I did meet him. A group of us went to breakfast at Ma Fischer's, an all-night grill on the East Side. I felt awkward. I had thought so much about his music, but I didn't have the courage to ask him about any of it. Mostly I just listened. He seemed grateful for the company. He had been off the road for a year, getting his life in order, and was full of the changes he was going through. He had stopped drinking, so we talked into the early morning over coffee. At 4 A.M., he left to drive back to Nashville. The last song he had sung that night had been "Midnight Rider," and I knew I would now hear a loneliness in it that I had never heard before.

I found a good position at the University of Utah, so Barbara and I headed for Salt Lake City in the fall of 1983. We knew nothing about Utah. Before the interview I had to look it up on a map to figure out where exactly it was. We were just following the jobs, but neither of us had the heart for moving, and I had started to sense it even before we left. I spent the summer of our departure obsessed with dying. It filled my dreams, night and day. I distracted myself by planning my funeral. The songs were the most important thing.

They were mostly about the road, about where the road went away from, where it went to, and how long it went on. Though they all had lines about dying, the songs were truly about enduring, which is what life was coming down to for me. A couple of spirituals, "Peace in the Valley" and an early song by Young, "Many Rivers," suggested a longing for something else. I liked the line in "Peace in the Valley" about the lion lying down with the lamb and the line in "Many Rivers" about being free:

> *Father you have made me many rivers.*
> *And I followed them from the mountains to the sea.*
> *Now would you make me one*
> *That flows beyond the sun?*

I wanted Utah to fulfill the promise I saw written in its rugged landscape. But everything in Salt Lake was overstated, a conspiracy against the laid-back ways of the desert. I felt physically displaced, as if nothing could give me any clues as to where I was. The street system in the city is supposed to leave no room for doubt. It's organized to tell you where you are in relation to the Mormon Temple at every moment. But I lacked some sense of direction to make the system work and was disoriented most of the time. I never got over that sense of uneasiness, and I spent my years there plotting an escape.

I found a watering hole for exiles at Junior's, a dark joint down on East 500 South. Junior's was a Midwestern tavern transported to the West: just a line of bar stools, a couple of booths, and a pool table in the back. The music was '50s jazz. I hated that, but I wasn't finding much new music anyway. And it was the price I had to pay for clientele that was literate, jaded, and mostly from somewhere else. We celebrated our alienation from the official culture with sarcasm and droll humor. We even had a theme song of sorts. At the end of happy hour, John, one of the owners, always played Warren Zevon's "Werewolves of London." He handed out tambourines, drumsticks, pots and pans, and the whole bar played rhythm and sang along: *Aaaaaaaaaaaa-oooh*. It was the best moment in the day.

On a hungover morning in the late spring of 1986, life started to change. Barbara looked at me and without malice in her voice said, "You are getting to be just like your mother." That I would end up like Mama was my secret fear for as long as I could remember. I knew I drank too much, but I had never really thought about it the same way I thought of Mama's problem—as an addiction. But that was what she was saying, though "your mother" was as close as she could get to the words. I vowed to stop in a way that was too casual for the circumstances. It proved harder than I'd thought it would be, but after a rough time getting started, I did stop. Quitting drinking didn't save our marriage, though. It just showed how many things we had let go unattended. Barbara and I separated the following February and divorced a year later.

Recovery stories are a lot alike: People put their lives back together by learning how to react in new ways. I had to break many old habits. I quit going to Junior's, stopped smoking, and started running. And I didn't listen to Steve Young for over two years. I still loved the songs, but I just couldn't bear to hear them. They were too painful in an all-new way.

I had lost track of Young after we left Milwaukee. He had been without a recording contract since *To Satisfy You*, an early '80s album on Rounder, and I had no idea that he had made a couple of albums in Europe. Instead I wore out an old Eric Anderson album, *Blue River*, and listened to Rosanne Cash, Leonard Cohen, and Nanci Griffith, though all lacked some soulful element I was after. For a time I listened to nothing but Van Morrison and wondered if I would ever love country music again. I still paid attention to it, though. I watched the *Grand Ole Opry* show on The Nashville Network every Saturday night. Sometimes I cried. I had given up a lot of the things that had connected me to where I came from—a way of speaking, a way of believing, a sense of family—and now I had given up my way of masking the pain of those losses as well. The music seemed to be about all I had left as a connection.

I decided I would try to turn my love of country music into academic work. If I couldn't have the music in the old way, perhaps I could find a new way of being connected to it. I drafted a sabbatical proposal for a study of country music fans. In the spring of 1990 I left for Nashville, but my life as a country music researcher was short-lived.

I followed the fans around town for about a month until one hot day in June at Fan Fair, Nashville's annual opportunity for country music fans to mingle with the stars. I was sitting in the grandstand at the start of the festival, listening to Kathy Mattea, a singer I liked better than many who would appear during the week, when I realized that I had no interest in *this* music or *these* fans. I was looking for pilgrims, like those in the old photos of the crowds that came to the Ryman in the 1940s and '50s and had no eyes to see these new versions. These fans wore their allegiances on t-shirts and hats, went to shows and receptions sponsored by the fan clubs, bought items at the gift shops, waited in long lines for autographs, paraded by the stage en masse for photos, and were thrilled that the Fan Fair ticket also got them a day at Opryland, Nashville's now-defunct theme park. What could I have been thinking? I had never really been interested in country music as something to study. I didn't have an insider's knowledge about any aspect of it. To me the music was a personal, intense, and dramatic telling of my own story.

Still, I was fascinated with Nashville. I went out to the clubs. Some of my old favorites—Townes Van Zandt, Guy Clark, Gail Davies, and Emmylou Harris—played occasionally. And there were a few other singers I liked as well—Alison Krauss, Walter Hyatt, Dave Olney, and David Ball. But what touched me most were the people who had come to Nashville to play, sing, and write songs. They were from all over now, more varied in their music, and many of them college educated. Every waiter or bartender had a song or wanted to sing one. I lived just off Music Row. My apartment building was a way station for songwriters who came and went. I loved to hear the music coming under the doors when I walked down the hall.

Steve Young had moved away from Nashville the year before I arrived, first to Austin and then to L.A. After nine years without a new record in the U.S., he had a deal with a Texas label for an album to be titled *Switchblades of Love*. He came through town in the spring with Butch Hancock, and they did a show at the Bluebird Café. I was thrilled to hear him again. The years had brought balance to his performance. He was steadier, more self-assured. He could still write a sad song, but the music reflected a more spirit-filled vision of life and focused on themes of forgiveness, renewal, and self-acceptance:

> *I will bow down to the stars*
> *I'll ask forgiveness for the scars*
> *That I have made*
> *In the name of love.*

When it was time to go back to Salt Lake City, I felt like I had made a home for myself in Nashville and didn't want to go back. Middle Tennessee State University offered me a position, and I accepted. I have lived in Nashville for more than ten years now. When I am asked why I live here, I always say "the music," and I mean it. But it's more complicated than it sounds. The dreamy longings that brought me here have mostly disappeared. Nashville's a city of pretensions, a show-business town dedicated to the next big formula. "It's the music that matters," the music business people say again and again, but that's really just longhand for "sales." And the city communicates that worldview through billboards, banners, guest lists for shows, receptions for big sellers, showcases, publicists, syrupy reviews, and mostly timid journalism. The level of hype creates a good deal of nostalgia for "the good old days," when the town was smaller, the business was simpler, and the music was really country. I, too, miss the voice of Merle Haggard and the occasional well-crafted song on the radio, but my bet is that showbiz has ruled here from the start and that Nashville is, in fact, more interesting and varied today than it ever was.

Country music cultivated a broad mainstream audience and produced its most bland, pop-flavored product in the '90s. And yet, as hollow as that music has been, Nashville developed a vital live music scene made up of performers who recorded mostly on the independent labels. This music, the kind of roots music I have loved all these years, made a minor comeback and even received a name, Americana. I started to become conscious of the change in February of 1994, when Young came back to play a string of songwriter shows organized by Lucinda Williams, who had just moved to town from Austin. The shows left me longing for more. I went out to hear Williams every time she played and also became a fan of R.B. Morris, a songwriter-poet from Knoxville. Soon I was going to a lot of other shows as well: Steve Earle, Buddy and Julie Miller, the Del McCoury Band, Gillian Welch, Amy Rigby, Mathew Ryan, Tim Carroll, Duane Jarvis, Kevin Gordon, Paul Burch, Malcolm Holcombe, and BR5–49.

For a couple of years I went out to hear music two and three nights a week. I don't go that often now, but I still love live music enough to suffer all the inconveniences—the waiting around, the bad sound systems, the smoke, the late nights, the spotty opening acts, and the unevenness of even my favorite music. And it's not just for the wonderful moments that I go, though there have been a few of those: Steve Earle gets out of prison and joins Guy Clark and Townes Van Zandt for a show at the Bluebird; Lucinda Williams gets up to perform "On the Wings of a Dove," with Nanci Griffith and Gillian Welch singing backup, at a CD release party; Merle Haggard plays swing tunes with a small group on Lower Broadway; Iris Dement joins Earle for a duet of "I'm Still in Love with You" with the Del McCoury Band at the Station Inn; Bob Dylan sings Hank Williams's "Honky Tonk Blues" at the Municipal Auditorium. The music can still be full of life even when nothing so dramatic happens. Sometimes, while waiting for the music to begin, I wonder why I have come out on a Tuesday night to hear R.B. Morris at 12th & Porter. And then Morris and the band take the stage, and I wonder how I could be anywhere else.

Even a tired, stagey show like the *Opry* has its moments. The *Opry* has started wintering at the Ryman in recent years, and I went the night that Ralph Stanley was inducted. It was the usual show with the same intros and jokes you hear week after week. But you are much closer to the action at the Ryman, there's the aura of the place, and there were a few more stars added, too. On the night I was there Reba McEntire and Patty Loveless played the show. The audience couldn't get enough of Reba, and she pranced and preened and used a ten-piece band. The stage didn't rotate, as in coliseums, and there were no dancers, but it was all very contemporary. And then Ralph Stanley came on and sang "Pretty Polly" with Patty Loveless in that spare, unaffected, high lonesome sound he and his brother Carter made famous, and it was a kind of witness to something else that the music has been and occasionally still is.

Steve Young was in town to play the other night. He's been coming back about once a year for three or four years. We have developed a friendship through these visits, and it's always good to see him. This time he played a show at the Unitarian Church, a beautiful room with a decent sound system and acoustics, and there were more than a hundred people there. He has an album out on Appleseed, *Primal Young*. It has some new songs, and he covers a number of popular and traditional ones from his youth. The album, which pays tribute to the joys, sorrows, and hopes of common people, is the most plainspoken of his albums, and mostly it's about the enduring power of music:

> *There's a jig in my mind*
> *I hear it all the time.*
> *Dance to that jig in my mind.*

He opened the night with "Jig," and then he worked about half of the new CD around his classics. For some years now Young has strung his songs together in a loose story of his career. The story gives the songs a place, allowing a bit of distance for the singer, a useful distance particularly for those early dark songs. These newly recorded tunes about black-dirt farmers and displaced workers find their place amidst the intensely autobiographical ones and alter in a small but important way the story that the show tells. Some of my favorites get lost in the process, but it's a broader vision of what matters, and I was moved that night more deeply by a performance than I had been in years. The anguished outsider of "Montgomery in the Rain" and the contrite pilgrim of "Switchblades of Love" still have their time, but it's the tradition of song as much as the struggle of the singer that seems to matter now:

> For the jig's not impressed
> with who's doing the best
> It's just looking for life's feel.

There are still sad songs, but the new ones render a feeling that is at once specific to the singer and at the same time just part of the way things are, a sorrow that is an essential part of life. These songs from *Primal Young* remind me in ways the old ones never did that there is nothing new in the joys and sorrows we live out or in the songs we sing about them. I feel sure that this attitude toward sorrow is there in the songs, but I think it's in me, too.

> Little birdie, what makes me love you so?
> It's because you see me in my sorrow
> But I am searching for a patch of blue
> Just like you.

I have found the form of my life in the lines of Steve Young's songs. They were my words of parting when I left and my words of longing when I wanted to go back. They were my endearments when I found love and my curses when I lost it. They were my words of comfort when I grieved. And when I couldn't grieve, they were angry words that passed for grief. Those lines live on in me still, but I don't take them so personally anymore. At fifty-five, two years older than my father ever lived to be and two years shy of my mother's last birthday, I face my own questions about what endures. So I am happy to hear this familiar voice and this new version of a very old tune:

> Little birdie, come sing me one song.
> I've got a short time to be here.
> I've got a long time to be gone.

CARL WILSON

With Joey Gone, I Finally Get the Diana Fetish

The gangling shadow of Joey Ramone looms over indie rock this week, with the punk avatar's Easter demise after a long, unpublicized battle with cancer.

Given the date, it's tempting to be punkishly blasphemous, to evoke Joey hanging over his absurdly tall mike stand, as if nailed to it, with a crowded nightclub for his own private Calvary (that's the C in CBGB). The Ramones were punk's evangelists by example; new bands would spring up behind them armed with three chords and the truth. Upon this rock 'n' roll, Joey built his church.

But hold on. Joey was a Jew, born Jeff Hyman in Queens, and nobody's martyr. Anyway, I'm more reminded of—wait for it—Princess Di. His peril was kept so quiet that the news came as a sudden blow. And like Diana, Joey had so outlived his moment (many of his comrades burned out long ago) that it came to seem unnatural that this monster-movie man-child would age, much less die. His weirdness looked indestructible, despite the vulnerability of his stuffed-up singing and the alienated "Gabba Gabba Hey" chant he swiped from Todd Browning's 1932 circus-sideshow film, *Freaks.*

Like a paper-bag princess, what he had was purity. He never got rewarded the way heirs such as Green Day did. Like Diana Spencer, he spun fantasy from manner alone, his squint and his strut, as well as an up-from-nowhere myth, though this one was a rags-to-more-rags story. So now I finally get why people are so obsessed with that simpering, spoiled and spurned royal icon. So far, I'd granted their fetish nothing but contempt, but they'd feel the same about mine.

Calling Joey's death "tragic" would be pompous. At 49, he died prematurely, not young; these things happen. He was no Kurt Cobain. So it's hard to address the void he leaves, the way something good has gone out of the world. Joey Ramone embodied a knowingly innocent desire, the pain-pleasure of want. Half his songs were titled *Now I Wanna* something, or *I Don't Want to* something else. And isn't that what tabloid princesses are all about, too?

They often say "what Diana wanted is what we all want," but we don't all share her dream of love and luxury. We do all want to want, in itself. That's what the whomp of energy in every Ramones song reminds me, while the dopey-smart, repetitive lyrics intimate that we'll still be left wanting in the end. And if I can make Joey my dashboard Jesus, my saint of wanting, and play Sleater-Kinney's *I Want to Be Your Joey Ramone* over and over, you can make Diana yours, and sniffle along with *Candle in the* fucking *Wind*.

Or else you could head out into the night in Toronto on Wednesday and see Guided By Voices and Spoon, two bands that wrestle with those urges that go back to the Ramones and beyond. Robert Pollard of the cult-favourite GBV is a former schoolteacher whose quest for the perfect pop tune has spawned a sprawling body of songs, many just fragments, pursued and abandoned. On recent albums such as the new *Isolation Drills*, he tries to flesh his ideas out, but the results are needlessly complex, duller than the desperate futility of the past.

Spoon seeks the same musical grail with less hubris and more success, parrying Elvis Costello–like cleverness off the Ramones' kissable simplicity and repetition. Spoon's new *Girls Can Tell* includes the rapturous *Believing is Art*, and its first verse (and last verse, as Joey would shout, "same as the first") can stand as an epitaph, until—as it always did in the fast-and-furious Ramones world—something better comes along:

Things everybody would say:
Believing is hard, believing is art.
Things everybody should know:
The end will come slow,
And love breaks your heart.

Gabba Gabba Hey.

OTHER NOTABLE
ESSAYS OF 2001

Alex Abromovich, "Vintage Violence" (*Feed*, March 22, 2001)

Noah Adams, "Far Appalachia" (*DoubleTake*, Spring 2001)

Grant Alden, "When the Fallen Angels Fly" (*No Depression*, March/April 2001)

Liz Armstrong, "Strange in a Strange Land" (*Chicago Reader*, July 20, 2001)

Larry Brown, "The Whole World's Out There to Write About" (*No Depression*, May/June 2001)

Jeff Chang, "Bang the Drum" (*Vibe*, November 2001)

Robert Christgau, "Ghost Dance" (*The Village Voice*, September 19–25, 2001)

Chris Colin, "Jonathan Richman" (*Salon.com*, September 4, 2001)

Jim DeRogatis, "The Giant Stirs: Generation Y in the Wake of September 11" (*Salon.com*, September 19, 2001)

Lee Durkee, "Jim White's Yellow Mind" (*Oxford American*, Fifth Annual Music Issue, 2001)

Bill Friskics-Warren, "Delta Dawning" (*No Depression*, November/December, 2001)

James Gavin, "The Most Democratic Music: Homophobia in Jazz" (*JazzTimes*, December 2001)

Tim Hall, "Muscle Shoals: A Pilgrimage to the Heart of Southern Soul" (*New York Press*, September 12–18, 2001)

Greg Kot, "Wilco's Dark Victory" (*Chicago Tribune Magazine*, October 14, 2001)

Enrique Lavin, "Aterciopelados: The Velvet Revolution" (*CMJ*, April 9, 2001)

Calvert Morgan, "What'd You Do, Son? Finding Unexpected Revelation in the Music of Elvis Presley" (*Oxford American*, Fifth Annual Music Issue, 2001)

David Pecoraro, "Mouse on Mars: Idiology" (*Electronic Music Reviews*, Spring 2001)

Ben Ratliff, "Fixing, for Now, the Image of Jazz" (*The New York Times*, January 7, 2001)

Alex Ross, "The Searchers: Radiohead's Unquiet Revolution" (*The New Yorker*, August 20–27, 2001)

Seth Sanders, "Liliput/Y Pants" (*Chicago Reader*, March 9, 2001)

Roni Sarig, "Six Meditations on Living in the Present" (*Creative Loafing*, November 9, 2001)

David Segal, "Surly? They Jest" (*The Washington Post*, July 8, 2001)

Philip Sherbourne, "Without Whom" (*Neumu*, October 12, 2001)

Jennifer Spiegel, "Love Rescue Me: Entering the Holy of Holies" (*Image: A Journal of the Arts*, Winter 2000–2001)

Hank Stuever, "The Kids Are Alright" (*The Washington Post*, February 18, 2001)

Greg Tate, "Intelligence Data" (*The Village Voice*, September 26–October 2, 2001)

Bill Werde, "The D.J.'s New Mix: Digital Files and a Turntable" (*The New York Times*, October 25, 2001)

Armond White, "Summer in the Noir City" (*New York Press*, May 23–29, 2001)

Jessica Willis, "Tori Amos" (*New York Press*, November 7–13, 2001)

LIST OF
CONTRIBUTORS

Charles Aaron grew up in Asheboro, North Carolina, and Rome, Georgia, where Lynyrd Skynyrd tried to teach him to be a simple kind of man. But he just never learned. A resident southern alien in Brooklyn, New York, since the 1980s, Aaron is Music Editor of *SPIN* Magazine. He has never carried a lighter.

Franklin Bruno has written about music for *The Village Voice*, *Spin*, *L.A. Weekly*, *Los Angeles New Times*, and *Puncture*, and his poems have appeared in *Zzyzyva*, *Ribot*, and *Faucheuse*. He has released five albums as a member of Nothing Painted Blue and three as a solo artist, the most recent being *A Cat May Look At A Queen* (Absolutely Kosher). A native Southern Californian, he lives and works in Los Angeles.

David Cantwell lives in Kansas City, Missouri, where he is a free-lance writer and college English instructor. He's written about music for *No Depression*, *Country Music*, *Oxford American*, *Salon.com*, and the *Nashville Scene*. His *Heartaches by the Number: Country Music's 500 Greatest Singles*, co-written with Bill Friskics-Warren, will be published in early 2003.

Nik Cohn was born in London in 1946, and spent his childhood and adolescence in Derry, Northern Ireland. He is the writer who spawned *Saturday Night Fever*, and is the author of several books on rock and pop culture, including *Awopbobaloobopalopbamboom*, *Ball the*

Wall and *Rock Dreams* (with Guy Peellaert). *Yes We Have No*, his most recent book, was published by Secker & Warburg in 1999. He now lives in Shelter Island, New York.

Erik Davis is a San Francisco–based writer whose book, *TechGnosis: Myth, Magic, and Mysticism in the Age of Information*, is currently being translated into six languages. Davis is a contributing editor for *Wired* and *Trip*, and has also contributed articles and essays to a number of magazines and book anthologies. Some of his work can be accessed at *http://www.techgnosis.com*.

Matthew C. Duersten is a Wisconsin-bred, Los Angeles–based writer whose most recent work has appeared in the coffee-table book *LA Now* (Pasadena Art Center College of Design). He is a contributing writer for *LA Weekly*, *New Times*, *Flaunt* and *Black Book* and his writing has also appeared in *Variety*, *Jalouse*, *Front Desk LA*, *Buzz*, *Glue*, *Time Out-New York*, *Los Angeles* and *Total Movie & Entertainment*.

David Eason teaches journalism and communication at Middle Tennessee State University. His critical essays about the mass media and popular culture have appeared in varied books and journals. He is the former editor of the journal *Critical Studies in Mass Communication*.

Steve Erickson is the author of *The Sea Came in at Midnight*, *Days Between Stations*, *Rubicon Beach*, *Tours of the Black Clock*, *Leap Year*, *Arc d'X*, *Amnesiascope*, and *American Nomad*. He has been acclaimed as one of the most individual and important contemporary novelists by Thomas Pynchon, Greil Marcus, William Gibson, and many others.

Kodwo Eshun lives and works in London. He is the author of *More Brilliant than the Sun: Adventures in Sonic Fiction* and the editor of the forthcoming *Afrofuturist Reader*.

Sasha Frere-Jones is a musician and writer living in New York City.

David Gates is the author of the novels *Jernigan* and *Preston Falls*, and a short-story collection, *The Wonders of the Invisible World*; he is currently at work. Don't ask. He writes about books and music and what-not for *Newsweek*.

Gary Giddins has written the *Village Voice's* "Weather Bird" column since 1974. In 1986, he and the late John Lewis introduced the American Jazz Orchestra, which presented repertory concerts for seven years. Giddins adapted as PBS documentaries his biographies of Charlie Parker and Louis Armstrong, which are available from Da Capo, along with *Riding on a Blue Note*, *Rhythm-a-ning*, and *Faces in the Crowd*. His most recent books are *Visions of Jazz*, which won the National Book Critics Circle Award for criticism in 1998; and *Bing Crosby: A Pocketful of Dreams*, which won the Ralph J. Gleason Music Book Award and Theater Library Association 2002 Book Award.

Michael Hall graduated from the University of Texas at Austin in 1979. Before joining *Texas Monthly* in 1997, he was an associate editor of *Third Coast Magazine* and the managing editor of the *Austin Chronicle*. Hall won two 2001 Katy Awards: one for Best Reporter Writing Portfolio and one for Personality Profile/Interview for his July 2001 story "Lance Armstrong Has Something to Get Off His Chest." He has also written for *Trouser Press*, the *Austin American-Statesman*, and *Grammy Magazine*.

Mark Jacobson has been listening to Bob Dylan for 40 years, which makes him considerably older than he ever thought he'd be. A magazine journalist for many publications and author of two novels, *Gojiro* and *Everyone and No One*, Jacobson is currently finishing a book about travelling around the world with his wife and three children. He lives in Brooklyn.

Lenny Kaye is a writer, record producer, and musician. He is a longtime guitarist with Patti Smith, and has also worked with Jim Carroll, Suzanne Vega, and Allen Ginsberg. His anthology, *Nuggets*, has achieved renown as one of the first "garage-rock" anthologies, and he co-wrote Waylon Jennings' autobiography, *Waylon*. He is currently working on a book about the crooners of the early 1930s.

Monica Kendrick is a staff writer for the *Chicago Reader*. She has also contributed to *The Wire* and *The Journal of Country Music*, and sometimes writes poetry and fiction.

John Leland is a reporter at the *New York Times* who writes frequently about music and popular culture. He lives in the East Village with his wife and son.

Greil Marcus is the author of *Lipstick Traces*, *The Old, Weird America* and *Double Trouble*, among other books. His column "Days Between Stations" appears eight times a year in *Interview* and "Real Life Rock Top 10" biweekly in *Salon.com*. In 2000 he taught the American Studies seminar "Prophecy and the American Voice" at the University of California at Berkeley and at Princeton University.

Geoffrey O'Brien's books include *Castaways of the Image Planet*, *The Browser's Ecstasy*, *The Phantom Empire*, *Dream Time: Chapters from the Sixties*, and *Hardboiled America*, and his poetry has been collected in *Floating City: Selected Poems 1978–1995*. He is at work on *Jukebox Sonata*, a book about listening to popular music. He lives in New York City where he works as editor-in-chief of The Library of America.

The Onion is a satirical newspaper and website published in New York City, NY; Chicago, IL; Madison, WI; Milwaukee, WI and Denver, CO. It can be found on the web at *www.theonion.com*.

Simon Reynolds writes about pop culture for *Spin* (where he is a senior contributing writer), *New York Times*, *Village Voice*, *The Wire*, and *Uncut*. He is the author of *Generation Ecstasy: Into the World of Techno and Rave Culture; The Sex Revolts: Gender, Rebellion and Rock-'n'Roll* (co-written with Joy Press), and *Blissed Out: The Raptures of*

Rock. Currently he is working on a book about post-punk 1979–84, due for publication in 2004. He also operates a website at *http://members.aol.com/blissout/front.htm*.

Kelefa Sanneh writes about popular music for the *New York Times*. He is also deputy editor of *Transition*, an international review of race and culture.

Luc Sante's books include *Low Life* and *The Factory of Facts*. He is the improbable owner of a Grammy (for liner notes). The two songs he wrote with the Del-Byzanteens can both be found on the soundtrack of Wim Wenders's *The State of Things*.

RJ Smith is a senior editor and media critic at *Los Angeles* magazine. He has been a Visiting Scholar at the Getty Research Institute, and is currently working on a book about African American Los Angeles in the 1940s. He has written for the *Village Voice*, *New York Times Magazine*, and *Grand Royal*.

Kate Sullivan lives in L.A. and writes about music, film, radio, and the people who make (and sometimes destroy) them. Since her essay ("J. Lo vs. K. Sul") was written, she's become a prominent contributor to *Spin* Magazine (which she stacks openly in her living room). Kate also writes frequently for *City Pages* and her blog (*www.katesullivan.blogspot.com*). She would like to thank Keith Harris and Jim Walsh for midwife services on the piece—and for staying gold.

Joey Sweeney is a contributing editor at *Philadelphia Weekly*.

Carl Wilson has been a senior features editor and music columnist at *The Globe and Mail*, Canada's national newspaper, since 1999. He is also a columnist for Canadian art magazine *C*, and his work has appeared in *The Nation*, *Newsday*, *Saturday Night*, *Hour* and *This Magazine*, among others. He lives in downtown Toronto, where he takes tickets at Trampoline Hall Lectures.

CREDITS